Refugee Resettlement

STUDIES IN FORCED MIGRATION
General Editors: Tom Scott-Smith and Kirsten McConnachie

This series, published in association with the Refugees Studies Centre, University of Oxford, reflects the multidisciplinary nature of the field and includes within its scope international law, anthropology, sociology, politics, international relations, geopolitics, social psychology and economics.

For a full volume listing, please see back matter.

Refugee Resettlement

POWER, POLITICS, AND HUMANITARIAN GOVERNANCE

Edited by
Adèle Garnier, Liliana Lyra Jubilut,
and Kristin Bergtora Sandvik

berghahn
NEW YORK • OXFORD
www.berghahnbooks.com

First published in 2018 by
Berghahn Books
www.berghahnbooks.com

Library of Congress Cataloging-in-Publication Data
Names: Garnier, Adèle, editor. | Jubilut, Liliana Lyra, editor. | Sandvik, Kristin
    Bergtora, editor.
Title: Refugee Resettlement: Power, Politics, and Humanitarian Governance /
    edited by Adèle Garnier, Liliana Lyra Jubilut, and Kristin Bergtora Sandvik.
Description: New York: Berghahn Books, 2018. | Series: Studies in Forced
    Migration; 38 | Includes bibliographical references and index.
Identifiers: LCCN 2018016463 (print) | LCCN 2018021400 (ebook) | ISBN
    9781785339455 (eBook) | ISBN 9781785339448 | ISBN 9781785339691
Subjects: LCSH: Refugees–Services for. | Humanitarianism. | Power (Social
    sciences)
Classification: LCC HV640 (ebook) | LCC HV640 .R41835 2018 (print) |
    DDC 362.87/83–dc23
LC record available at https://lccn.loc.gov/2018016463

British Library Cataloguing in Publication Data

A catalogue record for this book is available from the British Library

ISBN 978-1-78533-944-8 hardback
ISBN 978-1-78533-969-1 paperback
ISBN 978-1-78533-945-5 ebook

To those who build a longer table, not a higher fence

Contents

Part III. Resettlement Bureaucracies and Resettled Refugees in Local Contexts

Abbreviations

AMEP	Adult Migrant English Program
ASAV	Associação Antonio Vieira
BNLA	Building a New Life in Australia
BPA	Brazil Declaration and Plan of Action
BPEAR	Bureau for the Placement and Education of African Refugees
CIA	Central Intelligence Agency
CIC	Citizenship and Immigration Canada
CONARE	Comitê Nacional para os Refugiados (National Committee for Refugees)
CPA	Comprehensive Plan of Action for Indo-Chinese Refugees
ERCM	Emerging Resettlement Countries Joint Support Mechanism
EU	European Union
GAR	government-assisted refugee
GBV	gender-based violence
HIAS	Hebrew Sheltering and Immigrant Aid Society
IC	individual case
ICARA	International Conference on Assistance to Refugees in Africa
ICMC	International Catholic Migration Commission
IGCR	Intergovernmental Committee on Refugees
ILO	International Labour Organization
IOM	International Organization for Migration

IRC	International Rescue Committee
IRCC	Immigration, Refugees and Citizenship Canada
IRO	International Refugee Organization
IRPA	Immigration and Refugee Protection Act
Mercosul	Mercado Comum do Sul (Southern Common Market)
MIDI	Ministère de l'Immigration, de la Diversité et de l'Inclusion
MPA	Mexico Declaration and Plan of Action
NGO	nongovernmental organization
NTCA	Northern Triangle of Central America
OAU	Organization of African Unity
ORR	Office of Refugee Resettlement
PSR	privately sponsored refugee
RLC	Refugee Landed in Canada
RSD	refugee status determination
RWTN	Refugees Welcome to Norway
SGBV	sexual or gender-based violence
SHG	self-help group
SUR	Strategic Use of Resettlement
UN	United Nations
UNECA	United Nations Economic Commission for Africa
UNESCO	United Nations Educational, Scientific and Cultural Organization
UNHCR	United Nations High Commissioner for Refugees
USAID	U.S. Agency for International Development

Introduction

Refugee Resettlement as Humanitarian Governance

Power Dynamics

*Adèle Garnier, Kristin Bergtora Sandvik,
and Liliana Lyra Jubilut*

Introduction

Refugee resettlement is defined by UNHCR, the United Nations High Commissioner for Refugees, as "the transfer of refugees from an asylum country to another State that has agreed to admit them and ultimately grant them permanent settlement" (UNHCR n.d.). This definition has evolved over time,[1] yet refugee resettlement has established itself as one of UNHCR's three "durable solutions" to forced displacement in the international refugee regime alongside local integration of refugees in their country of asylum and refugees' voluntary repatriation to their country of origin. More and more countries have instituted resettlement programs since the 1990s. Sixteen states had such schemes in 2008, and twenty-seven in 2016; these were mostly industrialized countries (UNHCR 2009, table 21; and see Cellini, this volume). However, as the UNHCR definition indicates, refugee resettlement relies on the goodwill of states. It is not a right, and a majority of states do not engage in it. The number of resettled refugees remains very low compared to the number of refugees hosted by countries of first asylum, which are mostly located in the Global South.

This book sets out to provide a comprehensive, knowledge-based analysis of global resettlement practices to academics, practitioners, and readers interested in refugee protection and humanitarianism. We believe such a contribution is particularly timely in light of the current political climate and unprecedented efforts to undermine both a common humanitarian tradition and how we construe our facts about the world. Resettlement has traditionally been understood by scholars and practitioners as a part of global refugee management, with a particular focus being given to the scarcity of resettlement slots (Fredriksson and Mougne 1994; Newland 2002; Betts et al. 2008). This edited volume takes a different tack by understanding refugee resettlement as a form of *humanitarian governance* at the international, national, and local levels.

As is further explored below, we understand humanitarian governance as involving care *and* control: it is driven by a humanitarian ethos of helping the most vulnerable but in doing so involves practices ruling the lives of the most vulnerable without providing them with a means of recourse to hold the humanitarians accountable for their actions (Harrell-Bond 1986; Hyndman 2000; Verdirame and Harrell-Bond 2005; Nyers 2005; Feldman and Ticktin 2010; Agier 2011; Pallister-Wilkins 2015). This analytical approach allows a more comprehensive understanding of the political, social, and symbolic properties of contemporary resettlement practices. Although resettlement is an important tool for protecting vulnerable civilians, it is also an unaccountable, costly process permeated by inequality. To examine resettlement as a form of humanitarian governance, we rely on three analytical approaches.

First, we take a lifespan approach to our discussions of resettlement, emphasizing movement in space and time. As refugee resettlement is presented as a "durable solution" to displacement, we believe that it is essential to understand refugee resettlement as a process that does not start when a refugee is chosen for resettlement. Selection procedures often take years, if not decades, and are simultaneously transnational and deeply local in nature. Similarly, resettlement does not magically stop once resettled refugees land at the airports of resettling states. A lifetime of vulnerability and resilience does not disappear because one crosses borders, and neither does the bureaucratic disciplining of refugees as humanitarian subjects. Thus, we label refugee resettlement an instrument of durable humanitarian governance.

Second, we analyze this spatial and temporal trajectory through the theoretical prism of power. We believe that it is essential to explore the *power relationships* among the many organizations, states, and individuals who have a stake in the definition and implementation of refugee resettlement. Such power relationships are shaped by the context of *global inequality,* which is the trigger for the need for resettlement programs in the first place, and exacerbated by the scarcity of resettlement slots.

Third, we assess resettlement as a *multilevel* form of humanitarian governance that can be analyzed by exploring and unpacking how resettlement is constituted at the international, national, and local levels as policy and practice.

Compared to other aspect of international refugee management, refugee resettlement has received relatively little academic attention and only recently has become more wide ranging and multidisciplinary. This includes studies in political science, international relations, history, legal sociology, anthropology, geography, and health sciences. Three main themes can be identified. There is, first, a focus on specific resettlement policies and the population groups in question, such as the resettlement of Indo-Chinese refugees (Viviani 1984; Robinson 1998, 2004), the Sudanese "Lost Boys" (Bixler 2005), or Browne's (2006) account of resettled refugees' journey to Australia. A smaller number of studies has also been devoted to emerging resettlement countries in the Global South (Jubilut and Carneiro 2011; Ruiz 2015; Menezes 2016). This line of inquiry also incorporates analyses of the significance of states' interests in the emergence of international cooperation on refugee resettlement (Suhrke 1998; van Selm 2003; Garnier 2014).

A second theme is the assessment–often through ethnographic methods (Horst 2006; Sandvik 2009, 2010, 2011; Thomson 2012) or advocacy research (Verdirame and Harrell-Bond 2005)–of refugees' experiences of the selection process and the accountability problems it engenders. This literature often frames investigations of refugees' vulnerability and resilience and the motivations, actions, and omissions of resettlement bureaucrats at different levels. While scholarship on resettlement, vulnerability, and gender has significantly expanded, other issues, such as refugees' disability and age, have been less explored (but see, respectively, Mirza 2011; Seibel 2016). A third theme, which has received the most attention, is the integration and adaption of resettled refugees, with a strong emphasis on the many challenges they face (Waxman and Colic-Peisker 2005; Nawyn 2006; Hugo 2011; Hyndman 2011; Ott 2013; Crock 2015; Darrow 2015; Losoncz 2015; Garnier 2016b). Drawing on lifespan approaches, a few studies connect the second and third themes (Mirza 2011; Spivey and Lewis 2015).

Across these thematic clusters, there is a concern with humanitarian governance, especially with the role and power of UNHCR as an international protection actor (Sandvik and Lindskov Jacobsen 2016). However, no comprehensive analytical treatment of resettlement as a form of humanitarian governance exists in the literature. To that end, this multidisciplinary volume brings together contributions from anthropology, law, international relations, social work, political science, public policy, and gerontology to offer a discussion of contemporary resettlement processes and the ways in which resettlement epitomizes both the international community's unprecedented formal commitment to protect civilians, including refugees, and the reality of an often ineffective and unchecked resettlement bureaucracy. It also shows how past resettlement practices bear on current developments.

The volume complements and expands existing knowledge on resettlement selection processes and reception, with a geographical scope covering the Democratic Republic of Congo, Tanzania, Brazil, Chile, Australia, Canada, the United States, Norway, and the European Union. Because we offer multidisciplinary perspectives grounded in a common understanding of refugee resettlement, we believe that the volume is greater than the sum of its parts. We argue that it constitutes a stepping stone to further advance refugee resettlement research but also to offer suggestions for improving resettlement practice, and therefore, refugee protection.

In the following, we lay out our conceptual framework. We then put it to use in an exploration of refugee resettlement as humanitarian governance from international, national, and local perspectives. This exploration leads us to highlight a number of paradoxes at the core of refugee resettlement and briefly show how future research could address these paradoxes. Finally, we introduce the volume's contributions.

Refugee Resettlement as Humanitarian Governance

Historically, humanitarian governance has been construed as an act of benevolence aiming to help suffering people in need. Michael Barnett has described it as "the increasingly organized and internationalized attempt to save the lives, enhance the welfare, and reduce the suffering of the world's most vulnerable populations" (Barnett 2013: 379). Humanitarian governance is situated within recent international relations literature as a subfield of global governance, which we understand as the multiple governmental, intergovernmental, and nongovernmental efforts and mechanisms to manage common public goods and address international issues (Barnett and Duvall 2004).

An expanding body of literature shows how the practical deployment of this ethics of care (Barnett 2011) goes hand in hand with discourses and practices of control. Starting with Harrell-Bond's (1986) revelatory anthropological study *Imposing Aid,* studies from various disciplines have investigated how Western states and global elites define situations as "crises" (Pandolfi 2003; Nyers 2005) and engage in undemocratic and unaccountable humanitarian governance operations. This has been notably exposed in the context of refugee camps (Hyndman 2000; Agier 2011; Ilcan and Rygiel 2015) and border policing practices (Pallister-Wilkins 2015). More broadly, in practices including day-to-day hospital care as much as adjudication of asylum claims and military interventions in foreign countries, Fassin (2012), Fassin and Pandolfi (2013), and Feldman and Ticktin (2010) have shown how "the humanitarian reason," or caring on behalf of humanity at large, could substitute a focus on human rights and justice with an emphasis on compassion.

Compassionate rhetoric and actions may help alleviate acute suffering yet not sustainably reduce global and local inequality produced by conflicts and disasters at various scales. Rather, they may contribute to reproduce inequality because of a short-term and ad hoc focus on needs alleviation in lieu of making crisis-affected societies sustainably peaceful and equitable (see also Keen 2008). These critical accounts are thus concerned with the distribution of power between actors involved in and affected by humanitarian governance.

In this volume we draw on these insights to explore refugee resettlement as an instrument of humanitarian governance involving the cooperation of many actors at the local, national, and international levels. We argue that it is an instrument of *durable* humanitarian governance because refugee resettlement is constituted by practitioners, and especially UNHCR, not as a rapid response to an acute crisis but as a durable solution implying a long-term concern for particularly vulnerable individuals, from their selection in refugee camps to their integration in resettling states. This vision of a continuum in humanitarian governance over time also speaks to migration and refugee scholarship's increasing awareness of the need for a long-term focus in our analysis of migrant and refugee lives before, during, and after migration and flight (Griffith et al. 2013). Longitudinal studies show that many first-generation resettled refugees remain vulnerable in receiving societies (Colic-Peisker and Tilbury 2006).

The notion of a long-term, "durable" humanitarian governance continuum can, for instance, allow us to identify similarities in the ethics of care toward resettlement candidates, on the one hand, and in the context of their treatment in resettling states, on the other hand. It also allows a longitudinal investigation of mechanisms of control. Refugee resettlement is a comparatively costly instrument of international protection. This is because it comprises the identification of those considered the most vulnerable, a further (if orderly) displacement for the selected, and the fostering of their long-term integration, that is, investment in technologies of identification, selection, mobility, and settlement. Yet as an instrument of governance, refugee resettlement also lacks a "culture of accountability." Previous research has observed how accountability in refugee resettlement programs is interpreted as narrowly focused upward toward donor states and UNHCR's headquarters, excluding considerations of downward accountability toward refugees with respect to the equity and procedural fairness of the resettlement selection process (Garnier 2016c).

Refugee Resettlement and Power

Many of the abovementioned studies of humanitarian governance analyze the array of practices deployed to govern the humanitarian subjects and their contribution to entrenching global inequality. Agier (2011), for instance, focuses on instruments used to "manage" the "undesirables" in refugee camps. In this volume, and following Harrell-Bond's (1986; Verdirame and Harrell-Bond 2005) advice to not neglect the agency of refugees themselves, we explore the variety of power dynamics at the core of refugee resettlement. A common definition of power is "the capacity or ability to direct or influence the behavior of others or the course of events" (Oxford Dictionaries, n.d.).

Traditionally, power has often been assimilated with a resource, and this is a representation we find at the core of statements such as "money is power" and "knowledge is power." Focusing on authority, discursive power, and institutional power in global governance, Barnett and Duvall (2004) have challenged this view, pointing at the difference between the source of power and its actual execution, and have also questioned the nature of power: does the capacity to do something means that someone dominates someone else? Or does someone have the capacity to do something because he or she has the capacity to convince others to freely engage in an activity that requires cooperation? Building on Barnett and Duvall's concept of power, we argue for the need for a more systematic focus on the multileveled nature of an international regime, that is, how and to what extent this regime permeates day-to-day interactions—but also what kind of feedback effects can be expected from the ground to the core of the regime.

Doing so, we are indebted to critical scholarship on the governmentality of migration (Walters 2015) and international migration management (Geiger and Pécoud 2010) while being keen to emphasize the nuances of multileveled power dynamics. To that end, in this introduction we draw on political geographer John Allen's concept of power. Allen (2003: 2) defines power as "the relational effect of social interactions." Defined as such, power encompasses forms of power *with* others (such as persuasion and negotiation) and power *over* others (such as authority, which compels one to do something, and coercion, which forces one to do something). Allen focuses on the space in which forms of power are deployed, for instance on the proximity that is required for coercion to occur, or on the broader scale at which persuasion can be deployed.

From the vantage point of power relationships, a particularly confounding aspect of refugee resettlement is that it is not codified in hard international refugee law: the 1951 Refugee Convention does not mandate it. However, UNHCR has been very prolific in codifying its understanding of refugee resettlement into soft law though numerous guidelines and handbooks. The lack of a binding legal framework means that the implementation of refugee resettlement requires considerable political resources and near-constant mobilization of international and domestic advocates to *persuade* decision makers to deploy the instrument, and *negotiations* are often requited to settle the size and nature of resettlement contingents. Scholarship on the politics of persuasion has argued that associating resettlement's humanitarian objectives with concerns more pressing to the state, such as security and economic well-being, may be effective (Betts 2009). However, the international community's failure to even set a modest resettlement target in the context of the Syrian crisis has cast a shadow on these expectations.

Still, at the local level, UNHCR's soft law often has *authority* or even *coercive power* when implemented by selection officers toward resettlement candidates who can be considered to have no option but to adhere as closely as possible to the selection criteria to be considered for resettlement. Yet, UNHCR exerts these forms of power over resettlement candidates with very limited accountability. Misappropriation (or just lack of use) of soft law instruments such as the *Resettlement Handbook,* or the failure to detect and dismantle corruption schemes, can lead to distortion or nonimplementation of core humanitarian values and refugee protection objectives (Sandvik 2011), and this can eventually weaken UNHCR's *persuasive power* at the global level.

Coercion can also be an issue when resettled refugees are faced with forms of social control because of their difficulties to gain footing in the formal labor market, and thus be either subjected to social control deployed by welfare professionals or to labor exploitation. However, it would also be a mistake to ignore the ways in which refugees exert their agency to *negotiate* access to resources and *persuade* bureaucrats and employers of their credentials. Local bureaucrats involved in resettlement, even though their margin of maneuver is reduced by scarcity of resources, also adapt their practice and aim to preserve their negotiating power.

Drawing on these concepts, the remaining of this introduction investigates the power dynamics of refugee resettlement as an instrument of durable humanitarian governance. We start by focusing on the role of UNHCR in defining refugee resettlement and promoting it in the international community as a durable solution to forced displacement. This will illustrate UNHCR's power of persuasion and negotiation in the international sphere as well as the modalities of institutionalization of these forms of power in soft law. We then focus on how individual resettling states are approaching refugee resettlement and to what extent UNHCR is able to convince these states to align their resettlement priorities with its own. Lastly, we address the machinery of refugee resettlement at the local level, as a bureaucratic and social process both in states in which refugees are selected for resettlement and in resettling states. Here, we discuss how UNHCR's soft law tools are implemented and to what extent it has authority or even coercive power, but also whether and how local actors, and especially refugees, are also able to use their power of negotiation and persuasion so as to achieve their goals.

Exploring Multileveled Power Dynamics

UNHCR and the International Promotion of Refugee Resettlement

As mentioned earlier, the definition of refugee resettlement has evolved over time. Scholarship on refugee resettlement in the interwar period and in the aftermath of World War II insists on the mix of demographic, economic, geopolitical, and humanitarian considerations in the selection of refugees for resettlement, which reached its highest numbers ever in the 1950s (Kunz 1988; Miles and Kay 1992; Wyman 1998; Neumann 2004; Karatani 2005; Long 2013). Clearer humanitarian contours were given to refugee resettlement as UNHCR was established in 1950 and the Refugee Convention adopted in 1951, which, until the 1967 Protocol, only applied to refugees fleeing the aftermath of World War II (Holborn 1975; Loescher 2001) and still allows its application only to European refugees.[2] Legal, financial, and institutional hurdles thus limited UNHCR's capacity to develop an extensive body of knowledge codifying resettlement as well as its power of persuasion over states in regards to whom to resettle. This was of particular concern for African refugees, as Sandvik explores in this volume.

The willingness of Western states to engage in large-scale refugee resettlement dwindled in the context of diminishing labor needs and a shift in the geographical focus of forced displacement from the Global North to the Global South. In 1975, the Indo-Chinese refugee crisis resulted in large-scale global resettlement efforts toward non-European refugees, yet also led to a crisis of confidence of Western states in the ability of UNHCR to screen "genuine refugees" for resettlement (Viviani 1984; Robinson 2004). Whereas one in twenty refugees identified by UNHCR was resettled in 1979, only one in four hundred was resettled in 1993 (Fredriksson and Mougne 1994: 5). Only a handful of states kept regular resettlement programs, most notably the United States, Australia, Canada, and Scandinavian countries, and these programs did not necessarily focus on resettling UNHCR identified resettlement cases (see also next section). The decline of refugee resettlement, and limited prospects for repatriation in many cases regardless of UNHCR's increased focus on this "durable solution," fueled protracted displacement in the Global South as well as an increase of asylum claims in the Global North (Chimni 2004; Shacknove 1993).

Following an influential internal review of refugee resettlement in the 1994 (Fredriksson and Mougne 1994; Garnier 2014; and see Sandvik; van Selm, this volume), UNHCR engaged in a conceptual and organizational resurgence of refugee resettlement. Refugee resettlement was redefined in major policy documents such as the *Agenda for Protection* (UNHCR 2003) as an instrument of international protection focusing on the most vulnerable refugees (a humanitarian instrument)[3] but also to contribute to international solidarity by complementing other "durable solutions" to forced displacement (a strategic instrument). Resettlement practice was to be aligned with this redefinition with the development of an increasingly extensive body of resettlement guidelines to be used in the field, most significantly the *UNHCR Resettlement Handbook,* published for the first time in 1997.

UNHCR made significant efforts to convince additional states to engage in resettlement, notably in Central Europe and Latin America, and to promote international resettlement cooperation with the establishment of regularly meeting multilateral resettlement fora. It also expanded its capacity to refer resettlement cases to resettling states, allowing UNHCR to stress the existence of a gap between resettlement needs and resettlement places (see UNHCR 2010: 2, 2012: 2). In this context, UNHCR has expanded its partnerships with NGOs, which may take core responsibilities within the resettlement process, such as the identification of resettlement cases and preparation of resettlement submissions (Piper and Thom 2014: 43f; UNHCR 2015). Major NGOs seconding UNHCR in these tasks are the Hebrew Sheltering and Immigrant Aid Society (HIAS),[4] the International Catholic Migration Commission (ICMC), International Rescue Committee, and Refuge Point. Finally, UNHCR increasingly engaged in knowledge production and dissemination on the integration of resettled refugees (UNHCR 2011: 52f; Casasola 2016).

UNHCR's power of persuasion in redefining refugee resettlement is undeniable. As van Selm explores in this volume, a number of resettlement initiatives have been launched under the auspices of the Strategic Use of Resettlement (SUR), most notably the multiyear resettlement of over 100,000 Bhutanese refugees from camps in Nepal to several resettling countries. It has also supported multilateral resettlement initiatives not explicitly promoted as SUR but focusing on specific refugee groups, including Burmese refugees from Thailand, the Sudanese Lost Boys and Somali minorities from Kenya, Burundian refugees from Tanzania, and Liberian refugees from Guinea and Sierra Leone (UNHCR 2011: 57f; Casasola 2016). More broadly the ratio of refugees accepted for resettlement on the basis of UNHCR selection criteria has increased (UNHCR 2011: 50; and see Garnier, this volume).

UNHCR has also been directly involved in the design of the European Union Joint Resettlement Program established in 2012 (Garnier 2014), in the design and implementation of emerging resettling states such as Brazil and Chile, and in the elaboration of multilateral resettlement initiatives in Latin America (see Jubilut and Zamur; Vera Espinoza, this volume). Going beyond what was originally advocated in its 1994 review, but in line with UNHCR's stronger ties with the private sector, UNHCR is also involved in public-private partnerships aiming to promote privately sponsored refugee resettlement (Garnier 2016a). This is a substantial achievement if one recalls the drastic decrease of resettlement places and, more broadly, the 9/11 attacks.

Yet there are obvious limits to UNHCR's power of persuasion. UNHCR's efforts have not been followed by a sustainable increase of resettlement places. The recent upswing in the offering of resettlement places was mostly related to the resettlement of Syrian refugees, and sharply declined (46 percent) in 2017 (UNHCR 2018: 30). Moreover, focus on Syrian resettlement was accompanied by a tightening of asylum systems and a stronger focus on repatriation for other refugee populations in many countries of the Global North (see van Selm, this volume). UNHCR has also been unable to achieve the inclusion of a global resettlement target of 10 percent of the world's refugees in the New York Declaration on Refugees and Migrants adopted in September 2016 by the UN General Assembly (Garnier 2016a).

The US withdrawal from the negotiations of the UN Global Compact on Migration, which aims to implement the New York Declaration, justified by the alleged lack of compatibility of this global initiative with US interests (Wintour 2017), will certainly further undermine UNHCR's efforts as it denotes an unwillingness to negotiate in the global arena (Jubilut 2017a). Finally, in spite of the ever-expanding production of knowledge on "best practices" regarding resettled refugees' well-being from their selection to their integration, UNHCR is at fault to ensure the large-scale deployment of such practices. The next section explores one of the factors limiting UNHCR's persuasive power: states' authority over the actual unfolding of national refugee resettlement program, while the following section is devoted to local challenges.

National Resettlement Discourses and Practices

Contrary to the provision of asylum, refugee resettlement is not, as mentioned, codified in hard international law. UNHCR provides advice on refugee resettlement that national governments are at their own discretion to follow or not. A state traditionally committed to refugee resettlement, yet suddenly suspending it (as did Denmark in 2016; see Kohl 2016), does not contravene any international legal standards. This volume's annex compiled by Amanda Cellini offers a detailed panorama of national resettlement diversity, on which the next paragraphs draw, and specific national cases are explored in various chapters. Here, to keep the overview concise, we only focus on current practices and discourses.

The offering of resettlement places is strikingly uneven. The United States has so far consistently offered the largest number of resettlement slots, even as it has declined sharply since 2016 (UNHCR 2017: 30). Canada and Australia have long followed, with each slightly above 10 percent of the global total over decades, even though the number of offered slots has in both cases significantly expanded in the context of the Syrian crisis. In this respect, Canada has in 2015–2017 proceeded to its largest-ever resettlement intake, with more than 40,000 Syrian refugees being resettled between November 2015 and February 2017 (IRCC 2017). Only two Scandinavian countries have sustainably offered above 1,000 resettlement places yearly: Sweden and Norway. Yet several countries have for the last few years, in the wake of the Iraqi and Syrian crises, offered larger numbers, including Germany, the United Kingdom, and Finland.

The setting of an annual resettlement figure is in some cases done by the executive branch of government, in other by the legislative branch. In either case, the decision follows consultations with "resettlement stakeholders" generally including UNHCR as well as public bodies and civil society organizations involved in resettlement from case selection to long-term integration. Such planning largely differs from the more confrontational and reactive nature of the elaboration of asylum policies (Alink et al. 2001). Yet, as in the case of asylum politics, broader advocacy toward the general public is also mobilized by "stakeholders," especially when they have the resources to do so.

Given the US role in resettlement, resettlement advocacy is particularly strong and diverse there, with, for instance, HIAS committing itself to "leading the American Jewish community to push for needed reforms in American and international policies that protect all refugees" (HIAS n.d.). Contrary to asylum/refugee status determination cases, the judiciary does not play a significant role in resettlement decisions. The means of recourse for refused resettlement candidates are very limited, largely because they are not on the territory of resettling states. This also limits the persuasive power of UNHCR, which often plays a significant advisory role in asylum decisions, but has long led to less domestic conflicts between government branches over the definition of who enters the country (on the Australian case, see Garnier 2014).

Time will tell whether President Trump's executive order to ban immigration from specific countries, including a temporary suspension of entrance of refugees already granted a visa to the United States and the permanent suspension of the resettlement of Syrian refugees, as well as a cut by half in US resettlement places constitute a dramatic shift away from such consensus (Yuhas and Sidahmed 2017). In any case, the ban followed a political conflict between US Republicans and Democrats at both federal and state levels (Ford 2016). Similarly, Reklev and Jumbert in this volume stress that refugee resettlement means different things to different political parties in Norway.

In political-administrative discourse, all resettling countries insist that their national resettlement program is an expression of humanitarian responsibility and international solidarity. The United States also presents it as a reflection of national values (see Darrow, this volume), while Australian governments repeatedly insist on the generosity of the country, which resettles more refugees per capita than any other–the fact that other countries host far more refugees per capita than Australia being rhetorically obscured (see Losoncz, this volume). Emerging resettlement states Brazil and Chile both present it as a tenet of humanitarianism. In addition, resettlement in Brazil can be seen as a tool for emerging innovative regional leadership (see Jubilut and Zamur, this volume) and Chile as a historical duty as it is itself a postauthoritarian state from which many have been resettled in the 1970s (see Vera Espinoza, this volume).

As for who is selected for resettlement, vulnerability is used as a criterion in all cases, yet some countries also legally require that resettled refugees demonstrate their ability to integrate into their society, even though implementation of the requirement varies (see Garnier on the Canadian case, this volume). Most countries include streams for various categories of resettled refugees, such as following the *UNHCR Resettlement Handbook,* Women-at-Risk, or Survivors of Violence and Torture. Yet especially major resettlement countries have categories for persons whose resettlement is not only advocated by UNHCR but also by domestic private actors, including the resettlement-involved NGOs mentioned earlier. The most prominent of these categories currently is Canada's private sponsorship stream, which allows established associations but also more informal groups of citizens to sponsor refugees (Hyndman 2011; Casasola 2016). It has been argued that the existence of private/community sponsorship, on top of providing additional resources to refugee resettlement, helps ensuring broad social support for refugees; however, the Canadian experience has proven so far hard to replicate beyond its borders (Garnier 2016a).

In all cases, the integration of resettled refugees is a multileveled process involving various levels of governance as well as civil society, whereby the actual configuration of responsibilities varies significantly (see Cellini, this volume, for details). Political incorporation depends on resettled refugees' legal status on arrival. Permanent residency and thus a pathway to citizenship is automatically granted on arrival in some countries, such as Canada, yet other countries, such as Germany, insist on the granting of a temporary permit at first. The timeline of expected socioeconomic integration into mainstream society also varies significantly, from an insistence on economic contribution within a few months for refugees in the workforce in the United States to the provision of specific welfare benefits for several years in Scandinavian countries.

Even though national governments have the authority to set the regulatory parameters of refugee resettlement, and UNHCR works toward persuading national governments of the value of its numerous resettlement guidelines, both the selection of resettled refugees and, to a lesser extent, their socioeconomic integration occurs at a distance from the headquarters of international and national institutions. Hence, the last section of this introduction focuses on refugee resettlement's power dynamics at the local level.

Local Resettlement Experiences

From selection to integration, resettlement locally relies on complex, multi-actor bureaucratic dynamics riddled with power imbalances. Resettlement candidates can be rejected at three different stages of the resettlement procedure. On the basis of an individual interview, a local protection officer from UNHCR, or a staff member from a seconding NGO (UNHCR 2011: 390f) can recommend resettlement for an "individual case" (an IC). Yet this recommendation can be disregarded by a resettlement officer (again from UNHCR or a seconding NGO), who may decide to not open a resettlement file for the IC. If the file is opened, the proper resettlement procedure starts, involving collection of documentation supporting the IC's claims as well as, eventually, an individual screening interview.

The resettlement candidate does not have the right to bring counsel to resettlement interviews. In practice, these interviews frequently take place without the aid of qualified interpreters. While the interviewee has a formal right to read through the resettlement form prior to signing it, many do not understand the legalistic language used in the form, and protection officers rarely have the time to explain how the interviewee's story fits with the various concepts and categories that determine eligibility. Regardless, the credibility of the IC is assessed on this basis. Following the interview, the quality of the submission is reviewed. Depending on the intensity of the violation, or risk of violation, of the refugee's rights and the need for resettlement the submission is categorized as "normal," "urgent," or "emergency."

If UNHCR's regional hub accepts the case, the resettlement dispatch is submitted to a potential resettlement country that has expressed interest in refugees with this nationality or personal profile. There are no formal requirements as to the timeliness of the decision. What constitutes "reasonable speed" depends on the size of the caseload and many other logistical, administrative, and financial factors. In the likely event of a negative response, the candidate only receives a standardized letter of rejection. Since many refugees have no permanent contact details, they may not receive notice, or they may receive it only after severe delays (Sandvik 2009, 2011).

Because of a resettlement candidate' limited recourse in case of a resettlement decision he or she considers wrong, and because of the lack of information on the development of his or her case, the refugee's power to persuade officers of the strength of his or her case and to negotiate a positive outcome is significantly constrained. The resettlement candidate appears to be coerced into accepting the decision and, even in the case of a positive outcome, to be subject to the symbolic violence of resettlement selection criteria. Nevertheless, resettlement candidates find ways to deploy persuasive power, for instance by *performing* their case as close as possible to the guidelines, whose existence they are well aware of, not only in resettlement interviews but also by producing letters and documents relating their experience, which they will attempt to deliver to who they consider to be the persons in charge of processing their case (Sandvik 2009).

Thomson, in this volume, explores some of these strategies as used by a Congolese resettlement candidate in a Tanzanian refugee camp. Collectively, resettlement candidates also stage protests at the front of highly visible UNHCR offices, infamously in the case of Sudanese refugees at the front of the UNHCR office in Cairo in 2006. The Sudanese refugees were motivated by an intense sentiment of being ignored by UNHCR and complained about their unfair treatment using the language of human rights law. In a nearby park, they self-organized locally as a community they considered safer and more social than their regular lives, in which they were scattered in slums in and around Cairo (Moulin and Nyers 2007). This collective dimension also speaks to scholarship on political organization of refugees in camps, whereby some wish to be resettled and some do not, which may affect collective political agency (Holzer 2012; Lecadet 2016).

Resettled refugees' integration equally involves structural imbalances and information scarcity but also opportunities for resettled refugees and involved organizations to overcome hurdles. Whereas performing vulnerability may be at stake during the selection process, the socioeconomic marginalization of many resettled refugees often means numerous encounters with welfare systems of host countries and their specific dynamics of care and control. In her chapter on the implementation of US refugee resettlement, Darrow, in this volume, insists on the structural constraints encountered by NGOs specifically mandated to integrate resettled refugees in the workforce as quickly as possible. She points at their strategies to negotiate the employment of particular individuals or group and emphasizes the justificatory discourse mobilized by these implementing partners and broader American society, which strongly stigmatizes the unemployed poor. Rapid employment is a slightly less pressing concern in the Canadian and Australian resettlement programs, which also have a stronger tradition of state-driven welfare than the United States.

Still, Garnier, this volume, and Losoncz, this volume, stress the individual and structural disadvantages resettled refugees face in the labor market, including limited proficiency in official languages, limited education, lack of recognition of foreign credentials and training, discrimination, and indiscriminate provision of settlement services to both immigrants and refugees. Garnier focuses, in this volume, on Canada and Quebec's discontinuity between a focus on resettled refugees' vulnerability as they are selected for resettlement and an emphasis on mainstream socioeconomic integration into the domestic middle class postarrival. She stresses that resettled refugees most successful on the labor market benefit from a conjunction of favorable personal attributes and of auspicious institutional measures. Vera Espinoza, in this volume, highlights the importance of mismatched expectations between local implementing agencies in Brazil and Chile and resettled refugees, noting that the better informed both parties were about the other party's expectations prior to the arrival of resettled refugees, the greater the ability of the latter to preserve their sense of agency postarrival.

Another critical source of both agency and constraints for resettled refugees is their family ties. This is explored in Lewis and Young's chapter in this volume recounting in diachronic perspective the resettlement experience of Cambodian and Karen refugees in the United States, pointing at cultural resilience but also at intergenerational conflicts in regard to the significance of cultural markers. Further, their chapter illustrates the enduring nature of difficulties faced by generations of refugees throughout the resettlement process. This can be seen to support the view that refugee resettlement, itself borne out of global and local inequality, fails to sustainably reduce it.

Refugee Resettlement's Paradoxes and Future Research Agenda

Our exploration points to the following paradoxes. First, we distinguish between types of power and this leads us to a paradox in regard to the visibility and invisibility of UNHCR's power in refugee resettlement. As the international organ overseeing refugee policy worldwide, UNHCR's persuasive power often seems mighty when it is in fact constrained by scarce resources and the political environment in which it is involved. By contrast, the local power of UNHCR is considerable, as it can make authoritative decisions changing the life of refugees and seems to even be able to coerce them into particular decisions; yet such power is a lot less visible to the international community. This *in/visibility paradox* could be more closely investigated in research on the multiple roles, and forms of power, of UNHCR in specific cases. Such research could bring together multisited ethnography, critical geography, international law, and policy implementation-focused scholars. It could also suggest pathways for UNHCR to be more accountable to refugees, while highlighting the nefarious impact, at the local level, that UNHCR's limited resources have on refugees.

Second, our comparative overview of national resettlement policies indicates a paradox relating to the processes of politicization and depoliticization of refugee resettlement in resettling states. Until recently, the issues of refugee protection and resettlement have not led to extensive political engagement by national communities in receiving states, a trend that might have been affected by the "refugee crisis" in the European Union and the Trump administration's travel bans (Jubilut 2017b). Specifically in terms of resettlement, there has been a relative lack of domestic political controversies around refugee resettlement as compared with asylum policy, or policies in regard to irregular migration may have preserved resources for resettlement and ensured its continuation and legitimacy.

However, depoliticization may also have led to the demobilization of domestic audiences around refugee resettlement, contributed to the stagnation of available resettlement slots, and contributed to the avoidance of focus on resettlement's failings. The presentation of refugee resettlement as the only well-accepted way to seek protection in some resettling states may also have contributed to threaten the legitimacy of asylum. To tackle this *de/politicization paradox*, studies combining critical discourse analysis and policy analysis could contrast the evolution of domestic resettlement discourses and the evolution of resettlement places, as well as compare political discourse on refugee resettlement with political discourse on asylum. Research findings may help suggest ways to develop a more political discourse on refugee resettlement, which advocates both more resettlement places and better resettlement policies.

Third, our focus on refugee resettlement as durable humanitarian governance hints at a paradox in the portrayal of the vulnerability and resilience of resettled refugees. Refugee resettlement is primarily motivated by humanitarian concerns. Resettled refugees are often portrayed as victims, and their considerable resilience seems obscured in discourses and practices of humanitarian governance. Yet, once in resettling states, the discursive and practical space for the vulnerability of resettled refugees is limited, as resettled refugees are generally expected to integrate, perhaps after a few months or a few years of transition, like the average immigrant.

This *vulnerability/resilience paradox* calls for more research into what prevents a focus on refugees' resilience before resettlement and into what impedes refugees' resilience in resettling states. This could include longitudinal, decade-spanning explorations of the fate of particular cohorts of resettled refugees, including analyses of the political discourses surrounding these particular groups. Such analyses could combine ethnographic, social work, and political science methods. Such research could also include policy analysis studies of the opportunities for and limits to domestic humanitarian constituencies promoting refugee resettlement. Results of such research may foster both discourses and practices preventing the stereotyping of resettled refugees while showing ways to decrease structural obstacles to the expression of their resilience.

Beyond the exploration of these paradoxes, we advocate more research into resettlement in the Global South.

The majority of refugees comes from, and stays in, the Global South; thus in-depth multidisciplinary investigations of existing Global South programs could point at both opportunities and challenges specific to particular regions. In this volume, Jubilut and Zamur, and Vera Espinoza do so in the cases of Brazil and Chile in the Latin American context, while Sandvik offers insights into intra-African resettlement experiences. Refugee resettlement initiatives could also be assessed as examples of South-South cooperation, or as vantage points to analyze power dynamics with a Global South focus or even the emergence of regional power as an important category in refugee protection (Jubilut and Zamur, this volume).

Pursuing this research agenda[5] would give greater insight into refugee resettlements' entrenchment in global inequality but also indicate some steps to reduce manifestations of said inequality. We are, however, aware that much more needs to be done to tackle global inequality: overcoming it would in fine means that refugee resettlement is not necessary anymore. We have perhaps never been further from such situation.

Presentation of Chapters

Joanne van Selm's chapter takes a political and juridical approach to investigate the role of the Strategic Use of Resettlement (SUR) in sustaining interest in resettlement writ large and adding to the refugee protection regime. The chapter relies on reports written on the subject of SUR from its introduction to the present, supplemented by some additional conversations with current policy makers regarding their thinking on whether SUR has continued potential. Introduced in 2003, SUR is intended to add a multiplier effect to the resettlement of refugees. In theory SUR offers opportunities for rethinking and refashioning not only resettlement but also the whole refugee protection regime—from orderly arrivals in developed countries to knock-on effects in terms of greater protection capacity in regions of origin. In both theory and practice, however, there are many pitfalls, including in the consequences of the language used (with the emphasis on strategy and multipliers, rather than protection) and in the devaluing of the resettlement activity itself.

Kristin Bergtora Sandvik's chapter proposes a critical legal history of international resettlement through a discussion of the gradual incorporation of African refugees into such schemes. Today, African refugees are prominent in the resettlement efforts of UNHCR and the major resettlement countries. Yet, until recently, African refugees were excluded from resettlement to the West. This chapter argues that this radical shift cannot be explained only by changes in quota allocations or domestic legal systems.

It surveys the historical evolution of the African resettlement candidate as a bureaucratic-legal category through three lines of inquiry: first, through the evolvement of resettlement in international refugee management; second, by unpacking the configuration of African refugees in UNHCR's interventions; and, third, by pointing to how the renewal and reform of resettlement that began in the mid-1990s produced rationales that not only undermined previous exclusion but also facilitated a greater inclusion of African refugees. In conclusion, Sandvik proposes that, as well as reflecting a more inclusive humanitarianism, the changing face of resettlement is linked to global migration management.

Liliana Lyra Jubilut and Andrea Cristina Godoy Zamur's chapter offers a case study of refugee resettlement in Brazil drawing on international law and international relations scholarship. Brazil has been praised as a model and a regional leader and has been a proponent of new ways of conceptualizing and implementing refugee resettlement in Latin America since the early 2000s. Relying on bibliography assessment, document analysis, exchanges with policymakers, and the authors' own experience with refugee protection in the country, Jubilut and Godoy aim to identify the power categories in Brazil's refugee resettlement in the program's current phase. The chapter concludes that Brazil's resettlement is both a case of positive achievement for an emerging resettlement country and an interesting case study in identifying power dynamics in resettlement, not least for being a thought-provoking example of the quest of soft power through humanitarianism and for suggesting a possible use of regional power in refugee resettlement.

Focusing on the US resettlement program, Jessica H. Darrow's chapter draws on social work literature and argues that US resettlement operates with a shifting view of resettled refugees. At admission, refugees are framed as deserving of the American humanitarian ethos, which is reflected in resettlement legislation. However, and similar to the framing of poor people of color in the United States, the moral worthiness of resettled refugees in the long term depends on the ability to integrate into the labor market. The latter largely relies on the role played by resettlement agencies' caseworkers, whose work Darrow has observed over several years using ethnographic methods. Darrow's chapter concludes with perspectives on refugee resettlement under the Trump administration, which is positioning itself as overtly hostile to refugees.

Adèle Garnier's chapter resorts to insights from scholarship on incorporation to analyze the relationships between the selection of resettled refugees and their labor market participation in Canada, more specifically the province of Quebec. Relying on regulatory analysis and interviews with settlement organizations and resettled refugees, the chapter argues that humanitarian constituencies in Canada effectively used their power of persuasion in the late 1990s to foster an increase in the admission of more vulnerable refugees from the early 2000s. Yet this power of persuasion is more limited in regard to integration in part because settlement is geared to offer services to all immigrants, whose overall profile is closer to the Canadian middle class than that of resettled refugees. This limits the negotiating power of more vulnerable resettled refugees as well as the bargaining power of service providers who aim to specifically support them. Garnier discusses the significance of these findings for Canada's resurgence as a global resettlement leader under the prime ministership of Justin Trudeau.

Ibolya Losoncz's chapter focuses on refugee resettlement in Australia, the third main contributor to international resettlement efforts. Concentrating on resettled refugees' labor market participation, it investigates the extent to which Australia's resettlement program delivers on its desired outcome of giving resettled refugees the same political, economic, social, and cultural rights as those enjoyed by nationals. Conceptually Losoncz combines insights from Merton, Granovetter, and Putnam and draws on data from the author's ethnographic study with recently settled South Sudanese refugees and a recently released large sample size longitudinal survey of humanitarian migrants (Building a New Life in Australia). The chapter shows how Australian government institutions fail to provide accessible pathways to resettled refugees to turn their personal resources and capabilities into economic and social participation, hence severely limiting their negotiating power and agency.

Linn-Marie Reklev and Maria Jumbert's chapter addresses the Norwegian political debate on burden sharing in refugee protection following the Syrian crisis, with a particular emphasis on resettlement. Based on a media analysis and interviews with key informants, it identifies three discourses that dominate the Norwegian refugee field: the cost-and-capacity discourse, the nation-state discourse, and the humanitarian discourse. The chapter argues that these three discourses take part in "discursive battles" in the political field and that the outcome of these battles shapes the political space for Norwegian resettlement initiatives in practice. Moreover, the chapter investigates how the image of Norway as a humanitarian power and peace nation has been contested in this process. The chapter shows that the cost-and-capacity discourse is the current hegemonic discourse that largely shapes and defines the values and interests of core actors in this area. Reklev and Jumbert conclude that the form and extent of future Norwegian resettlement initiatives depend on the hierarchy and power relations between the dominant discourses in the field.

Rooted in the disciplines of gerontology, family science, and human development, Denise C. Lewis and Savannah S. Young's chapter builds on extensive engagement with Cambodian and Karen refugees from Burma in the United States. The chapter relies on these refugees' narrative to explore similarities and differences in parallel past, present, and future experiences of resettlement in the United States. A reliance on refugees' voices brings to light needs not met by various response agencies, as well as families' collective actions to address those needs. The chapter focuses more strongly on the journey from home countries to resettlement and how refugees frame and respond to the stressors associated with those journeys to aid in successful integration of resettled refugees; the chapter also improves our own understanding of refugees' needs during and after resettlement. Rather than viewing refugees as powerless in the face of seemingly catastrophic events, this chapter acknowledges the power refugees possess as they navigate the terrain of flight and settlement. Lastly, Lewis and Young provide a critique of current US policy responses to refugee resettlement as they relate to our participants' narratives.

Marnie Thomson's chapter inquires into Congolese refugees' experiences with the selection process for resettlement, drawing from years of ethnographic research conducted in refugee camps, aid compounds, and government offices across Tanzania as well as in UNHCR regional and global headquarters. Refugees' stories reveal the ways in which resettlement selection varies case by case and depends on the discretion of case evaluators. Their stories also bring to light the risks refugees are willing to take to convince resettlement officials to select them. Some refugees admit to partaking in fraud; from their perspective such actions implicate corrupt resettlement officials or at least an unjust system. Resettlement selection decisions may represent aid workers' control over refugee lives, but being selected signals refugees' regaining power over their own lives.

Combining insights from critical geography and anthropological scholarship, Marcia A. Vera Espinoza's chapter draws on a broad range of qualitative data collected between 2013 and 2014 in Chile and Brazil to confront the expectations of Colombian and Palestinian resettled refugees with the expectations of resettlement organizations during the process of their integration in these two emerging resettlement countries. This allows exploring the complexities of resettlement, a process that is designed, experienced, and even resisted by different actors. The chapter highlights the translocality of resettled refugees' experience, that is, the simultaneous role of various locations in the construction of their identity. This revision of resettlement as an experience going beyond target numbers and policy can contribute to enhance our understanding of this durable solution in emerging resettlement countries and to reflect upon structural gaps in refugee resettlement more broadly.

Astri Suhrke and Adèle Garnier's concluding remarks insist on important characteristics of the global refugee regime: its structural fragmentation, normative diversity, and UNHCR's dependence on a handful of resettling states. A moral economy perspective on the resettlement regime suggests that resettlement, as much as it bears costs, serves important protection functions for at-risk refugees and reminds wealthy societies of their humanitarian obligations.

Amanda Cellini's annex offers a systematic comparison of all existing twenty-seven resettlement programs as of the end of 2016. Cellini focuses not only on respective resettlement statistics on their evolution in recent years but also on resettlement's national regulatory basis, main resettlement actors, eligibility criteria, and the involvement of UNHCR. No comparable database exists, and we believe the annex can be of great use to both practitioners and academics keen to further advance refugee resettlement research.

Adèle Garnier is a lecturer in the Department of Modern History, Politics and International Relations, Macquarie University, Australia. She holds a Ph.D. in Politics from the University of Leipzig, Germany and Macquarie University and has held research positions at the Interuniversity Research Centre for Globalization and Work (CRIMT), Université de Montréal, Canada, and the Group for Research on Migration, Ethnic Relations and Equality (GERME), Université Libre de Bruxelles, Belgium. She has published in *Refuge,* the *Journal of Ethnic and Migration Studies,* and *WeltTrends.*

Liliana Lyra Jubilut holds a Ph.D. and a Master's degree in international law from Universidade de São Paulo and an LL.M in International Legal Studies from NYU School of Law. She was part of the project Brazil's Rise to the Global Stage: Humanitarianism, Peacekeeping and the Quest for Great Powerhood of the Peace Research Institute Oslo. She has been working with refugees' issues since 1999. Currently she is a professor of the Postgraduate Programme in Law at Universidade Católica de Santos and a member of the IOM Migration Research Leaders Syndicate.

Kristin Bergtora Sandvik (Harvard Law School S.J.D.) is a research professor in humanitarian studies at Peace Research Institute Oslo and a professor in the faculty of law at the University of Oslo. Her research focuses on legal mobilization, gender-based violence, displacement and humanitarian ethics, technology, and innovation. Her work has appeared in *Polar: Political and Legal Anthropology Review, Refugee Survey Quarterly,* the *International Journal of Refugee Law, Disasters,* the *ICRC Review, Third World Quarterly,* the *Law and Society Review,* and many more.

Notes

1. This will be explored in greater detail later in this introduction.
2. For instance, Turkey has maintained the geographical limitation of the Refugee Convention and thus does not grant refugee status to people fleeing from outside

Europe. However, Turkey has adopted domestic legislation providing a binding asylum framework for all persons in need of international protection, and it provides temporary protection for Syrian refugees. As of December 2017, the Turkish Ministry of the Interior estimated that Turkey hosted 3.4 million refugees, 90 percent of whom originated from Syria (Refugee Rights Turkey 2017; European Commission 2017).

3. UNHCR's increasing focus on resettled refugees' vulnerability is part of the expansion of humanitarian hard law and soft law constructing vulnerability (see, for instance, Sandvik 2012).

4. HIAS was established in the late nineteenth century to assist the relocation of Jews expelled from Russia who sought protection elsewhere; it then expanded to foster the resettlement of persecuted Jews worldwide. In the past few decades, it has shifted its focus to other populations of refugees seeking resettlement, including in Africa and Latin America.

5. For more on the authors' take on a research agenda on resettlement, see Garnier, Sandvik, and Jubilut 2016.

References

Agier, Michel. 2011. *Managing the Undesirables: Refugee Camps and Humanitarian Government.* Cambridge: Polity.

Alink, Fleur, Arjen Boin, and Paul t'Hart. 2001. "Institutional Crises and Reforms in Policy Sectors: The Case of Asylum Policy in Europe." *Journal of European Public Policy* 8(2): 286–306.

Allen, John. 2003. *Lost Geographies of Power.* Oxford: Wiley-Blackwell.

Barnett, Michael. 2011. *Empire of Humanity: A History of Humanitarianism.* Ithaca: Cornell University Press.

———. 2013. "Humanitarian Governance." *Annual Review of Political Science* 16: 379–98.

Barnett, Michael, and Raymond Duvall, eds. 2004. *Power in Global Governance.* Cambridge: Cambridge University Press.

Betts, Alexander. 2009. *Protection by Persuasion: International Cooperation in the Refugee Regime.* Ithaca: Cornell University Press.

Betts, Alexander, Gil Loescher, and James Milner. 2008. *The United Nations High Commissioner for Refugees (UNHCR): The Politics and Practice of Refugee Protection into the 21st Century.* London: Routledge.

Bixler, Mark. 2005. *The Lost Boys of Sudan: An American Story of the Refugee Experience.* Atlanta: University of Georgia Press.

Browne, Peter. 2006. *The Longest Journey.* Sydney: University of New South Wales Press.

Casasola, Michael. 2016. "The Indochinese Refugee Movement and the Subsequent Evolution of UNHCR and Canadian Resettlement Selection Policies and Practices." *Refuge* 32(2): 41–53.

Chimni, B. S. 2004. "From Resettlement to Involuntary Repatriation: Towards a Critical History of Durable Solutions to Refugee Problems." *Refugee Survey Quarterly* 23(3): 55–73.

Colic-Peisker, Val, and Farida Tilbury. 2006. "Employment Niches for Recent Refugees: Segmented Labour Market in Twenty-First Century Australia." *Journal of Refugee Studies* 19(2): 203–229.

Crock, Mary, ed. 2015. *Creating New Futures: Settling Children and Youth from Refugee Backgrounds.* Sydney: Federation Press.

Darrow, Jessica. 2015. "Getting Refugees to Work: A Street-Level Perspective of Refugee Resettlement Policy." *Refugee Survey Quarterly* 34(2): 78–106.

European Commission. 2017. *Turkey Facts and Figures.* Accessed 18 December 2018. http://ec.europa.eu/echo/files/aid/countries/factsheets/turkey_syrian_crisis_en.pdf.

Fassin, Didier. 2012. *Humanitarian Reason. A Moral History of the Present.* Berkeley: University of California Press.

Fassin, Didier, and Mariella Pandolfi, eds. 2013. *Contemporary States of Emergency: The Politics of Military and Humanitarian Interventions.* New York: Zone Books.

Feldman, Ilana, and Miriam Ticktin. 2010. *In the Name of Humanity.* Durham: Duke University Press.

Ford, Matt. 2016. "Texas's Refusal of Refugees." *The Atlantic,* 21 September. Accessed 6 February 2017. https://www.theatlantic.com/news/archive/2016/09/texas-refugee-abbottwithdrawal/501038/.

Fredriksson, John, and Christine Mougne. 1994. *Resettlement in the 1990s: A Review of Policy and Practices.* Accessed 6 February 2017. http://www.unhcr.org/research/RESEARCH/3ae6bcfd4.pdf.

Garnier, Adèle. 2014. "Migration Management and Humanitarian Protection: The UNHCR's 'Resettlement Expansionism' and Its Impact on Policy-Making in the EU and Australia." *Journal of Ethnic and Migration Studies* 40(6): 942–59.

——. 2016a. "The Future of Refugee Resettlement: Will the September Summits Make any Difference?" *Norwegian Centre for Humanitarian Studies.* Accessed 6 February 2017. http://www.humanitarianstudies.no/2016/09/28/the-future-of-refugee-resettlement-will-the-september-summits-make-any-difference/.

——. 2016b. "Impact des Arrangements Institutionnels d'Admission et d'Insertion sur le Parcours Professionnel des Réfugiés." *Les Cahiers du CRIEC* 39: 40–58.

——. 2016c. "Narratives of Accountability in UNHCR's Resettlement Strategy." In *UNHCR and the Struggle for Accountability,* edited by K. B. Sandvik and K. Lindskov Jacobsen, 64–80. London: Routledge.

Garnier, Adèle, Kristin Bergtora Sandvik, and Liliana Lyra Jubilut. 2016. *Refugee Resettlement as Humanitarian Governance: The Need for a Critical Research Agenda.* Accessed 14 September 2016. http://fluechtlingsforschung.net/refugee-resettlement-as-humanitarian-governance/.

Geiger, Martin, and Antoine Pécoud. 2010. "The Politics of International Migration Management." In *The Politics of International Migration Management,* edited by M. Geiger and A. Pécoud, 1–20. Houndmills: Palgrave McMillan.

Griffith, Melanie, Ali Rogers, and Bridget Anderson. 2013. *Migration, Time and Temporalities: Review and Prospect.* COMPAS Research Resource Paper. Oxford: Oxford University.

Harrell-Bond, Barbara. 1986. *Imposing Aid: Emergency Assistance to Refugees.* Oxford: Oxford University Press.

Hebrew Sheltering and Immigrant Aid Society (HIAS). n.d. *Advocacy*. Accessed 6 February 2017. http://www.hias.org/work/advocacy.

Holborn, Louise. 1975. *Refugees, a Problem of Our Time: The Work of the Office of the High Commissioner for Refugees, 1951– 1972*. Metuchen: Scarecrow Press.

Holzer, Elizabeth. 2012. "A Case Study of Political Failure in a Refugee Camp." *Journal of Refugee Studies* 25(2): 257–81.

Horst, Cindy. 2006. "Buufis amongst Somalis in Dadaab: The Transnational and Historical Logics behind Resettlement Dreams." *Journal of Refugee Studies* 19(2): 143–57.

Hugo, Graeme. 2011. *Economic, Social and Civic Contributions of First and Second Generation Humanitarian Entrants*. Canberra: Department of Immigration and Citizenship.

Hyndman, Jennifer. 2000. *Managing Displacement. Refugees and the Politics of Humanitarianism*. Minneapolis: University of Minnesota Press.

——. 2011. *Research Summary on Resettled Refugee Integration in Canada*. Ottawa: United Nations High Commissioner for Refugees.

Ilcan, Suzan, and Kim Rygiel. 2015. "'Resiliency Humanitarianism.' Responsibilizing Refugees through Humanitarian Emergency Governance in the Camp." *International Political Sociology* 9(4): 333–51.

Immigration, Refugees and Citizenship Canada (IRCC). 2017. *#Welcome Refugees, Key Figures*. Ottawa: IRCC. Accessed 6 February 2017. http://www.cic.gc.ca/english/refugees/welcome/milestones.asp.

Jubilut, Liliana Lyra. 2017a. "Global Compacts on Migration and on Refugees: How They Should Intersect." *World Economic Forum Agenda Blog*. Accessed 18 December 2017. https://www.weforum.org/agenda/2017/12/compacts-for-migrants-and-refugees-can-be-separate-but-must-reflect-what-they-share.

——. 2017b. "Refugees Are Not the Creators of the Crisis. They Are the Victims." *World Economic Forum Agenda Blog*. Accessed 16 December 2017. https://www.weforum.org/agenda/2017/11/the-refugee-crisis-or-a-crisis-for-refugees/.

Jubilut, Liliana Lyra, and Wellington Pereira Carneiro. 2011. "Resettlement in Solidarity: A New Regional Approach towards a More Humane Durable Solution." *Refugee Survey Quarterly* 30(3): 63–86.

Karatani, Rieko. 2005. "How History Separated Refugee and Migrant Regimes: In Search of Their Institutional Origins." *International Journal of Refugee Law* 17: 517–41.

Keen, David. 2008. *Complex Emergencies*. Cambridge: Polity.

Kohl, Katrine. 2016. "The Evolution of Danish Refugee Resettlement Policy, 1978–2016." *Norwegian Centre for Humanitarian Studies*. Accessed 6 February 2017. http://www.humanitarianstudies.no/2016/11/24/the-evolution-of-danish-refugee-resettlement-policy-1978-2016/.

Kunz, Egon. 1988. *Displaced Persons: Calwell's New Australians*. Sydney: ANU Press.

Lecadet, Clara. 2016. "Refugee Politics: Self-Organized 'Government' and Protests in the Agamé Refugee Camp (2005–13)." *Journal of Refugee Studies* 29(2): 187–207.

Loescher, Gil. 2001. *The UNHCR and World Politics: A Perilous Path*. Oxford: Oxford University Press.

Long, Katy. 2013. "When Refugees Stopped Being Migrants: Movement, Labour and Humanitarian Protection." *Migration Studies* 1(1): 1–15.

Losoncz, Ibolya. 2015. "Goals without Means: A Mertonian Critique of Australia's Resettlement Policy for South Sudanese Refugees." *Journal of Refugee Studies* 30(1): 47–70.

Menezes, Fabiano L. de. 2016. "Utopia or Reality: Regional Cooperation in Latin America to Enhance the Protection of Refugees." *Refugee Studies Quarterly* 35(4): 122–41.

Miles, Robert, and Diana Kay. 1992. *Refugees or Migrant Workers? European Volunteer Workers in Britain, 1946–1951.* London: Routledge.

Mirza, Mansha. 2011. "Disability and Cross-Border Mobility: Comparing Resettlement Experiences of Cambodian and Somali Refugees with Disabilities." *Disability and Society* 26(5): 521–35.

Moulin, Carolina, and Peter Nyers. 2007. "'We Live in a Country of UNHCR'– Refugee Protest and Global Political Society." *International Political Sociology* 1(4): 356–72.

Nawyn, Stephanie. 2006. "Faith, Ethnicity and Culture in Refugee Resettlement." *American Behavioral Scientist* 49(11): 1509–27.

Neumann, Klaus. 2004. *Refuge Australia: Australia's Humanitarian Record.* Sydney: UNSW Press.

Newland, Kathleen. 2002. *Refugee Resettlement in Transition.* Washington, D.C.: Migration Policy Institute. Accessed 6 February 2016. http://www.migrationinformation.org/Feature/display.cfm?ID=52.

Nyers, Peter. 2005. *Rethinking Refugees: Beyond State of Emergency.* London: Routledge.

Ott, Eleanor. 2013. *The Labour Market Integration of Resettled Refugees.* Geneva: UNHCR.

Oxford Dictionaries. n.d. "Power." Accessed 6 February 2017. https://www.google.be/search?q=power+definition&ie=utf-8&oe=utf-8&client=firefox-b-ab&gfe_rd=cr&ei=TesRWM3dM6PS8AfQhoHQAQ.

Pallister-Wilkins, Polly. 2015. "The Humanitarian Politics of European Border Policing: Frontex and Border Police in Evros." *International Political Sociology* 9(1): 53–69.

Pandolfi, Mariella. 2003. "Contract of Mutual (In)Difference: Governance and the Humanitarian Apparatus in Contemporary Albania and Kosovo." *Indiana Journal of Global Legal Studies* 10(1): 369–81.

Piper, Margaret, and Graham Thom. 2014. *Removing the Stumbling Blocks: Ways to Use Resettlement More Effectively to Better Protect Refugee Minors.* Sydney: The University of Sydney/Amnesty International.

Refugee Rights Turkey. 2017. *Introduction to the Asylum Context in Tukey.* Accessed 18 December 2017. http://www.asylumineurope.org/reports/country/turkey/introduction-asylum-context-turkey.

Robinson, W. Courtland. 1998. *Terms of Refuge: The Indo-Chinese Exodus and the International Response.* London: Zed Books.

——. 2004. "The Comprehensive Plan of Action for Indochinese Refugees, 1989–1997: Sharing the Burden and Passing the Buck." *Journal of Refugee Studies* 17(3): 319–33.

Ruiz, Hiram. 2015. *Evaluation of Resettlement Programmes in Argentina, Brazil, Chile, Paraguay and Uruguay.* Geneva: UNHCR.

Sandvik, Kristin Bergtora. 2009. "The Physicality of Legal Consciousness: Suffering and the Production of Credibility in Refugee Resettlement." In *Humanitarianism and Suffering: The Mobilization of Empathy,* edited by R. D. Brown and R. A. Wilson, 223–244. Cambridge: Cambridge University Press.

———. 2010. "Framing Accountability in Refugee Resettlement." In *Accountability for Human Rights Violations of International Organizations,* edited by J. Wouters, E. Brems, and S. Schmitt, 287–307. Antwerp: Intersentia Publishers.

———. 2011. "Blurring Boundaries: Refugee Resettlement in Kampala–Between the Formal, the Informal, and the Illegal." *PoLAr: Political and Legal Anthropology Review* 34(1): 11–32.

———. 2012. "The Politics and Possibilities of Victim Making in International Law/As Políticas e Possibilidades da 'Construção de Vítimas' no Direito Internacional." *Revista Da Faculdade De Direito Do Sul De Minas* 27(2): 237–257.

Sandvik, Kristin Bergtora, and Katja Lindskov Jacobsen, eds. 2016. *UNHCR and the Struggle for Accountability.* London: Routledge.

Seibel, Kimberly. 2016. "Bureaucratic Birthdates: Chronometric Old Age as Resource and Liability in US Refugee Resettlement." *Refuge* 32(3): 8–17.

Shacknove, A. 1993. "From Asylum to Containment." *International Journal of Refugee Law* 5(4): 516–33.

Spivey, Savannah E., and Denise C. Lewis. 2015. "Harvesting from a Repotted Plant: A Qualitative Study of Karen Refugees' Resettlement and Foodways." *Journal of Refugee Studies* 29(1): 60–81.

Suhrke, Astri. 1998. "Burden-Sharing during Refugee Emergencies: The Logic of Collective versus National Action." *Journal of Refugee Studies* 11(4): 396–415.

Thomson, Marnie Jane. 2012. "Black Boxes of Bureaucracy: Transparency and Opacity in the Resettlement Process of Congolese Refugees." *PoLAR: Political and Legal Anthropology Review* 35(2): 186–205.

United Nations High Commissioner for Refugees' Office (UNHCR). Various years. *Statistical Yearbook.* Geneva: UNHCR.

———. 2003. *Agenda for Protection.* Geneva: UNHCR.

———. 2009. *Statistical Yearbook.* Geneva: UNHCR.

———. 2010. *Progress Report on Resettlement.* Executive Committee of the High Commissioner's Programme, EC/61/SC/CRP.11. Geneva: UNHCR. Accessed 6 February 2017. http://www.unhcr.org/4c0526409.htm.

———. 2011. *Resettlement Handbook.* Geneva: UNHCR.

———. 2012. *Progress Report on Resettlement.* Executive Committee of the High Commissioner's Programme, EC/63/SC/CRP.12. Geneva: UNHCR. Accessed 6 February 2017. http://www.unhcr.org/5006a6aa9.html.

———. 2015. *UNHCR-NGO Toolkit for Practical Cooperation on Resettlement: A Repository for Exchanging Ideas on Resettlement Partnerships.* Geneva: UNHCR. Accessed 6 February 2017. http://www.unhcr.org/protection/resettlement/4ce54a949/unhcr-ngo-toolkit-practical-cooperation-resettlement-repository-exchanging.html.

———. 2018. *Global Trends 2017: Forced Displacement at a Glance.* Geneva: UNHCR. Accessed 28 June 2018. http://www.unhcr.org/5b27be547.pdf.

———. n.d. "Resettlement." Accessed 6 February 2017. http://www.unhcr.org/resettlement.html.

van Selm, J. 2003. "Public-Private Partnerships in Refugee Resettlement: Europe and the US." *Journal of International Migration and Integrationale* 4(2): 157–75.

Verdirame, Guglielmo, and Barbara Harrell-Bond. 2005. *Rights in Exile.* Oxford/ New York: Berghahn Books.

Viviani, Nancy. 1984. *The Long Journey.* Melbourne: Melbourne University Press.

Walters, William. 2015. "Reflections on Migration and Governmentality." *Movements. Journal for Critical Migration and Border Regime Studies* 1(1). Accessed 5 December 2017. http://movements-journal.org/issues/01.grenzregime/04.walters–migrati on.governmentality.html.

Waxman, Peter, and Val Colic-Peisker, eds. 2005. *Homeland Wanted: Interdisciplinary Perspectives on Refugee Resettlement in the West.* Hauppauge: Nova Science Publishers.

Wintour, Patrick. 2017. "Donald Trump Pulls US out of UN Global Compact on Migration." *The Guardian,* 3 December. Accessed 5 December 2017. https:// www.theguardian.com/world/2017/dec/03/donald-trump-pulls-us-out-of- un-global-compact-on-migration.

Wyman, Mark. 1998. *DPs: Europe's Displaced Persons, 1945–51.* Ithaca: Cornell University Press.

Yuhas, Alan, and Mazin Sidahmed. 2017. "Is This a Muslim Ban? Trump's Executive Order Explained." *The Guardian,* 30 January. Accessed 30 January 2017. https://www.theguardian.com/us-news/2017/jan/28/trump-immigration-ban- syria-muslims-reaction-lawsuits.

Part I

Refugee Resettlement in International and Regional Perspectives

1

Strategic Use of Resettlement

Enhancing Solutions for Greater Protection?

Joanne van Selm

Introduction

"Getting the biggest bang for the buck" is a suggestion that comes up in interviews with officials in many governments and organizations when discussing the Strategic Use of Resettlement (SUR). It seems straightforward—get the most out of efforts to resettle refugees. The question is, however, is it that simple? Does having motives beyond the resettlement of a refugee individual or family actually assist in the search for solutions or protection?

The SUR was introduced by Canadian-led Working Group on Resettlement in 2003 and defined as follows:

> The strategic use of resettlement is the planned use of resettlement in a manner that maximizes the benefits, directly or indirectly, other than those received by the refugee being resettled. Those benefits may accrue to other refugees, the hosting state, other states or the international protection regime in general. (UNHCR 2003)

The concept of SUR, at heart, can be read as a simple statement: if deployed carefully, the very conscious and deliberate act of resettling a refugee for protection and a durable solution in a safe country can be given additional purpose. This additional purpose could be found in consequences for other refugees and for countries, as well as for the international refugee protection and humanitarian regime more broadly. In other words, resettlement does not stand alone. It is part of a bigger picture, and by being strategic (or at least tactical) in offering the limited number of resources available for actual resettlement, states could, in theory, bring benefits beyond the positive outcomes for the individuals and families resettled.

The central question for this chapter is whether SUR presents a practical path to increased protection broadly and more focused resettlement activity in particular, or whether SUR could better be considered as simply a concept. In the latter case, SUR would just be a thought to bear in mind when making choices about situations in which resettlement could play a role. A third alternative might be that the concept is too clumsy to be useful. One of the key ways to assess SUR's potential, and match that up against its emerging reality, is to look at the language used and motives given for various resettlement policy decisions around the world.

An underlying issue in approaching this question is an understanding of the distribution of power in both the refugee protection and solutions regime broadly and in resettlement in particular. In this context, reflections on power can relate both to traditional state power, and the potential sway of international organizations, and to the more subtle power of persuasion. The focus here will be on the subtle power of persuasion and on the power of ideas in terms of cross-fertilization and targeted use of an approach to stimulate or sustain interest in other areas. Here again, the language used and motives given for resettlement decisions demonstrate a certain use of power.

This chapter will survey the role of SUR and the closely associated "enhanced resettlement" in sustaining interest in resettlement writ large and adding to the refugee protection regime. It will rely on reports written on the subject from 2003 (its introduction) to today. The analysis of those reports is supplemented by conversations with policy makers over several years regarding their thinking on whether SUR has continued potential. The approach taken is one of policy analysis. It is qualitative and based on political and juridical thinking: while offering some data, it has to be noted that there is limited work or research on SUR and, as such, this chapter offers as much a process of thought as it does a thorough academic argument.

In theory, SUR offers opportunities for rethinking and refashioning not only resettlement but also the whole refugee protection regime–from orderly arrivals in developed countries to knock-on effects in terms of greater protection capacity in regions of origin. In both theory and practice, however, there are many pitfalls, including in the consequences of language used (with the emphasis on strategy and multipliers, rather than protection) and in the devaluing of the resettlement activity as a good in and of itself.

If SUR has had any success since its inception, it has lain in the power of the idea–the notion that resettlement can be employed or deployed for other purposes. However, the very danger that SUR brings to resettlement could be that if used for a purpose other than a durable solution for refugee protection needs, then resettlement could easily be abused or misused, undermining this very valuable solution tool.

How Did SUR Emerge?

SUR was introduced in 2003 as part of the Convention Plus initiative led by the United Nations High Commissioner for Refugees (UNHCR). This initiative flowed from the Agenda for Protection, itself an outcome of the Global Consultations marking the fiftieth anniversary of the 1951 Convention Relating to the Status of Refugees. That anniversary came in a period in which the convention was being called into question on many sides, with political parties in various developed states suggesting that it was no longer useful or relevant, and amid North-South tensions over the issue of solidarity and the location and financing of refugees and their protection.[1]

Interest in SUR specifically flowed from the confluence of three major trends that gave rise to a desire to reinvigorate or recast the traditional durable solution of resettlement. First there were serious limitations placed on the biggest resettlement program globally (that of the United States) following the terrorist attacks of 9/11 in 2001. Second, this was a time when European states were experiencing what then seemed like an asylum crisis (the events of 2015–2016 cast that in a different light), and not (yet) conducting any significant levels of resettlement. Third, existing resettlement countries and UNHCR had been seeking new partners in expanding resettlement for the benefit of the overall systems and a more solutions-oriented approach (van Selm 2003; Sandvik, this volume; Garnier 2014).

Over time, a renewed focus on comprehensive solutions also emerged, into which SUR played perfectly (van Selm 2004, 2013). Protracted refugee crises, stagnant for years or even decades in some cases (Thomson, this volume), might be resolved if some of the caseload were to be resettled, opening the way for others (perhaps dependent on specific group characteristics) to return home or achieve substantive local integration (on this, see Losoncz, this volume).

The intended appeal of SUR is clear: encourage more resettlement and more thoughtfulness in resettlement choices by focusing not only on the relatively small number of refugees who are resettled but also on any added benefits for others that can be gained through that resettlement. Officials who have been central to the development of SUR over the past decade often cite their search for "the multiplier effect."[2] By achieving a multiplication of impacts, there could also be an increase in willingness to resettle, and thus in both places available and destination countries involved (Jubilut and Zamur; Vera Espinoza, this volume).

The more cynical practitioners, perhaps naturally, have focused on issues such as why there cannot simply be more resettlement, because in and of itself resettlement, as a durable solution and "burden-sharing" tool is a "good thing."[3] Why would one have to layer other solutions or outcomes into the equation? Others have asked whether the significant resources needed for each individual resettlement case could be better channeled into a stronger and more direct approach in regions of origin, including in conflict prevention and resolution and in support to neighboring states hosting hundreds of thousands of displaced persons (Loescher and Milner 2003). So, it can reasonably be said that while SUR offers opportunities, it is also replete with pitfalls and challenges.

To be clear, it is far from being the case that all resettlement is, or ever would be, "used strategically"–although, as will be seen below, there is an increasing push toward developing "enhanced resettlement" that might be viewed as a more positive version of essentially the same approach.

This chapter is concerned only with that resettlement that is either labeled a "Strategic Use of Resettlement" or "Enhanced Resettlement" or talked of in strategic terms and could therefore be easily construed of as being intended to be SUR. Indeed a fundamental line of argument will be that one of the greatest challenges to "genuine SUR"–the seeking of a *positive* multiplier effect–is governments making use of resettlement offers to seek gains that serve nonprotection, or even what might be called antirefugee protection and certainly anti-(im)migration, interests.

Setting Up a Winning Situation

The notion of SUR did not bear immediate fruits in the mid-2000s, but later in the decade major resettlement countries and UNHCR were starting to identify situations in which they could apply or adapt the concept.

As noted above, SUR was developed in the context of the Convention Plus initiative. In the early 2000s, this initiative sought to elicit commitments from all key actors in multilateral processes to strengthen refugee protection based on the convention. It was very much an initiative intended to bridge the North-South divide in refugee protection. This divide is evident in the location of refugees (predominantly in the South) and the tone of discourse on asylum and on protection (particularly harsh in the North). It is also manifest in the issue of solidarity or responsibility sharing, both in a practical and financial sense, and in the sense of support and a managed approach (Betts and Durieux 2007; Pressé and Thomson 2008). The actors involved were receiving states in the developed world and less developed states in regions of origin, UNHCR, and implementing partners, including NGOs.

The three strands of Convention Plus were resettlement, targeted development assistance to support refugee protection, and the management of irregular secondary movements (UNHCR n.d.). The resettlement strand bore fruit in the form of the SUR working paper and discussions. However, its implementation was predicated on it being part of an overarching initiative including all three Convention Plus strands–and work on the other two elements was significantly less successful. Indeed the initiative as a whole has been characterized as a failure (Betts 2009: 150–52). As such, broad progress on SUR was impeded. Although the notion had been planted, it was not nurtured in isolation from the other Convention Plus strands but lay dormant until a context for its further development arose. It was, however, in the intervening period, used as support for decisions on groups of refugees to be resettled by the United States in particular, as will be seen below.

A UNHCR position paper in 2011 reignited the concept (UNHCR 2011a) and UNHCR's 2011 *Resettlement Handbook* talks of maximizing "the potential benefits from the application of this scarce resource" and how "with the active involvement of States, refugee and civil society, resettlement can open avenues for international responsibility sharing and, in combination with other measures, can open possibilities for self-reliance and integration" (UNHCR 2011b: 39). Used strategically, resettlement can, according to the handbook, "bring about positive results that go well beyond those that are usually viewed as a direct resettlement outcome" (ibid.).

UNHCR suggests the benefits of SUR can be maximized when states coordinate among themselves and with UNCHR. SUR has, or should have, greatest impact when it turns into a coordinated, comprehensive effort, not just to "use" resettlement but to develop a protection outcome that satisfies individuals, states, and societies and allows all durable solutions (so also integration and repatriation) to be applied. UNHCR and states (particularly the United States and Canada) point to a couple of successes. One was the closure of the Al-Tanf camp for Palestinians, which was achieved in part through the resettlement of ex-Iraq refugees with nowhere else to go (UNHCR 2012: 56). Another was the coordination of the Core Group on Bhutanese refugees in Nepal, which has seen a multiyear commitment to resettle tens of thousands of the 100,000 or more refugees (van Selm 2013).

Some question these apparent successes. Most Bhutanese were resettled to the United States, which was seeking to increase its own resettlement program and needed a relatively straightforward caseload, and the anticipated returns of others to Nepal did not really materialize (Banki 2008). SUR appears to some to have primarily been a tool or mantra under which resettlement decision makers in the United States could focus on groups who did not have the misfortune to be representative of those religions or ethnicities that Western states have difficulty accommodating in a time of extremist terrorism. Yet, one could also say that the concept of SUR at least presented an opportunity to focus on some of these groups and to achieve their resettlement, and durable solutions, even if it could just be a cover for avoiding some more difficult choices.

Indeed, the US resettlement program could have dwindled in the face of political opposition following 9/11. Instead UNHCR and the officials responsible for the program initially held back and then moved the program toward cases such as the Bhutanese in Nepal and the Burmese in Thailand, maintaining resettlement arrival numbers without challenging domestic US political concerns and perceptions about who was arriving. This simultaneously assisted UNHCR in clearing some backlogs and opening opportunities for other solutions for those who were not resettled from those specific situations (van Selm 2013: 36ff). This "Strategic Use of Resettlement" had an additional outcome in keeping the United States fully engaged in resettlement to the benefit of the international protection regime, as covered by the definition given by the 2003 Working Group definition of SUR. It kept the United States' refugee resettlement program open and active. By 2016 the resettlement targets of the program had grown numerically, and groups such as Syrians in Jordan and Lebanon were getting access and a solution (for additional perspectives on resettlement in the United States, see Darrow; and Lewis and Young, this volume).

In this maintenance and growth of the United States' resettlement program until 2016, we can observe the power of the idea. In essence, a small group of policy makers in various government agencies, as well as staff of nonprofit institutions involved in resettlement and the local UNHCR bureau, were able to employ the notion of SUR to help keep the resettlement program alive in a time of intense political pressure. Having done that, the program remained intact, ready to grow again when international developments and national politics required and permitted it.[4]

States and UNHCR frequently note that resettlement is a very scarce resource in the face of massive international (and internal) displacement (see, e.g., UNHCR 2003: para. 5).[5] One of the intended outcomes of SUR was an increase in the resource, and indeed some countries have started to participate in resettlement over the past thirteen years, even if the overall number of places has not increased dramatically (yet), and certainly not in proportion to global needs (Garnier 2014; Cellini, this volume).

SUR has primarily been called upon as a way of focusing resettling states and UNHCR's attention on long-standing refugee populations, in which there has been little or no movement and seems to be no end to the standstill other than through a game changer such as resettling one particular subgroup in order to achieve return or local integration for others (or indeed simply resettling an entire refugee community). Applying SUR for newer refugee groups might, perhaps, be seen as too much "strategy."

However, UNHCR has pushed for SUR, or as it has recently more often been labeled "enhanced resettlement," in the case of Syrians in Lebanon and Jordan (Cochetel 2015). Syrians are the focus of more resettlement efforts and resources than any crisis since the Indo-Chinese in the 1970s and 1980s. The following provides an illustration of this development, although the figures do not present the full picture of actual resettlement (pledges often exceeding the reality of arrivals). The United Kingdom has offered 20,000 places over five years, although actual arrivals since the announcement have been very slow, giving rise to concern that the target will never be met (House of Commons 2016). Germany has pledged almost 40,000 resettlement places for Syrians over a four-year period and has seen not only on-track arrivals of resettling refugees leaving Lebanon and Jordan but also the major part of the asylum arrivals during the 2015 crisis (UNHCR 2016a; Rietig and Müller 2016).

Canada resettled almost 40,000 Syrian refugees by January 2017 under the mix of its government-assisted and privately sponsored programs and promised more than twice that number of places (Immigration, Refugees and Citizenship Canada 2017; also Garnier, this volume). The United States had resettled its target of 10,000 Syrians for the year by August 2016 (Department of State 2016), and more than 50,000 had gained admission in total, in spite of extremely rigorous and lengthy background and security controls (UNHCR 2016a). All of this could have burden-sharing benefits for refugees remaining in Lebanon and Jordan as those countries see that they do not face the Syrian displacement crisis entirely alone, meeting some of the criteria defining SUR.

However, many of the governments do not actually refer to these resettlement situations as either SUR or enhanced resettlement–which in itself is a complicating aspect of assessing what SUR really is and how great its impact has been. A major finding of a 2013 UNHCR Policy Development and Evaluation Service (PDES) review of SUR was that policy makers meant different things when talking about the concept and that even lines of communication between UNHCR and resettlement countries on the subject were confusing (van Selm 2013). Goals were set out–the strategy–resettlement was applied, but whether the aims were achieved or not seemed immaterial. In 2011, UNHCR had even stated that "not achieving goals does not mean failure." The review called for improved communication and a more evidence-based approach. Part of the problem was that in a semantic sense "strategic use" sounds very solid (and if not militaristic, then at least strongly goal oriented and determined to enact specific and well–thought through plans to achieve defined consequences).

From a policy and communication perspective, therefore, the shift from "Strategic Use of Resettlement" to "Enhanced Resettlement" is interesting and important to consider when thinking of the opportunities and challenges of the approach. The semantic shift seems to have been intimated around the time of the 2011 *Resettlement Handbook* (UNHCR 2011b). However, even in the 2015 *Global Resettlement Needs* report, the term "Strategic Use of Resettlement" was used to refer to the Core Group on Syrian Refugees, and the introduction included an overview on the effective implementation of SUR (UNHCR 2014).

By the time of the 2017 *Global Resettlement Needs* report, the terminology had shifted to "upscaling" and "alternative pathways," with the term "strategic" reserved for the "strategic response" broadly of UNHCR to solutions and protection needs (UNHCR 2016b). The move seems to have taken the positive elements–taking a comprehensive approach, destination state coordination, relieving the burden on countries of first asylum, multiyear planning–and termed them positively as an enhancement to resettlement. Meanwhile, it appears that the semantically and politically more complex notion of a strategy for using resettlement is gradually being dropped– although there does not appear to be any official definition of "enhanced resettlement" that takes it beyond the 2003 working group definition of SUR.

Overreaching: SUR Being Used or Misused?

The SUR faces many challenges, which were highlighted in the 2013 review of SUR for UNHCR: being able to pinpoint the targeted outcomes, achieving those goals and having the evidence to underpin the achievement, coordinating between states and organizations involved in an effort at SUR, increasing numbers and participants so that there is a real chance of achieving goals and having the right language and approach to convey intentions (van Selm 2013).

The shift away from the use of "strategic" to "enhanced," and even beyond that to "upscaling" and finding "alternative pathways" that effectively offer similar protection and solutions to resettlement, may be an effort to overcome the semantic challenge. These shifts might also reflect the balance in the power of persuasion. The effort in 2016 and for the foreseeable future is likely to be to focus attention on resolving the situation of Syrian displaced persons, as a separate category from longer-term refugee populations. Resettlement as a long-term policy tool potentially has a different focus from the short- to medium-term goals of stemming the irregular flow of Syrian asylum seekers by finding a more managed approach to their arrival in Europe.

The establishment of core groups to coordinate approaches or at least collectively think through goals is another shift. Resettlement countries have increased in number, although there are many more potential destination countries that do not yet participate, and numbers have risen somewhat.

The fact that many resettlement countries now have specific programs for Syrians, in some cases in addition to broader resettlement programs, is also a demonstration of not only how numbers have risen but also how appeals can lead to some targeting (see also Reklev and Jumbert, this volume). However, SUR, or enhanced resettlement, continues to face challenges.

Even with the move to the language of "enhanced resettlement," it is important to ask, for example, how many priorities there can really be. In the 2013 UNHCR PDES review cited above, it was noted that it is difficult to unite the urgent language of "strategic use" with the fact that UNHCR offers "priorities for the Strategic Use of Resettlement" in dozens of situations around the world at once (van Selm 2013). This trend has continued, as can be seen in the 2015 assessment of *Global Resettlement Needs,* which sees priorities in the cases of Eritreans in Eastern Sudan, Congolese in Tanzania, Syrians in Egypt, Burmese in Thailand, Congolese in Malawi, Colombians in Costa Rica, Iraqis in Lebanon, Afghans in Iran, Congolese in Rwanda . . . and the list goes on (UNHCR 2014). In the 2017 *Global Resettlement Needs* report, there are nine "priority situations" listed, and groups of refugees to be resettled are assigned a priority category of "normal," "urgent," or "emergency" (UNHCR 2016b: 61, 64). Using the term "enhanced resettlement" partially removes the sense of urgency inherent in "strategic use," but the question remains of whether "priority" has the force intended when spread so liberally.

However, the bigger issue is that resettlement may not be used as originally intended. For those countries facing an asylum crisis, resettlement can look like a golden solution. The destination state gets to select the refugees, determine their status while they are still in their region of origin, say how many to move and when to move them, and determine their first destination on arrival in the resettling state. It sounds so orderly and organized when compared to the images of boats arriving unpredictably, carrying hundreds of people, who, once they have the energy, seem to fan out across a continent, deciding for themselves where to stop and ask for protection. The temptation to say that the strategic way to employ resettlement is a counterbalance to asylum arrivals is great. Although it has not been said exactly this way, it is not a stretch to read examples such as the EU-Turkey migration pact as a strategy employing resettlement to achieve other goals, in particular a reduction in irregular asylum arrivals.

The EU member states have committed many places to resettlement of Syrians from Jordan, Lebanon, and Turkey as well as to relocation from Greece. EU member states have pledged 38,000 places for Syrians (European Commission n.d.), and fourteen of the member states now have annual resettlement programs covering arrivals from around the world, with about 7,000 places made available annually (Cellini, this volume). The places for Syrians are supposed to be in addition to the annual resettlement quotas.

Sixteen of the EU member states also have relocation programs to admit refugees who initially sought protection in another EU member state (European Commission n.d.).

During 2015, Europe received an unprecedented number of arrivals: more than one million people, primarily from Syria, Africa, and South Asia, arrived in Europe, about 95 percent of them arriving by boat in Greece and Italy in particular (e.g., International Organization for Migration 2015). The vast majority of these migrants intended to reach Germany (McDonnell 2016). Many did, but a great many also found their way blocked as any semblance of an EU asylum system crumbled, Schengen and other freedom of movement rules were thrown into doubt, and borders were reinforced and, at least temporarily, closed (Mohdin 2016).

The overwhelming majority of Syrian arrivals by sea were coming from Turkey. In an effort to stem the flow, and after several unsuccessful attempts to do so by other means or to face the crisis in mutual solidarity, EU member states made an agreement with Turkey (European Council 2016). A key part of that agreement was a one-for-one, highly strategic, resettlement program, under which for each Syrian asylum seeker arriving irregularly in Greece from Turkey who was sent back another Syrian refugee would be resettled from Turkey to the EU. The potential for returns to Turkey, with the designation of "safe country" by EU governments, was met with a blistering critique by the human rights and refugee protection community (e.g., ECRE 2016a). The European Council on Refugees and Exiles also commented strongly on the resettlement aspect of the deal: "However, making any resettlement program conditional on an exchange which involves people risking their lives to seek protection establishes a morally repugnant precedent. Resettlement should be treated as distinct from readmission and other deterrence measures" (ECRE 2016b).

By mid-July some 800 Syrians had been resettled from Turkey to EU member states under the mandate of the 8 March 2016 pact, while some 8,250 Syrians had been resettled to the EU in the year since the July 2015 Resettlement Scheme had been agreed on (European Commission 2016). Meanwhile 482 migrants had been returned from Greece to Turkey since 10 March, and the population of migrants stranded in Greece had, by late August 2016, reached 67,250–a 43 percent increase since 10 March (International Organization for Migration 2016).

The major argument from the point of view of this chapter on SUR is that although such a one-for-one deal as the EU struck with Turkey might seem like a *strategy using resettlement,* it is not what the conceptualizers envisioned as SUR, and in essence it is an abuse both of resettlement itself and of the notion that resettlement can provide additional benefits.[6] The "benefit" of limiting asylum flows and preventing people from seeking protection is, one could argue, limited to voter relations for governments overseeing a migration and asylum system during a period of major conflict and displacements. That "benefit, however, does not constitute effective management of the international protection system grounded in the 1951 Convention relating to the Status of Refugees, the mandate of UNHCR and various international and regional human rights instruments. What is more, it has the potential to undermine any positive steps taken in building a more robust solutions approach, with resettlement as a core element.

Conclusion

Thirteen years on from the conceptualization of SUR, resettlement numbers have, or at least had until early 2017, risen somewhat, but any goal of a long-term orderly refugee arrival approach remains distant.[7] Refugee and displaced person numbers, globally, have risen significantly, and states' concerns about who exactly is among asylum and irregular arrivals have not diminished–in fact they have only heightened.

The central question for this chapter was which of three understandings of SUR was valid. Does SUR present a practical path to increased protection broadly, and more focused resettlement activity in particular? Could SUR be better considered as simply a concept, a thought to bear in mind when making choices about situations in which resettlement could play a role? Or is the concept too clumsy to be useful?

The overview and discussion above seem to show that in practice some greater protection focus can emerge from taking a SUR or enhanced resettlement approach–but that it cannot possibly be applied consistently across the board by all actors at all times. There are various factors influencing choices in undertaking resettlement. While any given government could claim that the resettlement they choose is driven by a desire to maximize its "multiplier effect," actually systematically making multiyear plans, coordinating with other governments and UNHCR, setting out specific and clear priorities and goals and achieving them (particularly when that includes prompting countries to accept returnees or allow a greater level of local integration in countries of first asylum) are very complicated and difficult. As such, the concept seems primarily to be useful as a support to explaining resettlement decisions at present; however, over time, with demonstrated successes and increasing quotas, it could become a more focused and solid element to increase protection more broadly.

The notion of SUR or enhanced resettlement encourages governments to think of resettlement not just as opening their doors to a very limited and select group of refugees–the chosen few, an almost perverse type of elite whether in terms of the exclusivity of their situation, or their vulnerabilities, or whatever the resettlement criteria applied–but as a tool in their protection kit that can open more than just a solution for the few selected. Perhaps the most important aspects of SUR for the long-term prospects of not only resettlement but the whole international protection regime are the multiyear approach and coordination.

Employing resettlement effectively, in both protracted situations and relatively new ones, requires flexibility. Much more resettlement of Syrians from Lebanon and Jordan in particular and sooner might have avoided the massive nature of the Mediterranean Sea crossings during 2015 and 2016–and might have meant that the protection-undermining pact between the EU and Turkey would not have been necessary, for example. The power of the idea of resettlement in this case came too late–and the ultimate persuasive factor might have been the actual presence of hundreds of thousands of asylum seekers and migrants and prospect of many more coming.

SUR has perhaps opened opportunities: it has given UNHCR and states a potentially powerful concept to persuade others (and in some cases for ministries to persuade political leaders domestically) that certain caseloads, or higher numbers, for resettlement could make sense. The very word "strategic" lends persuasive power to the idea, although at the same time it sets up an ethical conundrum when it is about the "use" of what most people in the field would prefer to see as an essential "good." Some might argue that employing SUR to increase the resettlement of the Bhutanese from Nepal, or Burmese from Thailand, demonstrates the manipulation (or persuasion) of a system by interested parties within a bureaucracy. However, they might also say that it shows weakness–choosing the easier caseloads. Perhaps one could approach it rather as examples that show the power of the idea in tackling a long-standing, protracted situation and, as a positive outcome, keeping the United States' resettlement program, in this instance, alive and operational for future caseloads. Writing in early 2017, the question might be whether SUR is the approach that could be used to once again restart the US refugee program. Would it have that power? Only time will tell.

Applying resettlement effectively to the benefit of more than the resettled refugees requires good coordination and communication, effective leadership, and an increasing number of committed governments willing to accept a resettlement caseload that, for the foreseeable future, is only likely to increase. It requires careful and open evaluation of where the policy has succeeded and where, how, and why it has failed, so that the benefits of SUR can be maximized for all concerned. It demands focus and probably means that some crises that might look like potential priorities are actually left on the back burner for some years but constantly monitored for when the time is ripe to employ resettlement to unlock the solutions potential for all concerned. It also requires governments to actively select refugees for migration to their country even if the electorate appears reluctant to accept immigration, and even while asylum seekers arrive seeking protection on their own timetable. Neither resettlement itself nor its enhanced or strategic use is an easy path, but if it could achieve its objectives it might well be worth pursuing.

Joanne Van Selm holds a Ph.D. in international relations from the University of Kent at Canterbury, United Kingdom and is an independent consultant on migration and refugee issues. She has previously held positions at Georgetown University, the Migration Policy Institute, the University of Amsterdam, and Vrije Universiteit. She was a coeditor at the *Journal of Refugee Studies* (2000–2011), was president of the International Association for the Study of Forced Migration (2003–2005), and is the author of numerous books, articles, studies, and reports on resettlement and other migration and refugee protection issues.

Notes

1. Betts (2009, 143–74) sketches the origins of Convention Plus; see also Feller (2001).
2. Interviews conducted for the UNHCR review of the Strategic Use of Resettlement and cited in van Selm 2013.
3. van Selm (2013).
4. Conclusion based on interviews and discussions 2010–2013 on SUR and the US resettlement program with staff of the US Department of State, Department of Homeland Security, UNHCR, and several nonprofit organizations with offices in Washington, D.C.
5. This is also a statement often made during interviews and conference presentations on the subject, for example.
6. This chapter is not concerned with characterizing the deal as a success or failure—that discussion is beyond the present scope.
7. The consequences of *Executive Order: Protecting the Nation from Foreign Terrorist Entry* of 27 January 2017 alter this statement, at least temporarily. That order suspended all resettlement to the United States for 120 days and all Syrian resettlement indefinitely. https://www.whitehouse.gov/the-press-office/2017/01/27/executive-order-protecting-nation-foreign-terrorist-entry-united-states.

References

Banki, Susan. 2008. "Resettlement of the Bhutanese in Nepal: The Durable Solution Discourse." In *Protracted Displacement in Asia,* edited by H. Adelman, 59–82. London: Routledge.

Betts, Alexander. 2009. *Protection by Persuasion: International Cooperation in the Refugee Regime.* Ithaca: Cornell University Press.

Betts, Alexander, and Jean-Francois Durieux. 2007. "Convention Plus as a Norm-Setting Exercise." *Journal of Refugee Studies* 20(3): 509–35.

Cochetel, Vincent. 2015. "What Do We Mean by 'Strategic Resettlement?'" EMN Norway's National Conference Oslo, 12 June. Accessed 6 February 2017. https://

www.udi.no/globalassets/global/european-migration-network_i/konferanse filer/vincent-cochetel—strategic-use-of-resettlement-emn-national-meeting-oslo-12-june-2015.pdf.

Department of State. 2016. *#RefugeesWelcome: US Admits 10,000 Syrian Refugees This Year.* Dipnote US Department of State Official Blog, 30 August. On file with the author.

European Commission. 2016. *Relocation and Resettlement: Positive Trend Continues, but More Efforts Needed.* Press release, 13 July. Accessed 6 February 2017. http://eu ropa.eu/rapid/press-release_IP-16-2435_en.htm.

——. n.d. *Resettlement and Relocation.* Factsheet. Accessed 6 February 2017. https:// ec.europa.eu/home-affairs/sites/homeaffairs/files/what-we-do/policies/europe an-agenda-migration/backgroundinformation/docs/relocation_and_resettle ment_factsheet_en.pdf.

European Council. 2016. *EU-Turkey Statement.* Press release, 18 March. Accessed 6 February 2017. http://www.consilium.europa.eu/en/press/press-releases/2016/ 03/18-eu-turkey-statement/.

European Council on Refugees and Exiles (ECRE). 2016a. *The EU-Turkey Deal in Practice: Jeopardising the European Asylum System,* 8 April. Accessed 6 February 2017. http://www.ecre.org/the-eu-turkey-deal-in-practice-jeopardising-the-european-asylum-system/.

——. 2016b. *EU-Turkey Deal: Trading in People and Outsourcing the EU's Responsibilities,* 8 March. Accessed 6 February 2017. http://www.ecre.org/eu-turkey-deal-trading-in-people-and-outsourcing-the-eus-responsibilities/.

Feller, Erika. 2001. "International Refugee Protection 50 Years On: The Protection Challenges of the Past, Present and Future." *International Review of the Red Cross* 83(843): 590–94.

Garnier, Adèle. 2014. "Migration Management and Humanitarian Protection: The UNHCR's 'Resettlement Expansionism' and Its Impact on Policy-Making in the EU and Australia." *Journal of Ethnic and Migration Studies* 40(6): 942–59.

House of Commons. 2016. *The Work of the Immigration Directorates (Q1 2016),* 25 July. Accessed 6 February 2017. http://www.publications.parliament.uk/pa/ cm201617/cmselect/cmhaff/151/15105.htm#_idTextAnchor024.

Immigration, Refugees and Citizenship Canada. 2017. *#WelcomeRefugees: Canada Resettles Syrian Refugees.* Ottawa: Government of Canada. Accessed 7 February 2017. http://www.cic.gc.ca/english/refugees/welcome/.

International Organization for Migration. 2015. *Irregular Migrant, Refugee Arrivals in Europe Top One Million in 2015.* Press release, 22 December. Accessed 6 February 2017. https://www.iom.int/news/irregular-migrant-refugee-arrivals-eu rope-top-one-million-2015-iom.

——. 2016. *Mixed Migration Flows in the Mediterranean and Beyond, Compilation of Available Data and Information, Reporting Period 22 August–24 August 2016.* Accessed 6 February 2017. http://migration.iom.int/docs/WEEKLY percent20Flows per cent20Compilationpercent20No23percent2025percent20Augustpercent202016 .pdf.

Loescher, Gil, and James Milner. 2003. "The Missing Link: The Need for Comprehensive Engagement in Regions of Refugee Origin." *International Affairs* 79(3): 595–617.

McDonnell, Tim. 2016. "Here's Why So Many of Europe's Migrants Have Their Hearts Set on Germany: The Country Has Long Been the Most Receptive in Europe to Refugees." *Mother Jones,* 8 September. Accessed 6 February 2017. http://www.motherjones.com/politics/2015/09/heres-why-all-european-migrants-want-go-germany.

Mohdin, Aamna. 2016. "These Are the Routes Being Closed Off to Refugees Fleeing into Europe." *Quartz,* 10 March. Accessed 6 February 2017. https://qz.com/635110/these-are-the-routes-being-closed-off-to-refugees-fleeing-into-europe/.

Pressé, Debra, and Jessie Thomson. 2008. "The Resettlement Challenge: Integration of Refugees from Protracted Refugee Situations." *Refuge* 25(1): 94–99.

Rietig, Victoria, and Andreas Müller. 2016. *The New Reality: Germany Adapts to Its Role as a Major Migrant Magnet.* Migration Information Source, 31 August. Accessed 6 February 2017. http://www.migrationpolicy.org/article/new-reality-germany-adapts-its-role-major-migrant-magnet.

United Nations High Commissioner for Refugees (UNHCR). 2003. *The Strategic Use of Resettlement (A Discussion Paper Prepared by the Working Group on Resettlement),* 3 June. Geneva: UNHCR. Accessed 6 February 2017. http://www.unhcr.org/refworld/docid/41597a824.html.

——. 2010. *Position Paper on the Strategic Use of Resettlement.* Annual Tripartite Consultations on Resettlement, Geneva, 6–8 July. Accessed 6 February 2017. http://www.refworld.org/pdfid/4c0d10ac2.pdf.

——. 2011a. *Implementation of the Strategic Use of Resettlement.* Working Group on Resettlement, Geneva, 11–12 October. Accessed 6 February 2017. http://www.refworld.org/docid/4ff147912.html.

——. 2011b. *Resettlement Handbook.* Geneva: UNHCR. Accessed 6 February 2017. http://www.unhcr.org/en-us/protection/resettlement/46f7c0ee2/unhcr-resettlement-handbook-complete-publication.html?query=resettlement.

——. 2012. *State of the World's Refugees.* Geneva: UNHCR. Accessed 6 February 2017. http://www.unhcr.org/3d464bc14.pdf.

——. 2014. *Global Resettlement Needs 2015.* Geneva: UNHCR. Accessed 6 February 2017. http://www.unhcr.org/en-us/protection/resettlement/543408c4fda/unhcr-projected-global-resettlement-needs-2015.html.

——. 2016a. *Resettlement and Other Admission Pathways.* Geneva: UNHCR. Accessed 6 February 2017. http://www.unhcr.org/573dc82d4.pdf.

——. 2016b. UNHCR, *Global Resettlement Needs 2017.* Geneva: UNHCR. Accessed 6 February 2017. http://www.unhcr.org/575836267.

——. n.d. *Convention Plus at a Glance.* Geneva: UNHCR. Accessed 6 February 2017. http://www.unhcr.org/403b30684.pdf.

van Selm, Joanne. 2003. "Refugee Protection Policies and Security Issues." In *Refugees and Forced Displacement. International Security, Human Vulnerability and the State,* edited by E. Newman and J. van Selm, 66–92. Tokyo: UNU Press.

——. 2004. "The Strategic Use of Resettlement: Changing the Face of Protection?" *Refuge* 22(1): 39–48.

——. 2013. *Great Expectations: A Review of the Strategic Use of Resettlement.* PDES report. Geneva: UNHCR. Accessed 6 February 2017. http://www.unhcr.org/research/evalreports/520a3e559/great-expectations-review-strategic-use-resettlement.html.

2

A Legal History

The Emergence of
the African Resettlement Candidate
in International Refugee Management

═══════════

Kristin Bergtora Sandvik

Introduction

The subject matter for this chapter is the emergence of the African refugee as a candidate for third-country resettlement. Across Africa, resettlement is a bureaucratic-legal arrangement with immense practical and symbolic significance, yet it has been subjected to limited doctrinal scrutiny in legal scholarship (Goodwin-Gill and McAdam 2007: 497–500; Troeller 2002; Noll and van Selm 2003; Hathaway 2005), and even less to critical legal approaches. The aim here is to explore African resettlement through the interface of three recent developments in international refugee management: the gradual recognition of the African refugee as a subject of international law, the reemergence of resettlement as a desirable humanitarian enterprise and viable mode of international protection, and the reform and renewal of resettlement by way of legalization, standardization, and human rights approaches.

The actual mechanisms of the resettlement process are largely unregulated by the 1951 Refugee Convention, which requires only limited facilitation.[1] The distribution of resettlement slots is managed by the United Nations High Commissioner for Refugees (UNHCR)'s branch offices and is regulated by updated versions of the *Resettlement Handbook* (most recently in 2011, but this chapter will focus on the 2004 handbook) and attendant soft law instruments. Throughout most of UNHCR's history, there has been a consistent gap between promoted and preferred durable solutions. Until 1985, voluntary repatriation was the preferred solution, while resettlement was promoted in practice (Chimni 2004). From the mid-1980s, resettlement became the "least preferred option" in policy and practice, until its resurgence in the late 1990s.

Beginning in the late 1990s, African refugees have been resettled by UN-HCR and through the largest country programs, those of Australia, Canada, and the United States, in increasingly great numbers. This development represents a remarkable break with the past. In 2003, UNHCR emphasized the seemingly universal heritage of resettlement: "Over the past fifty years, millions of people have been provided with the opportunity to build new lives for themselves, and their families, through resettlement" (UNHCR 2003: 2).

Yet, while the African refugee problem has been persistent since the early 1960s, until around 1980 only a very small number of African refugees had been resettled by UNHCR inside Africa, and no country (including Australia, Canada, and the United States) had quotas for African refugees. Not until the early 1980s were African refugees slowly being formally incorporated into extraregional resettlement schemes. In practice, even though UNHCR began to promote the possibility of out-of-Africa resettlement, and the three large resettlement countries molded their programs on the 1951 Refugee Convention and allocated quotas for African refugees, the numbers remained low until the late 1990s. What then is the explanation for the recent move toward the inclusion of Africans in the resettlement efforts of the international community?

This chapter aims to contribute to the critical legal literature on third-country resettlement by thinking about the various ways in which the African resettlement candidate as a quasijuridical category has been forged, reshaped, and distributed through international initiatives since the inception of the modern refugee regime. Reading UNHCR's descriptions of its contemporary resettlement activities, the relative prominence of African individual cases can be explained as the instrumental outcome of how soft law instruments, the standardization of management practices, a turn to human rights approaches, and new strategic considerations create linkages between the perceived need on the ground and the composition of the resettlement caseload. It is necessary to complicate the sentiments of progress and timelessness that converge in this narrative.

While the significant presence of African refugees in contemporary resettlement programs may be explained by pointing to the evolution of a more inclusive Western humanitarianism, to political factors such as changes in domestic quota allocations, or in the demands of home constituencies, these explanations are only partial. A more complete picture may emerge if the interplay between humanitarian emergencies, shifting political priorities, and changes in the form and content of international refugee law in the re-shaping of resettlement is studied. Examining the configuration of the legal status of African refugees will enable a better understanding of the degree to which the legal instruments, norms, and institutional practices of international organizations such as UNHCR are constituent of practice, in addition to the demands of realpolitik.

To that end, the chapter offers a two-part reading of historical regulatory approaches to resettlement and to the African refugee problem, followed by a discussion of developments in contemporary resettlement. It shows how the shifting national interests of resettlement countries and the subsequent changes in the policy designation of resettlement, the changing correlations made between the nature of the African refugee crisis and the predicament of African refugees. The chapter also explores the efforts to renew resettlement as a fair, accountable, and efficient regulatory mechanism have resulted in supplanting the erstwhile exclusion of African resettlement candidates, while forging stronger connections between resettlement and global migration management.

The chapter pursues three lines of interrogation. The first part surveys how the perceived function of resettlement programs and the preferred attributes of resettlement candidates have shifted with successive international initiatives, beginning with the efforts of UNHCR's predecessors, the Intergovernmental Committee on Refugees (IGCR), and the International Refugee Organization (IRO). The second part takes the complex African refugee crisis as the starting point for an account of the historical exclusion of resettlement as a durable solution to the African refugee problem. The topic for the third part is the reform and renewal of the institution of resettlement, which was instigated in the mid-1990s and is still continuing.

The chapter considers how legalization, standardization, and a reorientation toward human rights have combined to engender the recognition of African refugees as ideal marginal beings. The result is a larger and more diverse pool of African resettlement candidates in terms of gender, age, sexuality, religion, and profession. By way of conclusion, the importance of connecting the dots is highlighted. The chapter argues that it is the emphasis on suffering and vulnerability that has allowed African refugees to slip into the category of most preferred resettlement candidates. As a result, the designation of a small group of "vulnerable" individuals facilitates the application of the label "illegal" to the majority. Further critical legal analysis of the deployment of resettlement as a solution to the African refugee problem in international refugee management should be connected to discussions about the politics of global migration management.

From the Baltic Preference to the Boat People Crisis

This part locates the exclusion of African refugees in the context of the changing political priorities and institutional regimes that have governed resettlement in the aftermath of World War II. The events that shaped UNHCR's resettlement operations may broadly be described as phases of reordering (managing populations during postwar reconstruction), ideology (fighting the Cold War), and, finally, containment and decline (protecting borders and demoting resettlement). The historical legacy of this policy seems to have been the de facto omission of African refugees from the resettlement efforts of the international community.

The Immediate Postwar Effort

In the interwar years, successions of international refugee organizations were charged with resettling Jews and others who were fleeing Nazi persecution. IGCR was created on the basis of the 1938 Evian Conference to negotiate with Germany regarding Jewish migration. Described as largely ineffectual, and with limited achievements until its eventual demise in 1947, the IGCR nevertheless initiated negotiations with a number of countries in Europe and overseas (Stoessinger 1956: 39–44; Loescher 2001: 33). IGCR also concluded a number of agreements with European, North African, and Latin American countries that were later taken over by the IRO (Holborn 1975: 18–19).

IRO was created in 1946 and was operational until 1952. IRO's main function was resettlement (Loescher 2001: 38). In 1948, IRO's resettlement activities, which had focused on intra-European resettlement, shifted to overseas migration (Stoessinger 1956: 121). During its time of operation, IRO resettled well over a million people, four-fifths outside Europe, while repatriating a mere 73,000 (Colville 1993: 4–8). Despite these efforts, a hard core of 40,000 "undesirable" refugees, who were aged, sick, or handicapped or had been considered unfit by selection missions, remained scattered in camps across Europe, some until the early 1960s (Loescher 2001: 40).

The pretext for the mass resettlement schemes after World War II was neither completely utilitarian nor exclusively based on generosity and compassion: in the early postwar era, humanitarian motivations dovetailed with security concerns and with the continued expansion of the world economy that generated a significant labor shortage (Holborn 1975: 114). Hence, the resettlement agreements that the IRO concluded with European, Latin American, and Oceanic countries shared some important features with respect to how they identified desirable resettlement candidates. In contrast to American, British, and Continental traditions, which emphasized deserving and morally suitable recipients of charity and scientific philanthropy, or contemporary projections of resettlement as a durable solution for refugees with particular personal attributes or specific social or medical circumstances, the original resettlement programs were focused on external capabilities. They were explicitly designed to ensure the selection of candidates who were suitable (physically and mentally fit) for domestic labor markets (which required labor-intensive, unsafe, or strenuous work); were of appropriate nationalities, ethnicities, and religions; and had acceptable family compositions.

A number of countries agreed to take refugees on the understanding that they submitted to compulsory labor contracts. In effect, these contracts turned those resettled into indentured laborers, although the enforcement varied greatly in practice. In 1946, Great Britain admitted 2,500 manual laborers under the Balt Cygnet program. This scheme was the first formal accord between IRO and a resettlement country, and it became the standard for later agreements. In 1948, Great Britain initiated the scheme "Westward Ho," whereby 50,000 refugees from the three Western Zones of Austria and Germany contracted to undertake employment selected by the Ministry of Labour. Following the British example, Australia accepted refugees who agreed to a compulsory two-year term of government-designated labor as the price for Australian citizenship after five years (for a comparison with current-day practices, see Losoncz, this volume).

Also modeled on British practice, a Belgian scheme agreed to admit 50,000 refugees who would sign up for a two-year period of manual work in the coalmines. However, while the British program relaxed the labor requirements once the hardship caused to the refugee laborers became evident, the Belgian authorities rigorously enforced the contracts, to great dissatisfaction among the refugee population. In contrast, Canada placed "work orders" with IRO for 100,000 refugees, but without a legal compulsion to remain at the job in the case of "undue hardship" (Stoessinger 1956: 113–41; for a comparison with contemporary practices, see Garnier, this volume).

With respect to their personal status, eligible candidates were subjected to stringent requirements. In the British programs, candidates had to be single, as unmarried workers were thought to be more productive. In cases where married candidates were admitted, dependents had to be left behind, causing some 4,000 refugees to return to their home countries (Stoessinger 1956: 117–18, 122, 129). Although the IRO emphasized the positive benefits of receiving refugees with professional expertise, racial and religious considerations continued to be prominent. Most receiving countries, including the United Kingdom, Belgium, the United States, Australia, New Zealand, Canada, Brazil, Chile, Argentina, and Venezuela, expressed a preference for white Baltic refugees.

With the exception of the Dominican Republic, Latin American countries involved in resettlement, such as Argentina, Chile, and Brazil, openly or more covertly rejected refugees of Jewish origin, irrespective of their professional status. Brazil had an explicit prohibition on "Asiatics" (for contemporary Latin American practices, see Vera Espinoza; Jubilut and Zamur, this volume). The U.S. national origins quota system was based on the Asian Exclusion Act of 1924 but indirectly worked against Jewish and Catholic refugees too (Davis 1996).

Resettlement during the Cold War

UNHCR was created in 1950 to function as a permanent organ under the authority of the General Assembly (Goodwin-Gill 2007: 426). After overcoming a difficult start, including a complicated overlap with IRO, poor financing, and initial American resistance,[2] the organization grew rapidly during the 1950s. During its initial time of operation, the resettlement program remained largely unchanged from the IRO period. UNHCR continued the effort to empty European refugee camps, and resettlement was guided by the erstwhile objectives of ensuring stability around the allied reconstruction efforts and alleviating labor shortages. But as the Cold War came to dominate international affairs, resettlement gradually emerged as a highly potent administrative device in the evolving East-West conflict paradigm. Consequently, the profile of preferred candidates changed from those considered suitable for arduous labor to those who had "valid objections" to returning to countries that were incorporated into the Eastern Bloc.

The first instance of mass resettlement took place after the Soviet invasion of Hungary in 1956, which resulted in 200,000 refugees fleeing to Yugoslavia and Austria (Loescher 1993: 58). During the 1960s and 1970s, decolonization led to the formal dissolution of European administrative-military apparatuses and the creation of new international borders. Post-colonialism and Cold War politics generated independence struggles and civil wars, which caused large North-South refugee movements. With the exception of the anti-Castro Cubans and the anticommunist Vietnamese, few of these refugee populations were considered politically important by Western powers, and resettlement was only used intermittently on purely humanitarian grounds. Most significantly, resettlement was deployed when Idi Amin expelled nonnational Ugandan Asians in 1972, eventually leading to the resettlement of some 40,000 individuals to a total of twenty-five countries (UNHCR 1973a). During the 1970s and 1980s, resettlement was also offered to victims of military dictatorships in South and Central America.

The premise that repatriation was not considered an option for people fleeing from oppressive communist regimes or colonial oppression faded rapidly as the Cold War ended and global migration began to increase drastically. In particular, the Vietnamese refugee crisis came to define the use of resettlement until well into the 2000s. A massive exodus followed the collapse of the Saigon regime in 1975. By 1979, a major protection crisis had developed as certain asylum countries refused to accept more refugees, and over 200,000 refugees were languishing in camps. The first Conference on Refugees from Indo-China, in 1979, decided on a blanket resettlement for the Vietnamese boat people arriving in first-asylum countries in Southeast Asia (Robinson 2004).

However, as 1986 saw a massive increase in the number of boat people for apparently economic factors, the exodus was relabeled from a humanitarian crisis to a "boat people crisis" (Thomas 2000: 3). The second Conference on Indo-Chinese Refugees, in 1989, adopted a Comprehensive Plan of Action (CPA), which removed blanket resettlement and introduced screening procedures for individual refugees. The CPA did reduce the refugee flow, but, until its expiration in 1997, it also contributed to the prolonged detention of tens of thousands of unsuccessful Vietnamese resettlement seekers, particularly in Hong Kong (Towle 2006).

Containment and Decline

In the 1980s, the increased pool of would-be migrants, as well as their ethnic and religious diversity, increasingly frightened Western states. By the late 1980s, resettlement was considered to have become the chief pull factor in a mass migration movement in which people left their homeland primarily for economic and social reasons (UNHCR 2001). What Aleinikoff (1996) describes as "the calls to rethink the exilic bias of international refugee law" resulted in a variety of responses. The 1984 ExCom meeting formally ranked resettlement as the "least desirable and most costly" solution (Stein 1986). In subsequent years, the West increasingly shifted its management of population flows toward control and deterrence.

Pragmatic objections to resettlement programs, including negative effects on other durable solutions, the risk of creating pull factors or incentives for corruption were supplemented by liberal and communitarian perspectives. These argued that forced exile violated the right to return and that an emphasis on resettlement failed to appreciate the important link between human dignity and organic communities (Aleinikoff 1996: 261). As stated by the 1995 World Refugee Survey (92): "Resettlement is in some senses the antithesis of the proactive, preventive and homeland oriented approach to the refugee issue which the international community has started to adopt in recent years" (cited in Ferris 1996). In the period 1985–1993, voluntary repatriation came to be promoted as the durable solution. Chimni (2004: 55) explains that, in 1993, the notion of "safe return" was introduced in the context of temporary protection regimes established in Western Europe and sought to occupy the middle ground between voluntary and involuntary repatriation. In lieu of adequate support from Western countries, UNHCR proposed a doctrine of imposed return in 1996.

Due to the skepticism of its donors, the UNHCR remained apprehensive about resettlement throughout the 1990s (UNHCR Resettlement Section 1997). This skepticism was not exclusively caused by the increase in the number of resettlement seekers. As resettlement came into disrepute in the 1980s, Fredriksson and Mougne (1994) observe that UNHCR was "slow to adjust its procedures and allocation of resources to the new realities." In their 1994 report, they pointed out a number of institutional weaknesses, such as the absence of clear policies, inconsistent application of refugee doctrine, staffing problems, an insufficiently professional approach to case selection, and unclear command lines. The politics of containment in combination with the crisis of legitimacy set the stage for the discussion of contemporary resettlement later in the chapter.

Configuring the African Resettlement Candidate

This part traces the development of international resettlement through the growing UNHCR involvement in Africa, the gradual legalization of the African refugee, and the initial efforts to incorporate African refugees into international resettlement schemes.

UNHCR's Early Involvement in Africa

Throughout the 1960s and 1970s, Africa was plagued by independence struggles, proxy wars, and regional strife, which led to a substantial growth in the refugee population. In 1963, the continent harbored an estimated 310,000 refugees (UNHCR 1966a). This number grew to nearly 735,000 by early 1967, although unofficial figures at that time suggested that the total might have been as many as 1,300,000 (Rubin 1974). In 1973, UNHCR's statistics suggested that the number had grown to more than a million (Gallagher 1989). Africa's first modern refugee crisis occurred with the outbreak of Algeria's independence struggle (1954–1962). As Tunisia and later Morocco appealed for international assistance, following the influx of Algerians, the UNHCR became the first UN presence in Algeria. Throughout the 1960s UNHCR assisted the victims of independence wars and of internal turmoil in locations such as Angola (1961), Guinea-Bissau (1962), and Mozambique (1964; Holborn 1975: 509, 825, 830).

A number of factors limited the nature of UNHCR's involvement. Holborn (1975: 830, 848) observes that in the early 1960s, a certain European obliviousness persisted with respect to the impact and permanence of the African refugee problem, and the crisis was little discussed in UN fora. The increased participation of African states in the UN, the greater presence of the UN in Africa, and the gradual expansion of an African presence at the UNHCR ExCom changed this. Furthermore, according to the 1951 Refugee Convention, whose territorial scope was limited to Europe, the UNHCR was not mandated to intervene in Africa. In 1961, the General Assembly gave the UNHCR the authority to assist refugees within its "good offices." Aiming to bridge the gap between the 1951 Convention Mandate and UNHCR's statute, the category of prima facie refugees was introduced with the creation of UNHCR's good offices, by way of Resolution 1673 (XVI) of the UN General Assembly on 18 December 1961.

This legal innovation enabled the organization to raise funds and extend material assistance to African countries, without getting involved in sensitive postcolonial politics. To that end, the mode of approach in Africa was explicitly nonlegal. UNHCR's position was politically tenuous and required extensive diplomatic efforts. The organization had to strike a delicate political balance between assisting refugees and avoiding antagonizing colonial powers and emerging African states by accusing them of persecuting their subjects (Loescher 1993: 80; Holborn 1975: 440–43, 849). In this situation, mandate determination was viewed as a political and thus hostile act, not a technical humanitarian effort.

Part of the problem pertained to a difficult working environment for UNHCR officers. As noted by Loescher (2001: 119), the responses to the refugee crisis in Africa usually took place in an ad hoc manner. The refugees fled to poor countries in need of infrastructure, funds, and technical assistance, where UNHCR started from scratch in terms of organization and administration. Serious logistic shortages meant that protection was constantly underemphasized. Loescher explains that during this initial period, the UNHCR office for East and Central Africa had five staff members to cover the entire region from Tanzania to Senegal. There were no Africans on the staff, and the UNHCR relied almost entirely on its operational partners, who also lacked expertise on Africa.

While UNHCR encouraged new African states to ratify international agreements, the lack of specific domestic refugee legislation continued to hamper UNHCR's efforts to offer international protection. To the extent that refugee populations were regulated under national legislation, it was usually under immigration law. Traditionally lenient in their dealings with refugee flows, African governments based their engagement with UNHCR on a desire for material assistance. They were less interested in offering legal protection to populations that could destabilize the political situation (Loescher 2001).

According to Holborn (1975), the apparent permanence of the African refugee crisis demanded "a new pragmatism regarding the very nature of permanent solutions for refugees." Gallagher comments that, unlike in Europe, the functions to be performed in Africa were not diplomatic and legal in nature. Rather, they concerned the monetary support for and the development of direct assistance programs for refugees (Gallagher 1989). The then high commissioner, Felix Schnyder, expressed his belief that "in situations as those in Africa, the major and immediate need of refugees was for emergency assistance, rather than international legal protection" (Loescher 2001: 117). The focus was on material assistance, as it was presumed that settlements would lead to assimilation. The objective was to make the refugees self-sufficient and able to contribute to the local economy (Loescher 1993: 82).

The focus on development approaches at the expense of legal protection has intermittently reoccurred (Crisp 2001). In the 1960s, ideas about zonal development became prominent. Together with other UN bodies, UNHCR began to carry out this strategy in Burundi and Zaire in 1963 (Lui 2004). Although the emphasis was put on self-sufficiency, by 1973 African rural settlements consumed three-quarters of UNHCR's budget (Rogge 1981). The reconceptualization of displacement as a development problem at the 1981 and 1984 International Conference on Assistance to Refugees in Africa (ICARA I and ICARA II) engendered a "refugee aid and development" strategy (Gorman 1986). With ICARA II, the bulk of UNHCR expenditure shifted from Europe to Africa, as the organization left a "limited subsistence approach" and embarked on the large-scale organization of rural settlement schemes, inspired by World Bank–guided "integrated rural development land settlement schemes" (Loescher 2001: 22).

The African Refugee and the Politics of Difference

The previous subsection suggested that international law was marginalized during UNHCR's initial interventions in Africa. In addition, it is also important to note that African refugee flows, from the beginning, were conceptualized as different in terms of size, character, and needs (Holborn 1975: 825). In the 1960s, the African refugee movements were perceived to represent a unique type of displacement. While European refugees had been governed as political subjects, African refugees were constituted as subjects of development (Lui 2004: 55). The idea of "mass solutions" as appropriate for mass movements stood in sharp contrast to the individual solutions designated for European refugees. Refugee management remained premised on Western ideas about the African host societies, where refugees would go through "spontaneous" local integration (Holborn 1975: 843) and where "traditional African hospitality" to refugees made third-country resettlement less of a need for that continent (Rogers 1994). In a remarkable contrast, the Ugandan Asians expelled by Idi Amin in 1972 were seen as "special cases" and quickly resettled to the West.

Beyond the development agenda, the international community hesitated to endow African refugees with the capacity to have legal problems. Legal protection was not seen as required; African refugees were considered too numerous, dispersed, premodern, and poor to make individual assessments to establish the elements of the refugee definition possible or necessary (Holborn 1975: 836). This, of course, was a political choice unrelated to the actual needs or traditions on the ground. Louise Holborn suggested the obvious in 1975:

> For the skilled and educated refugees moving to the cities the matter of an appropriate legal status is of the greatest urgency. Questions of residence permits, identity papers, the right to work or to receive an education, social security, public assistance, and travel documents are of the same importance to them as they have been to refugees in Europe in like circumstances. Eventually, because of increased urbanization and due to decreased tolerance for protracted refugee populations among African governments, UNHCR gradually shifted its view that legal integration would emanate from social and economic integration. All the same, because of the emphasis on material assistance, overseas resettlement was rarely offered to Africans. (293)

The Emergence of the African Resettlement Candidate: From Socioeconomic Resource to Cultural Problem

Intra-Africa Resettlement for Urban and Educated African Refugees

Until 1968, there was almost no resettlement of African refugees out of the continent. A few organized efforts took place inside Africa. In 1965, the American Presbyterian Mission resettled 500 Sudanese families in Ethiopia (Holborn 1975: 861), and 3,000 Rwandese left Zaire for Tanzania in the context of the Mwesi resettlement project.[3] Gradually, UNHCR expanded its protection function to include the growing numbers of educated but unskilled urban refugees, who encountered increasingly restrictive labor legislation in their country of refuge (ibid.: 863). The organization came to realize the need to expand resettlement efforts with respect to this group, in light of "the growing number of individuals who do not have an agricultural background and often cannot be settled in their country of first asylum in Africa" (UNHCR 1974). What UNHCR prescribed was resettlement to other African states.

When, in its 1968 session, the UNHCR paid particular attention to the problem of resettlement of individual African refugees, this was "identified as concerning essentially refugees who had received higher education." The problem was conceptualized as one of brain drain, and the organization of resettlement efforts in cooperation with African governments hoped to "encourage the refugees to exercise their profession in African countries" (UNHCR 1968). By 1966, the refugee bureau had been created within the OAU Secretariat to maintain close relations with UNHCR (UNHCR

1966b), and a cooperation agreement between UNHCR and the OAU was signed on 13 June 1969.

The Conference on the Legal, Economic and Social Aspects of African Refugee Problems, in Addis Ababa in 1967, recommended the establishment of a Bureau for the Placement and Education of African Refugees (BPEAR), with the objective of finding solutions to the problem of educated refugees.[4] BPEAR was established 1 March 1968 (Oloko-Onyango 1994). A joint venture between UNHCR and OAU, BPEAR was intended primarily as a clearing house for the designation and implementation of a continental placement system (Holborn 1975: 854). The bureau would also cooperate with ECA, UNESCO, the International Labour Organization (ILO), and the voluntary agencies (UNHCR 1966: para. 59).

Through the secondment of staff and financial support, UNHCR assisted the bureau in preparing lists of qualified refugees for consideration by governments (UNHCR 1973b: para. 58). The idea was that detailed dossiers on refugees, who qualified for temporary or permanent resettlement, could then be circulated to African governments (Holborn 1975: 944). A set of "national correspondents" was appointed by governments to act as local representatives for the bureau. The correspondents, generally officials employed with immigration or refugee departments, were seen as "the vital link in the resettlement chain." Each correspondent headed a small committee of representatives of those intergovernmental and voluntary agencies directly involved locally, including the UNHCR (Oloko-Onyango 1994; see Holborn 1975: 945, annex 35.3 for a description of procedures).

BPEAR found no mention in the 1969 OAU Convention (Oloko-Onyango 1994), and during its lifespan the achievements of the bureau remained limited. According to UNHCR, only 300 African refugees were resettled in 1971 (UNHCR 1973b: para. 58). A "very limited number" of refugees were resettled in 1972 (UNHCR 1974: para. 56). The number in 1973 was approximately 300 (UNHCR 1975: para. 53), and in 1975 the total reached 390 (UNHCR 1976: para. 89). Under various names and due to institutional oversights, the bureau tottered along until the early 1990s but did not make the transition to the African Union. Commentators offer a number of explanations for BPEAR's failure. Projects were poorly planned and executed. There were prejudices against rural refugees (Murray 2004). The system of national correspondents failed, as few correspondents were appointed and those appointed did not report to or attend meetings. There were also allegations of financial mismanagement toward the end of the 1970s, when money meant for national correspondents was diverted (Oloko-Onyango 1994).

Some of the problems were beyond BPEAR's reach: the records on students remained incomplete, and a mismatch persisted between Anglophone jobseekers and French placements (Oloko-Onyango 1994). BPEAR was not able to build on any preexisting administrative structure and had a limited budget. The bureau suffered losses of autonomy in 1971, when it was placed under the OAU Assistant Secretary General for Political Affairs, and, in 1974, when it was moved to OAU's Political Department. As BPEAR underwent a number of changes in nomenclature, its capacity remained weak. Finally, the bureau also failed due to the incompatible expectations of African states, OAU, and UNHCR. For African states, BPEAR was a vehicle for generating more slots for education, OAU's objective was to resettle freedom fighters, while UNHCR saw BPEAR as an opportunity to deal with intractable refugee situations without being compromised (Holborn 1975: 945).

The Emergence of Extraregional Resettlement Opportunities

During the 1960s and 1970s only a handful of African refugees left for permanent overseas settlement. According to Rogge, this was largely because the traditional immigrant-receiving states, such as the United States, Canada, and Australia, saw the African refugee problem as a local one for which local solutions were best, because it consisted mainly of rural immigrants who would not be able to integrate effectively into industrialized countries. There was a widespread perception that the identification of resettlement cases was impossible, that Africans did not wish to be resettled, and that they would not be able to integrate (Rogge 1985: 168–69). These assumptions were underpinned by discriminatory Western attitudes to Africans generally and African refugees in particular.[5] They were also founded on skepticism among African leaders. Before 1980, African governments and the OAU opposed out-of-Africa resettlement due to fears of brain drain and resistance to outside intervention.

In the 1970s and 1980s, the major receiving countries began to use the 1951 Convention as the basis for both determining refugee status and allocating resettlement quotas. Nevertheless, as Stein (1983) pointed out, while "the reliance on the U.N. Convention definition of refugee means that Canada, the United States, and Australia are likely to be accepting a wider range of refugees than before . . . the use of the definition . . . does not mean all refugees have an equal chance of admission, within numerical limits, because each country gives priority in resettlement to groups it considers of special interest." This observation proved accurate: Browne (2006: 20) observed that despite growing demands from countries like Sudan and Tanzania, change had been slow and that the pronounced bias against out-of-Africa resettlement persisted into the late 1990s.[6]

The White Australia policy deployed throughout the 1960s changed in 1973, when the Whitlam government signed the 1967 Protocol to the 1951 Convention. This required Australia to consider asylum applications irrespective of the origin of the applicant. The country began accepting African refugees in 1984. The first intake was 220, out of an overall caseload of 13,591 refugees and humanitarian visa holders (Rogge 1985: 168–69). Between 1982 and 1987, Australia received almost 75,000 people via resettlement programs, yet only 481 were from Africa (Browne 2006: 20). The Canadian government adopted the Refugee Convention definition of "refugee" in 1969 (Lanphier 1981). The 1976 Immigration Act came into effect in 1978. In 1979, the country adopted annual refugee admission plans (Stein 1983).

Canada introduced a quota of 500 Africans in 1981 and increased this to 1,000 in 1983 (Rogge 1985: 169). Despite this quota, Africans remained underrepresented: in 1993–1996, there were still proportionally few Africans accepted in the Canadian resettlement program (Canadian Council for Refugees 1997). The US Refugee Act of 1980 introduced a modest quota of 3,000 for African refugees. In 1982, 995 African refugees were resettled to the United States. The numbers stayed low over the next decade (Africa Rights Monitor 1985). Furthermore, as noted by Wong, the numbers reflect clear foreign policy objectives: out of the 17,493 African refugees who were resettled to the United States between 1982 and 1989, 94 percent were Ethiopian, revealing the temporarily close relationship between the United States and successive Ethiopian governments (Wong 1995).

A Parallel Scheme for African "Problem" Refugees

The idea of in-continent resettlement has been a recurrent topic in African refugee management. As UNHCR toyed with this idea throughout the 1990s, Ferris (1996) observed, "There has always been rhetorical support for intraregional resettlement. Infraregional resettlement in Africa, for example, is seen as a way of encouraging regional responsibility and addressing concerns of brain-drain." Such schemes were finally put into place again in the late 1990s, when groups of refugees from the Great Lakes region were resettled to Burkina Faso and Benin. The joint 1968 initiative between UNHCR and the OAU had primarily targeted educated refugees. This time it was the African refugee as a harbinger of problematic customs that was in focus.

Polygamous families have long posed a challenge to UNHCR's resettlement programs. Few resettlement countries accept such unions, which have potentially enormous family sizes. It has been reported that, in the past, some refugees selected for resettlement have felt pressured to abandon their extended families (Refugee Law Project 2002: 27). In the mid-1990s, these concerns led UNHCR to initiate a pilot project for polygamous families. From 1998 to 2003, approximately 130 refugees resettled in Benin. Between 1997 and 2000, seventy-five refugees (twenty-five cases) were resettled into Burkina Faso. According to the independent evaluation commissioned by

UNHCR, the project proved to be a fiasco: by March 2005, only thirty-nine of the seventy-five resettled refugees remained in Burkina Faso, and those who remained lived in dire poverty (McKeever 2005).

These programs illustrate a remarkable paradox: previously constituted as a valuable human resource in intraregional resettlement schemes, this geographical solution now designated the African refugee as the emissary of cultural and traditional mores unacceptable in the West. An evaluation by Sperl and Brădişteanu (2004) pointed to a number of reasons for this failure. In 1997, the head of the Resettlement Section recommended a feasibility study of the Pilot Project to be undertaken. This recommendation was never followed up. Among other shortcomings were inappropriate selection criteria, inadequate briefing of the refugees prior to departure, and the limited capacity of UNHCR's implementing partners. The integration program had been implemented on an ad hoc basis. The refugees had expected to be resettled to the traditional resettlement countries. Burkina Faso and Benin are among the least developed countries in the world. By comparison, all traditional resettlement countries rank among the most developed.

Furthermore, until 2001, other refugees were simultaneously being resettled out of Burkina Faso, to the United States and Canada in particular, on the basis of lack of local integration prospects. The frustration experienced by the resettled refugees manifested itself as a much-publicized hunger strike and the occupation of the cathedral of Ouagadougou by a group of eighty-six refugees in mid-2000 (McKeever 2005). The refugees felt betrayed by UNHCR and saw themselves as guinea pigs in a failed experiment. Interestingly, the most common explanation for the poor performance of the Pilot Project provided by UNHCR staff, government bureaucrats, and NGO implementing partners was the pessimistic and unconstructive attitude adopted by the resettled refugees (Sperl and Brădişteanu 2004).

On the basis of negative evaluations, these projects have been discontinued (U.S. Department of State 2001). Despite its failure, and its underlying rationale that African refugees could be resettled within Africa only, the basic premise of the BPEAR scheme represented a progressive view of African resettlement candidates and a dynamic conception of the resettlement process as beneficial to both the resettled persons and the host state. However, when in-continent resettlement was taken up again in the mid-1990s, the basis was very different. Resettlement was now proscribed as a response to the problematic social organization of African families. As evidenced by the evaluation reports, these projects were not only poorly planned and executed but also based on bygone conceptualizations of the African refugee as subjects of development and as disconnected from transnational North-South processes. This meant that no justification had to be provided for distributing resettlement candidates between Burkina Faso and Benin, on the one hand, and Australia, Canada, and the United States, on the other.

Contemporary Resettlement: Renewal and Resurgence

This part considers how the various components of resettlement reform facilitated a greater inclusion of African refugees.

Technologies of Renewal: Legalization and Standardization

This section examines the conceptual evolvement of resettlement as a regulatory mechanism by mapping the administrative and normative improvements in the management of international resettlement. In response to the generalized criticism of humanitarianism and the particular attacks on UNHCR in the mid to the late 1990s, the organization has given increased attention to legalization, standardization, and evaluation of its activities.

The soft law regulation of resettlement in the late 1990s represented a change in the international management of resettlement. The IRO had attempted to outline basic policy principles but had found it impossible to lay down specific rules and consequently put the emphasis on flexibility and polices tested and shaped according to varying circumstance and trends. The BPEAR selected resettlement candidates through dossiers, without any particular requirements for how these dossiers were created and communicated, and relied on the discretion of unpaid national correspondents, who functioned more as diplomatic facilitators than bureaucrats (Holborn 1975: 945). Today, UNHCR emphasizes "global consistency," and the procedural and substantive content of UNHCR's resettlement procedure is regulated through a set of "core policy documents."[7]

The first set of "Resettlement Guidelines" was published in 1990. These guidelines were thought to "represent a significant step forward toward more rigorous and systematic implementation of resettlement activities."[8] The influential 1994 report *Resettlement in the 1990s: A Review of Policy and Practice* recommended that the Resettlement Section and the Section for the Promotion of Refugee Law develop a manual for use in the field and that an updated compendium of the legal requirements, criteria, and practices of each major resettlement country be prepared (Fredriksson and Mougne 1994: 10). Among the new initiatives undertaken thereafter was the adoption of the comprehensive *Resettlement Handbook* in 1997. The 1998 version of the *Resettlement Handbook* included updated country chapters (UNHCR Resettlement Section 1997). The *Resettlement Handbook* was updated in 2002 and again in 2004 and 2011. The handbooks are the result of extensive roundtable consultations with governments, NGOs, and UNHCR personnel from all over the globe.

According to the 2004 *Resettlement Handbook,* "The newly revised *Resettlement Handbook* sets clear standards for referring individuals to prospective countries" (emphasis added). Moreover, "the emphasis on rationality and transparency has both a local and a global function, by strengthening the credibility of UNHCR in general and widening the confidence of refugees, resettlement countries and other partners" (UNHCR 2004: 34). The handbooks regulate the basic procedures to be followed in field office resettlement operations in detail, including case identification, case assessment and verification, conducting interviews, the preparation of a resettlement submission, the UNHCR submission decision, state decisions, the departure arrangements, and the monitoring of the case identification through the departure arrangements. The handbooks also provide an articulation of UNHCR resettlement criteria and address issues of standards, accountability, and safeguards in detail.

Within this new regime, the selection of resettlement candidates was to be based on a form of "rigorous and individualized processing" capable of identifying particular personal circumstances and characteristics. Detailed legal criteria for resettlement were developed. The idea in the 2004 *Resettlement Handbook* was that by constructing a rigorous procedure of individual selection, within the confines of asylum and host country quotas, only "deserving refugees" truly in need of protection would be found eligible for resettlement. This strategy has strengthened the legitimacy of international resettlement. According to UNHCR, standardization and strategic programming have improved the agency's capacity to identify appropriate candidates for resettlement, and thus to generate an increase in the overall numbers of resettlement candidates (UNHCR 2007). A few years after 9/11, the numbers of resettled refugees were indeed recovering, after the first setback in the 1980s, when resettlement became the "least favorable solution" and the second setback, which occurred after 9/11, when many states blocked or severely delayed the resettlement processing of certain nationality groups[9] (see van Selm, this volume).

Synergies of Vulnerability: Resettlement as Human Rights Protection

UNHCR has a reference to the Universal Declaration of Human Rights built into the preamble of the Refugee Convention.[10] Nevertheless, the organization has had an ambivalent relationship with the international human rights framework. Not until 1981 did the UNHCR Executive Committee draw upon basic human rights standards in formulating its Protection Conclusions (UNHCR 1981). In 1988, the Executive Committee recognized "the direct relationship between the observance of human rights standards, refugee movements, and problems of protection" (UNHCR 1988).

Some years later, following general developments in humanitarianism, UNHCR started to call itself a "human rights organization" and began to describe its activities as the promotion of human rights. As noted by Gorlick (2002), the lateness of UNHCR's human rights focus may have resulted from a wish to emphasize the "nonpolitical and humanitarian" nature of its mandate. Now, the organization actively refutes the existence of any tension. As explained in a 1995 UNHCR manual on human rights: "Placing greater reliance on human rights standards as a basis for UNHCR's work does not jeopardize the humanitarian character of our activities, since international human rights law is itself non-political and non-partisan" (UNHCR 1995).

Crucial to contemporary efforts to resettle African refugees is the nexus between human rights and vulnerability, whereby there has been a channeling of universal ideas about human rights protection to narrower imageries of vulnerability and victimhood (see Reklev and Jumbert; Darrow; Thomson, this volume). The 1988 ExCom Conclusion no. 85, paragraph (jj) offered a clear restatement of the resettlement candidate mindful of previously ignored vulnerabilities, when it focused on "individual refugees with special protection needs, individual women at risk, minors, adolescents, elderly refugees and survivors of torture" (Hathaway 2005: 963). The ensuing reorganization of resettlement allowed an expansion of the candidate pool through a fairer and more efficient procedural and substantive identification of refugees who were at risk or who were victims of human rights violations. As a result, since the first set of Resettlement Guidelines were issued, in 1990, the bureaucratic process has come to incorporate a larger number of victim categories in ways that were thought to make room for a more diverse group of vulnerable candidates presenting a wider range of personal narratives of suffering (for a parallel perspective on the narratives of suffering, see Lewis and Young, this volume).

The 2004 *Resettlement Handbook* focuses on whether fundamental human rights are at risk and identifies resettlement as "one possible tool at the disposal of field offices to address a refugee's particular vulnerability" (UNHCR 2004). The *Resettlement Handbook* defines eight categories of people for whom resettlement is the appropriate solution. The primary criterion is legal and physical protection needs. Resettlement is linked to legal and/or physical protection when a refugee's situation meets one or more of the qualifying conditions. These are, first, when there is an immediate or long-term threat of *refoulement* to the country of origin, or expulsion to another country from where the refugee may be refouled; second, when a refugee is under threat of arbitrary arrest, detention, or imprisonment or when their physical safety or human rights in the country of refuge are threatened, and this threat renders asylum untenable; or, third, when a refugee is a survivor of violence or torture, has medical needs, is a woman-at-risk, needs family reunification, or is a child or adolescent, an older refugee, or a refugee without local integration prospects.

The *Resettlement Handbook* emphasizes that the profile of resettlement cases has been increasingly characterized by more complex cases originating from national armed conflicts and needing specialized attention and treatment, such as victims of torture and women-at-risk. This approach privileges the type of difficulties typically experienced by African refugees. The African continent is witnessing ongoing massive displacement across international borders, and these refugee populations are most likely to find themselves in a "protracted" situation, meaning that they have lived in exile for more than five years and that they still have no immediate prospect of finding a durable solution to their plight. In practice, this form of permanent limbo has come to represent a fourth, "default," solution to the refugee crisis across Africa (UNHCR 2007).

Legal developments have helped to facilitate this evolution, as evidenced by the 2004 *Resettlement Handbook;* in recent years a more sophisticated view of local integration as a multidimensional process encompassing legal, economic, social, cultural, and political aspects has been adopted. This category now includes as potential human rights victims those in mixed marriages, gays and lesbians, people with particular disabilities, and refugees accused of witchcraft. Furthermore, UNHCR has continued to rely on prima facie refugee status to address the situations of mass displacement on the African continent. Previously, UNHCR held that where resettlement was considered for prima facie refugees, it would usually be necessary to conduct an individual eligibility assessment. The recommendation of the 2004 *Resettlement Handbook* that the prima facie recognition merely be substantiated amounted to a de facto acceptance of submissions on behalf of prima facie refugees as well.

Finally, the factual and legal basis for construing African refugees as human rights victims is accompanied by something less tangible, namely, the gradual alignment between vulnerability and "African suffering" in international legal discourse, as seen in the focus on sexual violence and the contentious politics of international criminal law.

Conclusion

This chapter has critically examined the notion that the belated rise of African refugees in international resettlement can be explained exclusively by pointing to current humanitarian and political considerations. The chapter has shown how the rationales for resettlement and for the regulation of the legal subjectivity of African refugees have shifted significantly over time. This relatively recent inclusion of African refugees is explained not only by a reorientation of humanitarian concerns but also by reform initiatives that aim to achieve greater degrees of human rights protection, administrative justice, and efficiency.

At the same time, this making of a category of humanitarian victims serves as the perfect legitimate foil for what Dauvergne (2003) describes as the redefinition of the overwhelming majority of people on the move as "illegal." Along similar lines, van Selm (2003) warns that there is a danger that states can make resettlement a "humanitarian alibi" for restrictive asylum policies. By forging a link between the international refugee protection regime and global migration control, displaced Africans may be effectively and publicly distributed into binary opposing categories of victims and perpetrators. Further research on resettlement as a regulatory mechanism must also be alert to the ways in which the substantive categories and procedural standards of contemporary resettlement are designed to provide global migration control with a gloss of humanitarianism.

Kristin Bergtora Sandvik (S.J.D., Harvard Law School) is a research professor in humanitarian studies at PRIO and a professor at the faculty of law at the University of Oslo. Her research focus is on legal mobilization, gender-based violence, displacement and humanitarian ethics, and technology and innovation. Her work has appeared in *Polar: Political and Legal Anthropology Review, Refugee Survey Quarterly,* the *International Journal of Refugee Law, Disasters,* the *ICRC Review, Third World Quarterly,* the *Law and Society Review,* and many more.

This chapter is a modified reproduction of Kristin Bergtora Sandvik. 2010. "A Legal History: The Emergence of the African Resettlement Candidate in International Refugee Management." *Int J Refugee Law* 22(1): 20–47. doi: 10.1093/ijrl/eeq002. As such, the chapter addresses developments up until the mid-2000s. I gratefully acknowledge the generous permission of Oxford University Press.

Notes

1. Art. 30 of the 1951 Refugee Convention concerns transference of currency and assets. Art. 33 addresses the issue of the mandatory versus voluntary nature of resettlement, stating that refugees are entitled to devise their own solutions (Hathaway 2005: 967).
2. For a detailed trajectory of the American involvement in international refugee management, see Loescher (2001: 53–57, 71–72).
3. For a description of this program, see UNHCR (1966a, 1966b).
4. "The Final Report for the Conference on the Legal, Economic and Social Aspects of African Refugee Problems in Addis Ababa" 1967: Recommendation xi.
5. G. Kibreab, "Why Do the OECD Countries Discriminate against African 'Refugees' in Their Resettlement Policies?'" (Mimeo 1990), cited in Rogers 1994.
6. Although Browne (2006: 21) suggests that this may be partially explained by the Balkan Wars, he argues that the hesitance to accept Africans as resettlement candidates must also be understood in light of a legacy of racially based preferences.
7. According to the UNHCR-NGO Joint European Advocacy Statement on Resettlement (25 June 2008, Geneva), core policy documents include *UNHCR Re-*

settlement Handbook 2007; UNHCR, *Multilateral Framework of Understandings on Resettlement,* UN doc. FORUM/2004/6, 16 September 2004; UNHCR, *Framework for Durable Solutions for Refugees and Persons of Concern,* 1 May 2003; UNHCR, *Refugee Resettlement. An International Handbook to Guide Reception and Integration,* September 2002.

8. The guidelines dealt with six vulnerable groups (women at risk, victims of torture/violence, physically or mentally disabled refugees, medical cases and family reunion, and a now abandoned category of "longstayers) but provided only limited guidance on the threshold for determining vulnerability and how vulnerability might be linked to a "best interest" consideration (Fredriksson and Mougne 1994: 4, 24–25).

9. The levels of 2002 (50,600 and 55,600, respectively) were the lowest number of resettlement arrivals since the early 1980s (UNHCR 2005: chap. 3).

10. The preamble of the Refugee Convention opens by stating that "the Charter of the United Nations and the Universal Declaration of Human Rights approved on 10 December 1948 by the General Assembly have affirmed the principle that human beings shall enjoy fundamental rights and freedoms without discrimination."

References

Africa Rights Monitor. 1985. "African Refugees: Patterns and Policy." *Africa Today* 32: 71–78.

Aleinikoff, Thomas Alexander. 1996. "State-Centered Refugee Law: From Resettlement to Containment." In *Mistrusting Refugees,* edited by E. V. Daniel and J. C. Knudsen, 257–278. Berkeley: University of California Press.

Browne, Peter. 2006. *The Longest Journey.* Sydney: University of New South Wales Press.

Canadian Council for Refugees. 1997. *Refugees Worldwide, Assessment of Global Resettlement Needs and Resettlement in Canada Statistical Overview 1993–1996.* Montreal: Canadian Council for Refugees.

Chimni, B. S. 2004. "From Resettlement to Involuntary Repatriation: Towards a Critical History of Durable Solutions to Refugee Problems." *Refugee Survey Quarterly* 23: 55–73.

Colville, Rupert. 1993. "Resettlement: Still Vital after All These Years." *Refugees* 94: 4–8.

Crisp, Jeff. 2001. "Mind the Gap! UNHCR, Humanitarian Assistance and the Development Process." *International Migration Review* 35: 168–91.

——. 2003. *No Solution in Sight: The Problem of Protracted Refugee Situations in Africa.* UNHCR New Issues in Refugee Research, Working Paper no. 75. Geneva: UNHCR.

Dauvergne, Catherine. 2003. "Making People Illegal." In *Critical Beings: Law, Nation and the Global Subject,* edited by P. Fitzpatrick and P. Tuitt, 83–100. Aldershot: Ashgate.

Davis, Michael G. 1996. "The Cold War, Refugees and US Immigration Policy 1945–1962." Unpublished doctoral dissertation, Vanderbilt University. [On file with author.]

Ferris, Elizabeth G. 1996. "Refugees: New Approaches to Traditional Solutions." Paper presented at the conference People of Concern, 21–24 November, Geneva. Accessed 10 February 2017. http://repository.forcedmigration.org/show_meta data.jsp?pid=fmo:1523.

Fredriksson, John, and Christine Mougne. 1994. *Resettlement in the 1990s: A Review of Policy and Practice*. UN doc. UNHCR EVAL/Res/14 Dec. Geneva: UNHCR.

Gallagher, Dennis. 1989. "The Evolution of the International Refugee System." *International Migration Review* 23: 579–98.

Goodwin-Gill, Guy S., and Jane McAdam. 2007. *The Refugee in International Law*. Oxford: Oxford University Press.

Gorlick, Brian. 2002. *Human Rights and Refugees: Enhancing Protection through International Human Rights Law*. UNHCR New Issues in Refugee Research, Working Paper no. 30. Geneva: UHNCR.

Gorman, Robert F. 1986. "Beyond ICARA II: Implementing Refugee-Related Development Assistance." *International Migration Review* 20: 283–98.

Hathaway, James C. 2005. *The Rights of Refugees under International Law*. Cambridge: Cambridge University Press.

Holborn, Louise W. 1975. *Refugees: A Problem of Our Time: The Work of the United Nations High Commissioner for Refugees 1951–1972, vols. I & II*. Metuchen: Scarecrow Press.

Lanphier, Michael. 1981. "Canada's Response to Refugees." *International Migration Review* 15: 113–30.

Loescher, Gil. 1993. *Beyond Charity: International Cooperation and the Global Refugee Crisis*. New York: Oxford University Press.

——. 2001. *The UNHCR and World Politics: A Perilous Path*. Oxford: Oxford University Press.

Lui, Robyn. 2004. "The International Government of Refugees." In *Global Governmentality*, edited by W. Larner and W. Walters, 116–35. London: Routledge.

McKeever, David. 2005. *Identifying Gaps in Protection Capacity*. UNHCR Burkina Faso Strengthening Protection Capacity Project. Geneva: UNHCR.

Murray, Rachel. 2004. *Human Rights in Africa: From the OAU to the African Union*. Cambridge: Cambridge University Press.

Noll, Gregor, and Joanne van Selm. 2003. *Rediscovering Resettlement*. Washington, D.C.: Migration Policy Institute.

Oloko-Onyango, Joe. 1994. "The Place and Role of the OAU Bureau for Refugees in the African Crisis." *International Journal of Refugee Law* 6: 34–52.

Refugee Law Project. 2002. *Refugees in the City: Status Determination, Resettlement, and the Changing Nature of Forced Migration in Uganda*. University of Makerere Working Paper no. 6. Kampala: Uganda.

Robinson, W. Courtland. 2004. "The Comprehensive Plan of Action for Indochinese Refugees 1989–1997: Sharing the Burden and Passing the Buck." *Journal of Refugee Studies* 17: 319–33.

Rogers, Rosemarie. 1994. "Entering through the Door of Refugee Resettlement." Paper presented at the workshop Immigration into Western Societies: Implications and Policy Choices, Charleston, SC, 13–14 May.

Rogge, John R. 1981. "Africa's Resettlement Strategies." *International Migration Review* 15: 195–212.

———. 1985. *Too Many, Too Long, Sudan's Twenty-Year Refugee Dilemma.* Lanham: Rowman and Littlefield.

Rubin, Neville. 1974. "Africa and Refugees." *African Affairs* 73: 290–31.

Sperl Stephan, and Irinel Brădişteanu. 2004. *Refugee Resettlement in Developing Countries: The Experience of Benin and Burkina Faso, 1997–2003–An Independent Evaluation.* UNHCR Evaluation and Policy Analysis Unit and Resettlement and Special Cases Section. Geneva: UNHCR.

Stein, Barry N. 1983. "The Commitment to Refugee Resettlement." *Annals of the American Academy of Political and Social Science* 467: 187–201.

———. 1986. "Durable Solutions for Developing Country Refugees." *International Migration Review* 20: 264–82.

Stoessinger, John G. 1956. *The Refugee and the World Community.* Minneapolis: University of Minnesota Press.

Thomas, Joe. 2003. *Ethnocide: A Cultural Narrative of Refugee Detention in Hong Kong.* Aldershot: Ashgate.

Towle, Richard. 2006. "Processes and Critiques of the Indo-Chinese Comprehensive Plan of Action: An Instrument of International Burden-Sharing?" *International Journal of Refugee Law* 18: 537–70.

Troeller, Gary. 2002. "UNHCR Resettlement: Evolution and Future Direction." *International Journal of Refugee Law* 14: 85–95.

UNHCR. 1974. *Report of the United Nations High Commissioner for Refugees.* UN doc. A/9012. Geneva: UNHCR.

———. 1966a. *Addendum to the Report of the United Nations High Commissioner for Refugees.* UN doc. A/6011/Rev.1/Add.1. Geneva: UNHCR.

———. 1966b. *Report of the United Nations High Commissioner for Refugees.* UN doc. A/6311/Rev. 1. Geneva: UNHCR.

———. 1968. *Addendum to the Report of the United Nations High Commissioner for Refugees.* UN doc. A/6711/Add.1. Geneva: UNHCR.

———. 1973a. *How They Did It. Resettlement of Asians from Uganda in Europe and North America.* UN doc. CDR REC/GEN/13 D, 1973/05. Geneva: UNHCR.

———. 1973b. *Report of the United Nations High Commissioner for Refugees.* UN doc. A/8712. Geneva: UNHCR.

———. 1974. *Report of the United Nations High Commissioner for Refugees.* UN doc. A/9012. Geneva: UNHCR.

———. 1975. *Report of the United Nations High Commissioner for Refugees.* UN doc. A/9612. Geneva: UNHCR.

———. 1976. *Report of the United Nations High Commissioner for Refugees.* UN doc. A/31/12. Geneva: UNHCR.

———. 1981. *UNHCR Executive Committee Conclusions No. 22 (XXXII): On the Protection of Asylum-Seekers in Situations of Large Scale Influx.* Geneva: UNHCR.

———. 1988. *UNHCR Executive Committee Conclusions No. 50 (XXXIX): General Conclusion on International Protection.* Geneva: UNHCR.

———. 1995. *Human Rights and Refugee Protection.* Training Module RLD 5. Geneva: UNHCR.

———. 2001. *New Directions for Resettlement Policy and Practice.* UN doc. EC/51/SC/INF.2. Geneva: UNHCR.

——. 2003. *The Strategic Use of Resettlement*. UN doc. EC/53/SC/CRP.10/Add.1. Geneva: UNHCR.

——. 2004. *UNHCR Resettlement Handbook and Country Chapters*. Division of International Protection. Geneva: UNHCR.

——. 2005. *Statistical Yearbook*. Geneva: UNHCR.

——. 2007. *Global Trends: Refugees, Asylum-seekers, Returnees, Internally Displaced and Stateless Persons*. Geneva: UNHCR.

UNHCR Resettlement Section. 1997. "Resettlement: An Instrument of Protection and a Durable Solution." *International Journal of Refugee Law* 9: 666–73.

U.S. Department of State. 2001. *Proposed Refugee Admissions for FY 2002—Report to the Congress*. Bureau of Population, Migration and Refugees. Washington, D.C.: U.S. Department of State.

van Selm, Joanne. 2003. "The Strategic Use of Resettlement: Changing the Face of Protection." *Refuge* 22: 39–48.

Wong, Madeleine. 1995. "Emerging Patterns of African Refugee Resettlement in the United States." Masters thesis, Florida Atlantic University. [On file with author.]

3

Brazil's Refugee Resettlement

Power, Humanitarianism, and Regional Leadership

Liliana Lyra Jubilut and Andrea Cristina Godoy Zamur

Introduction

A humanitarian initiative at its core, resettlement is an instrument of governance (see Garnier; Sandvik and Jubilut, this volume) and, therefore, is intrinsically connected to power. Because of this, it is relevant to unpack power dynamics in resettlement to better understand all its elements and practices, thus improving resettlement as a tool for refugee protection. This chapter offers an innovative analysis of how power plays out in the refugee resettlement policies of a southern resettlement country. While many states are often criticized for narrowing the humanitarian space of refugee protection, Brazil has been praised as a model in fields ranging from its Refugee Act (Murillo González 2010: 58; UNHCR 2003) to refugee resettlement (Fischel de Andrade 2015) and as a regional leader (Murillo González 2010). This chapter proposes to analytically describe Brazil's resettlement initiatives in a historical perspective, highlighting the construction and implementation of humanitarianism and power dynamics involved in it. To that end, the chapter uses a typology of categories of power drawing on interdisciplinary literature and develops a novel power category: that of *regional power*.

In light of this, the chapter proceeds as follows. First, the concepts and methods are set out with an account of power categories found in interdisciplinary scholarship, especially in political science, international relations, and critical geography. Then, the chapter puts forward a historical background of refugee protection and resettlement in Brazil up to its present stage for contextualization. With these two sets of foundations established, the chapter focuses on presenting the current phase of resettlement in Brazil (which started in 2000) and, simultaneously, applying the power framework to it. In this sense the chapter covers the beginning of the current program (2000–2003); the proposal and implementation of resettlement in solidarity in the framework of the Mexico Declaration and Plan of Action (2004–2014); and the actions in the aftermath of the Brazil Declaration and Plan of Action (2014–onward)–with a focus on power. In each phase of the current refugee resettlement scheme, the chapter analyzes Brazil's resettlement programs with the objective of fleshing out the intersection among power politics, humanitarian rationalities, and regional leadership. To conclude, the chapter suggests avenues for future research.

Concepts and Methods

Durable solutions do not constitute a legal obligation to state parties to the 1951 Refugee Convention and the international refugee regime. Yet, with the ever-increasing number of refugees and the average time a person remains a refugee having reached twenty years (UNHCR 2016a), the international community needs to commit to finding solutions to the plights of these human beings. Refugee resettlement is one of the three traditional durable solutions to refugees, alongside voluntary repatriation and local integration (UNHCR 2013: 28), and the United Nations High Commissioner for Refugees (UNHCR) estimated the world's resettlement need to have reached almost 1.2 million refugees in 2017 (UNHCR 2018b: 29). Out of 193 UN members, less than 20 percent are resettlement countries, and 85 percent of refugees under UNHCR's mandate are hosted by developing countries (ibid.: 2). It is therefore relevant to regard resettlement as both "a vital protection tool and an international responsibility-sharing mechanism" (UNHCR 2009) and, hence, as a strategic instrument in ensuring an adequate and human rights–oriented response to the challenges posited by the increasing number of refugees in the world (see van Selm, this volume).

In line with the volume's introduction, this chapter considers refugee resettlement as an instrument of humanitarian governance, which is why a focus on the power dynamics at the core of refugee resettlement is critical. This chapter regards power as intrinsically connected to politics (Lukes 2004: 30) and an "action in concert" (Arendt 1972), besides being situated in space (Allen 2003) and historically (Milner 2015). The concept of power is contested, nonconsensual, and value dependent (Lukes 2004: 30), but most definitions seem to establish that it derives from a relational effect. The different nature of the relationships allows for the establishment of varied and nuanced categories of power. In light of this, it is useful for the analysis of Brazil's refugee resettlement policies to resort to the following types of power:

– **Soft power:** the ability to engage others to cooperate without resorting to coercion, but by fostering attraction to the causes and values one defends, to the point that the first actor is able to shape the preferences of the second (Nye 2004: 5–7)–a unilateral act of the agent that can lead (indirectly) to the influencing of others' behaviors as they are inspired by it. It is a practice of "leading by example," which results in the augmentation of prestige due to the perception of legitimacy and, thus, creates power for the actor.

– **Legitimacy:** a concept that derives from the "belief in the normative legitimacy of the rule (or in the legitimacy of the body that generated the rule)," "providing an internal reason for an actor to follow a rule" or "an internal sense of moral obligation" (Hurd 1999: 387). It is interesting to note that sometimes the concepts of legitimacy and authority are used as synonyms (Milner 2015: 13), in the sense of a power "which bring about duties or obligations to obey," and that this notion "has been employed by UNHCR in its history to not only increase its autonomy from states, but also attempt to change state behavior" (ibid.).

– **Persuasion:** a category of power that involves shared outcomes and power to achieve them (Allen 2003: 126), a practice that can be summarized as convincing with arguments. It can be seen as one of the several strategies used for the achievement of soft power. It is, however, an act already destined to change others' behaviors (i.e., an act designed for at least a bilateral situation) through mainly the use of words and not other practices.

– **Negotiation:** "a communicative model of interaction" with no obligation of compliance (Allen 2003: 125), but "directed at reaching agreement over common ends" (ibid.), which means a practice that can be summarized as bargaining and that can be a practice that leads to persuasion.[1]

– **Inducement:** a form of hard power in which an actor uses incentives such as payments and bribes to reach the envisioned objective (Nye 2004: 8), a power category that involves "a predetermined choice to exercise power over others" (Allen 2003: 126).

– **Manipulation:** the use of knowledge (information and ideas) to produce intended outcomes (Milner 2015: 13).

– **Coercion:** a compliance based on "the threat of deprivation" (Lukes 2004: 21).

– **Institutional power:** the power one actor exerts on other indirectly, through "institutional diffuse relations" (Barnett and Duvall 2005: 51).

– **Structural power:** a power category that relates to "co-constitutive, internal relations of structural positions," such as "master-slave" or "capital-labor" (Barnett and Duvall 2005: 52–53); in this sense, structural power "concerns the determination of social capacities and interests" (ibid.: 53).

– **Productive power:** a power type that is "the constitution of all social subjects with various social power" (Barnett and Duvall 2005: 55) through the use of discourse, knowledge, and claims to legitimacy (Milner 2015; Barnett and Duvall 2005) and that has at its center "the ability of actors to create and enforce new realities" (Milner 2015: 20).

– **Empowerment:** a currently fashionable and increasingly used but still ill-defined term (Calvès 2009) that can mean a process through which power can change and expand to "help people [or entities such as states] gain control over their own lives" (Page 1999: 2).

It is also important to include in the typology a novel category in the assessment of power in resettlement created for the analysis conducted in this chapter:

– **Regional Power:** the ability of a state to inspire and/or incentivize other states in its region to debate and adopt norms, actions, and approaches to international topics (such as refugee protection), thus increasing its soft power and role as a norm entrepreneur.

Resettlement is an initiative based on international cooperation, political will, and governance, thus a focus on power categories is highly relevant. Furthermore, all of the abovementioned power categories can be found in each of resettlement's phases (establishment of a resettlement scheme, resettlement *in se,* and after resettlement), so it is relevant to assess individual situations to be able to identify which are in fact present in each situation.

Empirically, drawing on insights from international law and international relations scholarship, the chapter applies this conceptual framework to the regional and domestic regulatory frameworks, actions, and discourses at the core of Brazil's refugee resettlement initiatives, including regional soft law, the use of migration in the country's international discourse, Brazil's partnership with UNHCR, and the initiatives of refugee resettlement in Brazil. Building upon previous works by the authors on resettlement (Jubilut and Carneiro 2011; Jubilut 2007) and refugee protection in Brazil (Jubilut 2006, 2007; Jubilut et al. 2016), the chapter combines the use (i) of publicly available legislative and regulatory materials; (ii) of primary data on current resettlement programs obtained via exchanges with UNHCR-Brazil, the National Committee on Refugees of Brazil (CONARE), and NGOs that are involved in the resettlement process in the country; (iii) of secondary sources, relying on bibliography for the historical part of the analysis; and, indirectly, (iv) of experiences drawn from the authors' practical work in the refugee regime in Brazil.

Brazil's Beginnings as a Resettlement Country

Resettlement prior to the 1997 Refugee Act
(Early Twentieth Century to the End of the 1990s)

Brazil's history of receiving resettled refugees began prior to the current resettlement schemes in a much less systematic way. Brazil accepted a small number of refugees during the interwar period. These persons, however, were not received based on humanitarian considerations but only if they met immigration requirements, which were introduced with the enactment of the 1934 Brazilian Constitution and were increasingly restrictive and unfavorable to migrants and refugees (Fischel de Andrade 2015: 154).

The first group of resettled refugees in Brazil was approximately 2,000 Russians fleeing the 1917 Russian Revolution, who arrived at the end of the 1930s (Fischel de Andrade 2015: 154–55). In the same period, Brazil also welcomed Jewish refugees, having received about 40,000 Jews in the previous years. After the 1937 Constitution, however, Brazil started to accept only Jewish refugees who had converted to Christianity (ibid.: 156–57). After 1945, as more active participation in the international community became one of the country's foreign policy goals (ibid.: 158), Brazil started to show a new willingness to accept resettled refugees.

However, Brazil used a lot of rhetoric but lacked real commitment, making it clear that humanitarian assistance would be "conditional to the satisfaction of both domestic expediency and needs" (Fischel de Andrade 2015: 159). By January 1952, out of the 1,038,750 refugees resettled by the International Refugee Organization, only 28,996 had gone to Brazil (ibid.: 158–61). Between 1952 and the late 1950s, over 13,000 refugees of different origins were resettled in Brazil. Since Brazil had not ratified the 1951 Refugee Convention, but only signed it, refugees were treated as regular migrants at the time. In 1960, Brazil signed the 1951 Refugee Convention (upholding the geographical limitations) and resettled 700 refugees of European origin who were in Hong Kong (ibid.: 161–62).

In contrast to previous decades, when Brazil was a country to which persons were resettled, in the context of Brazil's decades-long military dictatorship (1964–1985), the country became a country from which persons were resettled in the 1970s and 1980s. About 20,000 refugees from Argentina, Bolivia, Chile, and Uruguay were resettled from Brazil to Australia, Canada, Europe, New Zealand, and the United States (Fischel de Andrade and Marcolini 2002: 37). There were also resettlements to Sweden and France.

At the same time, some of these South American (de facto refugees) decided to live irregularly in Brazil–mainly from Argentina, Chile, and Uruguay (Fischel de Andrade 2015: 163)–and between 1979 and 1981, 150 Vietnamese and thirty-five Cuban refugees were resettled in Brazil. All of them were given residency permits instead of refugee status due to the maintenance of the geographical limitation stipulated by the 1951 Convention (which was only lifted in 1989 [ibid.: 164] despite Brazil's ratification of the 1967 Protocol in 1972 [Jubilut 2006: 24]) and the dictatorship's attitude toward refugees. In 1986, the country received fifty Iranian families of Baha'i roots (Jubilut 2007: 173).

In the mid-1980s and throughout the 1990s the main changes were in the context of human rights in Brazil, as the country experienced redemocratization after the dictatorship, adopted a human rights–oriented Federal Constitution (in 1988), and started to commit to human rights both internally and internationally. These changes paved the way for the enactment of the Brazilian Refugee Act in 1997 (Law 9.474/97) and the beginning of the current refugee resettlement scheme in Brazil, whose characteristics and power dynamics will be explored next.

The Beginning of the Current Resettlement Program (2000–2003)

At the end of the 1990s, UNHCR was pushing for a renewed emphasis on resettlement as a tool of the international refugee regime and was actively looking for new resettlement countries (UNHCR 2001; Garnier 2013; Sandvik, this volume). At the same time, Brazil's 1997 Refugee Act not only incorporated the 1951 Refugee Convention into domestic law but also set forth provisions with basic rules on refugee resettlement (Articles 45 and 46) and introduced novel provisions that, for instance, expanded the refugee definition to encompass gross and generalized violations of human rights as a cause for refugee status (article 1[III] of the 1997 Refugee Act), as expressed in the Cartagena Declaration of 1984 (Jubilut and Carneiro 2011: 67).[2]

The Cartagena Declaration is a 1984 regional soft law instrument that was adopted by Latin American countries; transformed into national norms in Argentina, Belize, Bolivia, Brazil, Chile, Colombia, Ecuador, El Salvador, Guatemala, Honduras, Mexico, Nicaragua, Paraguay, Peru, and Uruguay[3]; and later accepted by the Organization of American States.

In 1999, the Agreement for the Resettlement of Refugees in Brazil was signed between the Brazilian government and UNHCR, which led the way for the development of resettlement initiatives (Jubilut 2007: 200; see the annex of this volume for more on emerging resettlement countries). UNHCR perceived Brazil as an attractive option for the implementation of a new resettlement project due to the country's recently acquired interest in deepening its commitment to the protection of refugees, the quality of RSD procedures stated in its legislation, and its long-standing history as a country of migrants, with a vast territory and a tradition of tolerance for diversity (Jubilut 2007: 37). In terms of being an effective durable solution for refugees, upon their arrival in Brazil, refugees enjoy the same rights as Brazilian nationals, with the exception of political rights, and receive financial assistance for their basic living expenses funded by UNHCR for up to twelve months (UNHCR 2013: 6; ASAV 2016). Resettled refugees receive a temporary residency permit, which may be converted to permanent residency after four years. Finally, with four years of permanent residency, refugees may apply for citizenship (UNHCR 2013: 5).

In March 2001, UNHCR conducted visits to four different cities in Brazil–Mogi das Cruzes, Natal, Porto Alegre, and Santa Maria Madalena–to prospect the possibilities of developing pilot projects for refugee resettlement (UNHCR 2001: 2). They were chosen based on their diversity in terms of size, economic activity, and the ethnic origin of the residents (ibid.). Out of the visited cities, in the aftermath of the 9/11 attacks against the United States, only one remained in the resettlement project: Porto Alegre, where twenty-three Afghans were resettled in 2002 (Jubilut 2007: 39). In 2003, another sixteen resettled refugees arrived, mostly Colombians (Jubilut and Carneiro 2011: 78). The integration of Afghan and Colombian refugees was perceived very differently. The majority of the Afghan refugees requested voluntary repatriation after the fall of the Taliban regime. The Colombian group had a better resettlement outcome, with all refugees having successfully integrated, with the exception of three cases (ibid.: 79).

The emergence of a resettlement program illustrates the role of migration issues in Brazil's foreign policy agenda. At the time, migration was perceived as a suitable vehicle for ascertaining Brazil's new position as a protagonist in multilateral fora by differentiating the country from the "rich" countries (Reis 2011). Drawing on the chapter's power typology, it can be argued that Brazil's refugee resettlement became an instrument for enhancing the country's *soft power.*

Resettlement in Solidarity and the Mexico Plan of Action (2004–2014)

In parallel with the beginning of the resettlement program, the Brazilian government started to work with UNHCR on a "new approach to a traditional durable solution" (Jubilut and Carneiro 2011: 63) to be presented to other states of the region. Brazil proposed the idea of resettlement in solidarity (or solidarity resettlement) for adoption in the Mexico Declaration and Plan of Action (MPA) in 2004 (Mexico Declaration and Plan of Action

2004). The MPA is a document of the revisional process of the Cartagena Declaration. Such a process has meetings that take place every ten years from the Cartagena Declaration's adoption, aiming to reassess refugee protection in Latin America and approve new soft law instruments. The first of said documents was the San José Declaration on Refugees and Displaced Persons of 1994. The MPA was the second and was adopted by twenty Latin American states–Argentina, Belize, Bolivia, Brazil, Chile, Colombia, Costa Rica, Ecuador, El Salvador, Guatemala, Guyana, Honduras, Mexico, Nicaragua, Panama, Paraguay, Peru, Suriname, Uruguay, and Venezuela.[4]

The main objectives of the MPA were to strengthen existing protection mechanisms and to craft innovative solutions to protect refugees and other persons of concern in the region (Mexico Declaration and Plan of Action 2004: preamble and chap. 1). The MPA was divided into two sections, covering protection and durable solutions, respectively. The durable solutions component, in turn, was composed of three parts: (i) cities of solidarity, (ii) frontiers of solidarity, and (iii) resettlement in solidarity.

Resettlement in solidarity was conceived as a regional approach to a regional crisis, namely the large numbers of Colombian refugees in Colombia's neighboring countries (Jubilut and Carneiro 2011: 66, 71–72). The core premise of resettlement in solidarity, and one of its chief contributions, is the idea of responsibility sharing instead of the more conventional notion of "burden sharing" (compare Reklev and Jumbert, this volume). As the name implies, the influence of the principle of solidarity here is paramount and emphasizes the collective responsibility for the protection of refugees (Jubilut and Carneiro 2011: 70). In November 2004, Brazil and Chile (see Espinoza, this volume, for more on resettlement in Chile) were the first countries to implement resettlement in solidarity, followed by Argentina in January 2005, and Paraguay and Uruguay in June 2007 (Harley 2014: 39).

The MPA is a soft law document and, as it highlights cooperation, can be said to illustrate a situation in which power is not a zero-sum game, but rather "a positive-sum scenario where all" refugees, first countries of asylum, resettlement countries and UNHCR, as well as the international refugee regime "may benefit" (Allen 2003: 123). Furthermore, it can also be seen as an effort in humanitarian diplomacy, that is, a practice said to contribute to the promotion of international interests to be achieved through peaceful means (Smith 2007: 59), carried out within the obligations established by international humanitarian law, refugee law, and human rights law. Although typically executed by humanitarian aid workers, humanitarian diplomacy may also be undertaken by states (Régnier 2011: 1213) when engaged in humanitarian assistance (ibid.: 1217). In connection with the categories of power, humanitarian diplomacy is able to "negotiate compromise, to use persuasion and to seek and obtain genuine non–zero sum solutions in what are often seen by outsiders as intractable conflicts" (Smith 2007: 38).

Moreover, the proposal of resettlement in solidarity by Brazil and its consequent adoption in the MPA is an example of power through *persuasion* and *negotiation,* counting on the *legitimacy* of UNHCR, which lent its legitimacy to the idea of resettlement in solidarity championed by Brazil's CONARE, as it supported the construction of the concept and advocated its advancement in the MPA negotiations and adoption (Jubilut and Carneiro 2011: 72). It is also an illustration of the creation of *soft power* and of *productive power* (through the employment of the rhetoric of responsibility sharing and solidarity). Brazil's proposal can be seen as an act in humanitarianism that leads to the increase of *soft power* with an idea by the country resulting in the regional adoption of a new concept and initiative in resettlement.

Relating to the quest for *soft power,* the main motives seem to be the facts that "the resettlement program was connected also to the cooperation dimension in the South-South axis; was a possibility of closer relations with UNHCR (by complying to its demand) at the same time that it didn't represent 'heavy social and economic burdens' to the country" (Moreira 2015: 144, unofficial translation). With this initiative, Brazil was able to market itself as both promoter and practitioner of humanitarian policy in the international arena (compare Darrow; Garnier; Losoncz, this volume). Brazil was able to present "itself as one of the main speakers for the Global South, while also striving to be recognized as a potential member of the North" (Valença and Carvalho 2014: 76), thus accumulating *legitimacy* and *soft power* in different international settings.

In addition to political considerations, altruistic, logistical, and pragmatic concerns also played a role in motivating Brazil to spearhead this initiative, more specifically its eagerness to promote human rights–focused policies, the international rebirth of resettlement, and the reopening of UNHCR's office in Brazil in March 2004 (Jubilut and Carneiro 2011: 71).

Implementing Resettlement in Solidarity in Brazil

As priorities for resettlement Brazil selected cases of refugees with legal and physical protection needs, of women-at-risk, and of family reunification (Jubilut and Carneiro 2011:79). Brazil also showed a preference to resettle refugees from urban environments (White 2012:12). Selection missions included representatives of the government (through CONARE), NGOs, and UNHCR (Jubilut and Carneiro 2011: 80; White 2012: 12). By the end of 2005, Brazil had resettled eighty-five refugees through the resettlement in solidarity initiative: eighty-one Colombians and four Ecuadorians.

The initial implementation of resettlement in solidarity in Brazil was not without obstacles. One of the first barriers was to overcome a preference of refugees for being resettled in developed countries (Jubilut and Carneiro 2011:

79; see also Thomson, this volume). In 2006, in order to present Brazil as a more attractive alternative and to improve protection to applicants with severe physical security concerns, Brazil adopted a fast-track procedure that would enable the possibility of immediate relief (Jubilut and Carneiro 2011: 79). Fast-track decisions, which must be unanimous, are implemented up to seventy-two hours after the submission of the case by UNHCR (UNHCR 2013: 3–4).[5]

Another challenge had to do with Brazil's unique cultural background in the region (Jubilut and Carneiro 2011: 80; White 2012: 13). Unlike the Latin American countries of origin or of first asylum of the refugees being resettled, Brazil is the only country in the region where Spanish is not the native language. Challenges comparable to the ones found in other resettlement programs in the region were also noted, such as access to employment and housing (White 2012: 13).

In 2007, following a request from UNHCR, Brazil pledged to resettle just over 100 Palestinians who had been living in a camp in Jordan, having fled persecution in Iraq. The group was made up by Palestinians, people of other nationalities (Jordan, Lebanon, and Iran), and one stateless person. As they all arrived in the scenario of the closing of Palestinian refugee camps, they are loosely referred to as Palestinians (Jubilut and Carneiro 2011: 83). There is no agreement on the number of Palestinians arrivals, which varies from 104 to 109 persons, depending on the source (either CONARE or UNHCR-Brazil). This expanded the reach of the resettlement in solidarity initiative beyond the regional scope (ibid.) and can be seen as an effort in *persuasion* due to the *legitimacy* of UNHCR.

The scenario of the Palestinian refugees while still in Jordan seems to illustrate examples of, at the very least, *inducement* and, in the worst case, *manipulation* and *coercion*. In order to find a solution for the refugees as the camp was about to be closed and given that several other avenues of protection were unsuccessful, it seems that there was misleading information about Brazil prior to the acceptance of being resettled and of arriving in the country, not a unique case in terms of refugee camps (see Sandvik, this volume). The resettlement of these refugees was conducted through dossier (Jubilut and Carneiro 2011: 82–83), a procedure employed when it is unfeasible to carry out in-country selection (UNHCR 2013: 3). The Palestinians' resettlement in Brazil is considered a less successful experience than the previous ones with Afghans and Colombians (White 2012: 12).

Both from the host country and from the refugees' perspective, among the most serious and complex challenges faced by the Palestinian refugees were the question of adaptation and the difficulty of managing expectations (Hamid 2012: 140; and see Espinoza, this volume. For a temporal perspective on integration, see Lewis and Young, this volume). First, as mentioned, the information refugees received prior to their arrival was allegedly inaccurate or involved promises of benefits that could not be fulfilled (Hamid 2012: 141). The key points of dissatisfaction related to the refugees' territorial distribution, the choice of housing, access to health services, and the quality of Portuguese classes (ibid.: 140). The Palestinians' resettlement also became an issue for internal groups trying to influence Brazil's foreign policy in relation to the Israel-Palestine conflicts once the refugees were in Brazil and became a complex caseload both for UNHCR and the government, which led, in practice, to a slowdown in Brazil's resettlement program (Jubilut and Carneiro 2011: 84).

MPA and the Brasilia Declaration

Despite these challenges, the resettlement in solidarity program was still praised because it provided a "diversification of resettlement in the international arena" (White 2012: 4). The 2010 Brasilia Declaration on the Protection of Refugees and Stateless Persons in the Americas encouraged the application of the MPA framework, pointing out that there needed to be greater technical and financial support from the international community to continue the consolidation of the initiative (Brasilia Declaration 2010).

Funding, particularly, was seen as a key obstacle. The UNHCR Progress Report on Resettlement from 2014 stressed the vital need that "Latin American resettlement countries . . . assume increasing responsibility for their resettlement processing and integration programs in the coming years" (Executive Committee of the High Commissioner 2014: 3). The demand for diversification of sources of financial support "to include private and public funding, combined with the use of existing and currently untapped networks" (White 2012: 19) was stressed, as it directly affects the sustainability of the initiative in the long run (ibid.: 19; Menezes and Kostas 2017). The need to provide funds, however, could jeopardize one of the main factors that attract emerging resettlement countries: the possibility of being engaged in solutions to the refugee regime without bearing the costs (Reis 2011; Stuenkel 2016; Moreira 2015)–because the expenses of the resettlement program in Brazil were covered by UNHCR–that is, of enhancing their *soft power* with minimum engagement of financial resources. There was an expectation that the Brazilian government would assume the costs from 2017. There is no prevision of private funding so far.

The Brazil Declaration and Plan of Action (2014–onward)

The Search for Innovative Solutions

As mentioned, the difficulties in the Palestinian resettlement have slowed down refugee resettlement in Brazil. However, the scheme was not terminated. Between 2008 and 2013, 210 refugees were resettled in Brazil. Apart from four Palestinians, all arrivals were intraregional, with Colombian, Ecuadorian, and Venezuelan refugees. Despite these relatively small numbers, Brazil once again took the leadership in the resettlement *negotiations* for the Brazil Declaration and Plan of Action (BPA), which was adopted 3 December 2014.

The BPA–the third soft law instrument conceived in the revisional processes of the Cartagena Declaration–was adopted by twenty-eight states and three territories of Latin America (Antigua and Barbuda, Argentina, Bahamas, Barbados, Belize, Bolivia, Brazil, Cayman Islands, Chile, Colombia, Costa Rica, Cuba, Curacao, El Salvador, Ecuador, Guatemala, Guiana, Haiti, Honduras, Jamaica, Mexico, Nicaragua, Panama, Paraguay, Peru, Saint Lucia, Suriname, Trinidad and Tobago, Turks and Caicos, Uruguay, and Venezuela).[6] The BPA continued to have resettlement as a relevant aspect of refugee protection in the region, as it called for the continuation and reinforcement of the resettlement in solidarity program in Latin America (BPA: 24th preamble paragraph, and chap. 3). Resettlement in solidarity endures in Latin America. Between 2005 and 2014, 1,514 refugees were resettled under the auspices of resettlement in solidarity, 363 of whom came from countries outside the region (Ruiz 2015: 4). In Brazil, over 690 refugees were resettled during that period, of which 85 percent still remained in the country in 2015 (ibid.: 10).

Acknowledging the relevance of resettlement in solidarity in the region, the BPA tackled two specific situations (BPA: chap. 3). The first was the need for determining which cases to prioritize in the future in the resettlement in solidarity program as different countries raised concerns about the disconnection between the priorities set out in terms of vulnerabilities or prospects of successful integration and the actual characteristics of the selected refugees (Ruiz 2015: 12). It was noted that the rates of success in integration and in achieving self-sufficiency seemed to be higher for refugees who were resettled due to their lack of security (ibid.: 13). Second, the possibility of establishing a voluntary cooperation fund was presented to address the funding issue mentioned. Both situations expose states' concerns that in terms of power may be seen as related to *empowerment.* On the one hand, empowering refugees would better assist in their integration and therefore in their integral protection, that is, their human rights and refugee rights (Jubilut and Apolinário 2008). On the other hand, better funding could economically empower states to better implement their resettlement programs.

The BPA also brought forward a new initiative, also proposed by Brazil: a "labor mobility" program. Presented as a new approach to resettlement ten years after the MPA, it was directed at facilitating the transit of persons who had already been recognized as refugees in one of Mercosur's members or associate states (mainly Colombian refugees living in Ecuador) to other countries where they would have better employment opportunities; it was also a combined effort to promote local integration and self-sufficiency (BPA: chap. 3).

In 2014, UNHCR and the Brazilian government reached an agreement to develop and implement a pilot project of labor mobility by agreeing to resettle 200 Colombian refugees living in Ecuador to Brazil until 2016.[7] The criterion for selection would be based on the refugee's determination to achieve self-sufficiency through work,[8] reinstating an integration and labor-based approach that has a long history in refugee schemes (see, for instance, Kunz 1988; Kay and Miles 1992).

The language put forward in the BPA built upon the *soft power* and *productive power* of the solidarity component expressed in the MPA. To date, the labor mobility remains only a proposal (CONARE 2016a; ASAV 2016). In theory, though, it is relevant to note the *empowerment* aspect to which this initiative is both based and dependent upon: it seems to establish a new criterion for resettlement selection grounded on possibilities of self-reliance, simultaneously taking into account the planning of better integration opportunities afterward (compare Darrow; Garnier; Losoncz, this volume).

Brazil as a Regional Leader

Regarding its role as a regional leader, Brazil's resettlement is an interesting case in terms of power dynamics. In a regime where "Southern states had very little ability to influence the North" and where there appears to be a North-South impasse (Betts 2009), Brazil's refugee resettlement emerges as an example of a southern state (Brazil) influencing other southern states (Latin American countries). Brazil was the proposer of two regional initiatives regarding resettlement (i.e., resettlement in solidarity and labor resettlement) that were subsequently incorporated into soft law documents in Latin America (the MPA and the BPA).

It is a case that involves, to a lesser extent, *institutional power,* with Brazil influencing the other Latin American states in the institutional setting of the Cartagena Declaration and its revisional processes and the establishment of the normative basis for resettlement in solidarity. One can also interpret Brazil's engagement as involving two other power types, namely *structural power* (as it is through the MPA that the relationship of resettled refugees with resettlement countries is established) and, to a higher extent, *productive power* (the adoption of the responsibility sharing and solidarity logics, the embracing of a humanitarian idea, and the creation of the resettlement in solidarity initiative) through *persuasion* and *negotiation* (and UNHCR's *legit-*

imacy). It can also be seen as a case that may be relevant in a scenario in which, as mentioned, the vast majority of refugees is based in the Global South.

There are, however, different interpretations of the effectiveness of the MPA and the future of the BPA, with questioning of Brazil's ability to rise as a regional leader based on such initiatives. To some, the resettlement in solidarity initiative lacked real implementation, as "strategic interests" that would have motivated the countries in the region to effectively commit to cooperating were not met, thus failing to provide sufficient alleviation to the refugee plight in Latin America (Menezes 2016: 135–41). Nevertheless, this situation still adds a new dimension to power dynamics analysis in the refugee regime as it prompts the question of whether *regional power* is a force that needs to be taken into consideration among the typologies of power.

From one point of view, it is a regional interpretation of the above presented power concepts with one country's actions influencing the development of regional approaches to resettlement. Alternatively, it could be interesting to assess whether the creation of regional approaches to resettlement and regionally focused resettlement programs (as seems to be the case of Latin America) may aid in the actual protection of refugees and be a way forward in terms of durable solutions in the refugee regime, influencing the general power dynamics in resettlement. In both areas, *regional power* dimensions and how they can contribute to resettlement and refugee protection seem to be new avenues for investigation.

Assessing Brazil's Continued Resettlement Program

Brazil's resettlement program is an ongoing activity as well as a potential blueprint for future initiatives. In March 2016, the Brazilian government divulged that it had started talks with Germany to consider a partnership to receive Syrian nationals currently hosted there or whose move to Germany was being planned (Chade 2016). By June 2016, however, it was broadcasted that further *negotiations* in this respect had been halted, at least for the time being (Fellet 2016; Stuenkel 2016). Another possible initiative in refugee resettlement is the use of private sponsorships when "companies, foundations, individuals and charitable institutions offer direct support to the reception and integration of refugees, with its own private resources" (Brasil. Ministério da Justiça 2016, unofficial translation). Brazil has been engaged since 2016 in exchanges with Canada–a model in this area–to increase knowledge on private sponsorship (for instance with a visit by representatives from Canada to Brazil to discuss its experiences in February [ibid.] and by taking part in an international conference in Ottawa in December[9]).

Even though the progress of this initiative is still unclear, it seems to contest the traditional logic that states should be the only actors concerned with refugee resettlement and creates opportunities for new countries to engage in the resettlement practice (Kumin 2015: 1). This could affect the power dynamics of resettlement by opening new humanitarian spaces and, thus, also reflecting on resettlement as humanitarian governance. However, there is uncertainty regarding the new proposals in the resettlement scheme in Brazil, which may be due to changes stemming from the political and economic crisis in the country.

As mentioned, the number of arrivals for resettlement in Brazil has decreased in the past couple of years. The number of NGOs that are UNHCR implementing partners for resettlement in Brazil has also decreased: if in the beginning there were three NGOs in three different regions of the country, now there is only one: Associação Antonio Vieira (ASAV). The numeric trend held true for 2014, which saw forty-three arrivals, and 2015, with fourteen resettled refugees. However, in this period, the program restarted to look outside the region by receiving resettled refugees from Afghanistan and Palestine, as well as, for the first time, from Sri Lanka and Syria. In 2016, thirty-one individuals (twenty-five Colombians and six Ecuadorians) were resettled to Brazil, and in 2017 two Cubans arrived as resettled refugees. A Sudanese family of four was supposed to arrive at late 2017, early 2018, but their resettlement has not occurred yet. As of April, there were no new arrivals in 2018.

Reasons for the decline in the number of resettled refugees may include the abovementioned problems faced by the resettlement program with the Palestinian caseload, the political climate of the country, and the effect of the sudden increase in the number of asylum requests registered in the same period. In relation to the numbers, with only 8,863 recognized refugees, Brazil saw the number of asylum requests escalate 2,868 percent between 2010 and 2015 (CONARE 2016b). From 966 asylum requests in 2010, the numbers reached almost 30,000 applications in each 2014 and 2015 (ibid.). In 2018 it was divulged that there are 86,000 pending refugee status determination cases to be assessed by the country (Franco 2018), which can be explained by the fact that applying for refugee status was until 2017 the only avenue for people wanting to stay in the country for humanitarian reasons and still is the only alternative with a solid legal basis.[10] With the resulting work amount from the escalation of RSD assessments, the resources, both human and financial, are strained, which is also reflected in the resettlement program.

Resettlement in Brazil is an initiative that is aligned with human rights and that may aid in the protection of refugees regionally and even worldwide, but it is still far from achieving its full potential. In this sense, it is relevant to describe some of the program's main challenges as a way to address them and enhance the program as a form of humanitarianism.

First, there is the mentioned necessity of securing additional and specific funding mechanisms, which would enable resettlement to be less susceptible to external influences.

Second, there is a perceived flaw of all refugee-oriented programs in Brazil: the lack of an overarching guideline to direct their implementation. Policies in various areas, from RSD and resettlement to integration, seem to be formulated on an ad hoc basis. And, although "refuge is a state policy and it is understood as a part of [the country's] democratic values" (Brazil quoted in Fischel de Andrade 2015: 174), it does not seem to be, in practice, part of a long-term plan or a systemic and systematic approach to the protection of refugees.

The lack of firmly established public policies for refugee protection is the third challenge. There are indications of negative impacts in access to rights by all migrants, including refugees, such as difficulties accessing rights due to language barriers, accessing economic and social rights such as housing and employment, and securing documentation (Jubilut et al. 2015). These obstacles in accessing rights can be said to be the fourth challenge.

A fifth challenge is the question of quotas for resettlement. Brazil does not have a set quota for resettled refugees per year (UNHCR 2013: 3), and the annual target for resettlement is the product of power dynamics through *negotiation* among the government, UNHCR, and NGOs "based on the existing protection needs and availability of financial resources" (ibid.). While, on one hand, this is a positive characteristic, meaning that there is flexibility in the final decision of cases and in the number of accepted refugees, on the other hand, it may also generate a lack of commitment from the government, since there is not even a promise by Brazil to accept a specific number of refugees for resettlement yearly. This lack of commitment, however, is not a challenge exclusive to Brazil; it exists in all resettlement countries, as quotas can be changed at any time.

The sixth and seventh challenges are technical. Statistical data are scarce and the available information is often inconsistent and imprecise, with different sources involved in the resettlement process providing different information at times. Also, monitoring and evaluation tools should be in place so that the quality of resettlement can be better analyzed, and as a way to pay closer attention to the voices of resettled refugees. This would allow for power dynamics to include and policies to be built with the participation of the direct beneficiaries, also guaranteeing respect to rights through *empowerment* by *negotiation*.

An eighth challenge refers to the small number of resettled refugees. Although this can be criticized, it can also be justified given that the first resettled refugee arrivals in the current resettlement program happened less than fifteen years ago.

In light of these challenges, it is important to wait and see whether Brazil will continue to regard refugee resettlement as an exercise in humanitarianism, a topic of its regional leadership, and a way of enhancing its *soft power,* or if the practice will lose space for others in the countries' political agenda. An announcement of a pilot project to resettle about sixty to seventy refugees from the Northern Triangle of Central America (NTCA)—encompassing Guatemala, Honduras, and El Salvador—currently in Mexico and Costa Rica, in 2017,[11] was made but it does not allow us to be sure of the future of the program: on the one hand, it seems to be a step in the right direction but, on the other, this new project has not been put in practice so far.

Conclusion: The Road Ahead

This chapter has shown how the practices and discourses of the different phases of the current refugee resettlement scheme in Brazil can be analyzed via the prism of power categories.

Brazil's resettlement program can be said to have had a dynamic and optimistic start, but since then, due to difficulties in light of specific caseloads and changes in politics and policies, fewer cases have been resettled each year. The positive note is that the countries' refugee resettlement scheme was not abandoned. The difficulties also did not prevent Brazil from advancing proposals for new regional approaches to refugee resettlement, which have been included in soft law instruments of refugee protection in the region. Brazil has been able, thus, not only to create new approaches to be adopted internally but also to influence other states in Latin America to adopt them as regional initiatives.

This is positive because the refugee regime—and especially its humanitarian governance—can benefit from the combination of regional and international solutions. Regionalism "would not compete with existing efforts but would aim to complement them" (Jubilut and Ramos 2014: 66) and should not be taken blindly as an absolute positive development in international refugee law, but it brings a "greater possibility of uniform agreement between nation states in the region" (Harley 2014: 29–30) and is ultimately a way of fostering regional stability (ibid.). Regional solutions may be a way to cooperate with global governance of the refugee regime as, out of the 10.1 million refugees from the five major countries of origin, 89 percent found safety in a neighboring country (UNHCR 2016a: 21).

The MPA and the BPA offered valuable regional cooperation frameworks and developed the regional logic of solidarity. This seems to be an unremitting necessity as forced displacement continues in Latin America, with, for example, Colombia as the tenth major source country for refugees in 2015 (having an estimated 340,200 refugees; UNHCR 2016a: 17) and the ongoing crises in the NTCA, where asylum seekers rose from 20,900 in 2012 to 109,800 in 2015 (over a fivefold increase; ibid.: 7), as well as in Venezuela, with 170,169 asylum-seekers and 507,353 persons counting on alternative forms of stay in the region as of April 2018 (UNHCR 2018a). This alone justifies the continuation and further improvement of resettlement in solidarity programs throughout Latin America, in general, and in Brazil, specifically.

This fosters the prospect of adding a new dimension to power dynamics in resettlement, that is, *regional power,* to the still developing analysis of power in the refugee regime. Brazil's case also illustrates how such an analysis can exist in terms of specific case studies, as it involves several types of power relations, therefore demonstrating the need for the abovementioned spatial and historically situated assessments.

Finally, resettlement in solidarity can be used to expand protection spaces for refugees in Latin America (Harley 2014: 41), coming from the region or elsewhere, as a way to encompass "urgent protection needs, wherever they may arise" (Ruiz 2015: 26). This seems to be an idea aligned with the concept of responsibility sharing on a global level, given that at the end of 2017, there were 68.5 million displaced persons due to conflict or persecution in the world, of which 25.4 are refugees (UNHCR 2018b: 2).

For all of the above, it seems that, even with all its shortcomings, Brazil's resettlement is both a case of positive achievement for an emerging resettlement country and an interesting case study in identifying power dynamics in resettlement, not least for being a thought-provoking example of the quest of *soft power* through humanitarianism and for suggesting a possible use of *regional power* in refugee resettlement.

Liliana Lyra Jubilut holds a Ph.D. and a Master's in international law from Universidade de São Paulo and an LL.M. in international legal studies from NYU School of Law. She was part of the project Brazil's Rise to the Global Stage: Humanitarianism, Peacekeeping and the Quest for Great Powerhood of the Peace Research Institute Oslo (PRIO). She has been working with refugees' issues since 1999. Currently she is a professor of the Postgraduate Program in Law at Universidade Católica de Santos and a member of the IOM Migration Research Leaders Syndicate.

Andrea Cristina Godoy Zamur holds an LL.M. from Harvard Law School. She is Coordinator of Policies for Immigrants and for the Promotion of Decent Work at São Paulo's Municipal Secretariat for Human Rights and Citizenship, and was part of the project Brazil's Rise to the Global Stage: Humanitarianism, Peacekeeping and the Quest for Great Powerhood at PRIO. Zamur was a lawyer/refugee status determination officer and protection officer at the Refugee Center of Caritas Arquidiocesana de São Paulo (Brazil), a UNHCR implementing partner, and a member of the research group Direitos Humanos e Vulnerabilidades.

Notes

1. For Allen, negotiation and persuasion can be seen as part of an overarching category–i.e., associational power–but as the chapter proposes a nuanced analysis of power categories, the option was to present them separately, as they are different practices.
2. The Cartagena Declaration (1984) states in its 3rd Conclusion: "To reiterate that, in view of the experience gained from the massive flows of refugees in the Central American area, it is necessary to consider enlarging the concept of a refugee. . . . Hence the definition or concept of a refugee to be recommended for use in the region is one which, in addition to containing the elements of the 1951 Convention and the 1967 Protocol, includes among refugees persons who have fled their country because their lives, safety or freedom have been threatened by generalized violence, foreign aggression, internal conflicts, massive violation of human rights or other circumstances which have seriously disturbed public order."
3. According to http://www.acnur.org/t3/recursos/bdl/.
4. According to http://www.unhcr.org/455443b30.pdf.
5. Until February 2016, 218 had been resettled to Brazil using the Fast Track procedure.
6. According to http://www.acnur.org/cartagena30/pt-br/declaracao-e-plano-de-acao-do-brasil/.
7. See http://www.acnur.org/portugues/quem-ajudamos/solucoes-duradouras/mo bilidade-regional-e-insercao-economica-de-refugiados/. Accessed 9 February 2017.
8. See CONARE's Normative Resolution 20, which elaborates on the project. http://www.lex.com.br/legis_26436048_RESOLUCAO_NORMATIVA_ N_19_DE_18_DE_DEZEMBRO_DE_2014.aspx. Accessed 9 February 2017.
9. See http://www.unhcr.org/news/press/2016/12/58539e524/global-refugee-spo nsorship-initiative-promotes-canadas-private-refugee.html. Accessed 9 February 2017.
10. Brazil has recently adopted humanitarian stay visas, which are now present in the new Migration Law (Law 13.445/2017). The visas have already benefited Haitians and Venezuelans.
11. See http://m.folha.uol.com.br/mundo/2016/12/1841584-brasil-vai-reassentar-ref ugiados-de-honduras-el-salvador-e-guatemala.shtml. Accessed 9 February 2017.

References

Allen, John. 2003. *Lost Geographies of Power.* Oxford: Blackwell Publishing.
Arendt, Hannah. 1972. *Crises of the Republic.* New York: Harvest Books.
Associação Antonio Vieira (ASAV). 2016. Exchange of information with the authors through email.
Barnett, Michael, and Raymond Duvall. 2005. "Power in International Politics." *International Organization* 59(1): 39–75.

Betts, Alexander. 2009. *Protection by Persuasion: International Cooperation in the Refugee Regime.* Ithaca: Cornell University Press.

Brasil. Ministério da Justiça. 2016. *Brasil, ONU e Canadá Discutem Financiamento Privado para Reassentamento e Integração de Refugiados,* 26 February. Accessed 9 February 2017. http://www.justica.gov.br/news/brasil-onu-e-canada-discutem-financiamento-privado-para-reassentamento-e-integracao-de-refugiados.

Brasilia Declaration on the Protection of Refugees and Stateless Persons in the Americas. 2010. Accessed 9 February 2017. http://www.unhcr.org/protection/basic/4cdd3fac6/encouraged-declaration-protection-refugees-stateless-persons-americas-brasilia.html.

Brazil Declaration and Plan of Action. 2014. Accessed 9 February 2017. http://www.refworld.org/docid/5487065b4.html.

Calvès, Anne-Emmanuèle. 2009. "Empowerment: The History of a Key Concept in Contemporary Development Discourse." *Revue Tiers Monde* 200(4): 735–49.

Cartagena Declaration on Refugees. 1984. Accessed 9 February 2017. http://www.refworld.org/docid/3ae6b36ec.html.

Chade, Jamil. 2016. "Brasil se Oferece para Acolher Refugiados Sírios da Alemanha." *O Estado de São Paulo,* 31 March.

Comitê Nacional para os Refugiados (CONARE). 2016a. Exchange of information with the authors through email.

——. 2016b. *Sistema de Refúgio brasileiro Desafios e perspectivas.* Brasília: CONARE. Accessed 9 February 2017. http://www.acnur.org/fileadmin/scripts/doc.php?file=fileadmin/Documentos/portugues/Estatisticas/Sistema_de_Refugio_brasileiro_-_Refugio_em_numeros_-_05_05_2016

Executive Committee of the High Commissioner. 2014. *Progress Report on Resettlement.* EC/65/SC/CRP.11, 6 June. Geneva: UNHCR.

Fellet, João. 2016. "Governo Temer Suspende Negociação com Europa para Receber Refugiados Sírios." BBC Brasil, 17 June.

Fischel de Andrade, José H. 2015. "Refugee Protection in Brazil (1921–2014): An Analytical Narrative of Changing Policies." In *A Liberal Tide: Immigration and Asylum Law and Policy in Latin America,* edited by David J. Cantor, Luisa Feline Freier, and Jean-Pierre. Gauc, 153–83. London: University of London–ILAS.

Fischel de Andrade, José H., and Adriana Marcolini. 2002. "Brazil's Refugee Act: Model Refugee Law for Latin America." *Forced Migration Review* 12: 37–38.

Franco, Mariana. 2018. "Brasil tem 86 mil estrangeiros aguardando resposta sobre refúgio e 14 funcionários para avaliar pedidos." *G1,* 3 March.

Garnier, Adèle. 2013. "Migration Management and Humanitarian Protection: The UNHCR's 'Resettlement Expansionism' and Its Impact on Policy-making in the EU and Australia." *Journal of Ethnic and Migration Studies* 40(6): 942–959.

Hamid, Sônia C. 2012. *(Des)Integrando Refugiados: Os Processos do Reassentamento de Palestinos no Brasil.* Brasília: UnB.

Harley, Tristan. 2014. "Regional Cooperation and Refugee Protection in Latin America: A 'South-South' Approach." *International Journal of Refugee Law* 26(1): 22–47.

Hurd, Ian. 1999. "Legitimacy and Authority in International Politics." *International Organization* 53(2): 379–408.

Jubilut, Liliana L. 2006. "International Refugee Law and Protection in Brazil: a Model in South America?" *Journal of Refugee Studies* 19(1): 22–44.

——. 2007. *O Direito Internacional dos Refugiados e Sua Aplicação no Ordenamento Jurídico Brasileiro*. São Paulo: Método.

Jubilut, Liliana L. et al. 2015. "Migrantes, Apátridas e Refugiados." *Projeto Pensando o Direito 57*. Brasília: IPEA and Ministério da Justiça. http://pensando.mj.gov.br/wp-content/uploads/2015/12/PoD_57_Liliana_web3.pdf. Accessed 13 April 2018.

Jubilut, Liliana L., and Wellington P. Carneiro. 2011. "Resettlement in Solidarity: A New Regional Approach towards a More Humane Durable Solution." *Refugee Survey Quarterly* 3(1): 63–86.

Jubilut, Liliana L., and Silvia M. de O. S. Apolinário. 2008. "A população refugiada no Brasil: em busca da proteção integral." *Universitas: Relações Internacionais* 6(2): 9–38.

Jubilut, Liliana L., and Érika P. Ramos. 2014. "Regionalism as a Strategic Tool for Dealing with Crisis Migration." *Forced Migration Review* 45: 66–67.

Jubilut, Liliana L., Camila Sombra, and Camila Gilberto. 2016. "Human Rights in Refugee Protection in Brazil." In *Human Rights and the Refugee Definition–Comparative Legal Practice and Theory,* edited by Bruce Burson and David J. Cantor, 210–28. Leiden: Brill.

Kay, Diana, and Robert Miles. 1992. *Refugees or Migrant Workers? European Volunteer Workers in Britain, 1946–1951*. London: Routledge.

Kumin, Judith. 2015. *Welcoming Engagement: How Private Sponsorship Can Strengthen Refugee Resettlement in the European Union*. EU Asylum toward 2020 project. Migration Policy Institute Europe, December.

Kunz, Egon F. 1988. *Displaced Persons: Calwell's New Australians*. Sydney: ANU Press.

Lukes, Steven. 2004. *Power–a Radical View,* 2nd ed. London/New York: Palgrave.

Menezes, Fabiano L. de. 2016. "Utopia or Reality: Regional Cooperation in Latin America to Enhance the Protection of Refugees." *Refugee Survey Quarterly* 35: 122–41.

Menezes, Thais S., and Stylianos Kostas. 2017. "The Future of the Brazilian Resettlement Programme." *Forced Migration Review* 56: 51–52.

Milner, James. 2015. "Understanding Power and Influence in the Global Refugee Regime." Paper prepared for the workshop Power and Influence in the Global Refugee Regime, Carleton University, 23–25 September.

Moreira, Julia B. 2015. "Política Externa, Refugiados e Reassentamento no Brasil: uma análise sobre o período do governo Lula (2003–2010)." *Carta Internacional* 10: 133–151.

Murillo González, Juan Carlos. 2010. "A Importância da Lei Brasileira de Refúgio e suas Contribuições Regionais." In *Refúgio no Brasil: A Proteção Brasileira aos Refugiados e Seu Impacto nas Américas,* edited by Luiz Paulo Teles Ferreira, 48–51. Brasília: ACNUR, Ministério da Justiça.

Nye, Joseph. 2004. *Soft Power–The Means to Success in World Politics*. New York: Public Affairs.

Page, Nanette, and Cheryl E. Czuba. 1999. "Empowerment: What Is It?" *Journal of Extension* 37(5). https://www.joe.org/joe/1999october/comm1.php/php. Accessed 13 April 2018.

Mexico Declaration and Plan of Action to Strengthen International Protection of Refugees in Latin America. 16 November 2004. Accessed 9 February 2017. http://www.refworld.org/docid/424bf6914.html.

Régnier, Philippe. 2011. "The Emerging Concept of Humanitarian Diplomacy: Identification of a Community of Practice and Prospects for International Recognition." *International Review of the Red Cross* 93(884): 1211–37.

Reis, Rosana R. 2011. "A Política dos Brasil para as Migrações Internacionais." *Contexto Internacional* 33(1): 47–69.

Ruiz, Hiram. 2015. *Evaluation of Resettlement Programmes in Argentina, Brazil, Chile, Paraguay and Uruguay.* Geneva: UNHCR.

Smith, Hazel. 2007. "Humanitarian Diplomacy: Theory and Practice." In *Humanitarian Diplomacy: Practitioners and Their Craft,* edited by Larry Minear and Hazel Smith, 36–61. Tokyo: UNU Press.

Stuenkel, Oliver. 2016. "Brazil's Retreat from the International Stage Continues." *Post-Western World,* 17 June.

United Nations High Commissioner for Refugees (UNHCR). 2001. *New Directions for Resettlement Policy and Practice.* EC/51/SC/INF.2. Geneva: UNHCR.

——. 2003. *Refugiados no Sul da América do Sul: Argentina, Bolívia, Brasil, Chile, Paraguai e Uruguai.* Geneva: UNHCR.

——. 2009. *2008 Global Trends: Refugees, Asylum Seekers, Returnees, Internally Displaced and Stateless Persons.* Geneva: UNHCR.

——. 2011. *Discussion Note–Emerging Resettlement countries of Southern South America (Chile, Brazil and Argentina).* Geneva: UNHCR.

——. 2011. *Global Trends 2010.* Geneva: UNHCR.

——. 2013. *Resettlement Handbook, Country Chapters, Brazil.* Geneva: UNHCR.

——. 2016a. *Global Trends: Forced Displacement in 2015.* Geneva: UNHCR.

——. 2016b. *Projected Global Resettlement Needs 2017.* Geneva: UNHCR.

——. 2018a. *Venezuela situation informational portal.* Accessed 1 May 2018. https://data2.unhcr.org/en/situations/vensit.

——. 2018b. *Global Trends: Forced Displacement in 2017.* Geneva: UNHCR.

Valença, Marcelo M., and Gustavo Carvalho. 2014. "Soft Power, Hard Aspiration: The Shifting Role of Power in Brazilian Foreign Policy." *Brazilian Political Science Review* 8(3): 66–94.

White, Ana G. 2012. *A Pillar of Protection: Solidarity Resettlement for Refugees in Latin America.* New Issues in Refugee Research 239. Geneva: UNHCR.

Part II

National Policies and Ideologies of Refugee Resettlement

4

Working It Out in Practice

Tensions Embedded in the U.S. Refugee Resettlement Program Resolved through Implementation

Jessica H. Darrow

Introduction

The United States prides itself on a tradition of offering refuge to some of the world's most vulnerable people. Since the inception of the Refugee Admissions Program, the United States has led the world in total number of refugees resettled and in the expansive criteria for accepting incoming refugee applicants. The mission of the admissions program is to provide resettlement opportunities to people of "humanitarian concern" (United States Refugee Act of 1980, sec. 207), while also maintaining national security and rooting out fraudulent claims. Federal legislation, codified in the Refugee Act of 1980 (the Act),[1] supports the achievement of this mission.

Congressional debates leading up to the passage of the Act in 1979 focused on the issue of human rights, reflecting a larger societal awakening in the United States informed by the passage of the Civil Rights Act (Bon Tempo 2008). The Act includes multiple references to "humanitarianism" in refugee admissions policy–a word that represents a shift from a policy focused primarily on geopolitics to one focused more on a concern for human rights. Prior to 1980 the United States restricted its definition of a refugee to someone fleeing from a Communist country or from a Middle Eastern country. The Act broadened the U.S. definition to match that of the United

Nations High Commissioner for Refugees (UNHCR), a move that Congress intentionally made in order to remove the original discriminatory language and bolster a humanitarian focus (Anker and Posner 1981; Leibowitz 1983).

Data from refugee admissions over time demonstrate that this shift in focus went beyond rhetoric (also Sandvik, this volume). Before 1979 the United States resettled no refugees from Africa (ORR 2005), whereas in 1980, 0.4 percent of resettled refugees were from the African region (ORR 1980, 2005). After the Act passed in 1980, increasing numbers of refugees from Africa were admitted, and in 2016 the group of refugees most heavily represented in admissions was from the Democratic Republic of Congo (U.S. Department of State 2016). Beyond region for admissions, the United States has focused on the differential levels of threat between refugee groups. Since 1980, the United States has resettled more than 2.7 million refugees, who increasingly represent particularly vulnerable and "at-risk populations," such as single women, children, people who suffer from mental illness, or those who have survived torture (U.S. Department of State 2016; ORR 2015; Kerwin 2012; Barnett 2006).

Meanwhile, the goal of the U.S. Resettlement Program is to help new populations to access critical resources and become integrated in their local communities through labor market participation. The majority of policies in place to support this goal have an explicit focus on rapid employment and "economic self-sufficiency," and yet recent research on employment outcomes has shown that working refugees are not doing nearly as well as their immigrant or U.S. born counterparts (Capps et al. 2015; Desiderio 2016). The conclusion reached by refugee scholars and practitioners alike is that the U.S. employment-based resettlement policy might succeed in getting refugees to work, but that rather than getting them started on a career trajectory with upward mobility the refugee employment programs, at best, earn refugees access to "survival jobs" (Capps et al. 2015; Darrow 2015a; U.S. General Accounting Office et al. 1983; Halpern 2008; Kerwin 2012; Ong 2003).

Federal refugee resettlement policy is implemented by widely dispersed local resettlement agencies, the majority of which are contracted nonprofit organizations. The tension created by an admissions' focus on humanitarian resettlement and the associated practice of accepting the world's most at-risk populations, and a resettlement focus on getting refugees to work as quickly as possible, is played out in these local resettlement agencies. Resettlement workers are faced with the daily challenge of finding employment for their clients as quickly as possible, while contending with limited program resources and varying levels of client need and readiness for work.

The policy tension described here is paralleled in the American discourse relating to the poor. Just as the poor are at times and under certain conditions framed as worthy of government support or morally unworthy, refugees in the United States have been, on the one hand, conceptualized as morally worthy of our humanitarian generosity and, on the other hand, as morally suspect until gainfully employed and earning their way toward economic self-sufficiency. Thus, the image of the United States as a safe haven for the world's most vulnerable is complicated by resettlement policies that quickly transform the worthy refugee, accepted and admitted upon humanitarian principles, into a member of the unworthy poor, whose deservingness is determined and qualified by their success at entering the labor market and staying off public cash assistance (for contrasting domestic perspectives, see Reklev and Jumbert; Garnier; Losoncz; and Jubilut and Zamur, this volume). In fact, as will be discussed in the final remarks of this chapter, the very commitment to humanitarian resettlement is called into question as U.S. admissions policies for refugees are adjusted in the current political context.

This chapter, rooted in the social work discipline, asks the central question, what role does refugee resettlement policy play in the process of transforming refugees from one ideological category to the other? To answer this question, the chapter draws on data collected as part of an organizational ethnography of refugee resettlement policy implementation and argues that the structure of U.S. resettlement policy encourages a specific set of policy implementation choices by resettlement workers and is thus implicated in creating a bureaucratic process through which the refugee subject is transformed from worthy to unworthy.

The argument set forth in this chapter is closely aligned with the objective of this edited volume and is further developed in the introductory chapter. That is, the broader investigation of the performative aspects of refugee resettlement and their relationship to coercive power (Garnier, Sanvik, and Jubilut, this volume) is reflected in this chapter's focus on the structure of U.S. resettlement policy and the incentives that this structure creates for resettlement workers to prioritize the punitive dimensions of resettlement. However, while the editors of this volume do careful work to elaborate their conceptualization of *humanitarian governance* as combining the projects of aid (or care) and of social control, this chapter makes an effort to disentangle these entwined projects in the case of U.S. refugee resettlement.

Rather than seeing this endeavor as a deviation from the perspective of the present volume, I understand my articulation of the distinct aspects of U.S. refugee resettlement as a validation of the editors' conceptualization. This chapter moves away from a monolithic conception of the U.S. resettlement project that entwines social control and humanitarianism (which risks disguising the former by embracing the latter). The project of this chapter, then, is to specify where distinct values of aid and social control are archived in different aspects of U.S. resettlement policy and to engage in careful interrogation of the U.S. resettlement program and its underlying but dissonant values. In so doing, this chapter provides an empirical case of humanitarian governance. Herein I tease apart the practice of "humanitarianism," demonstrating distinct sets of refugee resettlement policies rooted in (1) the project of aid and an ideal of worthiness and deservingness, and (2) a set of practices and policies grounded in a project of social control and targeted at the unworthy/undeserving.

The Political Framing of the Worthy and Unworthy Subject

The dichotomous images of the poor as morally worthy or unworthy, or deserving and underserving of government support, have been deployed throughout the evolution of the American welfare state. Depending on the political, economic, and social context of the time, politicians, policy makers, and scholars have framed the poor as worthy or unworthy of public support. Political framing is a value-laden process through which elites use rhetoric to shape the meaning of events or issues in ways that direct public attention and weigh certain interests over others (Benford and Snow 2000).

For example, in the depths of the Great Depression when the majority of U.S. citizens was negatively affected by the vagaries of the labor market and faced decreasing wealth and increasing need, the welfare state was expanded to absorb more people, and politicians were more expansive and inclusive in their rhetoric about who deserved access to the social safety net (Piven and Cloward 1971). On the other hand, as the economic health of the nation improved and the numbers of people without work decreased, the welfare state contracted as people were pushed off the rolls of cash assistance and back to work. Along with this fraying of the safety net came a depiction of those who accessed it as less morally worthy than other Americans (Katz 1989; Mead 1992; Piven and Cloward 1971).

The idea that forms the basis for categorizations of the poor as unworthy or undeserving is that the poor are in some way responsible for their economic condition, that it is a moral failing that has led them to be poor. Arguments about the pathology of the poor can be subtle as well as brutal. Within this frame there is both an individual and an individual-structural explanation connected to the conceptualization of the unworthy poor. The individual frame unabashedly locates the problem of poverty in the poor themselves, claiming they have low morals and placing responsibility for poverty alleviation squarely on the subject (Lewis 1969).

A slightly more complex theory about the sources of poverty are those that acknowledge the role of policy in creating certain conditions that lend themselves to poverty production. These individual-structural arguments suggest that the poor lack an internal motivation to work, so it is the job of policy to address this inadequacy. This individual-structural argument is evident in the case built by Lawrence Mead (1992), who wrote, "To a great extent, nonwork occurs simply because work is not enforced" (134). From this perspective, the solution to the problem of a lack of discipline among the poor is to create policies that force them to work. Shortly after Mead wrote these words, President Bill Clinton passed a welfare reform policy that was designed to address the problem of poverty policy that might be perceived to create dependency. The 1996 welfare reforms took away entitlements to cash benefits for families who were economically eligible and made access to these benefits dependent on work (Personal Responsibility and Work Opportunity Reconciliation Act of 1996). Even its name, the Personal Responsibility and Work Opportunity Reconciliation Act, makes clear the policy perspective on the moral value of work. Since the passage of welfare reform in 1996, the image of the unworthy poor has repeatedly been utilized in order to justify ever more restrictive access to public cash assistance (Peck 2001; Soss et al. 2011).

Although poverty in the United States is not exclusive to one racial group, the framing of the poor as unworthy has a distinctly racial cast. Scholars have documented the phenomena of political elites blaming black people for their own condition of poverty and thus colluding in a system of oppression for whites over people of color (Wacquant 2010); of politicians using racially coded language during the lead-up to the 1996 welfare reform in order to condemn African Americans for creating unsafe conditions in inner cities, thereby associating poverty and immoral behavior with skin color (Soss et al. 2011); and of patterns of residential segregation in cities that have served to isolate black people in disinvested communities, thereby reifying the frame of the unworthy black poor and creating intersecting systems of racial oppression (Massey and Denton 1993).

Thus the ideological and racial framing of the unworthy poor has been explored and explained in the academy in ways that articulate the political and social dimensions of the process. Further, scholars have theorized the bureaucratic processes that form the mechanics of the shifting frames for the poor (Morgen 2001; Hasenfeld 2000; Handler and Hasenfeld 1991). But this body of work does little or nothing to incorporate refugees into the story of the framing of the American poor (Benson 2016), even as the racial cast of the unworthy frame for the poor in the United States has real implications for the resettled refugee population, which has increasingly become predominantly black and brown.

Connections and Contributions

Although there is a long tradition of theorizing the connection between the political framing of the poor as worthy or unworthy and the form that social policy directed at this population ultimately takes, as of yet there is not an analogous case made about the political framing of the refugee and its relationship to refugee policy. As others have argued, scholarship on refugee resettlement policies tends to be inward looking, analyzing the policies themselves but rarely drawing connections to other forms of social policy (Benson 2016). For example, recent refugee resettlement policy literature focused on policy politics has examined how various policies affect refugee integration (Capps et al. 2015; Desiderio 2016), how different resettlement policies affect particular groups of refugees (Ong 2003; Adelman 1982; Bach 1988; Choi et al. 2013; Tang 2015; see also Lewis and Young, this volume), and what the political and institutional role of resettlement agencies is in the policy implementation process (Darrow 2015a, 2015b; Nawyn 2006). To date, the connection has not been made between the political and ideological framing of the refugee subject and the parallel political project of framing the American poor.

To the extent that the refugee literature has taken up the framing of refugees and their relative worthiness, this area of study has traditionally focused on comparisons to other immigrant groups and has lacked much nuance. In the United States specifically, refugee scholars and resettlement advocates have taken a defensive stance toward the concept of worthiness, making moves to distance refugees from any association with other immigrants who might be deemed less worthy (Anker and Posner 1981; Zucker 1983; Haines and Rosenblum 2010). In addition, refugee studies have shown that due to the nature of UNHCR refugee determination policies and processes, refugees go to extraordinary lengths to tell their own persecution stories in ways that make them appear worthy of resettlement (Thomson 2012; Thomson, this volume; Sandvik 2009). In neither case does the relevant literature take up the questions of how or why refugees might be framed as unworthy, questions that are central to the focus of this chapter.

The work of this chapter, then, is to fill gaps in the literature by arguing that there are distinct ideological frames embedded in the structure of U.S. refugee admissions and resettlement policy that reflect broader ideological frames used to characterize poor people of color. Further, this chapter articulates the ways in which this ideologically bound political structure of refugee policy creates tensions for refugee workers as they make hard choices about the ways they serve their refugee clients. I argue that, ultimately, the majority of the kinds of practice choices these workers must make end up reifying the ideological frame of the refugee as taking up moral ground among the unworthy poor in the United States.

One part of the argument put forth in this chapter is that the individuals who arrive in the United States as survivors of violence begin their journey in one category, the worthy, and that as they are assimilated into U.S. society they are rapidly transformed to the other category, the unworthy. This transformation aligns with traditional American values, which are oriented toward both the humanitarian acceptance of the blameless victim and the simultaneous demand that each individual work to earn their way in society. Thus the sympathies of the American public align with the mission to offer safe haven to these vulnerable people (Haines and Rosenblum 2010; Halpern 2008; Kerwin 2012). The blameless that flee violence are deemed worthy of federal support, and the investment in bringing them to the United States to resettle is rooted in this sense of worthiness. However, once refugees arrive in the United States, they are quickly expected to enter the labor market, make a contribution to society, and avoid becoming a burden to society (Lugar 2010; cf Vera Espinoza, this volume). The mechanism for conveying this shift in social construction from the refugee as worthy to unworthy is the implementation of refugee resettlement policy.

The unworthy are expected not to rely on public benefits for survival but rather to work toward earning a living wage and becoming financially self-sufficient. This ideological expectation is clearly manifest in the articulation of policy goals in U.S. refugee resettlement: "The Federal agency administering . . . shall establish criteria for the performance of agencies under grants and contracts . . . and shall include criteria relating to an agency's efforts to reduce welfare dependency among refugees resettled by that agency" (1980: chap. 2(8)(A)). Refugees who resist this integration into the labor market, or who are unable to make the transition, are pathologized just as the American poor are. Data presented in this chapter demonstrate that refugee workers take action to sanction refugees for such behavior and to encourage behavior that is more compliant with the demand that refugees accept any job made available to them, regardless of skill match, personal preference, or even logistical convenience.

Methods

This chapter draws on data collected as part of a larger study that sought to understand the political development of refugee resettlement policy in the United States. The study conceptualized refugee resettlement policy as more than its legislative and program components and included in its scope the practices of resettlement workers tasked with implementing refugee policy. Protocol for the study received ethics approval from the institutional review board at the University of Chicago Chapin Hall and the School of Social Service Administration.

The study was conducted over two years between 2010 and 2012 as an organizational ethnography and included interviews with seventy-five refugee resettlement workers, refugee policy entrepreneurs, and other key informants. Over 600 hours of observation were conducted, following workers as they served their refugee clients. Observation, interview, and archival data were analyzed using both open coding and thematic coding. The rigor of the study was enhanced by gathering data from multiple sources and through ongoing peer review during the study design, data collection, and analysis. Further, the workers and other participants in the study were included in discussions about my findings and confirmed the resonance of these findings with their experience in the field.

U.S. Resettlement Policy: A Humanitarian Ideal

Politicians in the United States consistently return to arguments about the appropriate response to immigrant entry into the country, and the rhetoric on this issue was perhaps at its most polarized in the lead-up to the 2016 presidential election in which Islamophobia was utilized as a political tool. However, traditionally, the refugee resettlement program has maintained bipartisan support, due in part to its humanitarian principles (Zucker 1983). In fact, it can be argued that the United States has a history of exceptionalism in its humanitarian approach to refugee resettlement.

The evidence for this case is robust. First, the admissions policy language itself asserts the humanitarian intent of the program; the U.S. Refugee Admissions Program is targeted at those refugees who are "determined by the President to be of special humanitarian concern to the United States" (UNHCR 2016).

Second, the United States has historically set itself apart from the majority of other resettlement countries by not screening refugees for resettlement based on their education and work histories. In other words, criteria for admission to the United States has not been predicated on the extent to which individual refugees are work ready (Carens 2003). This expansive and arguably humanitarian approach to admissions has historically allowed the United States to position itself globally as a leader in the resettlement field. For example, on October 4, 2016 the U.S. Department of State issued a fact sheet related to 2016 refugee admissions in which it stated, "The United States is taking the lead in meeting the unprecedented challenge of the global refugee crisis" (U.S. Department of State 2016).

This leading role was directly associated in the report with the fact that "the U.S. resettlement program serves refugees who are especially vulnerable" and that "over 72 percent of the resettled refugees are women and children. Many are single mothers, survivors of torture, people who need urgent medical treatment, religious minorities, lesbian, gay, bisexual, transgender, or intersex (LGBTI) persons, or others imperiled by violence and persecution" (U.S. Department of State 2016). Indeed, the majority of refugee cases that the United States has prioritized align with UNHCR's priority categories for resettlement, namely, women-at-risk and unaccompanied children (UNHCR 2016).

Finally, the claim of U.S. leadership in this domain is supported by the fact that other resettlement nations have more recently expanded their own resettlement criteria to accept more and more vulnerable populations (Hathaway 1992; Ahmad 2016; Mayer 2016; on strategic resettlement, see van Selm, this volume).

At a time when tensions are running high about the potential risk of "radicalized" individuals penetrating the United States under the protection of the refugee program (Alvarez 2016), these categories of vulnerable refugees are presumably perceived to be the least threatening to the safety and security of Americans. This assumption is supported by the rhetoric employed by the politicians who support a robust refugee resettlement program. In the midst of the fraught Clinton-Trump presidential election cycle, these resettlement supporters repeatedly highlighted the disproportionate numbers of women and children who come as refugees to the United States, thus invoking the image of the worthy refugee in the face of charges that refugees present a security risk to the nation (Obama 2016; C-SPAN 2016).

At the same time, a single refugee mother whose family is identified overseas as particularly at risk and whose acceptance for resettlement and ultimate entry to the United States is predicated upon this risk faces a tremendous set of structural, institutional, and bureaucratic challenges once she arrives in her new home country. As the next sections of this chapter explain, refugee resettlement policy prioritizes rapid entry into the labor market, the organizations contracted to implement refugee policy are primarily evaluated based on their success at getting their refugee clients into jobs as quickly as possible, and the refugee resettlement workers tasked with getting jobs for their clients behave in ways that are aligned with the priority of work entry, often at the expense of other potentially important aspects of refugees' social integration.

Legislative Priorities

Structural Alignment and Challenges to the Humanitarian Ideal

The Refugee Act of 1980 is rooted in a political ideology that defines refugees as distinct from other immigrant groups and therefore worthy of federal assistance (Anker and Posner 1981; Zucker 1983). Debates about the original structure of the legislation focused on differences of opinion about who should decide how many refugees might be admitted and about how these decisions might be made, but all involved agreed that the Act was rooted in a humanitarian ideal. A major political player in the formation of the Act, Senator Edward Kennedy, wrote that with the Act, "Congress gave new statutory authority to the United States' longstanding commitment to human rights and its traditional humanitarian concerns for the plight of refugees around the world" (Kennedy 1981).

Ultimately, the language of the Act reflects two sets of values: one that aligns with the humanitarian ideal of refugee resettlement and one that is buoyed by the assurance that federal refugee assistance will be directed toward encouraging economic self-sufficiency (United States Refugee Act of 1980). While on its face this second set of values does not run counter to the humanitarian ideal, the rest of this chapter demonstrates how the legislative push toward economic independence for refugees who are not necessarily prepared for the U.S. work force creates real policy tensions for the workers who implement resettlement programs.

The Act is thus the legislative representation of the discordant values of refugee resettlement in the United States. And yet, the assumptions that undergird the legislation lead to conflicting priorities in refugee policy. Following from the humanitarian focus, the U.S. refugee admissions policies do not discriminate among refugees when considering them for resettlement.[2] As I explained earlier in the chapter, refugees are admitted to the United States based on their need for protection, and are not assessed for their fitness for the formal U.S. labor market.

This acceptance policy correlates with the frame of refugees as categorically worthy of U.S. support and can be seen as a parallel to the more inclusive frame of the worthy poor that was drawn upon during the expansion of the welfare state. At the same time, the U.S. resettlement program limits the duration of federal financial support to refugees and in this way encourages refugees to join the labor market as quickly as possible (Darrow 2015a; Kerwin 2012). Further, U.S. policy requires that refugees accept work, and if the refugee resists there are sanctions written into the legislation (United States Refugee Act of 1980: sec. 412 (e)(2)(C)). This set of resettlement policies represents a shift in the framing of the refugee, from worthy to morally suspect, and is a direct replica of the frame used to depict poor people of color as unworthy of government support unless they prove their willingness to work.

Various components of the Act are built on these dissonant values of humanitarianism and rapid labor market entry. For example, in keeping with the humanitarian mission, the Act authorizes as standard practice the use of federal funds to support the resettlement of all refugees equally, regardless of origin, via grants to states and local voluntary organizations (Leibowitz 1983; Zucker 1983). This pledge to distribute federal funds in an equitable manner across refugee groups demonstrates the egalitarian nature of the U.S. refugee program.

The Act also establishes the Office of Refugee Resettlement (ORR) within the Department of Health and Human Services, Administration for Children and Families to administer the majority of the resettlement programs. The

2015 ORR Annual Report states that "the Refugee Resettlement Program creates a path to self-sufficiency and integration for people displaced by war, persecution, and devastating loss. The first step on this path is helping refugees and other populations served by the program achieve economic self-sufficiency through ORR-funded employment services." (ORR 2015: 5). This language of economic self-sufficiency is characteristic of the Act writ large (United States Refugee Act of 1980). It represents a federal interest in providing financial support to refugees for as short a time as possible, which is rooted in ideology that locates worthiness and morality in labor market attachment.

Institutional Framework

Limited Financial Supports and a Push to the Labor Market

There are two federal agencies responsible for funding and oversight of refugee-specific social policies in the United States: the Department of State and ORR. These federal agencies do not provide actual resettlement service provision, but rather they contract with several national nonprofit agencies, which in turn hold subcontract service provision relationships with locally embedded organizations in communities throughout the country.

The Department of State's Reception and Placement program supports refugees and local implementing resettlement agencies for the first ninety days after refugee arrival. The goals of the Reception and Placement program, as stated in a 2012 Cooperative Agreement between the Department of State and a local implementing agency, include "providing refugees with basic necessities and core services during their initial period of resettlement" and "assisting refugees in achieving economic self-sufficiency through employment as soon as possible after their arrival in the United States in coordination with publicly supported refugee service and assistance programs" (Bureau of Population, Refugees, and Migration, 2012: 5) In pursuit of the goal of economic self-sufficiency, the Reception and Placement contract mandates that local resettlement agencies provide a myriad of goods and services to refugees, including staples such as housing, food, and clothing and core services such as employment support and community orientation.

All benefits and services mandated under the Reception and Placement program are meant to promote work readiness among the newly arrived refugees. Unlike many other immigrants who enter the United States, refugees are granted work permits upon entry (U.S. General Accounting Office et al. 1983). In order to support work access, the Reception and Placement program requires that refugees be assigned an employment case worker; that implementing agencies refer their refugee clients to English language classes with a vocational focus, as needed; and that these same agencies supplement refugee travel costs to and from employment interviews until program eligibility ends or employment begins, whichever comes first (Darrow 2015b).

The Department of State ends its involvement with resettled refugees after the Reception and Placement program ninety-day cutoff, yet these new arrivals are still eligible for various federally funded programs and services for up to five years (Halpern 2008). ORR distributes funds through both direct and indirect channels via a complex mix of formula and discretionary grants (ORR 2015). The largest of the ORR formula grants pays for the state-administered refugee resettlement program through which ORR repays states for 100 percent of the costs of offering newly arrived refugees Refugee Cash Assistance, Refugee Medical Assistance, and social services. Refugee Cash Assistance provides refugees with a small monthly cash benefit, but eligibility for this benefit ends when the refugee has been in the United States for eight months. Thus there is very real practical pressure built into the structure of the resettlement program that supports rapid labor market entry.

In addition to these benefit programs operated through the state welfare systems, ORR supports local implementing resettlement agencies more directly via formula grants such as the Refugee Social Services program. The formula for these grants is calculated using a retroactive look at the prior two years[3] of refugee arrivals to that state. One challenge that this formula creates for states and the organizations that implement refugee policy and rely on federal funding is the unpredictable and unreliable nature of the calculation. Due to the look-back formula, when there are several years of low refugee arrival numbers, followed by a surge of arrivals, the ORR formula funds will not follow until the next year. Several key informants reflected on the challenge that this formula funding structure creates. One program manager explains:

> This is where the right hand does not know what the left hand is doing. [The State Department] is ramping up arrivals, and we are laying off staff. As you know ORR's formula money to the states is based on arrivals of two years ago. . . . So, based on this antiquated formula, not only we lost money this year, but we will probably lose even more next year, because the last two years the numbers of arrivals were really low. So, as I said [the State Department] is ramping up and we are laying off, while we sat fully staffed for the last year looking at each other and hoping for arrivals.

These comments reflect one of the many ways that resettlement agencies are left to resolve the tensions embedded in the structure and design of the U.S. resettlement program. As this program manager makes clear, her agency must cope with any shortfall of federal funding, and the various ways to balance the agency books include laying off staff. This observation was made in 2012, a year when more refugees were resettled in the United

States than in either 2010 or 2011. As a result, the agency needed more staff to serve the arriving refugees, yet there were fewer funds than needed to maintain staffing levels due to the two-year look back. This same misalignment between arrivals and support funds was seen in 2016 as the State Department rapidly increased its refugee admissions numbers year over year in the face of the Syrian refugee crisis and the impending end of the Obama administration.

There are real tensions that result from having fewer staff than are needed to serve the refugees who agencies are mandated to resettle. These implementation challenges are explored in the following section of this chapter.

Implementation Challenges–Working It Out in Practice

The local organizations tasked with implementing the programs and policies mandated by the Act reflect the policy environment that is their domain. The service mandates described above require these agencies to stress work readiness and rapid employment, and these mandates are enforced through management technologies such as performance monitoring, which creates pressure through the threat of decreased funds or nonrenewal of contracts if agencies do not meet specific performance benchmarks (Darrow 2015a). Further, these local organizations are not provided with sufficient federal funding to fill their mandate, leaving them in the position of having to locate sufficient supplemental resources to serve all their clients. Inevitably, as with other kinds of social service agencies, refugee resettlement organizations are underresourced, as the level of demand for their service always rises to meet supply (Darrow 2015b; Lipsky 1980). As a result of this imbalance between resources and contract-related pressure, on the one hand, and client demand, on the other, the workers at the resettlement agencies included in this study used adaptive techniques to ensure that the resources they did have were focused on getting as many refugees to work as quickly as possible.

Response to Pressure Created by Mismatch between (Employment) Resources and (Client) Demands

Employment caseworkers in this study were responsible for finding job opportunities for their refugee clients, preparing these clients for job interviews, and then facilitating the process through which clients secured and maintained employment. Two issues that complicated this process for employment caseworkers were the limited number of employers who were willing to hire refugees and the competition among the five local resettlement agencies to secure jobs for their respective refugee clients in this resource-challenged environment.

One caseworker explained a key component for success in this work: "Because we are competing for scarce resources, we take any job we can get for 'em. I'm not moving one person who is unhappy over, 'cause I need that other position for the next one in line. Happy or not, you stay—someone else is desperate." This caseworker summed up a pattern that was routinely repeated by her peer employment workers as well: pushing refugees to take any job available and to keep that job even if they were unhappy, making room for other refugee clients to apply for and hopefully secure the next available work opportunity. Rather than taking more time to seek a "happy" fit between refugee and job opportunity, the caseworkers pragmatically erred in favor of securing whatever jobs they could for the most people as quickly as possible.

In order to maximize the potential for rapidly securing employment for as many refugee clients as possible, caseworkers worked to promote a work-ready mindset among their clients. For example, at one local agency a caseworker explained to a group of newly arrived refugees how their government cash assistance would work, and in so doing she stressed:

> The amount is not enough for you to live. They know you cannot survive on this money; this is temporary. After a short time they will be asking you, "Why is it taking so long to find a job?" The money is small because the government has no money to pay everyone to sit at home and do nothing, so you must work hard.

When asked about her motivation in stressing the insufficiency of federal cash supports, the caseworker explained, "I want to build a motivation to work. They need to understand this because they have to know they need to take any job they can get." At another resettlement agency, an employment caseworker summed up her own approach with clients in this way: "In my job I fight with people like no one else has to, with people who won't take any job. They have to understand, it is this or homelessness. They can't afford to be picky, and if they are we will make them see."

In both of these examples the employment caseworkers identified as part of their job the need to instill in their refugee clients a sense of urgency about work. As the analysis in this chapter has demonstrated, caseworkers operate in a policy context in which rapid work entry is the goal of refugee resettlement, and these workers clearly have internalized this goal and in turn made it the prioritized focus of their work with clients. Further, the language these workers use when talking about their clients reflects the judgment that refugee clients need to be motivated about their work readiness. In language reminiscent of Lawrence Mead's individual-structural argument about the questionable motivations of the American poor, these workers talked about the need to "make them see."

The moral judgments that employment caseworkers made of their refugee clients were demonstrated in multiple ways. Not only did workers make efforts to create a sense of urgency among their clients, they also talked about needing to train their refugee clients to behave in prescribed ways. For example, an employment caseworker explained how she responded when one particular group of refugee clients repeatedly and actively resisted accepting jobs they were not happy with: "I can't help them anymore. I mean they don't have the ethic for work. We have gotten most of them jobs, but some of them work two days and then walk off the job. I can't keep looking for them. And there are others who would go to [the factory]." When asked what these clients would do if the agency would not continue to help them find jobs, the caseworker adamantly asserted, "I feel like the goal is self-sufficiency. Not we pay your rent and you just hang out. They have to learn. So let them sit. And yes, we won't leave them; we will get them work. But let them sit for now and then they will see this is not the way to be." This worker was very explicit about her role in training her refugee clients to accept and keep the jobs she found for them, regardless of whether or not they liked the job.

Other caseworkers similarly talked about the need to train their clients to behave in certain ways. One caseworker explained, in reference to some clients who were late to an employment interview the week prior, "I won't ask them to come to the interview; they don't play by my rules; they don't play by anyone's rules." And another emphatically stated, "I can't do it for them. They have to put in the effort, but some of them won't do anything to help themselves."

In each of these cases caseworkers expressed frustration with their refugee clients for acting in ways that made it more difficult for the caseworker to help them secure employment. This frustration stems from the fact that in their day-to-day work employment caseworkers are held responsible for finding jobs for their refugee clients. To the extent that their clients make this job more difficult, caseworkers locate the problem in their clients rather than in the policy that demands early work in the first place or in the fact that the agencies are understaffed and insufficiently resourced. These examples demonstrate how employment caseworkers reify the unworthy categorization of their refugee clients when they act in ways that align with the policy priority of getting their clients to work as quickly as possible. Thus the goal for these workers is to mold their clients into a more worthy category of work-ready subject.

Exceptions to the Norm

The practice of prioritizing rapid work entry in ways that pushed clients to take any job available was not the only style of employment practice that caseworkers engaged in. In fact, the data collected for this study demonstrated that workers used their discretion to make different kinds of practice decisions at different times and that some practices were more aligned with an humanitarian ideal, ultimately responding to clients in ways that reflected a frame of worthiness. For example, one employment caseworker talked about his clients in ways that focused on their individuality: "I represent each and every one of them. They are all different and together we decide what they need. Because we are building tools not just for jobs, but for life. And they each have different lives." This caseworker's way of talking about refugee clients not just as a category of clients who need to be trained to work but as individual partners with whom decisions need to be made reflects a deep sense of respect for the refugees themselves. This sense of respect finds its roots in the frame of worthiness.

Unlike his peers in the examples above, this caseworker expressed frustration with the job opportunities made available for his refugee clients, rather than with the clients themselves:

> I did not realize the job quality would be so low. My goal is to help them achieve a good life. . . . My definition of a good life would be to be able to come home and spend some time with family instead of going right back to work, to earn some money and survive financially.

Rather than suspecting his clients of shirking their moral responsibility to work, this employee identifies refugees as people like any others who have no less right to a job and a life they enjoy.

This caseworker was not the only one who spoke of refugees in this way, nor was he the only one who engaged in routines that challenged the frame of the refugee as an unworthy subject. For example, after one caseworker found out his client had missed a job interview he called the client and reassured him, saying, "How about the next job; we will call you. Don't worry about this one. Don't worry, I will remember to call you the next time." In this example the caseworker did not hold it against the client that they missed the interview, rather he worked to reassure the client that there would be other opportunities. In this example the caseworker resists the practice of blaming the refugee, and in so doing the worker makes a choice that aligns him with the humanitarian ideals of resettlement.

In both of these cases the caseworkers moved beyond the dichotomy of the worthy/unworthy frame, instead shaping their expectations for clients in terms that reflect a set of rights. This rights-based approach to working with resettled refugees could offer a way out of the rhetorical trap represented in the worthy/unworthy frame. The problem with the dichotomous frame is that the only way to combat the image of refugees as morally suspect is to prove their worthiness. This very engagement reifies the dichotomy rather than breaking it down. On the other hand, a rights-based frame moves beyond the choices or behaviors of any individual refugee, instead rooting entitlement to services and respect simply in existence.

Conclusion

This chapter explores the conflicting values embedded in U.S. refugee policy: an admissions policy that is rooted in human rights and a humanitarian ideal and a resettlement program that is targeted at rapid labor market attachment for as many refugees as possible. The argument developed here asserts that the values of admissions and resettlement reflect patterns in the broader construction of the welfare subject in the United States, in which poor people of color are framed as either worthy or unworthy of government support, depending on an apparent willingness to work. Further, this chapter asserts that the humanitarian principles of refugee admissions serve to frame arriving refugees as morally worthy of government largesse but that the refugee is quickly transformed into an unworthy subject, who must be coerced into a work-ready mindset. The mismatch between humanitarian ideals and a push for labor market attachment is ultimately worked out by refugee resettlement caseworkers. As happens with other social policies, these caseworkers are the ones who define the meaning of resettlement policy when they use their discretion in ways that align with one or the other of these constructions.

When resettlement workers implement resettlement programs, they make choices about how to enact the policy in real time, and these choices represent one of the two sets of values characteristic of refugee policy, but not both. The different sets of decisions represented by the varying approaches to working with refugee clients represent different underlying assumptions about the worthiness of refugee clients. Even if the workers' themselves do not make moral judgments about their clients, the actions they take are rooted in a resettlement policy that is based on the assumption that refugees must work in order to earn a place in society.

The choice to apply sanctions to a refugee who resists a particular work opportunity represents an interpretation of refugee policy that is rooted in the push for self-sufficiency. The refugee who refuses to take any job offered is, in effect, delaying the time it will take to become independent of public financial aid and thus challenging the push for self-sufficiency. Therefore, sanctioning this refugee is a rational choice based on the principle.

On the other hand, when a resettlement worker chooses not to sanction a refugee who refuses a particular work opportunity, but rather makes an effort to find a job opportunity that better suits that refugee's interests (be it schedule, religious principles, or another reason for declining the job), that worker's decision might be seen as grounded in the humanitarian ideal of the policy. The caseworker that insists on identifying and addressing the individuality of each refugee client upholds the humanitarian vision of a refugee program. This vision is aligned with a conception of each refugee as worthy of service, worthy of support, and worthy of care, regardless of their suitability to the workforce. Further, there is potential in this kind of policy implementation to resist the dichotomous frames altogether, forging a new identity of refugee service based in rights.

However, the opportunity for caseworkers to engage in this radical rights-based work is structurally unsupported and therefore unlikely to become a norm. The structure of resettlement policy creates incentives for workers to make choices that support the unworthy construction of their refugee client. Through grant reviews and renewals, workers and resettlement agencies are held accountable for securing as many jobs for their refugee clients as possible. Therefore, when workers act in ways that uphold the humanitarian ideal of refugee resettlement, they commit to an act of unsanctioned generosity.

This chapter has demonstrated that in the United States there is more nuance in the social construction of the refugee subject than has previously been identified. Whereas refugee scholars and advocates of the admissions program have traditionally defined the refugee subject as morally worthy, I have shown how U.S. resettlement policy quickly transforms the refugee into a category of unworthy political subject who, just like other people of color who are poor, must prove their worthiness through work. However, in a devastating turn of political events, even this more nuanced conception has been upended. In the 2016 presidential election the United States elected a president who ran a campaign rooted in xenophobia, Islamophobia, misogyny, and racism. President Trump's executive orders relating to refugee admissions run counter to the very premise that refugees are categorically worthy of U.S. support.

President Trump's administration has specifically targeted Muslims and has fought to end refugee admissions to the United States from Syria and curtail admissions from several Muslim nations (Executive Orders 13769, 13780). This partitioning of refugees into religious categories, and the condemnation of an entire religious group, introduces a drastic shift in frames, away from a humanitarian ideal and into uncharted territory in which the United States can no longer claim it is a leader in its human rights approach to refugee admissions. In this new era of U.S. refugee admissions policy based on religious criteria, one can only assume that the current dichotomy of worthiness based on willingness to work will be further exacerbated and complicated as racism and Islamophobia are sanctioned at the highest levels of government.

In setting the presidential determination for a refugee admissions ceiling at 45,000 for 2018, Trump sent the unequivocal message to the international community that the United States is no longer a leader in the humanitarian sphere of resettlement. Not only has the Trump administration actively withdrawn from the conception of a United States committed to humanitarian ideals as exemplified in the welcoming of the world's most vulnerable, but it has also reframed the skeletal remains of the U.S. refugee resettlement project as a selective, criteria-based initiative (Newland 2017).

Specifically, the *Report to the Congress* (U.S. Department of State et al. 2017) states that the U.S. Departments of State and Health and Human Services "will work closely with UNHCR to ensure that, in addition to referrals of refugees with compelling protection needs, referrals may also take into account certain criteria that enhance a refugee's likelihood of successful assimilation and contribution to the United States" (8). This language indicates a shift away from the traditional framing of refugee admissions rooted in humanitarian ideals, wherein the worthiness of the refugee is found in their very political identity as persecuted individuals or groups, to one that is perhaps more aligned with the framing this chapter has identified as associated with the postresettlement project, one that identifies a refugee's worthiness in their suitability for the labor force.

Further, the Trump administration has introduced an added layer to its framing of refugee subjects that draws on the fears of the American people. The executive orders and political rhetoric relating to them include overt references to refugees as potential threats to national security (Executive Orders 13769, 13780). Despite a lack of evidence that refugees in the United States pose any threat to national security, or that they ever have, the administration makes repeated and consistent rhetorical moves using just such a divisive frame (Nowrasteh 2017). This shift in frames has already been associated with an unprecedented politicization of the U.S. Refugee Admissions Program (Richard 2017). Evidence of this politicization can be found in the content and tone of committee hearings on the subject in the U.S. House of Representatives (U.S. House of Representatives et al. 2017).

The combined effects of introducing selection criteria into the admissions screening process, reducing the admissions cap to record low numbers, and reframing refugees as potential threats to the safety of the United States could be to fundamentally alter the role of the United States in the realm of refugee resettlement. As other nations grapple with their own political debates over immigration, they will look to the United States and observe the current model of heightened nationalism and restrictionist policies toward refugees. States that have traditionally engaged in refugee resettlement, as well as others new to the practice, will find justification for limiting the scope of their commitments to UNHCR. While refugee resettlement placements dwindle across the globe, the quality of those placements could also diminish as nations fashion their policies for resettlement with the Trump administration's restrictive and racist policies serving as a template.

Jessica H. Darrow holds a Ph.D. from the School of Social Service Administration, University of Chicago, where she is a lecturer. Darrow's published work grapples with the organizational-level challenges in implementing refugee resettlement policy. Her ongoing research agenda is focused on the role of nongovernmental actors in carving out nontraditional spaces of citizenship for refugees in the United States and seeks to understand the lived experiences of resettled refugees over time. Darrow has also worked with refugees and local communities in Rwanda and served as executive director of the grassroots nongovernmental organization Cosmos Education.

Notes

1. The United States Refugee Act of 1980 is an amendment to the broader Immigration and Nationality Act (8 U.S.C 1001 et seq).
2. At the time of publication, this very fact was in question as the Trump administration repeatedly made efforts to insert discriminatory language into refugee selection and admissions policies.
3. At the end of federal fiscal year 2017, ORR announced a change to this funding formula, reducing the retroactive look back to one year.

References

Adelman, Howard. 1982. "American Indochinese Refugees: Are They Welfare Bums?" *Refuge* 2(2): 1–3.

Ahmad, Tariq. 2016. "Canada." In *Refugee Law and Policy in Selected Countries*, edited by Law Library of Congress, 40–55. Washington, D.C.: Library of Congress.

Alvarez, Priscilla. 2016. "What Should the U.S. Do about Refugee Resettlement?" *The Atlantic*, 29 March. Accessed 7 February 2017. https://www.theatlantic.com/politics/archive/2016/03/refugee-resettlement-united-states/474939/.

Anker, Deborah E., and Michael H. Posner. 1981. "The Forty Year Crisis: A Legislative History of the Refugee Act of 1980." *San Diego Law Review* 19: 9–90.

Bach, Robert L. 1988. "State Intervention in Southeast Asian Refugee Resettlement in the United States." *Journal of Refugee Studies* 1: 38–54.

Barnett, Don. 2006. *Backgrounder: A New Era of Refugee Resettlement*. Washington, D.C.: Center for Immigration Studies.

Benford, Robert D., and David A. Snow. 2000. "Framing Processes and Social Movements: An Overview and Assessment." *Annual Review of Sociology* 26: 611–39.

Benson, Odessa G. 2016. "Refugee Resettlement Policy in an Era of Neoloberalization: A Policy Discourse Analysis of the Refugee Act of 1980." *Social Service Review* 90: 515–49.

Bon Tempo, Carl J. 2008. *Americans at the Gate: The United States and Refugees during the Cold War*. Princeton: Princeton University Press.

Bureau of Population, Refugees, and Migration. 2012. *Cooperative Agreement*. Washington, D.C.: U.S. Department of State.

Capps, Randy, Kathleen Newland, Susan Fratzke, Susanna Groves, Gregory Auclair, Michael Fix, and Margie McHugh. 2015. *The Integration Outcomes of US Refugees: Successes and Challenges.* Washington, D.C.: Migration Policy Institute.

Carens, Joseph. 2003. "Who Should Get In? The Ethics of Immigration Admissions." *Ethics & International Affairs* 17: 95–110.

Choi, Sam, Cindy Davis, Sherry Cummings, Christina Van Regenmorter, and Molly Barnett. 2013. "Understanding Service Needs and Service Utilization among Older Kurdish Refugees and Immigrants in the U.S.A." *International Social Work* 58(1): 63–74.

C-SPAN. 2016. *Secretary of State John Kerry Foreign Policy Address,* January 2013. Accessed 7 February 2017. https://www.c-span.org/video/?403114-1/secretary-state-john-kerry-foreign-policy-address.

Darrow, Jessica H. 2015a. "Getting Refugees to Work: A Street-Level Perspective of Refugee Resettlement Policy." *Refugee Survey Quarterly* 34(2): 78–106.

———. 2015b. "The (Re)Construction of the Department of State's Reception and Placement Program by Refugee Resettlement Agencies." *Journal of the Society for Social Work and Research* 6(1): 91–119.

Desiderio, Maria Vincenza. 2016. *Integrating Refugees into Host Country Labor Markets: Challenges and Policy Options.* Washington, D.C.: Migration Policy Institute.

Haines, David W., and Karen E. Rosenblum. 2010. "Perfectly American: Constructing the Refugee Experience." *Journal of Ethnic and Migration Studies* 36: 391–406.

Halpern, Peggy. 2008. *Refugee Economic Self-Sufficiency: An Exploratory Study of Approaches Used in Office of Refugee Resettlement Programs.* Washington, D.C.: U.S. Department of Health and Human Services.

Handler, Joel, and Yeheskhel Hasenfeld. 1991. *The Moral Construction of Poverty: Welfare Reform in America.* Newbury Park: Sage Publications.

Hasenfeld, Yeheskhel. 2000. "Organizational Forms as Moral Practices: The Case of Welfare Departments." *Social Service Review* 74: 329–51.

Hathaway, James. 1992. "The Conundrum of Refugee Protection in Canada: From Control to Compliance to Collective Deterrence." *Journal of Policy History* 4: 71–92.

Katz, Michael. 1989. *The Undeserving Poor: From the War on Poverty to the War on Welfare.* New York: Pantheon Books.

Kennedy, Edward M. 1981. "Refugee Act of 1980." *International Migration Review* 15: 141–56.

Kerwin, Donald. 2012. "The Faltering US Refugee Protection System: Legal and Policy Responses to Refugees, Asylum-Seekers, and Others in Need of Protection." *Refugee Survey Quarterly* 31: 1–33.

Leibowitz, Arnold H. 1983. "The Refugee Act of 1980: Problems and Congressional Concerns." *Annals of the American Academy of Political and Social Science* 467: 163–71.

Lewis, Oscar. 1969. "The Culture of Poverty." In *On Understanding Poverty: Perspectives from the Social Sciences,* edited by D. P. Moynihan, 187–220. New York: Basic Books.

Lipsky, Michael. 1980. *Street-Level Bureaucracy: The Dilemmas of the Individual in Public Services.* New York: Russell Sage Foundation.

Lugar, Richard. 2010. *Abandoned upon Arrival: Implications for Refugees and Local Communities Burdened by a U.S. Resettlement System That Is Not Working: A Report to the Members of the Committee on Foreign Relations, United States Senate, One Hundred Eleventh Congress, Second Session, July 21, 2010.* Washington, D.C.: U.S. Government Printing Office.

Massey, Douglas S., and Nancy A. Denton. 1993. *American Apartheid: Segregation and the Making of the Underclass.* Cambridge, MA: Harvard University Press.

Mayer, Matthias. 2016. *Germany's Response to the Refugee Situation: Remarkable Leadership or Fait Accompli?* Washington, D.C.: Bertelsmann Foundation.

Mead, Lawrence. 1992. *The New Politics of Poverty.* New York: Basic Books.

Morgen, Sandra. 2001. "The Agency of Welfare Workers: Negotiating Devolution, Privatization, and the Meaning of Self-Sufficiency." *American Anthropologist* 103: 747–61.

Nawyn, Stephanie J. 2006. "Making a Place to Call Home: Refugee Resettlement Organizations, Religion, and the State." PhD Diss., University of Southern California.

Newland, Kathleen. 2017. *The U.S. Falls Behind as Others Take on New Leadership amid Record Humanitarian Pressures.* Washington, D.C.: Migration Policy Institute.

Nowrasteh, Alex. 2017. *President's Trump's New Travel Executive Order Has Little National Security Justification.* Cato Institute, 25 September.

Obama, Barack. 2016. *Remarks by President Obama at Leaders Summit on Refugees.* New York: United Nations.

Office of Refugee Resettlement (ORR). 1980. *Annual Report to Congress.* Washington, D.C.: U.S. Department of Health and Human Services, Administration for Children and Families, Office of Refugee Resettlement.

——. 2005. *Annual Report to Congress.* Washington, D.C.: U.S. Department of Health and Human Services, Administration for Children and Families, Office of Refugee Resettlement.

——. 2015. *Annual Report to Congress.* Washington, D.C.: U.S. Department of Health and Human Services, Administration for Children and Families, Office of Refugee Resettlement.

Ong, Aihwa. 2003. *Buddha Is Hiding: Refugees, Citizenship, the New America.* Berkeley: University of California Press.

Peck, Jamie. 2001. *Workfare States.* New York: Guilford Press.

Personal Responsibility and Work Opportunity Reconciliation Act of 1996. Public Law 104-193. 104th U.S. Congress.

Piven, Frances Fox, and Richard Cloward. 1971. *Regulating the Poor: The Functions of Public Welfare.* New York: Random House.

Richard, Anne C. 2017. *Bringing Refugees to America: Obama and Trump Administration Policies.* Public Lecture. Chicago: University of Chicago.

Sandvik, Kristin B. 2009. "The Physicality of Legal Consciousness: Suffering and the Production of Credibility in Refugee Resettlement." In *Humanitarianism and Suffering the Mobilization of Empathy,* edited by R.D. Brown and R.A. Wilson. Cambridge: Cambridge University Press.

Soss, Joe, Richard Fording, and Sanford F. Schram. 2011. *Disciplining the Poor: Neoliberal Paternalism and the Persistent Power of Race.* Chicago: University of Chicago Press.

Tang, Eric. 2015. *Unsettled: Cambodian Refugees in the NYC Hyperghetto.* Philadelphia: Temple University Press.

Thomson, Marnie Jane. 2012. "Black Boxes of Bureaucracy: Transparency and Opacity in the Resettlement Process of Congolese Refugees." *PoLAR: Political and Legal Anthropology Review* 35: 186–205.

Executive Order 13769, C.F.R.–Protecting the Nation from Terrorist Attacks by Foreign Nationals. 2017.

Executive Order 13780, 3 C.F.R.–Protecting the Nation from Foreign Terrorist Entry into the United States. 2017.

United Nations High Commissioner for Refugees (UNHCR). 2016. *UNHCR Resettlement Handbook and Country Chapters.* Accessed 7 February 2017. http://www .refworld.org/docid/542134777.html.

United States Refugee Act of 1980. Public Law 96-212. U.S. Code, Title 8, Chapter 12, Subchapter IV, Section 1522, INA: Act 412–Authorization for Programs for Domestic Resettlement of and Assistance to Refugees. 96th U.S. Congress.

U.S. Department of State. 2016. *Fact Sheet: Fiscal Year 2016 Refugee Admissions.* Washington, D.C.: U.S. Department of State.

U.S. Department of State; U.S. Department of Homeland Security; U.S. Department of Health and Human Services. 2017. *Proposed Refugee Admissions for Fiscal Year 2018. Report to the Congress.* Washington, D.C.: U.S. Department of State; U.S. Department of Homeland Security; U.S. Department of Health and Human Services.

U.S. General Accounting Office, U.S. National Technical Information Service, University Publications of America. 1983. *Greater Emphasis on Early Employment and Better Monitoring Needed in Indochinese Refugee Resettlement Program.* Washington, D.C.: General Accounting Office.

U.S. House of Representatives, Judiciary Committee, Subcommittee on Immigration and Border Security. 2017. Oversight of the United States Refugee Admissions Program.

Wacquant, Loïc. 2010. "Class, Race and Hyperincarceration in Revanchist America." *Daedalus* 139(3): 74–90.

Zucker, Norman L. 1983. "Refugee Resettlement in the United States: Policy and Problems." *Annals of the American Academy of Political and Social Science* 467: 172–86.

5

Resettled Refugees and Work in Canada and Quebec

Humanitarianism and the Challenge of Mainstream Socioeconomic Participation

Adèle Garnier

Introduction

"We're Canadians. We're here to help." These were the final sentences of Canada's Prime Minister Justin Trudeau as he addressed the United Nations General Assembly's 71st session in September 2016 for the first time after almost a year in office (Trudeau 2016). This vision of Canada as a helping hand speaks to Canada's resurging humanitarianism under the Trudeau government. Trudeau positioned himself as a champion of the United Nations, and a key aspect of the resurgence of Canadian humanitarianism is the resettlement of close to 40,000 Syrian refugees between November 2015 and February 2017 (IRCC 2017). Yet Trudeau also stressed that the objective of this resettlement operation was for Syrian refugees to integrate into the Canadian middle class and to contribute to Canada's diversity, one of the main strengths of his country. Tellingly, Canada's current immigration minister, Ahmed Hussen, himself arrived to Canada as a refugee from Somalia. Beyond inspiring examples, the Syrian refugees' inclusion would be facilitated, Trudeau believed in 2016, by the fact that most Syrian refugees coming to Canada had belonged to Syria's middle class (Trudeau 2016).

With his double focus on Canada's humanitarianism and its middle class, Trudeau hinted at a key issue of refugee resettlement, namely linkages between the selection of resettled refugees and their long-term socioeconomic participation in resettling states. However, data collected on resettled Syrian refugees have revealed that most cannot be considered "typical middle-class arrivals" (IRCC 2016b). For instance, education levels among Syrian refugees were on average significantly below that of Canadian nationals and other immigrant categories (ibid.). In any case, socioeconomic positioning is not the reason Syrian refugees were selected for resettlement: their vulnerability is.

This chapter argues that humanitarian constituencies in Canada effectively used their power of persuasion in the late 1990s to foster an increase in the admission of more vulnerable refugees from the early 2000s. Yet this power of persuasion is more limited in regard to socioeconomic participation in part because settlement services in Canada are geared to offer services to all immigrants, whose overall profile is closer to the Canadian middle class than that of resettled refugees. This limits the negotiating power of more vulnerable resettled refugees as well as the bargaining power of service providers who aim to specifically support them.

The chapter investigates this outcome in the specific context of the province of Quebec. The immigration and integration policies of the Francophone province are the most autonomous of all Canadian provinces. In slight departure from Canadian multiculturalism (Hiebert 2016; Griffith 2017), Quebec has long insisted on its specific "intercultural" immigrant integration model taking into account the province's linguistic and historical characteristics (Rocher and White 2014). In addition, the labor market participation gap between native born and foreign born is significantly higher in Quebec than on average in Canada (Vérificateur Général du Québec 2017: chap. 4). Yet it is shown that issues discussed in this chapter are also relevant to Anglophone Canada.[1]

Conceptually, I draw on the notion of humanitarian governance and on the power typology presented in this volume's introduction, as well as literature on the institutional and social setting of immigrant incorporation. My methodology combines secondary analysis of federal and provincial regulation of the admission of resettled refugees and of statistical data on resettled refugees' labor market participation and earnings, with interviews conducted in Montreal and two regional cities in Quebec.

The chapter is structured as follows. The next section situates the chapter in the literature and details its approach and method. I then focus on the persuasive power of humanitarian constituencies in promoting the arrival of vulnerable refugees from the early 2000s. The following section focuses on the limited negotiating power of resettled refugees and settlement service providers in regard to labor market participation and thus illustrates the limited influence of humanitarian constituencies over time and across policy sectors. Finally, I discuss the conceptual and empirical implication of findings for Canadian resettlement and whether lessons can be drawn internationally from the Canadian case.

Overview: Refugee Resettlement in Canada and Quebec

Over the past decade and before the increased arrival of Syrian refugees, Canada, as the second-largest resettling country behind the United States, resettled between 10,000 and 20,000 resettled refugees annually (see annual figures since 2006 in Cellini, this volume). There are three main categories of resettled refugees in Canada: government-assisted refugees (GARs), privately sponsored refugees (PSRs), and blended sponsorship refugees. Canada is the only resettling country to have a long-standing private sponsorship program, which allows not just established humanitarian groups and faith-based organizations but also groups of citizens to facilitate the arrival and settlement of resettled refugees (Hyndman et al. 2017). Whereas the Canadian government covers the cost of GARs' settlement in Canada for a year after admission via the Resettlement Assistance Program, private sponsors commit to do the same for PSRs, and costs are shared in the case of blended sponsorship refugees.

In 2015, the country resettled 9,488 GARs, 9,746 PSRs, and 811 blended sponsorship refugees. Canada also accepts refugees after an asylum claims, and 12,070 such refugees were admitted in 2015 (IRCC 2015). While the admission of refugees after an asylum claim is decided federally, the province of Quebec, in the context of the Canada-Quebec Agreement of 1991, is responsible for the admission of GARs and PSRs destined for the province, although these refugees have to be admissible according to federal regulations. Quebec is the only Canadian province to have such a prerogative regarding the selection of resettled refugees (Becklumb 2008). In 2015, Quebec admitted 1,631 GARs and 2,967 PSRs in the province–the first time since 2006 that arrival of privately sponsored refugees significantly outnumbered the arrival of government-sponsored refugees (MIDI 2017).

As mentioned above, and in contrast to the United States under President Trump (see Darrow, this volume), Canada is aspiring to be a global resettlement leader. The admission of Syrian refugees was Canada's largest ever resettlement intake in one year (Griffith 2017). The Trudeau government was very vocal in its support of resettlement at the New York Summit on Refugees and Migrants in September 2016 and actively fosters the dissemination of knowledge on private refugee sponsorship as part of the Global Refugee Sponsorship Initiative launched at this summit (Hussen 2017).

Approach

This chapter relies on the concepts of durable humanitarian governance and power presented in the book's introduction (Garnier, Sandvik, and Jubilut, this volume). Briefly, we conceive of refugee resettlement as a tool designed to help the most vulnerable refugees (hence resettlement's humanitarian rationale) not only to escape unsustainable life conditions but also to live stable and fulfilling lives in the long term (hence the durable element). Yet we don't say durable *solution* (as refugee resettlement is labeled by the United Nations High Commissioner for Refugees, UNHCR) because we consider that resettled refugees' vulnerability does not disappear overnight once they land in resettling states. Vulnerability often continues not only to be part of resettled refugees' experience but also to be part of the frames of reference used in social interactions with individuals and institutions.

In line with the volume's introduction, I draw in this chapter on John Allen's definition of power as "the relational effects of social interactions" (Allen 2003: 2), and, as he does, I differentiate between types of power *with* others and types of power *over* others. Here, I am particularly concerned with persuasion and negotiation as forms of power with others and authority as a form of legitimate power over others. Even though much literature on Canada and Quebec's immigration and refugee policy is concerned with power, this is rarely done explicitly.[2]

However, literature investigating the significance of institutional and social factors for the political incorporation of immigrants clearly addresses power dynamics–if somewhat implicitly. In particular, Bloemraad (2006), in her seminal comparison of immigrants' political incorporation in the United States and Canada, has pointed at the importance of the national institutional setting, including the provision of financial resources, to support a local social environment favorable to immigrants' citizenship acquisition. Translated into our power vocabulary, Bloemraad shows that a state that has the authority and resources to foster political incorporation emboldens local social initiatives to support refugees' citizenship acquisition and political participation. This chapter argues that the labor market participation of resettled refugees cannot be supported in the same way through the mobilization of humanitarian constituencies.

As noted by Wilkinson and Garcea (2017), Canadian literature on refugees' labor market participation has not focused very strongly on its institutional setting. Rather, scholarship has emphasized the significance of individual characteristics, such as age and gender, as well as factors pertaining to access to the labor market, such as proficiency in official languages and recognition of foreign credentials (Krahn et al. 2000; Xue 2006: 7; Hyndman 2011; Renaud et al. 2003; CIC 2011). Being relatively young, male, and proficient in official languages are predictors of better access to the labor market. A few studies have evaluated the significance of ethnic and social ties for refugees' labor market participation and argued that ethnic ties are rather detrimental to upward labor market mobility, whereas social networks ties have a more positive impact (Lamba 2003).

Wilkinson and Garcea (2017), drawing on relatively recent pan-Canadian and Western Canadian survey data, include findings on the significance of the institutional context. They observe that refugees' lack of information on their rights, services to which they have access, and capacity constraints among service providers impede refugees' labor market trajectories. This chapter aims to build upon such findings with a specific focus on the articulation between the Canadian federal level and the province of Quebec, while developing the approach presented in this volume's introduction. The significance of humanitarian constituencies and of power dynamics is investigated in this context.

Methodologically, the research combines secondary analysis of law and policies regulating the admission of resettled refugees in Canada and Quebec and of available statistical data on resettled refugees' labor market participation and earnings with semistructured interviews conducted in 2015 and 2016 with resettled refugees (seven participants) and staff of organizations supporting refugees' labor market participation (six participants) in three locations: Montreal and two smaller municipalities within a 100-kilometer radius of Montreal, Saint-Jérôme in the Laurentides region, and Saint-Hyacinthe in the Montérégie region.

Montreal had about 1,650,000 inhabitants at Canada's 2011 census, Saint-Jérôme about 66,000, and Saint-Hyacinthe 54,000. A total of 22.6 percent of the Montreal population was foreign born as of 2011, 4.0 percent of the population of Saint-Jerome, and 3.0 percent in Saint-Hyacinthe. Refugee participants were selected based on their length of time in Canada (at least five years, to gain a midterm perspective on their labor market trajectories) and labor market activity (they had to be employed or looking for employment). Staff supporting labor market participation was either employed at an immigrant settlement agency or employability support services catering to the needs of the general population. I focused on participants with several years of experience in their position.

Recruiting refugee participants proves to be a challenge because refugees long settled in Canada are harder to identify in the community than newly arriving refugees or migrants, who have stronger interactions with settlement service providers and employment services. Chicha (2009: 52) makes a similar point in regard to the qualitative exploration of the professional careers of immigrant women who have been in Quebec for more than five years. In addition, it is also easier to recruit participants of one particular type of resettled refugee (GARs), who have more interactions with settlement services providers than PSRs (IRCC 2016a).

Drawing on the observations made on the ethics of refugee research by Jacobsen and Landau (2003), Oxford University's Refugee Studies Centre (Refugee Studies Centre 2007), and Gifford (2013), interactions during interviews aimed to respect both the agency of participants and their potential vulnerability. My research was approved by the University of Montreal's ethics committee. Participants were given the opportunity to withdraw from any questions they did not want to answer, to read interview transcripts, and to withdraw consent from data use. Open-ended questions to refugee participants focused only on their labor market experience, primarily post-admission. There were no specific prompts regarding prearrival labor market experience and prearrival experience more broadly, yet most refugee participants opted to discuss them. In addition, my involvement in a collaborative project on refugee employability in Quebec (Blain et al. 2017) led to informal exchanges with settlement service providers' representatives.

Having done fieldwork in three different locations in Quebec helps in accounting for the diversity of situations in the province. I am aware that my fieldwork is a small "n," nonrepresentative study with numerous limits (Ott 2013: 23–25) and can be considered an interpretive, hypothesis-generating case study (Lijphart 1971).

Resettled Refugees' Admission: Persuasive Power of Humanitarian Constituencies

Resettled refugees are admitted to Canada mostly on the basis of humanitarian considerations, in line with the 1951 Refugee Convention as well as other international human rights treaties ratified by Canada. Yet according to primary legislation, they also have to demonstrate their "ability to become successfully established in Canada," for instance through their knowledge of the country's official languages or the presence of relatives in Canada (Immigration and Refugee Protection Regulations s.139(1)(g)). However, the implementation of the current primary legislation, the Immigration and Refugee Protection Act (IRPA), which entered into force in 2002, differs from the letter of the law. This evolution in implementation contrasts with the implementation of previous primary legislation on immigration and can be considered the result of long-standing humanitarian mobilization.

Refugee advocates, migrant rights groups, and the UNHCR have long opposed the use of an integration-focused selection criterion for resettled refugees. As a result, immigration officers selecting resettled refugees started to apply this criterion more liberally in the 1990s, although this led to inconsistencies in practice (Canadian Refugee Council 1999). Tasked with the design of an overhaul of Canada's immigration law and policy at the end of the 1990s, the Immigration Legislative Review Advisory Group made a recommendation to scrap the integration criteria for resettled refugees (Legislative Review Advisory Group 1997: recommendation 88). Refugee advocates praised recommendation 88, yet they criticized the review's broader focus on the admission of immigrants most likely to satisfy Canada's short-term labor market needs (see, for instance, Canadian Refugee Council 1998: 15; UNHCR 1998; Hyndman 1999). Recommendation 88 was, however, watered down in a subsequent white paper (CIC 1999: 41). Advocates in turn demanded that immigration officers consistently prioritize vulnerability over the "ability to become successfully established" in the selection of resettled refugees (Canadian Refugee Council 1999).

Humanitarian lobbying had an impact. Whereas, as mentioned above, IRPA still requires the application of the integration selection criterion to all prospective permanent residents, administrative guidance to immigration officers recommends in the case of resettled refugees a focus primarily on vulnerability. Secondary legislation also explicitly exempts from this criterion refugees deemed at great risk for their personal safety or in urgent need of protection (CIC 2009: 67). Quebec's own regulations entail both a similar integration requirement and similar exemptions for vulnerable refugees (Règlement sur la Sélection des Ressortissants Étrangers: sec. 27). In addition, IRPA exempts refugees from inadmissibility in Canada on the grounds of "excessive demand" on the country's health system (Immigration and Refugee Protection Act s.38(2); see Guyon [2011]).

Regulatory change led to the evolution of resettled refugees' profiles. Post-IRPA resettled refugees were found to have lower levels of proficiency in Canada's official languages as well as lower levels of education at the time of admission. There was also an increase in the proportion of arrivals over the age of sixty-five as well as an increase in the proportion of resettled women as principal applicants and an increased arrival of spouses and dependents (CIC 2011: 22, 2012a, 2012b; IRCC 2016a). Assessments in Quebec noted the increasingly "complex profile" of GARs (TCRI 2009: 11) as well as their increased medical needs (Guyon 2011: 3).

In sum, the persuasive power of humanitarian constituencies effectively swayed the regulators to change practice, and this with significant impact on subsequent cohorts of resettled refugees who were more vulnerable than previous ones. This shows that there are trade-offs in the definition of who to admit and that regulatory change occurs in response to social mobilization. At the same time, the fact that primary legislation continues to list integration criteria for all prospective permanent residents illustrates the weight of the existing legislative framework but also perhaps the readiness of humanitarian constituencies to settle for discretionary, and not legal, change. Thus focus on particularly vulnerable refugees remains subject to the interpretation of the immigration bureaucracy. Renewed social mobilization may be necessary to persuade the bureaucracy of the critical importance of this focus on vulnerability in the selection of resettled refugees if said bureaucracy were inclined, or were politically swayed, to again insist more strongly on integration criteria.

Some actors among humanitarian constituencies were proactive in anticipating integration challenges posed by an increased arrival of more vulnerable resettled refugees. For instance, the UNHCR office in Ottawa, which has had long-standing good relationships with Canadian immigration bureaucrats, expanded its focus on refugee integration in parallel to the early 2000s' regulatory change.[3] The following section shows that resettled refugees' labor market participation remained, nonetheless, a challenge and investigates how institutional and social dynamics constrain the negotiating power of resettled refugees and labor market support providers.

Resettled Refugee's Labor Market Participation: Limited Negotiating Power of Humanitarian Advocates and Refugees

Like Canada's other provinces, Quebec is responsible for the delivery of settlement services, yet its funding model and organizational dynamics are distinct. Quebec's government autonomously manages an annual budget it receives from the federal government to fund settlement support (Becklumb 2008; Griffith 2017). This budget is primarily used by the Quebecois ministry of immigration (currently called Ministère de l'Immigration, de la Diversité et de l'Inclusion [MIDI]). However, several other ministries are involved in settlement support, notably the ministry of employment in regard to employability support and career development (Chicha and Charest 2008: 19–21; TCRI 2009).

Frontline service delivery is provided by nonprofit organizations relying on funding agreements with ministries for many of their activities. The "community sector" has historically had strong autonomy (Vaillancourt 2002, and this autonomy has long been supported by Quebec's provincial government (White 2012). In regard to employment, the community sector has funding agreements with Emploi Québec, the ministry of employment's agency supporting employment and workforce development (Chicha and Charest 2008). No organization exclusively caters to the needs of resettled refugees; however, one immigrant settlement organization in each of the thirteen municipalities receiving GARs is tasked with assisting them in the first year after their arrival to Canada (Guyon 2011). These municipalities include Saint-Jérôme and Saint-Hyacinthe, where fieldwork discussed in this chapter was conducted along with Montreal.

Like preceding cohorts of resettled refugees, post-IRPA resettled refugees show remarkable resilience, with levels of labor market participation being initially low yet increasingly steadily over a decade. Yet unemployment levels are high and earnings remain significantly below the Canadian average, especially in Quebec.[4] As far as their economic trajectory is concerned, first-generation resettled refugees thus appear excluded from the Canadian middle class.[5] This is a major worry to them. Resettled refugees report employment as one of their main concerns alongside mental health and housing (Hyndman 2011). It can be said that resettled refugees are very keen to address the issue. Their use of immigrant settlement services is higher than that of other immigrant categories (ibid.; Wilkinson and Garcea 2017), and refugees more broadly report being particularly eager in engage in skills training (Esses et al. 2012).

In my fieldwork, all refugee participants were GARs. This may reflect their higher use of support services compared to PSRs, as I recruited most refugee participants via settlement organizations. Geographic origins included Southeastern Europe, Latin America, and sub-Saharan Africa. Five participants had arrived in Canada in 2011, one in 2007, and one in the mid-1990s. Two participants were men and five were women. The two male participants' level of education (one with a university education, the other near high school completion) was significantly higher than that of the women participants (either no formal education or primary school completion). I met all female participants in Saint-Hyacinthe, and the two male participants respectively in Saint-Jérôme and Montreal. All participants had worked in their countries of origin. Several participants with no formal education had worked in the fields from childhood. Some had also worked in the countries from which they were resettled. In the following, all names used are pseudonyms.

Puran, a participant who had been born in a refugee camp and was completing his secondary education in this camp as he was selected for resettlement, worked on construction sites outside the refugee camp during school holidays. Monique, who had completed primary school, had had the opportunity to train and work as a baker in the refugee camp in which she spent several years. This is remarkable given the scarcity of employment opportunities in many refugee camps (Garnier 2014). All participants had focused on learning French on arrival before looking for employment—"francization" on arrival is a priority of Quebec' integration policies (MIDI 2015).

At the time of the interviews, only the two males, who were better educated, had steady employment. All female participants were then unemployed. Several were still learning French while looking for work, and their labor market trajectories had alternated between long periods of unemployment and short periods (a few weeks, at most a few months) as low-wage workers in conditioning and packing plants, as well as internships in a recycling plant and a secondhand clothes store. Several unemployed participants despaired of their inability to find a good job, or any job at all, without completing secondary education, and this influenced their view of the local labor market. For instance, Monique, insisting on her years of experience in several jobs, regretted that no employer in Saint-Hyacinthe would give her a chance because of her lack of secondary education. In contrast, Puran, who had found long-term employment as a kitchen hand, stated that what mattered to his employer in Saint-Jérôme had been his ability to learn on the job.

The male participants in my sample share individual characteristics predicting better opportunities in the labor market; these are presented in this chapter's second section. First, they are male and had a higher level of education than most other participants on arrival in Canada. Additionally, they were resettled at a younger age than the female participants (between eighteen and twenty-five years old, in contrast to an age range between thirty and forty) and were somewhat proficient in English—yet not proficient at all in French—whereas most other participants had no command of either language on arrival. The fact that both had an ascendant career with one employer is an indication that their respective employers found them effective and knowledgeable enough individuals, that is, to have enough "soft skills," to be inclined to promote them. Yet immigrant settlement services in Canada and Quebec are not designed to cater to the specific needs of resettled refugees—nor, more broadly, of any particular immigrant category. Rather, a broad range of settlement services is offered to those in all categories. Particular groups can be singled out for particular projects and activities, for instance youth or refugee women, but these groups are not differentiated by an official immigrant category.

In interviews, settlement and employment services providers argued that the diversity of profiles within the resettled refugees' population but also the small size of the contingent of resettled refugees as compared to other immigrant categories may not justify settlement services specifically targeting them. Indeed, resettled refugees, or even refugees as a whole, represent a small proportion of the yearly arrivals of permanent residents, whose largest proportion is skilled migrants (Garnier 2016c). Even accounting for the significant Syrian refugees–focused increase of refugee admission, more than 60 percent of permanent residents remain skilled migrants as of 2016 (Griffith 2017).

From an employment support perspective, they also represent a small proportion of particularly vulnerable job seekers. They thus may be considered a potential target for programs for people who for a long time have not been integrated into the labor market—as such and not as resettled refugees.[6] In addition, it was mentioned that refugees themselves did not focus on this label when looking for work, as this was not perceived as conducive to availing themselves of opportunities in the labor market. In response to such concerns, and perhaps because of her own view on the subject, one immigrant settlement service provider had removed the label "refugee" from an employability program targeting young refugees and instead focused on their youth.[7] Lack of concerted focus on resettled refugees does not foster the cohesion of humanitarian advocacy in regard to socioeconomic participation.

Another factor limiting such cohesion is the lack of coordination between stakeholders involved in the socioeconomic participation of resettled refugees. This includes the federal/provincial divide in regard to the provision of settlement services. A former manager of a federally funded employability program for immigrant and refugee youth in Saint-Jérôme noted, for instance, that disjuncture between the federal and provincial funding framework meant that her program participants had no access to Emploi Quebec–funded support measures while they were enrolled in the program. Instead of having a concerted effort to support resettled refugees, support measures were thus dispersed. Others mentioned that ministerial fragmentation in regard to immigrant and refugee integration in Quebec was detrimental to refugees, echoing Chicha and Charest's (2008) observation regarding the impact of ministerial fragmentation on immigrant settlement in Montreal.

Finally, humanitarian constituencies are affected by the "advocacy chill" (Shields 2013) resulting from increasingly managerial and cost-saving practices by public decision makers. The employability coordinator at TCRI, the Montreal-based umbrella body for nonprofit agencies supporting refugees and immigrants, was critical of the increasing divergence between the community sector's interpretation of its mandate as an agent of social change and the view of the current government of Quebec. The latter has been strongly focused on austerity measures, pushing for a command-and-control approach in funding agreements, and thus has increasingly challenged the long-standing consensus regarding the autonomy of the community sector (see also Depelteau et al. 2013).

Beyond interviews mentioned in this chapter, immigrant settlement service provider staff, in informal conversations not specifically referring to resettled refugees, also reported that they had targets to achieve in terms of job placements in order to fulfill their funding agreements. This led to privileging the search for any job in the short term rather than potentially longer, more selective searches for good quality jobs. This is an indication that the province of Quebec is catching up with neoliberal practices already well established in the rest of Canada (White 2012; Shields 2013).

To what extent can we say that the weakening of humanitarian advocacy is particularly an issue for the most vulnerable resettled refugees? Perhaps because more vulnerable refugees need more time, as well as more support services, to acquire the resources that are necessary to get on an upward trajectory in the labor market. Yet, as mentioned above, a managerial approach reduces the array of services available and attempts to increase the speed at which immigrants and refugees are considered self-sufficient. In this context, the bargaining power of more vulnerable refugees, and that of agencies aiming to help them, is restricted—and this restriction is due to the authority of public institutions over the practices of contracted nongovernmental settlement services providers.

Still, this does not mean that this bargaining power is completely nonexistent, and this is reflected in the role of support services in the upward career trajectory of the two male, better educated participants in my fieldwork. Puran, after failing to complete his secondary education in Saint-Jérôme, enrolled locally in newly established vocational training focusing on the hospitality industry. As part of this training he did an internship as a kitchen hand in a restaurant and was hired there at the end of his internship. Puran benefited from the cooperation of his educational provider with employers keen to develop new vocational training open to "atypical" profiles such as his. The other man, Dobrilo, who had gained some tertiary education in his country of origin, "climbed the ladder" within the Montreal-based settlement agency that had assisted him after he had been resettled.

His first job at his settlement agency had been funded through an Emploi Quebec subsidy, and he benefited from a one-year extension of the subsidy to continue funding its work. This extension was granted thanks to the persuasive power of his then manager at Emploi Quebec. He then became responsible for assisting a large group of incoming refugees whose language he spoke. At the time of the interview, he was a settlement services coordinator for GARs at the settlement agency. On this basis, Dobrilo can be said to have joined the ranks of the Canadian middle class, while Puran appeared to be on the way to belonging to it in the relatively near future. The individual characteristics of the two men as much as the mobilization of the bargaining power of local actors can be said to have created their upward employment trajectories.

Discussion and Perspectives

Focusing on refugee resettlement in Canada and Quebec, this chapter has highlighted the regulatory construction of humanitarian governance and shown the critical role of the mobilization of humanitarian constituencies as well as political and institutional constraints faced by these constituencies. This exploration can be contrasted with the chapters in this volume investigating the regulatory construction of resettlement's humanitarian governance at the international level (see van Selm; Sandvik, this volume), at the national level in the case of Norway (Reklev; Jumbert, this volume), and in a regional context in Brazil (Jubilut and Zamur, this volume). In regard to the admission of resettled refugees, humanitarian constituencies managed to effectively perform in the public sphere and to remind the Canadian and Quebecois governments of the humanitarian objectives of refugee resettlement. Yet regulatory change mostly occurred at the discretionary level (administrative practice), whereas primary legislation remained the same– limiting the structural impact of humanitarian constituencies and thus humanitarian governance in immigration legislation.

In the longer term, the limits of humanitarian constituencies' persuasive power have been shown in the context of the labor market. Because of their dependence on state and provincial regulations, which are driven by a promarket rationale, humanitarian constituencies do not have the authority to impose regulatory change facilitating the labor market inclusion of the most vulnerable resettled refugees. Humanitarian constituencies also do not have the resources to ensure that settlement and employability service providers are in a situation to implement the existing regulatory framework in a way that would consistently strengthen the labor market position of the most vulnerable resettled refugees, because they cater to the needs of the entire immigrant population, whose profile and needs are closer to that of the Canadian middle class than that of resettled refugees. Scarcity of resources makes constant mobilization and advocacy with federal and provincial authority difficult.

Finally, humanitarian constituencies find themselves dispersed because of the lack of coordination between the various stakeholders involved in the socioeconomic participation of resettled refugees and can be hampered by the regulatory divide between the provincial and the federal levels. Compared to Bloemraad's findings mentioned in the chapter's second section, the national institutional setting of the socioeconomic incorporation of resettled refugees in Canada thus appears less likely to foster social mobilizations at the local level than the national institutional setting of the political incorporation of immigrants in this country. This echoes the Canadian findings of Wilkinson and Garcea (2017) and the Quebecois findings of Blain et al. (2017). Beyond the country's borders, the socioeconomic marginalization of resettled refugees in Canada shows similarities with resettling states investigated in this volume, namely the United States (Darrow; Lewis and Young, this volume), Australia (Losoncz, this volume), Chile and Brazil (Vera Espinoza, this volume).

Nonetheless, an investigation of local dynamics in the Montreal area has shown that close relationships between various settlement stakeholders (settlement and employability services providers, educational providers, employers, and Emploi Quebec) can have a positive effect on resettled refugees' access to the labor market and career development. Such relationships of proximity thus support the agency and negotiating power of resettled refugees on the labor market. Yet in our investigation, resettled refugees who have benefited from such networks also had individual characteristics that made them more likely to have upward employment trajectories than more vulnerable refugees, such as a higher level of education and being male. This complements this volume's investigation of the agency and negotiating power of women resettlement candidates in Tanzania (Thomson, this volume) and of resettled Cambodian and Karen refugees in the United States (Lewis and Young, this volume).

It is not impossible that particularly vulnerable resettled refugees also benefit from close relationships between local stakeholders, especially in a context of enduring local labor market demand; yet this is a big ask. Closer relationships over a single issue are difficult to achieve because each settlement stakeholder is pursuing multiple goals at the same time and stretching its resources in doing so. Imposing a hierarchy of goals in favor of resettled refugees' labor market participation seems already difficult for immigrant and employability services catering to the needs of broader population groups, even though this does not exclude the development of specialized resettled-focused expertise within such organizations, which could ensure continuity in the pursuit of this goal. Yet it seems even harder for employers, educational providers, and agencies such as Emploi Quebec.

Institutional obstacles to refugees' socioeconomic participation have recently gained in visibility in Canada and Quebec. In late 2017, both Canada's federal auditor-general and its provincial equivalent in Quebec released two reports recommending significant change to better address the needs of Syrian refugee newcomers (in the federal case, see Auditor General of Canada 2017) or more broadly of newcomers (in Quebec, see Vérificateur Général du Québec 2017). The federal report noted that an increase of integration funding that occurred in response to the arrival of Syrian refugees was adequate and that most Syrian newcomers had access to language and needs assessments.

However, funding delays had led to the temporary shutdown of support services and there was no appropriate management of waiting lists preventing rapid access to settlement services. The Quebec report was far more critical toward the MIDI. It noted that in spite of the official focus on "francization" in Quebec's official integration policy, the MIDI failed to track what happened to non-Francophones who did not access its language support services. Perhaps even more worryingly, a majority of those who participated in language courses considered them insufficient for their level of needs, and thus not adequate to support rapid labor market participation in the province.

Perhaps a greater awareness of these challenges will lead to policy shifts: under Prime Minister Justin Trudeau, Canada has demonstrated a political commitment to humanitarianism and social inclusion, and the country's immigration policy is often described as "evidence based" (Griffith 2017). At the same time, most vulnerable newcomers, and this is the case of many resettled refugees, are at a systemic disadvantage in a system that is geared to catering to the needs of "mainstream newcomers," while labor market support services cater to the needs of "mainstream job seekers"–notwithstanding the admirable engagement of many individual staff members (see also Blain et al. 2017).

Still, what could make a difference is large-scale social mobilization, and it is often said that Canada's success as an immigration country is largely based on its social acceptance of immigration. However this acceptance goes with the reckoning that immigration is economically useful, as well as with the strong involvement of various social groups in immigration and refugee intake planning at the federal and provincial levels (Blain et al. 2017; Hiebert 2016). The harder the obstacles resettled refugees face, the more difficult it is for resettled refugees to contribute to the Canadian and Quebecois socioeconomic fabric. This should be kept in mind when assessing the sustainability of Trudeau's ambition for Canada to be a global leader in refugee resettlement.

Other Canadian particularities should not be forgotten in this respect. As opposed to most other resettling countries, Canada is "lucky" (Hussen 2017) to be geographically very isolated and hence to have a degree of control over immigration flows that most countries do not have. This may currently be challenged by the considerable increase of asylum claimants leaving the United States in fear of the Trump administration's hostile stance toward refugees and immigrants (Darrow, this volume), and time will tell whether a scenario of nascent hostility toward asylum seekers, as seen in Australia (Losoncz, this volume) may occur in Canada. It is notable that both Trudeau and Hussen insist on the need for the immigration and refugee intake to be orderly to be acceptable to the Canadian population (Hussen 2017). This aspect of the Canadian discourse is not very different from other resettling countries' rhetoric.

Another aspect to consider is the unique and entrenched character of Canada's institutional arrangements, especially private sponsorship of refugees (Hyndman et al. 2017; Wilkinson and Garcea 2017). Private sponsorship enjoys considerable social legitimacy in Canada and Quebec because of its enduring character, and this may be very hard to replicate beyond its borders. In Canada, sponsors and advocates deplore the mounting backlog of sponsorship applications in part created by the prioritization of the Syrian refugee caseload (Hyndman et al. 2017). The Trudeau government will have to deliver on its commitment to eliminate this backlog in order for Canada to remain a credible leader in refugee sponsorship.

Finally, Canada's resurgent humanitarianism remains very much concerned with the national agenda. Grayson and Audet (2017) show that Canada's financial contribution to UNHCR has more than doubled under the Conservative prime ministership of Stephen Harper, who by no means considers himself an internationalist. At the same time, the proportion of earmarked funding has considerably increased, which Grayson and Audet (2017) interpret as an indication of a desire to influence the UNHCR's agenda (on this more generally see Suhrke and Garnier, this volume). Future research will be needed to explore the extent to which humanitarian constituencies will be able to draw on Trudeau's humanitarian commitment to not only address obstacles to their influence in regard to the socioeconomic participation of resettled refugees at the domestic level but also tackle issues of priority alignment between Canada and the UN refugee agency.

Adèle Garnier is a lecturer at the Department of Modern History, Politics and International Relations, Macquarie University, Australia. She holds a Ph.D. in politics from the University of Leipzig, Germany and Macquarie University and has held research positions at the Interuniversity Research Centre for Globalization and Work (CRIMT), Université de Montréal, Canada and the Group for Research on Migration, Ethnic Relations and Equality (GERME), Université Libre de Bruxelles, Belgium. She has published in *Refuge,* the *Journal of Ethnic and Migration Studies,* and *WeltTrends.*

Notes

1. Canada is officially a bilingual country, and there are both Francophone minorities outside of Quebec and Anglophone minorities in Quebec, especially in Montreal. Yet French is institutionally and linguistically the dominant language in Quebec, and so is English in the rest of the country.
2. A search in widely used scholarly databases (EBSCO's Social Sciences Abstracts, Google Scholar, and JSTOR) for publications with "Canada," "power," and immigration- and refugee-related terms in their title led only to an essay by Leigh Binford called "From Fields of Power to Fields of Sweat: The Dual Process of Constructing Temporary Migrant Labour in Mexico and Canada" (Binford 2009). Drawing on Henri Lefebvre and Robin Cohen, Binford focuses on the forces at play (including workers' own subjectivity) in the social construction of migrant workers, yet the concept of power itself is never defined.
3. Interview with officer from the UNHCR Canada branch office in Ottawa, Montreal, 28 August 2015.
4. See Garnier (2016b) for a more detailed exploration of resettled refugees' earning trajectories, with a discussion of similarities and differences between government-assisted and privately sponsored refugees.
5. Similar to the children of immigrants in Canada. The children of refugees, however, achieve higher completion rates at university than Canadian-born counterparts, indicating that exclusion from the middle class is a temporary phenomenon (Hou and Bonikowska 2016).

6. This was the case of a program discussed by an employment support manager in Saint-Hyacinthe (14 July 2015). Echoing to an extent a discourse discussed at greater length by Darrow in the U.S. context in this volume, the manager framed this category of persons as in need of a "change of mentality." Yet this mentality was not perceived as something typical of "the poor" but rather of Quebecois people "born for a small loaf of bread" (*nés pour un petit pain*), a colloquialism that reflects the centuries of poverty of a large part of the Quebecois population.
7. Interview with settlement services provider, Montreal, 4 December 2015.

References

Allen, John. 2003. *Lost Geographies of Power*. Oxford: Wiley-Blackwell.
Auditor General of Canada. 2017. *Independent Auditor's Report. Report 3: Settlement Services for Syrian Refugees–Immigration, Refugees and Citizenship Canada*. Ottawa: Office of the Auditor General of Canada. Accessed 11 December 2017. http://publications.gc.ca/collections/collection_2017/bvg-oag/FA1-23-2017-2-3-eng.pdf.
Becklumb, Penny. 2008. *L'Immigration: l'Accord Canada-Québec*. BP 252-F. Ottawa: Canadian Parliament.
Binford, Leigh. 2009. "From Fields of Power to Fields of Sweat: The Dual Process of Constructing Migrant Labor in Mexico and Canada." *Third World Quarterly* 30(3): 503–17.
Blain, Marie-Jeanne, Pacale Chanoux, and Roxanne Caron, with the collaboration of Myriam Richard, Marie-Claire Rufagari, Nisrin Al-Yahya, Lisette Richard, Meriem Bichri, Adèle Garnier, and Noémie Trosseille. 2017. *Synthèse et Conclusions. Recherche-Action: Perspectives Exploratoires sur l'Employabilité des Personnes Réfugiées*. Montreal: TCRI/ERASME.
Bloemraad, Irene. 2006. *Becoming a Citizen: Incorporating Immigrants and Refugees in the United States and Canada*. Berkeley: University of California Press.
Canadian Refugee Council. 1998. *Refugees in Canada*. Canadian Refugee and Humanitarian Immigration Policy 1997 to mid-1998. Accessed 6 February 2017. http://ccrweb.ca/sites/ccrweb.ca/files/static-files/survey98.pdf.
———. 1999. *Comments on Building on a Strong Foundation for the 21st Century*. Accessed 6 February 2017. http://ccrweb.ca/en/white-paper-comments.
Chicha, Marie-Thérèse. 2009. *Le Mirage de l'Egalité: Les Immigrantes Hautement Qualifiées à Montréal*. Toronto: Fondation Canadienne des Relations Raciales.
Chicha, Marie-Thérèse, and Eric Charest. 2008. "L'Intégration des Immigrés sur le marché du travail à Montréal: politique et enjeux." *IRRP Choix* 14(2): 1–62.
Citizenship and Immigration Canada (CIC). 1999. *New Directions for Immigration and Refugee Policy and Legislation: Building on a Strong Foundation for the 21st Century*. White Paper White Paper. Ottawa: Citizenship ad Immigration Canada.
———. 2007. *Summative Evaluation of the Private Sponsorship of Refugees Program*. Ottawa: Citizenship and Immigration Canada. Accessed 6 February 2017. http://www.cic.gc.ca/english/resources/evaluation/psrp/psrp-summary.asp.

——. 2009. *Operational Manual 5: Overseas Selection and Processing of Convention Refugees Abroad. Class and Members of the Humanitarian-Protected Class.* Ottawa: Citizenship and Immigration Canada.

——. 2011. *Evaluation of Government-Assisted Refugees (GARs) and Resettlement Assistance Program (RAP).* Ottawa: Citizenship and Immigration Canada. Accessed 6 February 2017. http://www.cic.gc.ca/english/pdf/pub/gar-rap.pdf.

——. 2012a. *IMDB 2008 Immigration Categories Profile: Government-Assisted Refugees.* Ottawa: Citizenship and Immigration Canada. Accessed 6 February 2017. http://www.cic.gc.ca/english/pdf/pub/imdb/GAR_3.pdf.

——. 2012b. *IMDB 2008 Immigration Categories Profile: Privately-Sponsored Refugees.* Ottawa: Citizenship and Immigration Canada. Accessed 6 February 2017. http://www.cic.gc.ca/english/pdf/pub/imdb/PSR_3.pdf.

——. 2015. *Population Profile: Syrian Refugees.* Ottawa: Citizenship and Immigration Canada. Accessed 6 February 2017. http://lifelinesyria.ca/wp-content/uploads/2015/11/EN-Syrian-Population-Profile.pdf.

Depelteau, Julie, Francis Fortier, and Guillaume Hébert. 2013. *Les Organismes Communautaires au Québec. Financement et Évolution des Pratiques.* Montréal: Institut de recherche et d'informations socio-économiques.

Esses, Victoria, Meyer Burstein, Zenaida Ravanera, Stacey Hallman, and Stelian Medianu. 2013. *Alberta Settlement Outcomes Survey.* Calgary: Alberta Human Services. Accessed 6 February 2017. http://work.alberta.ca/documents/alberta-outcomes-settlement-survey-results.pdf.

Garnier, Adèle. 2014. "Arrested Development? UNHCR, ILO and the Refugees' Right to Work." *Refuge* 30(2): 15–25.

——. 2016a. "The Future of Refugee Resettlement: Will the September Summits Make Any Difference?" Norwegian Centre for Humanitarian Studies, 28 September. Accessed 6 February 2017. http://www.humanitarianstudies.no/2016/09/28/the-future-of-refugee-resettlement-will-the-september-summits-make-any-difference/.

——. 2016b. "Impact des Arrangements Institutionnels d'Admission et d'Insertion sur le Parcours Professionnel des Réfugiés." *Les Cahiers du CRIEC* 39.

——. 2016c. "Power Dynamics in the Selection and the Labour Market Integration of Resettled Refugees in Quebec." Brighton: Sussex Centre for Migration Research, Blog of the Refugee Resettlement Conference. Accessed 6 February 2017. http://www.sussex.ac.uk/migration/research/integrationcitizenship/refugeeresettlement/conference-blogs.

Gifford, Sandy. 2013. "To Respect or Protect? Whose Values Shape the Ethics of Refugee Research?" In *Values and Vulnerabilities: The Ethics of Research with Refugees and Asylum Seekers,* edited by K. Block, E. Riggs, and N. Haslam, 41–69. Samford Valley: Australian Academic Press.

Government of Canada. 1999. *Building a Strong Foundation for the 21st Century: New Directions for Immigration and Refugee Policy and Legislation.* Ottawa: Minister of Public Work and Government Services. Accessed 6 February 2017. http://publications.gc.ca/collections/Collection/Ci51-86-1998E.pdf.

Grayson, Catherine-Lune, and François. Audet. 2017. "Les Hauts et les Bas du Financement Canadien au HCR: Quelle Aide et pour Quels Réfugiés?" *Refuge* 33(1): 62–76.

Griffith, Andrew. 2017. *Building a Mosaic: The Evolution of Canada's Approach to Immigrant Integration.* Migration Policy Institute, 1 November. Accessed 11 December 2017. https://www.migrationpolicy.org/article/building-mosaic-evolution-canadas-approach-immigrant-integration.

Guyon, Sylvie. 2011. "La Réinstallation au Québec des Réfugiés Réinstallés de l'Étranger, un Secret Bien Gardé!" *Vivre Ensemble* 18(62): 1–5.

Hiebert, Daniel. 2016. *What's So Special about Canada? Understanding the Resilience of Immigration and Multiculturalism.* Washington, D.C.: Migration Policy Institute. Accessed 12 December 2017. https://www.migrationpolicy.org/research/whats-so-special-about-canada-understanding-resilience-immigration-and-multiculturalism.

Hou, Feng, and A. Bonikowska. 2016. *Educational and Labour Market Outcomes of Childhood Immigrants by Admission Class.* Analytical Studies Branch Research Paper Series. Ottawa: Statistics Canada.

Hussen, Ahmed. 2017. "Interview with the Honourable Ahmed D. Hussein, Minister of Immigration, Refugees and Citizenship, Canada." *International Migration* 55(4): 5–9.

Hyndman, Jennifer. 1999. "Globalization, Immigration and the Gender Implications of Not Just Numbers in Canada." *Refuge* 18(1): 26–31.

———. 2011. *Research Summary on Resettled Refugee Integration in Canada.* Ottawa: United Nations High Commissioner for Refugees.

Hyndman, Jennifer, William Payne, and Shauna Jimenez. 2017. "Private Refugee Sponsorship in Canada." *Forced Migration Review* 54: 56–59.

Immigration and Refugee Protection Act. S.C. 2001, c. 27.

Immigration and Refugee Protection Regulations. SOR/2002-227.

Immigration, Refugees and Citizenship Canada (IRCC). 2015. *Facts and Figures 2015: Immigration Overview: Permanent Residents–Annual IRCC Update.* Ottawa: IRCC. Accessed 11 December 2017. http://open.canada.ca/data/en/dataset/2fbb56bd-eae7-4582-af7d-a197d185fc93?_ga=2.165101375.1252848501.1512948298-11853 69781.1512695167.

———. 2016a. *Rapid Impact Evaluation of the Syrian Refugee Initiative.* Ottawa: IRCC. Accessed 11 December 2017. https://www.canada.ca/en/immigration-refugees-citizenship/corporate/reports-statistics/evaluations/rapid-impact-evaluation-syrian-refugee-initiative.html#toc1-4.

———. 2016b. *Evaluation of the Resettlement Programme.* Ottawa: IRCC. Accessed 6 February 2017. http://www.cic.gc.ca/english/pdf/pub/resettlement.pdf.

———. 2017. #Welcome Refugees, Key Figures. Ottawa: IRCC. Accessed 6 February 2017. http://www.cic.gc.ca/english/refugees/welcome/milestones.asp.

Jacobsen, Karen, and Loren B. Landau. 2003. "The Dual Imperative in Refugee Research: Some Methodological and Ethical Considerations in Social Science Research on Forced Migration." *Disasters* 27(3): 185–206.

Krahn, Harvey, Tracey Derwing, Marlene Mulder, and Lori Wilkinson. 2000. "Educated and Underemployed: Refugee Integration into the Canadian Labour Market." *Journal of International Migration and Integration* 1(1): 52–84.

Lamba, Navjot. 2003. "The Employment Experience of Canadian Refugees: Measuring the Impact of Human and Social Capital on Quality of Employment." *Canadian Review of Sociology* 40(1): 45–64.

Legislative Review Advisory Group. 1997. *Not Just Numbers: A Canadian Framework for Future Immigration, Executive Summary.* Ottawa: Citizenship and Immigration Canada.

Lijphart, Arend. 1971. "Comparative Politics and the Comparative Method." *The American Political Science Review* 65(3): 682–93.

Ministère de l'Immigration, de la Diversité et de l'Inclusion (MIDI). 2015. *Ensemble, Nous Sommes le Québec: Politique Québécoise en Matière d'Immigration, de Participation et d'Inclusion.* Québec: Gouvernement du Québec/MIDI.

——. 2017. *Présence et Portraits Régionaux des Personnes Immigrantes Admises au Québec de 2006 à 2015.* Québec: Gouvernement du Québec. Accessed 11 December 2017. http://www.midi.gouv.qc.ca/publications/fr/recherches-statistiques/PUB_Prese nce2017_admisQc.pdf.

Ott, Eleanor. 2013. *The Labour Market Integration of Refugees.* PDES 2013/16. Geneva: UNHCR.

Rea, Andrea, and Johan Wets. 2014. *The Long and Winding Road to Employment: An Analysis of the Labour Market Careers of Refugees and Asylum Seekers in Belgium.* Gent: Academia Press.

Refugee Studies Centre. 2007. "Ethical Guidelines for Good Research Practice." *Refugee Survey Quarterly* 26(3): 162–72.

Règlement sur la Sélection des Ressortissants Étrangers I-0.2, r. 4.

Renaud, Jean, Victor Piché, and Jean-François Godin. 2003. "'One's Bad and the Other Is Worse': Differences in Economic Integration between Asylum Seekers and Refugees Selected Abroad." *Canadian Ethnic Studies* 35(2): 86–99.

Rocher, François, and Bob White. 2014. "L'interculturalisme québécois dans le contexte du multiculturalisme canadien." *Étude IRPP* 49. Montreal: Institut de recherche en politiques publiques.

Shields, John. 2013. "Nonprofit Engagement with Provincial Policy Officials: The Case of Canadian Immigrant Settlement Services." Paper presented at the First International Conference on Public Policy, Grenoble, France, 26–28 June.

Table de Concertation des Organismes au Service des Personnes Réfugiées et Immigrantes (TCRI). 2009. *Rapport Annuel 2008–2009.* Montreal: TCRI.

Trudeau, Justin. 2016. *Prime Minister Justin Trudeau's Address to the 71st Session of the United Nations General Assembly.* Ottawa: Prime Minister of Canada. Accessed 12 December 2017. https://pm.gc.ca/eng/news/speeches.

United Nations High Commissioner for Refugees' Office (UNHCR). 1998. "*Comments on* Not Just Numbers: A Canadian Framework for Future Immigration Report of the Immigration Legislative Review Advisory Group." Accessed 6 February 2017. http://ccrweb.ca/sites/ccrweb.ca/files/staticfiles/hcrlegr.htm#(iv) percent20Prospects percent20for percent20Integration.

Vaillancourt, Yves. 2002. "Le Modèle Québécois de Politiques Sociales et ses Interfaces avec l'Union Sociale Canadienne." *IRPP Enjeux Publics* 2(3): 1–52.

Vérificateur Général du Québec. 2017. *Rapport du Vérificateur Général du Québec à l'Assemblée Nationale pour l'année 2017–2018.* Accessed 11 December 2017. http://www.vgq.gouv.qc.ca/fr/fr_publications/fr_rapport-annuel/fr_2017-2018-Autom ne/fr_Rapport2017-2018-AUTOMNE.pdf.

White, Deena. 2012. "Interest Representation and Organization in Civil Society: Ontario and Quebec Compared." *British Journal of Canadian Studies* 25(2): 199–229.

Wilkinson, Lori, and Joseph Garcea. 2017. *The Economic Integration of Refugees in Canada: A Mixed Record?* Washington, D.C.: Migration Policy Institute.

Xue, Li. 2006. *Initial Labour Market Outcomes: A Comprehensive Look at the Employment Experience of Recent Immigrants during the First Four Years in Canada.* Ottawa: Citizenship and Immigration Canada.

6

The Structural and Institutional Exclusion of Refugees in Australia

Ibolya Losoncz

Introduction

Successful resettlement of refugees depends both on individual resources and strategies of refugees and on the foundational principle of having the same rights as host communities. Stating the equality of rights is fundamental for the normative framework that determines refugee resettlement policy, and the state has an important responsibility in the clear articulation of these rights (Ager and Strang 2008; compare Jubilut and Zamur; Reklev and Jumbert, this volume). But is legislating and articulating equality of rights sufficient by itself? Or do governments also have a responsibility to use their power and their institutions to protect and advance the nondiscriminatory realization of these rights?

Focusing on the case of the economic participation of recently resettled refugees in Australia, this chapter argues that being granted the same rights underpins the successful integration of resettled refugees and that governments and their institutions have an important role in ensuring the realization of these rights. Failing to do this increases the structural imbalance of power in which refugees find themselves and negatively affects refugee integration. This chapter systemically explores the impact of social structures and institutional responses and practices on resettlement outcomes for refugees. Employment was chosen because it is an important pathway to economic and social inclusion and the settlement of refugees. It provides an income and a sense of security and enables the development of social networks and cultural skills vital for integration. Stable employment is at the top of the United Nations High Commissioner for Refugees' (UNHCR's) list of essential indicators of successful resettlement (UNHCR 2011). Employment and the economic participation of refugees also benefits the receiving country.

The chapter argues that current Australian resettlement policies are dominated by a strong emphasis on migrants' adopting their new country's normative goals and values without a corresponding emphasis on ensuring that there are effective pathways for refugees to achieve these goals (see similarly Darrow; Garnier, this volume). On the contrary, in some instances Australia's social structures and institutions constitute obstacles rather than facilitators to the economic and social inclusion of resettled refugees. For example, my findings will demonstrate how a simplistic application of mainstream recruitment mechanisms, such as the merit-based selection system, fails to recognize the relative disadvantage of refugees and thus restricts their access to jobs.

The chapter is structured as follows. The next section presents the chapter's theoretical framework. A brief account of the development of Australia's refugee resettlement programs then shows how the historical context has contributed to contradictions in current Australian resettlement policies. The rest of the chapter presents the results and analysis from two independent, yet related, datasets to reveal how Australian social structures and institutional practices thwart the social and economic inclusion of refugees admitted for settlement. I conclude by demonstrating that the structural imbalance of power in which refugees find themselves undermines their capacity and determination to economically and socially integrate and by shedding light on the chapter's contribution to the exploration of refugee resettlement as humanitarian governance.

Role of the State and Government Institutions: Theoretical Framing

In the past ten years, research on refugee resettlement has increasingly focused on the role of host societies and host states, including settlement policies and processes, such as housing, employment, education, health care, income support, and family reunion (Colic-Peisker and Tilbury 2007; Stewart 2009; Valenta and Bunar 2010; Valtonen 2004; and Lewis and Young; Vera Espinoza, this volume). Yet our knowledge of how social structures and mechanisms do or do not support resettlement and the processes involved remains limited.

In their conceptualization of refugee integration, Ager and Strang (2008) identify two main types of processes mediating between foundational principles and integration outcomes: facilitators and social connections. Social connections, such as social bridges, social bonds, and social links are important at the local level. Facilitators, aimed at providing pathways and removing structural barriers to integration, are often under the control of the state and are important at the national policy-making level. Ager and Strang noted that despite the importance of these processes, they are undertheorized and poorly understood.

One theoretical framework to set outcomes apart from the processes leading to these outcomes is Robert Merton's adaptation theory. The two main elements of the theory are goals, that is, culturally structured normative values, and social structures, that is, pathways structuring the capacities of individuals in the social groups. In other words, the cultural structure sets goals, while social structure provides pathways for making and implementing goals (Merton 1968).

Merton argued that valued goals of society, such as economic participation and success, are desired by all, but opportunities to achieve them are not equally distributed, and pathways for some are structurally blocked or restricted. Specifically, Merton saw social structures to be the reason most migrants were unable to reach economic success and became part of the most marginalized of their new country despite working hard, often in menial jobs (Merton 1968). In his adaptation theory, he argued that behaviors adopted by individuals, in terms of adaptation of or resistance to normative goals and their formal institutions, are structurally determined. That is, social structures make the means and actions to achieve cultural goals possible for groups occupying certain statuses within a society and difficult or impossible for other groups, such as refugees.

The other important analytical concepts, to explicate social connections, are Robert Putnam's social capital theory and Mark Granovetter's work on the role of small-scale interactions. Putnam saw social capital as the relationships between people and their social networks and the associated norms of trust (Putnam 2000). In the context of refugee integration, bonding and bridging networks are vital mediators of integration outcomes (Ager and Strang 2008). Bonding social capital is characterized by strong relationships, typically with people from the same ethnic community. Bridging social capital, on the other hand, are networks of looser connections beyond family, friends, and the diaspora. These connections, although weaker than the ties with friends and family, connect people to a multitude of outside worlds, providing a bridge to new work-related networks. As proposed by Granovetter (1983), it is these distinct forms of interactions that provide the capacity to be more successful at searching for and obtaining employment.

Indeed, the positive role of bridging social capital has been confirmed by a number of empirical studies (such as, Lancee 2010; Stone et al. 2003).

Australian Refugee Resettlement Policies in Context

Australia is an augmentative country, that is, a country that actively supports population growth through immigration (Kunz 1981). Nearly 30 percent, or 7 million, of Australia's current resident population was born overseas (Australian Bureau of Statistics 2016). Despite this history of immigration, Australia offers protection to far fewer refugees than many countries. Of the 2.45 million refugees globally who had their status recognized or were resettled in 2015, just 11,776, or less than 0.5 percent were assisted by Australia (UNHCR 2016). Yet, if one considers Australia's contribution as a proportion of the number of refugees resettled within the UNHCR resettlement program, Australia ranks third overall behind the United States and Canada (UNHCR 2016). This is consistent with the Australian government's long-standing position of giving priority to resettlement within the UNHCR program over on-shore applications for resettlement. For the past fifteen years, Australia has resettled between 6,000 and 12,000 refugees each year and has recently announced it will permanently increase its refugee intake to 18,750 a year by 2018–2019, in addition to its one-off special intake of 12,000 resettled refugees from the Syrian and Iraq humanitarian crisis (Kenny 2016 and see Cellini, this volume).

Until now, being a major contributor to the UNHCR's resettlement program has brought considerable reputational benefits in the international realm to Australia by promoting its global humanitarian image (Jupp 2007). Recently, the Australian government has also tried to use its strong support of UNHCR's resettlement efforts to justify its inhumane and punitive detention of asylum seekers, an act in violation of Australia's human rights treaty obligations (McBeth et al. 2011: 516).

In the domestic context, finding approval for Australia's resettlement program has been more challenging. The narrative aspects of providing permanent safety and resettlement for some of the most vulnerable refugees[1] appeals to some, but not all Australians (on vulnerability, see Thomson; Sandvik, this volume). Instead, the dominant domestic reasoning for admitting humanitarian migrants for resettlement is their potential contribution to Australia's workforce and population. In fact, historically, the Australian government's approach to humanitarian migrants is part of the broader immigration strategy of supporting population growth and subsequent economic prosperity. While in the late 1970s Australia developed a separate refugee policy, the dominant expectation that all immigrants, including refugees, should quickly benefit Australia economically has not changed (Jupp 2007).

The inappropriateness of this framework and the contradictions inherent in this policy are evident. After all, integration is a lengthy two-way process (Valtonen 2004). It involves societal and institutional adaptations to facilitate the settlement of new arrivals through reducing or eliminating barriers to social and economic participation (Ager and Strang 2008; Losoncz 2017a) and providing support services to assist the development of social connections and economic independence (Abur and Spaaij 2016; Ager and Strang 2008).

But the impact of this inappropriate framework and policy contradiction did not surface until recently, prompted by two main developments in Australian refugee resettlement policy in the past twenty years. First, there has been an increase in the proportion of humanitarian migrants from long-term conflict zones and from protracted situations (Department of Immigration and Citizenship 2011). Living for prolonged periods in conflict zones and refugee camps, which are characterized by insecurity, violence, and scant opportunity for education and employment, affects the physical and mental health and human capital development of refugees considerably (Loeescher and Milner 2009). As I will demonstrate in the two sections on results, a significant proportion of recent humanitarian migrants to Australia has relatively low human capital in terms of formal education and English proficiency—both important predictors of socioeconomic status.

While the characteristics and subsequent needs of humanitarian migrants have changed dramatically (Garnier 2014), investment in services and processes supporting the resettlement efforts of humanitarian migrants has not grown apace. On the contrary, this same period has also seen the second major change—a decline in the targeted support of the resettlement process of humanitarian migrants. Resettlement-specific support has been minimized, and economic and social integration has become the responsibility of the immigrant household, aided by a limited range of government-funded welfare services, coordinated by mainstream departments, and delivered by the third sector. The intersection of these two major changes, and a coinciding decline in the need for low-skilled labor in the manufacturing sector in Australia (Kelly and Lewis 2003; Waxman 2001), has resulted in diminished employment opportunities for immigrants with a low skill base; this subsequently has created an impoverished existence among refugees compared to other Australians.

The evident decline in economic participation and increase in welfare dependence (Hugo 2011) among refugees is a concern for the Australian government. But while the government acknowledges the role of settlement services and the influence of the willingness of Australian society to welcome new arrivals, the emphasis is on "the commitment of those arrivals to establishing a life in Australia" (Department of Social Services 2015: 3), rather than the effectiveness of resettlement policies and programs. Additionally, it is assumed that existing mechanisms, developed to ensure that institutions provide equal access to all members of Australian society, will also provide equal opportunities to immigrants accepted for resettlement. But this assumption is at odds with the reality for many migrants, especially those with a refugee background who are experiencing severe social and economic problems.

Methodology

Resettlement is enmeshed in historical events, legal structures, institutional powers, and individual actions. Its study requires an interdisciplinary approach and strong methodology to analyze the complex interplay between structural and systemic conditions, actors and their agency, and cultural norms and values. To analytically explicate the causal mechanisms producing change, these elements need to be treated in dialectical unity despite their different ontological planes. To address this methodological challenge I used a critical realist approach (Danermark et al. 2002) and a sequential mixed methods research design. The initial qualitative phase, informed by grounded theory, was followed by a quantitative phase. The use of a critical realist framework provided a robust method for capturing the interplay between the analytically distinct elements of migration research and to analytically explicate the causal mechanisms producing social change or reproduction (Iosifides 2012; Losoncz 2017b). The use of inductive analytic processes of grounded theory methodology (Charmaz 2006) allowed me to uncover how participants made sense of their new country, its normative values, and its social structures. Together, grounded theory and a critical realist framework allowed me to go beyond describing meanings among participants to examining and analyzing the structures that generate them. Subsequent quantitative analysis of a larger, more representative dataset of refugees provided a robust test of the generalizability of the propositions that arose from the qualitative phase.

Qualitative Data

The collection of qualitative data was part of my doctoral thesis research, and the results reported in the qualitative section draw on findings reported in an earlier publications (i.e., Losoncz 2017a). Qualitative data were collected between 2009 and 2012 through ethnographic engagement and individual interviews in four Australian cities with thirty-two South Sudanese men and women who had migrated to Australia less than ten years ago. In addition, nine Sudanese and non-Sudanese community workers who had close professional connections with the South Sudanese community (in the capacity of community development workers, refugee counselors, and school counselors) were interviewed for their insights into the resettlement experiences and challenges of the community. Ethics approval was sought and granted for this research by the Human Research Ethics Committee, Australian National University.

The South Sudanese population was chosen for two reasons: first, the relatively larger number of South Sudanese refugees, approximately 20,000 (Lucas et al. 2011), accepted for resettlement in Australia between 2003 and 2007; and, second, the concerns voiced by both the government and the South Sudanese community regarding their settlement outcomes (Dhanji 2009; Hebbani et al. 2010; Milner and Khawaja 2010; Murray 2010), indicating the community to be an "extreme" example of the failures of the resettlement processes. Selection of extreme cases are useful, as they often reflect the purest form of insight into the phenomenon being studied (Bazeley 2013).

Initial snowball and convenience sampling of participants progressed to purposive sampling as the research advanced. Participants were from a mix of South Sudanese ethnic groups, the majority being Dinka and Nuer. Their age ranged between eighteen and fifty years, and about one-third of them were women. A third of the participants stated that they had a tertiary education and another third a secondary education. Remaining participants had either a primary level of education or no formal education. About half of the participants were married but did not always cohabit with their partner. About one-third of the participants were employed, and nearly all participants were pursuing some form of education or training.

Formal interviews were between thirty- and ninety-minutes long. All participants were interviewed in English, which most could speak well.[2] Data were analyzed and increasingly abstracted using constant comparative methods of grounded theory. While interviews were the primary source of data, my engagement with the community, such as attending community celebrations and church services, helped to contextualize findings emerging from interviews. This use of multiple data sources brought layered, yet convergent meanings to the research (Bazeley 2013).

Quantitative Data

Quantitative data were drawn from Wave 1 of the Longitudinal Study of Humanitarian Migrants or Building a New Life in Australia (BNLA) survey performed in 2014. BNLA is a longitudinal survey of humanitarian migrants that was commissioned by the Department of Social Services and collected across Australia. The sample was drawn from a database of resettled refugees who had been granted visas through Australia's humanitarian program and had arrived in Australia three to six months prior to the interview.[3]

This chapter uses data from all 1,798 adult respondents between the ages of twenty-one and fifty-five.

Since results from the qualitative and quantitative analysis are reported in separate sections–as they are related to two different, although closely related samples–inferences and interpretations are integrated in the discussion section.

Results from Qualitative Research with the South Sudanese Australian Community

Participants were aware of the important role of employment for successful resettlement, and they reported a strong desire to work and to become economically self-sufficient. But, despite desiring and expecting economic participation, the unemployment rate of 30 percent among the Sudanese-born population is almost six times that of the overall Australian population (Australian Bureau of Statistics 2012). Further, those employed are often underemployed and/or clustered in low occupational status immigrant employment niches (Correa-Velez and Onsand 2009).

Participants saw employment as the main pathway to their goal to move from their refugee status and to become an included and contributing member of their new society. At a public event in Canberra celebrating the first anniversary of South Sudanese independence, the local community leader put the following public request to the minister for multicultural affairs:

> Many of our people from South Sudan are now educated at universities as economists, legal and health professional or are qualified workers in the fields of childcare, community work, or aged care, but they are not given the opportunity to work. We want the opportunity to contribute to this society. We do not want to stay refugees relying on service providers forever. (first anniversary celebration of South Sudan's independence, 21 July 2012, Canberra)

Employment was also seen as an important opening to become active members and to learn in their new social environment about its practices, norms, and values. It was also seen as an opportunity for both immigrants and members of the host society to learn about each other's culture and build social connections. As expressed by one of the participants:

> Employment is the best and the quickest way to integrate. . . . For example, if I work with you, then you can learn my culture and the others working in other companies–from there our image in the society gets communicated and we kind of, you know, will believe that we are part of this society. (young male South Sudanese participant)

Indeed, stable and meaningful employment is critical for successful settlement; it provides an income and a sense of security and enables the development of social networks and cultural skills, which are vital for integration. It also contributes to psychological and social well-being by enhancing self-esteem and self-sufficiency (Correa-Velez et al. 2015). Conversely, long-term unemployment among refugees is likely to negatively influence settlement, health, and well-being (Abdelkerim and Grace 2012; Fozdar and Torezani 2008).

The main reasons identified by participants for not being able to attain employment included lack of skills and English proficiency, lack of networks and knowledge of the local employment context, discrimination from employers, and a merit-based selection system that fails to recognize the relative disadvantage of refugees. These issues fall into the three conceptual categories of human capital, social capital, and systemic barriers.

Human Capital

Skills and English proficiency is a significant predictor of employment in Australia, and poor English speakers are disproportionately represented among the unemployed (Bureau of Immigration, Multicultural and Population Research 1996). All participants identified the importance of good communication and English skills for participating in the labor market. At the same time they were concerned that the current provision of the Adult Migrant English Program (AMEP) is inadequate for learning a new language, and its delivery does not take into account their limited formal education experience. As explained by one of the South Sudanese community workers:

> They've been to English classes, the CIT classes, for 510 hours without learning A, B, and C. They managed to teach them nothing. And I don't blame them. Many of us are coming from a village where only 1 percent of the women went to school. Just learning to hold a pen took time. (female South Sudanese community worker)

The participant's claim that the current provisions of English classes is inadequate is supported by educational research showing that the process of acquiring a new language requires seven to eleven years (Thomas and Collier 2002) and possibly longer for adult migrants.

Social Capital

Another challenge for obtaining employment identified by participants is the lack of social connections facilitating job search. As expressed by one participant:

"Getting opportunity is based on who you know, not what you know. And that's the problem for our community; we don't have that connection where you can easily access employment opportunities" (young male South Sudanese participant).

Social connections are one of the important domains of Ager and Strang's (2008) conceptual model. Bridging types of social capital (Putnam 2000) are particularly vital mediators of gaining employment.

While participants reported high levels of bonding social capital in their community, they also observed that the value of these connections for finding employment is limited, as very few people in their community have connections with Australian employers in their newly emerging community. Bridging social capital, on the other hand, was reported to be weak. Participants also noted that, despite the importance of these connections for finding a job, employment services did not help them to cultivate these connections.

Systemic Barriers

But the main issue for participants was what they called "hidden racism" in the forms of discrimination and systemic barriers in the Australian employment recruitment practices. A particular concern among participants was the large proportion of graduates in their community with a qualification from Australian universities who cannot find employment.

Many of us are doing factory work, even though we've got skills. We are trying hard to get into the education system so that we can get a better job. But most of us, even though we completed our degree in Australia, we are not getting employment. So we go to the factory. (male South Sudanese participant)

While the employment of first-generation adult refugee migrants in the lower echelons of the labor market is a relatively established trend in Australia, there is a new dimension to the problem: a large proportion of young African Australians with high-level qualifications from Australian universities who cannot find jobs. The "countless African Australian refugees with high-level qualifications who've found it virtually impossible to work in their field of expertise in Australia" even raised the concern of the then finance minister, who concluded that "professional employment opportunities are still heavily influenced by the informal connections of familiarity that attach to people who are well integrated into our society. Outsiders are subtly excluded by a complex web of invisible barriers" (Tanner 2008).

The next section explores whether the claims presented in this section can find support in quantitative analysis of a much larger and more representative sample of the most recent humanitarian migrants in Australia.

Results from Quantitative Analysis of the BNLA

Sample characteristics have confirmed the relatively low level of human capital in terms of formal education and spoken English, but they also indicated considerable personal resources. A considerable proportion, 15 percent, has never been to school and 70 percent reported not being able to speak English at all, or not well. A large proportion of survey respondents were born in long-term high-conflict zones, such as Iraq (40 percent) and Afghanistan (25 percent). Although 33 percent of respondents reported experiencing posttraumatic stress disorder (PTSD), 89 percent of participants had positive self-efficacy[4] and 93 percent reported positive attitudes toward self. Social capital among survey respondents was relatively low, with only 33 percent responding positively about their community support networks. In terms of deprivation, 23 percent of respondents reported experiencing more than one type of hardship due to a shortage of money, compared to only 8 percent in the broader Australian community.[5]

Despite a strong desire among participants to work and be economically independent, only 6 percent were in paid work after six months in Australia, which increased to 18 percent in the subsequent ten months.[6] Lack of published data restricted direct comparison with immigrants from other migration categories for the same period. But a report on settlement outcomes released in 2011 found that after four years living in Australia only 31 percent of humanitarian migrants were employed compared to 50 percent of family migrants and 84 percent of skilled migrants (Australian Survey Research Group Pty Ltd 2011).

Logistic regression of the BNLA data to predict employment found gender, age, time spent in Australia, and English proficiency to be significant predictors. Males were much more likely to be employed than females. Odds of employment increased slightly with age but decreased as people got older. Being employed also improved with time spent in Australia and with increased English proficiency. But education level and employment prior to coming to Australia were not significant predictors of being currently employed. A considerable proportion, 38 percent, held postschool qualifications and 58 percent had work experience prior to coming to Australia. Yet, these personal resources did not improve the likelihood of employment, indicating that current hiring practices undervalue the capabilities of humanitarian migrants. Similarly, while participants reported high self-sufficiency and self-reliance, these personal resources did not translate into improved employment prospects. Interestingly, PTSD did not show a negative impact on gaining employment either.

When looking for work, the majority of refugees turned to family and friends (64 percent), followed by Centrelink and employment agencies (55 percent), employers (48 percent), own community (46 percent), and newspaper and internet (37 percent). Only 19 percent reported looking for work through connections within other communities, confirming limited bridging-type social connections among the most recently arrived refugee communities in Australia.

In terms of the helpfulness of available services, the agency that they found the least helpful was the very agency tasked with helping job seekers find a job—employment agencies. Nearly 40 percent found them to be not at all helpful, and an additional 25 percent a little helpful. This confirms claims made by South Sudanese participants of the qualitative study: employment agencies are unresponsive to the needs of refugees.

The main reasons for finding it hard to get a job converge with reasons identified by the South Sudanese sample. Lack of Australian work experience followed by English proficiency were the leading reasons, with each selected by more than half of the respondents. Lack of skills and qualifications and not being able to get a job in the same occupation previous to coming to Australia were identified by about a third of the respondents. Discrimination, however, was only identified by 6 percent. This discrepancy could relate to the relatively short period survey participants had spent in Australia, compared to South Sudanese participants. As participants were still in the process of enhancing their English and accrediting their qualifications from overseas and acquiring Australian qualifications, the potential for discriminatory practices to arise has been limited.

Discussion

Such a low rate of employment among a population with high aspirational and personal resources, as well as capacities in the form of postschool qualifications and overseas work experience, raises the question of socially structured inequalities in Australian settlement policies and discrimination from employers. Indeed, a number of important large sample size quantitative Australian studies have found higher unemployment rates among refugees compared to other migrants even after controlling for differences in education and English proficiency. While their employment outcomes improved with duration of residence, it continued to lag behind other migrants (Cobb-Clark 2006; Thapa and Gorgens 2006; Vandenheuvel and Wooden 1999). Additionally, employment outcomes did not improve with time at the same rate for all refugees. Some groups, such as those from Africa, continue to experience higher levels of unemployment even after a considerable length of residence (Hugo 2011).

Despite this robust empirical evidence, both employers and the Australian government refuse to acknowledge the connections between policies and practices and the disproportional difficulties faced by refugee migrant groups in Australia in gaining employment. Instead they attribute it to lack of skills and personal characteristics. Employers claim that often refugees do not have the "cultural knowledge" or that they would not "fit in" with other staff. This was often stated as a "soft skill" related to "Australian-ness" (Tilbury and Colic-Peisker 2007). In other words, the subjective concept of "cultural difference" has become an admissible reason, at least in practice, for denying economic participation and inclusion.

As for the government position, the emphasis remains on the characteristics and so-called deficits of refugees. For example in 2016, when reporting on the low employment rate of 18 percent among humanitarian migrants after fifteen months in Australia, the Department of Social Services identified low levels of literacy, little formal schooling, and high rates of mental health problems as a main reason for such low levels of employment (Taylor 2016). This chapter argues that from a policy perspective, individual characteristic should not be seen as deterministic factors, but rather as capacities that can be turned into participation if appropriate pathways are provided. My finding that postschool qualifications and work experience prior to coming to Australia did not improve the odds of participants' employment indicates that the current pathways are inadequate.

For example, English proficiency is the strongest skill-based predictor for employment and is fundamentally linked to good settlement outcomes. But refugees come to Australia with vastly different English skills, and most of them have low levels of English. While English proficiency is viewed by the Australian government as one of the most important indicators of integration and resettlement (Department of Immigration and Citizenship 2006), the current provision of English classes, AMEP, does not deliver the desired outcome. Wave 2 results from the BNLA indicates that only 18 percent of the participants who reported not speaking English at all or not well in Wave 1 reported improved English proficiency a year later.[7]

AMEP provides up to 510 hours of English language tuition to humanitarian entrants and other migrants. In the 2016–2017 budget, the government announced that the AMEP program will be redesigned to improve client participation, including establishing two new service streams–social English and pre-employment English (Refugee Council of Australia 2016). The AMEP redesign is an encouraging development that may create better opportunities for refugees to become proficient in English and subsequently allow increased employment opportunities and effective settlement. Yet there are other important improvements needed. Recent community feedback identified flexible funding options to cater to the diverse needs of learners accessing the program and a more practical, practice-oriented structure and content as especially relevant. There are particular considerations for refugee women who have little or no experience in formal classroom settings while some women from Muslim communities are challenged by lack of access to private transportation, fear of using public transportation, not being allowed to travel unaccompanied, discomfort with mixed-sex classes, and lack of information (Federation of Ethnic Communities' Councils of Australia 2016).

Another area where recognized pathways to employment remain unsupported is fostering work experience opportunities and connections to potential employers—both acute needs among refugee migrant job seekers. Lack of Australian work experience prevents migrant jobseekers from competing with other applicants in the labor market. Their lack of connections beyond family and friends limits their capacity to be more successful at searching for and obtaining employment. As established by research, it is the ties beyond family and friends that provide a bridge to new work-related networks (Granovetter 1983). Yet employment agencies—private enterprises founded by the government—fail to assist in the development of connections to potential employers or opportunities for work experience. Both qualitative and quantitative results of this research found employment agencies to be unresponsive to the needs of refugees. Rather, they see their role as "expert mediators" between the unemployed and potential employers and providers of training to job seekers (Tilbury and Colic-Peisker 2007).

There are a number of potential reasons employment agencies are unresponsive to the needs of refugees, including institutional inertia, lack of appropriate skills, and contractual disincentives. Contractual arrangements and remuneration of employment services depend on the number of clients serviced and/or placed in employment. Refugees represent a relatively small proportion of the total client pool of mainstream agencies, yet they have very specific needs that require employment agencies to go outside of their routine activities. Under the current arrangement, responding to the specific needs of clients from a refugee background does not make a good business case.

Of course, labor market discrimination cannot be seen in isolation from government policy and lack of government action to fix the evident systemic flaw in Australian recruitment processes. As one non-Sudanese community worker commented:

> We should be a bit more thoughtful of what we are going to do with the people when they come to the country. Like 13,000 people a year is a lot of people when they don't know what they are doing and the support from the government is rather pathetic. They just give out the settlement grants to different organizations, but a lot of the people don't get any benefits. There are no structural responses from government. It is a kind of a minimalist approach. We take these people to keep the UN happy and then we give the funding to these organizations to look after them and hopefully it will work. (non-Sudanese community worker)

So what is the reason behind the Australian government's reluctance to fix the dissonance between pathways and programs as delivered and their policy objectives?

The standard method of recruitment in Australia applied to all job applicants, including those from a refugee background, is merit-based selection. The mechanism is believed to deliver equal access and opportunity to *all* members of Australian society. It follows an assessment based on the candidate's work-related and personal qualities, including demonstrated experience, preferably in Australia, of the skills required. This benchmark is hard to attain for most refugees, who, because of their refugee experience, are not entering the labor market on equal terms with people who grew up in Australia. In other words, the application of mainstream recruitment mechanisms, without provisions for disadvantaged groups, restricts access to refugees and other disadvantaged groups and thus systemically discriminates against them.

In summary, Australia's current resettlement practices are delivering poorly in both performative and practical dimensions. In the global context, the shortcomings of the Australian government's human rights obligations have been noted by the United Nations. Resettlement countries commit themselves to providing appropriate services, infrastructure, and support necessary for the integration of refugees, including the creation of equal access and opportunities to ensure participation and actively promote an inclusive and welcoming society (UNHCR 2011 and see van Selm, this volume). In its response to Australia's fifteenth to seventeenth periodic reports to the United Nations Committee on the Elimination of Racial Discrimination (UNCERD), the committee drew particular attention to the multiple forms of discrimination experienced by some groups, including African Australians. The committee recommended that Australia strengthen the racial and cultural dimensions of its Social Inclusion Agenda (UNCERD 2010: 3).

In the domestic context, many refugees experience severe social and economic problems. My analysis of the BNLA found that over 23 percent of participants experienced more than one type of hardship due to shortage of money, compared to only 8 percent in the broader Australian community.[8] Such economic marginalization of refugees prevents them from fully participating in or belonging to the broader community. In other words, while the Australian government gives legal permission to refugees to resettle in Australia, they are not afforded the same living standards and opportunities enjoyed by the broader Australian society.

Conclusion

This chapter critically examined Australia's refugee resettlement program and the reasons for adverse economic and social outcomes among refugees. I have argued that the main reason lies in labor market discrimination and lack of government action and policy to provide refugees accessible pathways for inclusion. Yet, Australia is not unique in failing to have effective policies and programs to assist the integration of refugees. Countries, such as Sweden, Norway, and Belgium, also have very high-level unemployment and subsequent marginalization of refugees (Eurostat 2014). Despite being given equal foundational principles and rights, a large number of them remain "outside the system."

Can we generalize from the findings of this Australian case study to explain general trends in economic outcomes for resettled refugees in so-called Western countries? I propose that we can. The findings of my study that by simply giving equal rights and equal access to social institution and structures will not lead to good integration outcomes is not limited to Australia. It applies to any situation in which the state fails to take additional steps to ensure that equal rights principles give people substantive rather than formal, equal opportunities. Following the approach to power presented in the volume's introduction, one could say that the inability of governments to ensure enforcement of the principle of equal rights for resettled refugees considerably reduces the negotiating power of many refugees, as it deprives them of options to improve their socioeconomic situation.

The failure to ensure equal rights is a more subtle way to exclude forced migrants from Australian society than the country's established policy of isolation of asylum seekers in faraway detention centers (Garnier 2014), yet it is equally concerning. Further, this points at the hypocrisy of the Australian government's insistence on the greater "humanitarian worth" of resettled refugees as opposed to asylum seekers and, in this context, at the limits of care at the core of Australia's official humanitarian migration program, whereas selection and admission control mechanisms are manifold. This chapter's analysis thus contributes to this volume's critical exploration of refugee resettlement as humanitarian governance.

Despite increasing evidence of the systemic exclusion of refugees it is generally not acknowledged, and the narrative is dominated by claims that particular migrant groups are prone to adopt nonfunctional behaviors. However, as argued by Merton (1968), it is not members of particular groups that have dysfunctional behavior; rather it is elements of institutions that are generally functional for some but dysfunctional for others. In other words, social structures affect not only outcomes for people but also the strategies and behaviors they adopt. The structural imbalance of power in which resettled refugees find themselves undermines their capacity and determination to economically and socially integrate. Difference-blind recruitment practices imposed by the government tends to block the pathways to economic participation of refugee migrants, while discrimination in the labor market seems to coerce refugees to be unemployed or underemployed. Lack of government action to address these structural problems, and scapegoating particular groups instead, can lead to the systemic marginalization of refugees and the stigmatization of particular communities.

Ibolya (Ibi) Losoncz holds a Ph.D. in regulation, justice, and diplomacy from the Australian National University, Canberra, where she is a postdoctoral research fellow at the School of Regulation and Global Governance (RegNet). Losoncz's research focuses on the interplay between individual and institutional elements of integration and their impact on the resettlement trajectories of humanitarian migrants and their families. Previously, she was a senior research analyst at various institutions. She has published in *Journal of Refugee Studies, Child Abuse and Neglect, Australian Social Policy,* and *The Australian and New Zealand Journal of Criminology.* Her broader research interests include the African diaspora, institutional legitimacy, empirical evaluation, and research design.

Notes

1. For example, women admitted under the woman-at-risk visa subcategory.
2. Participants had considerably higher levels of English proficiency than the wider South Sudanese Australian community. Follow-up discussion with participants indicated that the issues and experiences discussed are shared across the community, especially among those with greater cultural gaps and lower English proficiency.
3. Onshore visa holders had to have received their permanent protection visas in the same period.
4. Self-assessed ability to accomplish goals, think of good solutions, and handle whatever comes one's way.
5. Information on hardship for the broader Australian community is based on the author's analysis of data from the Household, Income and Labour Dynamics in Australia (HILDA) survey, Wave 13, 2013.
6. Results from Wave 2 data. The limited number of survey items collected in Wave 2 does not allow the use of this more recent data to identify significant predictors of employment.
7. Author's analysis of BNLA Waves 1 and 2.
8. Author's analysis of data collected from the HILDA survey, Wave 13, 2013.

References

Abdelkerim, A. Abdelkerim, and Marty Grace. 2012. "Challenges to Employment in Newly Emerging African Communities in Australia: A Review of the Literature." *Australian Social Work Journal* 65(1): 104–19.

Abur, William, and Ramon Spaaij 2016. "Settlement and Employment Experiences of South Sudanese People from Refugee Background in Melbourne, Australia." *Australasian Review of African Studies* 37(2): 107–18.

Ager, Alastair, and Alison Strang. 2008. "Understanding Integration: A Conceptual Framework." *Journal of Refugee Studies* 21(2): 166–91.

Australian Bureau of Statistics. 2012. *Labour Force, Australia.* Vol. 6202.0. Canberra: Australian Bureau of Statistics.

——. 2016. *Migration, Australia, 2014–15.* Vol. 3412.0. Canberra: Australian Bureau of Statistics.

Australian Survey Research Group Pty Ltd. 2011. *Settlement Outcomes of New Arrivals–Study for Department of Immigration and Citizenship.* Canberra: Department of Immigration and Citizenship.

Bazeley, Pat. 2013. *Qualitative Data Analysis: Practical Strategies.* London: Sage.

Bureau of Immigration, Multicultural, and Population Research. 1996. *English Proficiency and Immigrant Groups.* Vol. 1. Canberra: Bureau of Immigration.

Charmaz, Kathy. 2006. *Constructing Grounded Theory: A Practical Guide through Qualitative Analysis.* Thousand Oaks: Sage.

Cobb-Clark, Deborah. 2006. "Selection Policy and the Labour Market Outcomes of New Immigrants." In *Public Policy and Immigrant Settlement,* edited by Deborah Cobb-Clark and Siew Ean Khoo, 27–52. Cheltenham: Edward Elgar.

Colic-Peisker, Val, and Farida Tilbury. 2007. "Integration into the Australian Labour Market: The Experience of the Three 'Visibly Different' Groups of Recently Arrived Refugees." *International Migration* 45(1): 59–85.

Correa-Velez, Ignacio, Adrian G. Barnett, and Sandra M. Gifford. 2015. "Working for a Better Life: Longitudinal Evidence on the Predictors of Employment among Recently Arrived Refugee Migrant Men Living in Australia." *International Migration* 53(2): 321–37.

Correa-Velez, Ignacio, and Gerald Onsando. 2009. "Educational and Occupational Outcomes amongst African Men from Refugee Backgrounds Living in Urban and Regional Southeast Queensland." *The Australasian Review of African Studies* 30(2): 114–27.

Danermark, Berth, Mats Ekström, Liselotte Jakobsen, and Jan Ch. Karlsson. 2002. *Explaining Society. Critical Realism in the Social Sciences.* Abingdon: Routledge.

Department of Immigration and Citizenship. 2006. *The Evolution of Australia's Multicultural Policy.* Canberra: Australian Government.

——. 2011. *Refugee and Humanitarian Issues: Australia's Response.* Canberra: Australian Government.

Department of Social Services. 2015. *Settlement Needs Information.* Canberra: Australian Government.

Dhanji, Surjeet. 2009. "Welcome or Unwelcome? Integration Issues and the Resettlement of Former Refugees from the Horn of Africa and Sudan in Metropolitan Melbourne." *The Australasian Review of African Studies* 30(2): 152–78.

Eurostat. 2014. *Labour Force Survey: Ad Hoc Module on the Labour Market Situation of Migrants and Their Immediate Descendants.* Luxembourg: Eurostat.

Federation of Ethnic Communities' Councils of Australia. 2016. *Australia's Growing Linguistic Diversity: An Opportunity for a Strategic Approach to Language Services Policy and Practice.* Canberra: FECCA.

Fozdar, Farida, and Silvia Torezani. 2008. "Discrimination and Well-Being: Perceptions of Refugees in Western Australia." *International Migration Review* 42(1): 30–63.

Garnier, Adèle. 2014. "Migration Management and Humanitarian Protection: The UNHCR's 'Resettlement Expansionism' and Its Impact on Policy-Making in the EU and Australia." *Journal of Ethnic and Migration Studies* 40(6): 942–59.

Granovetter, Mark. 1983. "The Strength of Weak Ties: A Network Theory Revisited." *Sociological Theory* 1: 203–33.

Hebbani, Aparna, Levi Obijiofor, and Helen Bristed. 2010. "Intercultural Communication Challenges Confronting Female Sudanese Former Refugees in Australia." *Australasian Review of African Studies* 31: 37–61.

Hugo, Graeme. 2011. *Economic, Social and Civic Contributions of First and Second Generation Humanitarian Entrants.* Canberra: Department of Immigration and Citizenship.

Iosifides, Theodoros. 2012. "Migration Research between Positivistic Scientism and Relativism: A Critical Realist Way Out." In *Handbook of Research Methods in Migration,* edited by Carlos Vargas-Silva, 26–49. Cheltenham: Edward Elgar.

Jupp, James. 2007. *From White Australia to Woomera: The Story of Australian Immigration.* 2nd ed. Cambridge: Cambridge University Press.

Kelly, Ross, and Philip E. T. Lewis. 2003. *The Changing Pattern of Skill Demand in the Australian Economy.* Centre of Labour Market Research Discussion Paper Series, vol. 03/2, The University of Western Australia and University of Canberra.

Kenny, Mark. 2016. "Australia to Take Central American Refugees as Malcolm Turnbull Pledges to Do More at Obama Summit." *Sydney Morning Herald,* 21 September. Accessed 7 February 2017. http://www.smh.com.au/federal-politics/political-news/australia-to-take-central-american-refugees-as-malcolm-turnbull-pledges-to-do-more-at-obama-summit-20160920-grkcq9.html.

Kunz, Egon F. 1981. "Exile and Resettlement: Refugee Theory." *International Migration Review* 15(1/2): 42–51.

Lancee, Bram. 2010. "The Economic Returns of Immigrants' Bonding and Bridging Social Capital: The Case of the Netherlands." *International Migration Review* 44(1): 202–26.

Loeescher, Gill, and James Milner. 2009. "Understanding the Challenge." *Forced Migration Review* 33: 9–11.

Losoncz, Ibolya. 2017a. "Goals without Means: A Mertonian Critique of Australia's Resettlement Policy for South Sudanese Refugees." *Journal of Refugee Studies* 30(1): 47–70. http://jrs.oxfordjournals.org/content/early/2015/12/04/jrs.fev017.full.pdf+html.

——. 2017b. "Methodological Approaches and Considerations in Regulatory Research." In *Regulation, Institutions and Networks,* edited by P. Drahos, 77–95. Canberra: ANU Press.

Lucas, David, Monica Jamali, and Barbara Edgar. 2011. "The Sudan-Born in Australia: A Statistical Profile." *Australasian Review of African Studies* 32(2): 10–24.

McBeth, Adam, Justine Nolan, and Simon Rice. 2011. *The International Law of Human Rights.* Oxford: Oxford University Press.

Merton, Robert K. 1968. *Social Theory and Social Structure.* New York: Free Press.

Milner, Karla, and Nigar G. Khawaja. 2010. "Sudanese Refugees in Australia: The Impact of Acculturation Stress." *Journal of Pacific Rim Psychology* 4(1): 19–29.

Murray, Kate E. 2010. "Sudanese Perspectives on Resettlement in Australia." *Journal of Pacific Rim Psychology* 4(1): 30–43.

Putnam, Robert D. 2000. *Bowling Alone: The Collapse and Revival of American Community*. New York: Simon & Schuster.

Refugee Council of Australia. 2016. *2016–17 Federal Budget: What It Means for Refugees and People Seeking Humanitarian Protection*. Sydney: Refugee Council of Australia.

Stewart, Emma. 2009. *The Integration and Onward Migration of Refugees in Scotland: A Review of the Evidence*. New Issues in Refugee Research 174. Geneva: UNHCR.

Stone, Wendy, Matthew Gray, and Jody Hughes. 2003. *Social Capital at Work: How Family, Friends and Civic Ties Relate to Labour Market Outcomes*. Research Paper No. 31. Melbourne: Australian Institute of Family Studies.

Tanner, Lindsay. 2008. "African-Australians Confronted by Challenges." *Business Day Blogs*, 4 August. Accessed 7 February 2017. http://blogs.theage.com.au/busiess/lindsaytanner/2008/08/04/africanaustrali.html.

Taylor, David, producer. 2016. "Humanitarian Migrants Finding It Easier to Land a Job, Research Shows." *AM*, 6 July. Accessed 7 February 2017. http://www.abc.net.au/am/content/2016/s4495244.htm.

Thapa, Prem J., and Tue Gorgens. 2006. "Finding Employment after Migration: How Long Does It Take?" In *Public Policy and Immigrant Settlement*, edited by Deborah Cobb-Clark and Siew Ean Khoo, 53–86. Cheltenham: Edward Elgar.

Thomas, Wayne, and Virginia P. Collier. 2002. *A National Study of School Effectiveness for Language Minority Students' Long-Term Academic Achievement: Final Report*. Santa Cruz, CA: Center for Research on Education, Diversity and Excellence.

Tilbury, Farida, and Val Colic-Peisker. 2007. "Skilled Refugees, Employment and Social Inclusion: A Perth Case Study of Three Communities." In *Settling in Australia: The Social Inclusion of Refugees*, edited by Val Colic-Peisker and Farida Tilbury, 108–27. Perth: Centre for Social and Community Research, Murdoch University.

United Nations High Commissioner for Refugees (UNHCR). 2011. *UNHCR Resettlement Handbook*. Geneva: UNHCR.

———. 2016. *Global Trends: Forced Displacement in 2015*. Geneva: UNHCR.

United Nations Committee on the Elimination of Racial Discrimination (UNCERD). 2010. *Consideration of Reports Submitted by States Parties under Article 9 of the Convention: Concluding Observations of the Committee on the Elimination of Racial Discrimination, Seventy-Seventh Session*. Vol. CERD/C/AUS/CO/15–17. New York: CERD.

Valenta, Marko, and Nihad Bunar. 2010. "State Assisted Integration: Refugee Integration Policies in Scandinavian Welfare States: The Swedish and Norwegian Experience." *Journal of Refugee Studies* 23(4): 463–83.

Valtonen, Kathleen. 2004. "From the Margin to the Mainstream: Conceptualizing Refugee Settlement Processes." *Journal of Refugee Studies* 17(1): 70–96.

Vandenheuvel, Adriana, and Mark Wooden. 1999. *New Settlers Have Their Say—How Immigrants Fare over the Early Years of Settlement*. Canberra: Department of Immigration and Multicultural Affairs.

Waxman, Peter. 2001. "The Economic Adjustment of Recently Arrived Bosnian, Afghan and Iraqi Refugees in Sydney, Australia." *International Migration Review* 35(2): 472–505.

7

Shaping the Political Space for Resettlement

The Debate on Burden Sharing in Norway Following the Syrian Refugee Crisis

Linn Marie Reklev and Maria Gabrielsen Jumbert

Introduction

The Syria crisis has put the question of resettlement and so-called burden sharing on the top of the agenda of the international refugee protection regime, including governments, international organizations, and non-governmental organizations (NGOs). According to the United Nations (UN), by March 2016, more than half of the population had been forced to flee their homes (UN 2016). The situation has had major implications for Syria's neighboring countries, with more than four million Syrian refugees located in Syria's nearby region by May 2016 (UNHCR 2016b). Accordingly, the international community has recognized that Syria's neighboring states are hosting an unsustainable share of the refugee "burden." Burden-sharing initiatives including resettlement, humanitarian admissions, and financial aid have thus been launched in response (UNHCR 2016a).

This chapter will address the particular case of Norway, traditionally a significant humanitarian actor–in particular with regards to resettlement–on the international stage. More specifically, the chapter looks at the relationship between burden sharing as an international norm and Norwegian political discourses in the context of the Syrian refugee crisis. It asks the following question: How have the dominant discourses on Norway's responsibilities vis-à-vis populations displaced by the crisis in Syria and the hierarchy between these discourses shaped the political space–for action and, in the longer term, for burden sharing in refugee protection? This question is especially relevant because Norway, in line with the Scandinavian tradition, promotes itself both nationally and internationally as a humanitarian power and a "peace nation," and as a prominent actor in the field of refugee protection (for discussions of comparable national motivations, see Darrow; Garnier; Losoncz; Jubilut and Zamur, this volume).

As seen in the introduction to this volume, framing resettlement as a form of humanitarian governance, Norway's involvement is a means to not only take its share of the burden but also to influence how refugee resettlement is defined and implemented. Yet this approach has been contested in the debates on the Syria crisis. Political support to the humanitarian approach that has often been seen as almost a given has in this context competed with other political discourses that emphasize interests and values embedded in "the national." Thus, looking at these different discourses and the political space they create allows for a better understanding of how various policies and responses regarding refugee protection and resettlement come into being, how power works through such discourses, and how the image projected internationally is negotiated domestically (see, for instance, Barnett and Duvall 2005).

Norway is the sixth largest humanitarian donor to operations both within Syria and in the region (Norad 2015), as well as a significant actor in terms of physical burden-sharing initiatives. As of April 2016, Norway had pledged 9,000 resettlement places for Syrians (UNHCR 2016a). Yet, this has come about amid intense political debates on the domestic arena, and we posit here that how burden sharing is applied and implemented to a large extent depends on such domestic political processes. In the analysis, we draw upon theoretical and methodological insights from the disciplines of political science, sociology, and international relations.

The Norwegian political landscape has a tradition of being consensus based, with solidarity as a cornerstone value. Governments have in the past few decades shifted between right-wing coalitions and governments led by the Social Democrat Labor Party, until the latter had to enter a coalition with the Socialist Party and Centre Party in 2005 to ensure a majority. Overall, Norway has taken in relatively few refugees and resettles, compared to Sweden for example. Today, however, a rapidly growing immigrant population and the attacks on 22 July 2011 by a right-wing extremist provide some of the backdrop against which the debate unfolds. In addition, as Norway has grown wealthy thanks to its oil, the recent drop in oil prices has had implications for the resources made politically available for refugee protection initiatives, and has also affected the general perception of Norwegian society's capacity to receive. We identify three dominant discourses in the

Norwegian political field: a humanitarian discourse, a cost-and-capacity discourse, and a nation-state discourse.

The humanitarian discourse is based largely on international humanitarian and refugee protection norms and stresses the need for global solidarity. The cost-and-capacity discourse is heavily influenced by market liberalist economic ideas and emphasizes the importance of balancing international demands with (perceived) national capacities. Finally, the nation-state discourse encompasses a view of Norway as an independent and sovereign nation-state, which must act on the basis of its domestic interests. The chapter argues that these three discourses take part in discursive battles in the political field and that the outcome of these battles shapes the political space for action in terms of Norwegian burden-sharing initiatives. The hierarchy and power relationships between these discourses therefore have significant policy consequences.

The chapter proceeds as follows: first, we briefly discuss the role of burden sharing in the policy and academic literature and the methodological choices of the analysis. We then present the three dominant discourses and analyze the hierarchy between them. Further, we discuss the political space these discourses created for different forms of burden sharing. Finally, the chapter will review how the hierarchy of discourses has influenced Norwegian debates on burden sharing.

Concepts and Methodology

Burden sharing between states is a significant normative principle in international refugee protection (Feller 2006). The normative significance of burden sharing is particularly highlighted by the United Nations High Commissioner for Refugees (UNHCR)'s focus on encouraging increased burden sharing between states in its policy activities (Sandvik and Lindskov Jacobsen 2016). For instance, the UNHCR Executive Committee meeting in October 2004 provided a conclusion document titled *Conclusion on International Cooperation and Burden and Responsibility Sharing in Mass Influx Situations* that stressed the importance of solidarity with host countries of mass refugee populations and the value of, and need for, enhanced burden and responsibility sharing in these situations (UNHCR 2004). UNHCR (2015) also considers resettlement a durable solution to the refugee situation. Burden sharing has also been a significant topic in the academic literature addressing refugee protection issues, as seen notably through scholarly work on states' involvement in international cooperation on refugee resettlement (van Selm 2003; Garnier 2014; and van Selm, this volume).

Suhrke (1998) in her analysis in particular looks at the disincentives for regional or international burden-sharing schemes in the field of refugee protection, showing that states may to a greater extent than in other areas bank on "going it alone," rather than risking engaging in taking an unknown number of displaced persons in the future. Further, Thielemann (2003; Thielemann and Dewan 2006) operates with two logics of action, the "norm-based" and the "cost-benefit" logics, as conceptualized in political sociology, to analyze different drivers of engaging in burden sharing at the interstate level. However, there has been little focus in this field on how burden sharing is interpreted and implemented in specific national contexts, a criticism that also has been faced by the norms literature in international relations more generally (Hopf 2002). This chapter thus attempts to address this gap by focusing specifically on burden sharing in the Norwegian context.

The analysis is organized around two events that have shaped the political debate in Norway on this issue: the so-called Syria Agreement (*Syria-forliket*) and what has come to be referred to as the (European) "refugee crisis." The Syria Agreement is a political agreement on a special resettlement quota for Syrian refugees, developed in spring 2015 (Bergens Tidene 2015). The European refugee crisis in this context refers to the late summer and fall of 2015, when the number of migrants and refugees seeking to cross the borders of Europe rapidly increased. We address in particular the political debates and struggles in the period from late August 2015 until the EU meeting on relocation in Brussels on 14 September 2015, a relatively brief time period but characterized by extensive political debate and media coverage of the situation.[1]

Three Discourses in the Norwegian Political Landscape

A range of actors are involved in the field of refugee protection in Norway, including political parties and individuals within them, civil society, public institutions, and the research community. The quota for how many resettles Norway is to receive is decided politically in the Norwegian Parliament every year, and then the Ministry of Justice and Public Security decides which main groups to prioritize. The Norwegian Directorate for Immigration, situated under the ministry, is in charge of processing the applications for resettlement from the UNHCR and decides who gets to come. The sitting government (2013–2017)–with the Conservative Party and the Progress Party–generally promotes a strict refugee and asylum policy, and in particular, the Progress Party has made a tougher immigration policy a cornerstone of their policy. However, as a minority government, they are sensitive to competing discourses within the field. The Labor Party is the country's largest political party; it is situated in the center left of the political spectrum and promotes a center-oriented asylum policy.

Further, the government-supporting parties–the Christian Democrats and the Liberal Party (which is on the conservative side but close to the center)–have been active in the current debate, with a somewhat stronger focus on a humane asylum policy and international solidarity than the government parties have (Venstre 2018; Kristelig Folkeparti 2016). The Socialist Left Party is positioned to the left of the Labor Party and is arguably the strongest proponent of a liberal asylum policy in the Norwegian Parliament. In the Syria Agreement, both the Progress Party and the Socialist Left Party chose to leave the negotiations.

The Progress Party was against increasing the number of resettlements, arguing that they wished to concentrate on providing aid in Syria's neighborhood (Nesvik 2015). The Socialist Left Party, on the other hand, did not find the agreement ambitious enough (Sosialistisk Venstreparti 2015). A number of civil society actors have also been active in the debate, as exemplified by "The Syria Platform," created by eleven of the largest humanitarian NGOs in Norway through which they coordinate their national political advocacy activities. Moreover, the new volunteer organization Refugees Welcome to Norway (RWTN) experienced a large increase in members when refugees started to arrive in Norway in high numbers.

The core ideas identified in the textual analysis characterize and define the Norwegian political debate on burden sharing in the context of the Syria crisis. The textual analysis related to the Syria Agreement revealed different ideational positions concerning the following issues: (1) where to locate the help and how to prioritize between "helping them here or where they are," (2) the level of commitment to international values and normative obligations, and (3) what morality on behalf of political actors entails. As for the texts related to the European refugee crisis, we identified the following issues of contention: (i) Norway's role in Europe, and the importance of European solidarity, (ii) the relative importance of international solidarity versus (perceived) national interests, (iii) the policy implications of effective humanitarian initiatives, and (iv) the need to rethink mechanisms for burden sharing and refugee protection. These core ideas are partly constituted by the different discourses, while they also take part in constituting the different discourses themselves. Uncovering these ideas enables us to identify the three main discourses in the Norwegian political field: the humanitarian discourse, the cost-and-capacity discourse, and the nation-state discourse, which we will now review.

The Humanitarian Discourse

The humanitarian discourse draws upon ideas and norms embedded in international humanitarian law and the human rights framework. These include the responsibility to protect vulnerable people, in particular in situations of conflict, as well as the need to promote and protect political, social, and economic rights for the individual (see Sandvik; Thomson, this volume). In this way, the humanitarian discourse frames burden sharing as *responsibility* sharing because all states have a common responsibility to protect refugees. In the Norwegian context specifically, the humanitarian discourse is deeply rooted in the idea of Norway's heritage as a humanitarian nation. It also has a particular history with regard to refugee protection, in which the figure of Fridtjof Nansen is a central reference point. For instance, Pål Nesse (2015 interview) notes, "Norway is a country one looks to internationally in the refugee context . . . 'everybody' knows that Nansen was the first High Commissioner. . . . Norway has an international reputation when it comes to refugee work."

The Norwegian humanitarian discourse is largely constituted by domestic actors' perception of Norway as a country that acts upon humanitarian principles at home and abroad (compare Vera Espinoza; Lewis and Young, this volume). The UN plays a strong role in this discourse and is accorded significant moral authority and legitimacy, despite its arguably imperfect practice. Consequently, the discourse emphasizes that UN policy and principles must be guiding Norwegian politics independently of whether domestic actors perceive these recommendations as being inconvenient or undesirable for Norway's perceived self-interest (Vevstad interview 2015; Sosialistisk Venstreparti 2015; Egenæs et al. 2015). In general, a defining feature of the discourse is that international norms and principles must have a central place in the making of domestic policies.

More specifically, key concepts in the humanitarian discourse revolve around "solidarity," "morality," "*dugnad*" (Norwegian term for collective effort), and "human and political rights," which we will go through in the following. First, solidarity is a significant *nodal point* in the humanitarian discourse and provides the core argument for burden sharing (Thielemann 2003; UNHCR 2014; Sosialistisk Venstreparti 2015). Solidarity is understood in this discourse in two ways. First, solidarity is directed toward the refugees themselves, based on traditional humanitarian values, including the need to protect civilians and vulnerable persons independently of who they are. Second, the concept of solidarity refers to states in the region who are hosting a very large share of the refugee population, with a conception of the international community as being responsible for displaced populations. These understandings of solidarity are key drivers for concrete measures of responsibility sharing.

Since the beginning of the European refugee crisis, the humanitarian discourse has first and foremost applied the notion of solidarity in the European context. Some actors largely associated with the humanitarian discourse compare Norway's engagement explicitly with those of Sweden and

Germany, which have been in the lead of European refugee protection responses (Lysbakken 2015), and with that advocate a proactive humanitarian role for Norway in Europe. Interestingly, this notion of European solidarity has seemingly nothing to do with the question of EU membership. Instead, it emphasizes that Norway must act upon this solidarity simply because it takes part in a European community based upon shared commitments and responsibilities (NRK 2015b).

Each of the discourses promotes a specific perception of morality. In the humanitarian discourse, morality is first and foremost embedded in the international. Norway is understood as having a moral responsibility toward affected states and the refugees themselves. This moral responsibility can only be fulfilled if Norway provides financial aid abroad and protection to vulnerable refugees at home. Hence, with regard to the debate on "helping them here versus helping them where they are," which has been prominent in the Norwegian debate following the Syrian crisis, the answer is that both aspects are necessary (Egenæs et al. 2015; Arbeiderpartiet 2015). In particular, the humanitarian discourse emphasizes the need to provide protection in Norway to the *most vulnerable* who cannot be protected in the nearby area (Meyer 2015 interview).

Dugnad can be understood as another nodal point in the humanitarian discourse. It is applied in relation to both international and national refugee protection initiatives and encourages a joint voluntary effort on all levels of society because it is for the common good (Egenæs et al. 2015). As such, the concept is closely tied to burden sharing: everyone is encouraged to do what they can so that Norway can take its share of the international burden. The discourse emphasizes "innovation," "improvisation," and a need to "use all the tools in the toolbox" (Nesse 2015 interview; Meyer 2015 interview). Therefore, many of its adherents have criticized the lack of political will among the political leadership to undertake innovative measures. Simultaneously, the discourse suppresses concerns for capacities and costs, seen as something that will "work itself out" eventually.

Finally, the humanitarian discourse is also influenced by a strong emphasis on rights, although with differing perspectives according to the actors, which has also led to some tensions within the discourse (Meyer 2015 interview; Austenå 2015 interview). Although human rights and humanitarian discourses often support each other, notably in what has come to be called the human rights–based approach in humanitarianism (Sandvik 2013), they also have certain differences that may affect potential policy outcomes, as discussed notably by Fassin (2012) and Feldman and Ticktin (2010). For instance, certain humanitarian actors note that the dominance of the human rights perspective in the humanitarian field risks preventing the development of more innovative and efficient protection initiatives, which encompass the needs and interests of all stakeholders, including the population inside Syria and the host communities in the neighboring countries (Meyer 2015 interview).

The Cost-and-Capacity Discourse

A mix of political and economic ideas makes up the cost-and-capacity discourse. In particular, the cost-and-capacity discourse rests upon a notion of rationality and a priority given to cost-benefit considerations in all refugee protection initiatives. Key terms in the discourse relate to "efficiency," and it advocates a balanced relationship between national and international, with also its specific view on what is moral.

"Efficiency" is a nodal point in the costs-and-capacity discourse and is used as a "normative-political concept" that often justifies financial burden sharing over physical protection initiatives (Betts 2006: 151). Betts (2006: 152, 167) notes that this justification is largely based on the principles of the "optimum allocation of resources" and comparative advantage, which is derived mainly from economic theory. In particular, comparative advantage in the field of burden sharing is based upon states' comparative capacities for physical or financial forms of protection. Consequently, wealthy northern states such as Norway normally have a comparative advantage in terms of financial burden sharing. This argumentation has characterized much of the political debate on burden sharing in the wake of the crisis in Syria. In the "helping them here or helping them where they are" debate, the proponents of the cost-and-capacity discourse have continuously stressed that it is more efficient and effective to provide financial aid because you can then help more people with the same resources (Nesvik 2015; NTB 2015a).

As Nesvik (2015) phrases it: "We show political responsibility by using the resources to help where the help matters the most." The discourse shows a somewhat ambiguous relationship to humanitarian ideals. On the one hand it advocates that the help should reach the most people possible, and on the other it suppresses the emphasis of the humanitarian discourse on the need to help the most vulnerable by providing them protection in Norway when they cannot be sufficiently protected in the nearby region.

The cost-and-capacity discourse promotes a rather balanced view regarding the importance of the national and the international. The UN is still considered an important and legitimate institution whose recommendations are of value in the domestic political context. However, these must always be weighed against the concerns of national actors and institutions and their capacities (Hillestad 2015; NTB 2015b). The economic perspective is particularly important: since refugee protection is a costly process that demands great resources, the discourse promotes a careful approach to the implementation of international norms and principles.

The cost-and-capacity discourse also promotes a particular perception of morality and, more specifically, a form of "rational political morality." In this view, it is *morally* right to opt for a rational and efficient refugee policy founded on economic calculations, rather than conducting policies seen as driven by emotions and naivety. Such policies do hold symbolic value, as the cost-and-capacity discourse plays on an inherently humanitarian ethos over how to *best* help the Syrian refugees, yet it is the efficiency and effectiveness of the measures that matter (Nesvik 2015; NTB 2015a). Hence, the reasoning for why, how, and the extent to which we must help—and consequently the practical policy implications for burden-sharing initiatives that follow—are grounded in different ideational perspectives and worldviews.

The Nation-State Discourse

The nation-state discourse is characterized by a strong emphasis on internal national affairs, the preservation of national culture and togetherness, and a focus on Norway's role as an independent nation-state.

First, the focus on internal affairs gives relatively less space for considerations about the international community and international norms and principles (Ruud 2015). It also implies that Norway's international identity is not an important element in this discourse. It is, rather, framed as being in opposition, a sort of protest to discourses that emphasize the role of the international. An example of this is the humanitarian discourse, qualified here as naïve, politically correct, and repressive toward conflicting views and ideas, in particular those that are skeptical toward increased immigration. By attacking the deeply embedded notions of right and wrong, good and bad in the humanitarian discourse, the nation-state discourse delegitimizes it and the values it promotes.

The nation-state discourse includes significant elements from the other discourses, which is apparent in several of the analyzed texts. Most notably, actors identified by this discourse have drawn upon an anti-immigration discourse, a welfare discourse, and an efficiency discourse in their texts (Fremskrittspartiet 2015; Ruud 2015; NTB 2015a). Arguments referring to welfare, for instance, draw on the other ideas to support the overall argument that low numbers of immigrants, asylum seekers, and refugees are desirable, because they have a negative impact on Norwegian welfare. The discourse moves the political focus toward the need to protect the welfare state. However, the extent to which the nation-state builds on other discourses varies and consequently creates fractions and tensions within the discourse itself.

Political morality is here understood in mainly domestic terms. Political morality relates to the responsibility of political actors to its own society and its own people. National welfare, culture, and togetherness are public goods that must be preserved, and it is morally right to do so. High levels of immigration are seen as damaging for these public goods. In particular, the fraction of the nation-state discourse that relies heavily on an anti-immigration discourse emphasizes that these non-Western refugees pose a particular challenge to Norwegian culture and social togetherness. In consequence, Norway will not be able to "preserve the good and safe welfare state we have today" (Progress Party website 2015). Moreover, this fraction mainly represents Syrian refugees as a "burden" for Norwegian society and growing refugee flows as a "pressure" on European states (Ruud 2015). It arguably removes parts of the refugees' individuality and leads to a form of dehumanization, which may also be a mechanism that makes the overall focus on the national possible.

The Hierarchy between the Discourses and Power Relationships in the Norwegian Political Landscape

The findings from the textual analysis show that the current Norwegian government largely follows the cost-and-capacity discourse. In particular, the Conservative Party most clearly represents this discourse, by maintaining a pragmatic approach to the refugee issue, consistently emphasizing the cost element. Fractions of the Progress Party are also strongly influenced by this discourse, although the party is characterized by internal discursive fractions. As defined by Allen (2003), this discourse thus benefits from power defined both in terms of authority (because it is being held by actors in government) and in the form of persuasion (because it is shared by many actors, in government and elsewhere, even in the face of increased public support for the humanitarian discourse). It is thus arguably the more powerful political discourse on burden sharing in refugee protection.

The nation-state discourse is seemingly the weakest of the dominant discourses because only a few political actors defend it, although some of them are from the Progress Party, even in the government. This provides the discourse with power in the form of authority, as defined by Allen (2003). It can even be said to be disproportionately strong due to this position and the relatively small explicit support from political actors. Moreover, as several elements of the discourse are considered controversial, the representatives of this discourse receive significant media attention, which in turn increases their persuasive power and ability to shape the discursive field. Further, the approach that is skeptical of immigration enjoys considerable support among the public, and, as a result, the nation-state discourse still contributes significantly to shaping the political space for action on burden sharing.

The humanitarian discourse constitutes the views of a large group of actors within the political field, including a large share of civil society actors, NGOs, researchers, and political parties including the Socialist Left Party. Moreover, other smaller political parties, including the Christian Democrats and the Liberals, are also to an extent associated with this discourse, even though they also draw heavily on the cost-and-capacity discourse. As such, the humanitarian discourse has significant power in the political field through its persuasive capacity, which has increased as the wider public also became more aware and engaged due to the continued refugee crisis. It also possesses a form of "moral hegemony," as it is derived from the wider, international discourse of humanitarianism, a discourse that, as Barnett (2005: 731) notes, contains a high level of moral authority, with a different meaning of authority here than in Allen's definition (see also Joachim and Schneiker 2012). However, the discourse is simultaneously marginalized by the nation-state discourse and partly by the cost-and-capacity discourse, on this very basis. It also has less authority, in the sense that it is less shared by actors in government and because it partly isolates itself from the cost-and-capacity discourse.

The discursive frames that define the boundaries of the political field arguably changed from the Syria Agreement and during the European refugee crisis late summer/early fall 2015. Dramatic events contributed to the rapid change in actors' perspectives of the situation and what needed to be done. The growing civic engagement and grassroots activities were a notable change. The images of desperate refugees at the borders of Europe sparked a desire to "do something," as seen in particular with the work of RWTN. In particular, the movement's search for a politically neutral discursive framework attempted to break down the separation between traditional left and right in Norwegian politics. It attempted to prevent the Syrian refugee question from being about party politics, thus striving to reach a traditional humanitarian approach of neutrality, impartiality, and independence. In consequence, it contributed to granting the humanitarian discourse a stronger role in the field.

The general change in the public opinion appeared to affect the political discourses. For instance, Progress Party leader Siv Jensen modified her anti-immigration arguments during the electoral campaign as she was faced with this civic engagement (Vevstad, 2015 interview). Further, the Liberal Party and the Christian Democrats gradually moved toward a more explicit humanitarian discourse as the European refugee crisis evolved. This contributed to changing the power relations between the cost-and-capacity discourse and the humanitarian discourse, as both parties are support parties for the government. In general, the nation-state discourse was gradually accorded a weaker role, as many political actors moved further toward the humanitarian discourse.

The Political Space Created for Burden Sharing in Refugee Protection

The different discursive practices vary significantly in terms of the political space they create for action. The humanitarian discourse deliberately widens the scope for political action in the field, in particular by emphasizing the importance of developing new and innovative measures in refugee protection. However, the humanitarian discourse is also restrictive in that all measures in the refugee protection field must meet certain standards founded on human rights. Hence, in some ways, it also narrows the space for debating and considering certain policy alternatives, and thus the possibilities for efficiency measures and resource-saving initiatives because these often, although not always, risk affecting such standards. Finally, due to its prioritization of international humanitarian norms over national economic considerations, it is likely to suppress concerns for costs and resource capacities in its policy development. The dynamics between the discursive practice of the humanitarian discourse and that of the other discourses also emphasizes the potential and limitations of the power of persuasion.

The cost-and-capacity discourse's focus on efficiency frames a very limited and specific set of burden-sharing policies as possible and desirable, and costs will often take priority over human rights and humanitarian principles. This was arguably the case in the Syria Agreement in which adherents to the cost-and-capacity discourse maintained that protection in region of origin was preferable without making a clear exception for the most vulnerable–despite the UNHCR's recommendations. It expresses a conception of Norway as a rational political actor, which takes its international responsibility seriously but at the same time cannot accept demands that will have significant negative effects on the Norwegian economy and society (NTB 2015b).

The explicit value foundations of the nation-state discourse limit the political space to a greater extent than the other discursive practices. Since the discourse includes a strong anti-immigration element, it outright seeks to hinder Norway's involvement in physical protection initiatives. Instead it is likely to promote the strengthening of border control as a strategy to prevent increased immigration. Hence, financial burden sharing is seemingly deemed to be the only acceptable burden-sharing initiative within this discourse, as financial aid to the nearby region supports a strategy of containment that is believed to lead to fewer refugees arriving in Europe.

The cost-and-capacity discourse can be characterized as the provider of the core premises of the refugee protection debate in Norway: all political actors involved had to engage with the core ideas of this discourse, including efficiency, cost-benefit analysis, and resource constraints. Its normative-political foundation in liberal market economics and economic rationality, however, relies on an inherently economic understanding of efficiency. As

Betts has argued (2006: 152) this concept of efficiency in refugee protection "provides a legitimating discourse" yet limits the possibilities for developing a "more substantial conceptualization of efficiency" (Betts 2006: 168). This has also had concrete implications for how burden sharing has been approached, as it has narrowed the space for initiatives to be considered legitimate.

As the humanitarian discourse was granted a stronger role, the actors associated with the cost-and-capacity discourse were forced to seriously engage with the ideas embedded in it. For instance, the prime minister's explicit reference to the need for a national *dugnad* to implement the Syria Agreement (Hillestad 2015) implies that she is engaging directly with the core concepts embedded in the humanitarian discourse and seeing their potentially powerful impact, although she applied it in a slightly less ambitious manner. The government's decision in September to host a donor conference for states to raise money for UN programs in the nearby region can be seen as a way to meet the challenge raised by the humanitarian discourse. Solberg explained it with the need to "mobilize an international *dugnad*" (Hillestad 2015). The humanitarian discourse increasingly challenged the cost-and-capacity premises and pushed the boundaries of what can be defined as legitimate political responses in the field.

So why was there not a more substantive change in political practice following this discursive battle? There is seemingly little desire among the political leadership to develop more ambitious burden-sharing initiatives beyond participating in the European relocation scheme. The donor conference initiative primarily encouraged financial burden sharing and thus remained within the broader boundaries of the cost-and-capacity discourse—a limitation that can be explained by the relatively disproportionate power of the nation-state discourse. Moreover, despite the strong humanitarian engagement in large parts of the population, others also sensed increasing fear during the growing "crisis," which added to the Progress Party's political clout.

What Space for the Different Forms of Burden Sharing?

Different forms of burden sharing have been at the core of the political debates on refugee protection, including resettlement, financial burden sharing, temporary (collective) forms of protection, and other forms of complementary protection. First, resettlement has been a key focal point in debates on refugee protection and is the main mechanism in the Syria Agreement. Norway's special role in resettlement has been emphasized by a number of humanitarian actors, although it also touches upon points of contention within the humanitarian discourse itself. For instance, some have criticized the focus on resettlement, noting that its differentiated treatment between refugees is difficult to justify from a purely humanitarian viewpoint, when you could help many more with the same resources in the nearby region (Meyer 2015 interview), revealing some of the hegemonic power of the cost-and-capacity discourse. Yet, the textual analysis showed that most civil society actors associated with the humanitarian discourse stress that resettlement is an effective and necessary protection tool for the *most vulnerable.*

As a resource-draining and costly protection mechanism, resettlement is a policy area where fractions of the humanitarian and the cost-and-capacity discourses conflict with one another and where the hegemonic role of the latter has had significant implications on the space eventually given to resettlement. Further, there is a fear among certain political actors in this discourse and the nation-state discourse that (increased) resettlement will further promote Norway as a country of asylum (Ministry of Justice official 2015 interview). In the autumn and winter of 2015, Norway experienced a large increase, in relative terms, in asylum seekers arriving in the country.

Although the number of arrivals drastically decreased after the government imposed new policy regulations, there is still a perception among many political actors, and the public, that the system is stretched to its limits in terms of capacity and resources. The political hegemony of the cost-and-capacity discourse is thus likely to result in a prioritization of ordinary asylum processes—which Norway in the end cannot strictly control—over new resettlement initiatives, as the combination of the two is seen as too costly. The outcome of this discursive battle is yet unknown but is likely to be close to a status quo. As a Ministry of Justice and Public Security official (2015 interview) put it: "There is no question of not accepting any refugees for resettlement, but of how to prioritize different ways to help."

The current discursive hierarchy implies that financial burden sharing will be the most important burden-sharing initiative for Norway as the crisis in Syria continues. As financial burden sharing is seen as a necessary means by all the discourses, the question is no longer whether Norway will participate in financial burden sharing but the extent to which it will contribute. Actors associated with the humanitarian discourse continuously argue that Norway can and should do more financially: "We have increased the support to Syria, but not much to the UNHCR. The international donor community has not kept up with UNHCR's financial needs. . . . In 2010 Norway was the fifth largest donor . . . in 2014 Norway was the ninth largest" (Meyer 2015 interview).

However, the cost-and-capacity discourse promotes a more pragmatic financial burden-sharing policy, in which perceptions of existing resource structures determine the level of financial aid advocated. The nation-state discourse further strengthens this discursive practice due to its emphasis on the need to spend financial resources mainly on national welfare policies.

Norway is thus likely to remain an important contributor to financial burden sharing, although the financial contributions are unlikely to experience a dramatic increase.

The empirical material shows how temporary protection programs are a particularly sensitive political issue, especially from the point of view of the humanitarian discourse. The temporary protection scheme granted to Bosnian refugees in Norway during the 1990s is a strong reference point in this debate, with the main lessons learned being that the *temporary* aspect of such protection may have deeply problematic consequences for the individuals who are affected (Austenå 2015 interview; Igesund 2015 interview). As Austenå stresses: "It is about the lives of individuals. . . . People become rooted and have children."

The discussion, or lack of discussion, on temporary protection highlights the powerful rights perspective that is embedded in large parts of the humanitarian discourse. However, other actors in this discourse adopt a more pragmatic and effectiveness-focused approach and stress the necessity of implementing these schemes despite the challenges, as it will "provide protection to more people more quickly" (Vevstad 2015 interview). Interestingly, Nesse (2015 interview) also notes that temporary protection represents a protection solution that in some ways compromises between the humanitarian discourse and the cost-and-capacity discourse: "[The lack of debate on temporary protection] . . . has to do with the absence of discussion about how we can solve this situation. . . . it will force its way into the cost debate. . . . we will not have to take all the economic consequences at once."

However, temporary protection is also challenging for the cost-and-capacity discourse for other reasons, in particular the integration aspect. Bosnians being Europeans is seen as having made them more easily integrated, especially in the labor market (Koser and Black 1999: 533, 535). The cost-and-capacity discourse will prioritize refugees who are easily integrated, as this is more cost efficient. Hence, although this discourse is not founded upon explicit anti-immigration sentiments, the cultural and religious background of the Syrian refugees does matter here too. In general, due to the skepticism among many actors in the political field toward this protection initiative, it seems unlikely that Norway will take further initiatives in this area.

Finally, the empirical material shows that actors associated with the humanitarian discourse have provided several policy suggestions that can foster alternative ways of providing protection to Syrian refugees, including the provision of humanitarian visas and enhanced possibilities for family reunification. However, alternative forms of complementary protection have not been suggested by actors identified by the other discourses, and the cost-and-capacity discourse is likely to oppose most new policy initiatives that increase public spending, giving little room to the development of such initiatives.

Conclusion

Norway's efforts in the field of refugee resettlement are closely tied to Norway's broader ambitions as a peace builder and a humanitarian nation. Strong efforts in this field have contributed to supporting the image of Norway as an altruistic, morally sound actor. In turn, this gives Norway increased credibility in humanitarian and peace-building affairs more generally. It has shown that the country is willing to take its own share of the burden caused by war and conflict, including when it is resource demanding. Moreover, this has signalized a certain respect for the humanitarian and peace-building system and the UN–including its norms, institutions, and recommendations. Hence, the outcome of the recent debate on burden sharing may also have implications for Norway's ambitions as a peace nation and its ability to exert influence over international refugee management as well as over other states and possible candidates for hosting resettles.

Although Norway is a particularly significant actor within refugee resettlement, the findings of this study may offer insights into other European and non-European states. The versions of these dominant discourses presumably also exist in other states, which in different ways contribute to international cooperation, even if the power relations between them are different. The specific discourses largely reflect political sentiments and tensions well known in most national contexts, in the EU and beyond, relating to issues such as international solidarity, immigration concerns, questions of resource spending, and the protection of the welfare state. If Norway, as a prominent actor in refugee protection, experiences these tensions, it is likely that it also dominates the resettlement debates in other countries. Further, the study also provides general insights into how dominant discourses on burden sharing may interact and compete with each other and consequently shapes the space for burden sharing in a particular national context.

Thielemann and Suhrke have both focused on the drivers and disincentives for burden sharing in the international sphere. In particular, Thielemann has identified the significance of the cost-benefit approach in the international perspective. We have done this in the domestic perspective, but instead of perceiving this approach as a "logic," we have identified it as a hegemonic discourse that shapes and defines the values and interests of core actors in the Norwegian refugee field. In this regard, the hegemony of the cost-benefit approach benefits from power defined by both authority and persuasion, as in Allen's definition, despite lacking the moral authority conceptualized by Barnett. In consequence, this approach has significant implications for national burden-sharing initiatives in practice.

The debate on burden sharing following the Syrian refugee crisis, at least in the period addressed here, has highlighted issues concerning Norway's European identity and the extent to which Norway wants to play a prominent and proactive role in Europe in this field. As the situation has evolved, there has seemingly been a discursive change on this issue, with a growing consensus among political actors that Norway must contribute at the European level, although at which level varies among the political actors.

Certain tentative implications for Norwegian burden-sharing initiatives can be drawn from the discursive practices that have characterized the Norwegian response to the Syrian refugee crisis. It is clear that there is no real challenge to financial burden sharing in the discursive field, and financial burden sharing will thus remain the least controversial form of burden sharing in future refugee crises. Also in noncrises, Norway is generally a significant provider of humanitarian aid. However, the level of financial aid at a given time will depend on the hegemonic discursive practice as well as on nondiscursive factors, especially economic ones. If the oil crisis continues, for instance, Norway is likely to experience another economic reality during future refugee crises. This may in turn change the perceptions of actors in the political field and grant the cost-and-capacity discourse with an even stronger role.

Regarding physical protection initiatives, the question of implications is more challenging. Traditionally, resettlement is Norway's most significant contribution to physical burden-sharing initiatives. The Syrian crisis shows how special resettlement schemes may be established in future crises, although discursive practice set out by the nation-state discourse and the cost-and-capacity discourse shows that cultural and religious factors will matter in this regard. This implies that the scale of physical burden-sharing initiatives to a certain degree will depend on where the crisis takes place and who the refugees are. To what extent will depend on the hierarchy between the dominant discourses and is likely to shape the image that Norway projects of itself internationally as a key humanitarian contributor to refugee protection.

Linn Marie Reklev holds a M.A. in peace and conflict studies from the University of Oslo and a B.A. in politics and international relations from the University of York. She currently works for the PRIO Centre on Gender, Peace and Security at the Peace Research Institute Oslo (PRIO). She has previously worked for the Permanent Mission of Norway to the United Nations in Geneva, the Norwegian Directorate for Immigration, and as an adviser to the Permanent Delegation of Norway to the OSCE.

Maria Gabrielsen Jumbert holds a Ph.D in international relations and political science from the Institut d'Etudes Politiques, SciencesPo Paris (2010). She is Senior Researcher and Research Director at the Peace Research Institute Oslo (PRIO), and Director of the Norwegian Centre for Humanitarian Studies (NCHS). She led the project Brazil's Rise to the Global Stage (BraGS): Humanitarianism, Peacekeeping and the Quest for Great Powerhood (2014–2017). Her work focuses on how new information and surveillance technologies produce humanitarian and security practices, especially related to human mobility and borders, and how these practices and responses interact. Her work has appeared in, inter alia, the *Journal of Modern African Studies, Third World Quarterly,* the *International Review of the Red Cross,* and the *Review of International Studies.*

Note

1. The analysis is based upon empirical material: first an analysis of extensive media material (news articles and op-eds) and articles on the main political parties' websites relating to these two events selected to represent both the variety of actors involved and the variety of ideas and meanings regarding burden sharing; then a set of six articles related to the Syria Agreement (Fremskrittspartiet [Progress party's website] 2015; Nesvik 2015; Hillestad 2015; Arbeiderpartiet [Labor Party website] 2015; Sosialistisk Venstreparti [Socialist Left Party's website] 2015; Egenæs et al. 2015) and eight related to the European refugee crisis (Lysbakken 2015; NTB 2015a, 2015b; Ruud 2015; Torset and Foss 2015; Solsvik 2015; NRK 2015; Gullikstad 2015) were selected for a closer analysis, seen as representative of the broader views in the debates. The initial textual analysis enabled us to uncover a range of core ideas that characterized the political debate on this issue. However, we do not claim to cover the full range of actors and ideas present in the Norwegian debate. This analysis was then supplemented with interviews with key informants (four NGO representatives, two civil servants from the Ministries of Justice and Foreign Affairs, and a legal expert) chosen for their knowledge of, and hands-on experience with, Norwegian and international refugee and asylum politics.

References

Allen, John. 2003. *Lost Geographies of Power.* Malden: Blackwell Publishing.

Arbeiderpartiet. 2015. *Et godt svar fra Norge i en ekstraordinær situasjon* [A Good Response from Norway in an Extraordinary Situation]. Accessed 30 September 2015. http://arbeiderpartiet.no/Aktuelt/Internasjonalt/Et-godt-svar-fra-Norge-i-en-ekstraordinaer-situasjon.

Barnett, Michael. 2005. "Humanitarianism Transformed." *Perspectives on politics* 3(4): 723–40.

Barnett, Michael, and Raymond Duvall, eds. 2005. *Power in Global Governance.* Cambridge: Cambridge University Press.

Bergens Tidene. 2015. "Dette er Syria-avtalen" [The Syria Agreement]. 10 June. Accessed 30 September 2015. http://www.bt.no/nyheter/innenriks/Dette-er-Syria-avtalen-3378175.html.

Betts, Alexander. 2006. "What Does 'Efficiency' Mean in the Context of the Global Refugee Regime?" *The British Journal of Politics and International Relations* 8(2): 148–73.

Bratberg, Øivind. 2014. *Tekstanalyse*. Oslo: Cappelen Damm.

Egenæs, John Peder et al. 2015. "Kronikk: Nasjonal dugnad for syriske flyktninger" [Op-ed: National *dugnad* for Syrian Refugees]. *Verdens Gang,* 11 March. Accessed 25 September 2015. http://www.vg.no/nyheter/meninger/syria/kronikk-nasjo nal-dugnad-for-syriske-flyktninger/a/23412532/.

Fassin, Didier. 2012. *Humanitarian Reason. A Moral History of the Present.* Berkeley: University of California Press.

Feldman, Ilana, and Miriam Ticktin. 2010. *In the Name of Humanity.* Durham: Duke University Press.

Feller, Erika. 2006. "Asylum, Migration and Refugee Protection: Realities, Myths and the Promise of Things to Come." *International Journal of Refugee Law* 18(3–4): 509–36.

Fremskrittspartiet. 2015. *Innvandringen truer velferdssamfunnet* [Immigration Threatens Welfare Society]. Accessed 30 September 2015. https://frp.no/aktuelt/2015/05/ innvandringen-truer-velferdssamfunnet.

Garnier, Adèle. 2014. "Migration Management and Humanitarian Protection: The UNHCR's 'Resettlement Expansionism' and Its Impact on Policy-Making in the EU and Australia." *Journal of Ethnic and Migration Studies* 40(6): 942–59.

Gullikstad, Åsne. 2015. "Aktører: Dette bør gjøres" [Actors: This Should Be Done]. *Dagsavisen,* 10 September. Accessed 7 November 2015. http://www.dagsavisen .no/verden/aktører-dette-bør-gjøres-1.393910.

Hillestad, Linn Kongsli. 2015. "Vi kommer ikke til å ta i mot flyktninger hvis vi ikke har boliger til dem." *Dagbladet,* 10 June 2015. Accessed 16 September 2015. http://www.dagbladet.no/2015/06/10/nyheter/politikk/flyktninger/syria/ innenriks/39601651/.

Hopf, Ted. 2002. *Social Construction of International Politics: Identities and Foreign Policies: Moscow, 1955 & 1999.* New York: Cornell University Press.

Joachim, Jutta, and Andrea Schneiker. 2012. "New Humanitarians? Frame Appropriation through Private Military and Security Companies." *Millennium Journal of International Studies* 40(2): 365–88.

Koser, Khalid, and Richard Black. 1999. "Limits to Harmonization: The 'Temporary Protection' of Refugees in the European Union." *International Migration* 37(3): 521–43.

Kristelig Folkeparti. 2016. *Innvandring og integrering.* Accessed 5 May 2016. https:// www.krf.no/politikk/politikk-a-til-a/innvandring-og-integrering/.

Lysbakken, Audun. 2015. "Det er helt sant at flyktningene må hjelpes der de er. Og nå er de i Europa" [It Is True That the Refugees Must Be Helped Where They Are. And Now They Are in Europe]. *Aftenposten,* 1 September. Accessed 30 September 2015. http://www.aftenposten.no/meninger/kronikker/Det-er-helt-sant-at-flyktningene-ma-hjelpes-der-de-er-Og-na-er-de-i-Europa–Audun-Lysbak ken-8145408.html.

Nesvik, Harald Tom. 2015. "Derfor brøt vi forhandlingene om syriske flyktninger" [That Is Why We Broke Off the Negotiations on Syrian Refugees]. *Aftenposten,*

5 June. Accessed 7 November 2015. http://www.aftenposten.no/meninger/ kronikker/Kronikk-av-Frps-parlamentariske-leder-Derfor-brot-vi-forhandling ene-om-syriske-flyktninger-8046636.html.

Norad. 2015. *Syria*. Accessed 5 May 2016. http://www.norad.no/landsider/mid tosten/syria/.

NRK. 2015. *Venstre krever ny kikk på Syria-avtalen* [The Liberal Party Demands a New Look at the Syria Agreement]. Accessed 7 November 2015. http://www.nrk.no/ norge/venstre-krever-ny-kikk-pa-syria-avtalen-1.12535764.

NTB. 2015a. "Overbevist om at det er best å hjelpe i nærområdene" [Convinced That It Is Best to Help in the Nearby Areas]. *Dagens Næringsliv*, 6 September. Accessed 30 September 2015. http://www.dn.no/nyheter/politikkSamfunn/ 2015/09/06/1136/-overbevist-om-at-det-er-best–hjelpe-i-nromrdene.

———. 2015b. "Solberg avventende til EUs flyktningdugnad" [Solberg Is Hesitant towards the EU Refugee *dugnad*]. *Vårt Land,* 7 September. Accessed 7 November 2015. http://www.vl.no/nyhet/solberg-avventende-til-eus-flyktningdugnad-1.393066.

Orchard, Cynthia, and Andrew Miller. 2014. *Protection in Europe for Refugees from Syria*. Forced Migration Policy Briefing 10. Oxford: Refugee Studies Centre.

Regjeringen. 2016. *Regjeringens arbeidsprogram for samarbeidet med EU 2016*. Accessed 5 May 2016. https://www.regjeringen.no/no/dokumenter/program_eu/ id2473342/.

Ruud, Solveig. 2015. "Carl I. Hagen vil sende alle båtflyktninger i retur." *Aftenposten,* 19 August. Accessed 7 November 2015. http://www.aftenposten.no/nyheter/ iriks/politikk/Carl-I-Hagen-vil-sende-alle-batflyktninger-i-retur-8131466.html.

Sandvik, Kristin Bergtora. 2013. "The Multiple Tracks of Human Rights and Humanitarianism." In *Worlds of Human Rights: The Ambiguities of Rights Claiming in Africa,* edited by Bill Derman, Anne Hellum, and Kristin Bergtora Sandvik, 257–276. Nijmegen: Brill.

Sandvik, Kristin Bergtora, and Katja Lindskov Jacobsen, eds. 2016. *UNHCR and the Struggle for Accountability*. London: Routledge.

Shiblak, Abbas. 1996. "Residency Status and Civil Rights of Palestinian Refugees in Arab Countries." *Journal of Palestine Studies* 25(3): 36–45.

Solsvik, Anne. 2015. "Venstre vil ha hastemøte om flyktningsituasjonen" [The Liberal Party Wants an Emergency Meeting on the Refugee Situation]. *Venstre,* 7 September. Accessed 7 November 2015. http://www.venstre.no/artikkel/2015/09/07/ venstre-vil-ha-hastemote-om-flyktningsituasjonen/.

Sosialistisk Venstreparti. 2015. *Derfor brøt SV Syria-forhandlingene* [That Is Why the Socialist Left Party Broke Off the Syria Negotiations]. Accessed 30 September 2015. https://www.sv.no/blog/2015/06/10/sv-bryter-syria-forhandlinger/.

Suhrke, Astrid. 1998. "Burden Sharing during Refugee Emergencies: The Logic of Collective versus National Action." *Journal of Refugee Studies* 11(4): 396–415.

Thielemann, Eiko R. 2003. "Between Interests and Norms: Explaining Burden Sharing in the European Union." *Journal of Refugee Studies* 16(3): 253–73.

Thielemann, Eiko R., and Torun Dewan. 2006. "The Myth of Free-Riding: Refugee Protection and Implicit Burden Sharing." *West European Politics* 29(2): 351–69.

Torset, Nina Selbo, and Andreas Bakke Foss. 2015. "KrF-lederen: Norge må fravike Dublin-avtalen for Syria-flyktningene" [The KrF-Leader: Norway Must Waive the Dublin Regulations for the Syria Refugees]. *Aftenposten,* 20 August. Accessed

7 November 2015. http://www.aftenposten.no/nyheter/iriks/politikk/KrF-lede ren-Norge-ma-fravike-Dublin-avtalen-for-Syria-flyktningene-8144493.html.

United Nations (UN). 2016. *Joint Statement on Syria*. Accessed 21 May 2016. http:// www.un.org/News/dh/infocus/Syria/Joint percent20Humanitarian percent20St atement percent20on percent20Syria_En.pdf.

United Nations High Commissioner for Refugees (UNHCR). 2004. *Conclusion on International Cooperation and Burden and Responsibility Sharing in Mass Influx Situations*. Accessed 15 August 2016. http://www.unhcr.org/41751fd82.html.

——. 2014. *In Search for Solidarity: Resettlement and Other Forms of Admission for Syrian Refugees*. Accessed 20 August 2015. http://www.swedenabroad.com/ImageVault Files/id_26640/cf_347/In_Search_of_Solidarity_-_Resettlement_and_Other_F .PDF.

——. 2015. *Durable Solutions*. Accessed 7 November 2015. http://www.unhcr.org/pa ges/49c3646cf8.html.

——. 2016a. *Resettlement and Other Admission Pathways for Syrian Refugees*. Accessed 20 May 2016. http://www.unhcr.org/en-us/protection/resettlement/573dc82d4/ resettlement-other-admission-pathways-syrian-refugees-updated-29-april.html.

——. 2016b. *Syrian Regional Refugee Response*. Accessed 20 May 2016. http://data.un hcr.org/syrianrefugees/regional.php.

van Selm, Joanne. 2003. "Public-Private Partnerships in Refugee Resettlement: Europe and the US." *Journal of International Migration and Integration* 4(2): 157–75.

Venstre. 2018. *Tema: Retten til asyl*. Accessed 7 May 2018. https://www.venstre.no/ tema/innvandring-integrering/retten-til-asyl/.

Vevstad, Vigdis. 2015. *Europeisk byrdefordeling*. *Dagens Næringsliv,* 15 September. Accessed 5 November 2015. http://www.dn.no/meninger/debatt/2015/09/15/21 46/Flyktningkrisen/europeisk-byrdefordeling.

Interviews (all in 2015)

Ann-Magrit Austenå, 8 October
Solveig Igesund, 15 October
Johan Meyer, 6 October
Ministry of Justice and Public Security official, 26 October
Pål Nesse, 9 October
Beate Slydal, 13 October
Vigdis Vevstad, 14 October

Part III

Resettlement Bureaucracies and Resettled Refugees in Local Contexts

8

Parallel Pasts, Presents, and Futures

Narratives of Cambodian and Karen Refugees
in the United States

Denise C. Lewis and Savannah S. Young

The lives and needs of resettled refugee families are often shaped by trau-matic experiences before and during flight, yet this, along with the agency of the refugees themselves–that is, their will and rights to make decisions regarding their present and future–is often ignored in research and policy in the U.S. context. To ensure successful integration of resettled refugees, and improve our understanding of resettlement, there is a need to focus more strongly on the journey from home countries to resettlement, particu-larly how refugees frame and respond to the stressors associated with those journeys. Rather than viewing refugees as powerless in the face of seem-ingly catastrophic events within a context of managed migration (Geiger and Pécoud 2013; Walters 2015; also Sandvik, this volume), we focus on the power refugees possess as they navigate the terrain of flight and settlement (see also Thomson, this volume). We argue that when we, and others such as humanitarian service agencies and policy makers, clearly hear and respect refugees' voices, we can begin to cocreate responses to refugees' needs in collaboration with the refugees who, themselves, hold valuable everyday forms of wisdom surrounding what they need to live successfully in the United States.

The chapter builds on extensive engagement with two ethnic groups from Southeast Asia: Cambodians (from Cambodia), and Karen (an ethnic group from Burma). Fractured data fail to provide a comprehensive breakdown by individual ethnic groups within the category of Southeast Asian nations. Refugees from this region have formed a major immigrant population in the United States, beginning with the first waves of Southeast Asian refugees in 1975 and continuing with present-day Karen refugees (Bureau of Population, Refugees, and Migration, U.S. Department of State 2015).

The majority of the approximately 250,000 refugees from Cambodia arrived in the United States in the early to mid-1980s. Most settled along the east and west coasts, and a small group of approximately 125 families settled in Mobile County, Alabama. The Karen continue to be one of several ethnic groups originally from Burma who have been resettled in the United States in recent years due to decades of harsh ethnic violence in Burma and years of living in refugee camps in Thailand. In 2015 alone, for example, over 18,000 refugees from Burma were resettled in the United States (Office of Refugee Resettlement, U.S. Department of Health and Human Services 2016). Approximately thirty Karen families have resettled in a rural community near Atlanta, Georgia.

By listening to the voices of these groups, we explore how their experiences of resettlement in the United States are shaped by "parallel pasts, presents, and futures" to address the following three research questions: What are similarities and differences between these two resettled groups despite the passage of time? How is power distributed among those involved in resettlement processes, especially between refugees and systems within which they move? How can we listen to their voices now and in the future to understand and cultivate refugees' resettlement experiences in the United States?

We assert that refugees' voices bring to light needs not met by the managed migration practices (Geiger and Pécoud 2013; Walters 2015; for comparative domestic contexts, see Darrow; Garnier; Losoncz; Vera Espinoza, and Jubilut and Zamur, this volume) of various humanitarian response agencies, and we describe families' collective actions to address those needs. Because it is vitally important to recognize the power of refugees' stories and explanations of events they have experienced, we include refugees' own narratives describing their entire journeys, which include fleeing their homelands, their experiences in refugee camps, their resettlement, and rebuilding their lives as refugees in foreign lands. Lastly, we provide a critique of current U.S. policy responses to refugee resettlement as they relate to our participants' narratives.

Theoretical Foundations

The families we include in this chapter have experienced significant stress, individually and as families. Those stressors have influenced individuals' and family members' abilities to engage in instrumental, affective, and symbolic exchanges across generations. To better illuminate families' experiences, we combine theoretical perspectives from family science, human development, and gerontology. Family stress theory (McCubbin 1979; Robinson 1997), family systems theory (Bowen 1966), and the family exchange theoretical perspective (Lewis 2008) allow us to consider concepts of multigenerational transmission of various processes within family interactions.

Family stress theory (McCubbin 1979) provides a framework for understanding stress and resiliency (Robinson 1997) within families. Family systems theory (Bowen 1966) situates families as units engaging in complex, emotionally connected interactions. The family exchange theoretical perspective (Lewis 2008) is synthesized from life course (Elder 1985), social constructionist (Berger and Luckmann 1966), and social exchange (Dowd 1980) theories to place families' instrumental, symbolic, and affective exchanges into an interlinking structure that reveals meanings of family interactions. Although rarely applied to studying refugees' lives, family, human development, and gerontological theories provide unique pathways for understanding refugees' narratives of the disassembly, reconstruction, and redefinition of their lives (Lewis 2001, 2008).

Refugees' Voices

> For almost an hour he talked while occasionally glancing at sheets of notebook paper filled with handwritten Khmer. This was a story he wanted known. About all I did was nod and listen. . . . He spoke slowly with many long pauses between words, sentences, and thoughts. I wondered how he could stand to relate these horrifying stories to me. But it was obvious that he wanted to make sure that he told me as much of his history as possible. His description of the Communist takeover and the slaughter of his family were shocking, saddening, terrifying. I am surprised that I didn't cry because this was the first time I heard a firsthand account of a survivor. I suppose had he cried I would have cried with him. (fieldnotes from Lewis)

As C. Wright Mills stated, "Neither the life of an individual nor the history of a society can be understood without understanding both" (Mills 2000 [1959]: 3). We can understand through the voices of both resettled Cambodian and Karen refugees. The thirty-year span (mid-1970s to early 2000s) from the arrival of Cambodian refugees to the arrival of Karen refugees is filled with turmoil that continuously creates wave after wave of refugees and asylum seekers. Responses across multiple political boundaries have varied and include the imprisonment of those who flee, housing in megacamps, and humanitarian efforts by various groups and individuals. The focus of this chapter is on the lived experiences described by refugees, themselves.

We hope to inspire those who encounter refugees to listen for the untold stories and hear the silence between words spoken (Ghorashi 2007), in addition to understanding refugees' verbal narratives. Refugees' stories involve the dynamic interplay of ordinary and extraordinary circumstances across multiple levels, as well as constant negotiation of power between themselves and those with whom they interact, including both government and humanitarian organizations seeking to strategically move and place refugees according to agency and host country perceived needs. We include narratives as they are lived, experienced, told, and molded into text (Eastmond 2007). We assert that while the reasons for and responses to refugee crises may seem universal and predictable to many, narratives of refugees provide a widely varied story of leaving home countries, time in liminal positions, resettlement, and secondary migration that speaks to the power and resilience within the refugees themselves (see Pittaway et al. 2009; Sleijpen et al. 2016).

Methods

Ethnographic research methods, including participant observation, group meetings, and interviewing (Bernard 2011; Patton 2015; Wolcott 2008), allow a representation of narratives gathered from individual and family interviews with Cambodian and Karen refugees. Lewis originally established a relationship in 1996 with a Cambodian community near her home through her volunteer work teaching English. Cambodian, and other Southeast Asian refugees, have been settled and resettled in the United States in response to multiple wars and conflicts across Southeast Asia from the 1950s to the present day. In multiple periods between 1997 and 2014, she engaged with 125 individual Cambodians from approximately twenty families.

Multiple topics discussed over this thirteen-year period include war experiences and survival, traditional medicine, health beliefs and behaviors, and everyday life. Young completed interviews with fourteen individual Karen refugees from five families between 2014 and 2016 who lived near her home institution. Her original contact with the Karen community came about because of her interest in community gardening. Since the initial contact with the Karen community, we have created a program designed to work directly with refugee groups to determine immediate needs. The relationships with both the Cambodian and Karen communities are ongoing.

We engaged in participant observation and interviews with both groups. Culturally responsive participant observation was critical for building trust so that refugees were comfortable relaying their stories to us (Seponski et al. 2013). We participated in and observed everyday activities, special events, happy celebrations, and mundane tasks, all while maintaining distance and relative objectivity. Time spent included daylong encounters, a short two-week stay, and spending several months living with a host family.

Focus groups provided ways to articulate research goals and methods and discuss issues of confidentiality and informed consent (Bernard 2011). Less formal group meetings provided ways to listen while participants told broad, collective stories and raised community-specific issues. This allowed us to determine, with participants' input, the most relevant issues within these particular communities. We conducted unstructured interviews with no preconceived notion of the direction of the interview and used semistructured interviews guided by specific topics (Bernard 2011).

Ethnographic research involves constant analysis to uncover trends, patterns, issues, and themes as they unfold (Bernard 2011). It is the combination of ethnographic methods that allow a richness and depth toward understanding the social, cultural, and political processes that create the lived experiences of both groups of refugees. We began to discuss the similarities in Cambodian and Karen refugees' responses during the phase when we analyzed the Karen data.

Multilevel and long-term interactions revealed how families dealt with daily patterns of life in the United States that are remarkably different from life in their sending countries. The refugee families whose voices fill this chapter experienced secondary migration to rural enclaves where they continue their struggle to reconcile cultural and cognitive dissonance while maintaining a sense of family and cultural identity. The most powerful voices in this chapter are not from us as researchers but from refugees themselves as they navigate their journeys.

Voices

Personal life stories are rarely the dominant interactions with refugees due to hesitation to bring up traumatic experiences as well as pressure to prioritize basic needs (e.g., jobs, housing, food, and education). However, individual stories are vital for contextualizing and understanding lived experiences. The first step is establishing rapport and trust. It is only after engaging in conversations about more mundane aspects of everyday life that refugees open up about the most painful aspects of their lives. It is only their voices that can truly reveal their experiences of escape, trauma, and rebuilding as they navigate resettlement.

Fleeing

Both groups faced multiple disruptions to social order, community, home, and family. Many Cambodian refugees described how they fled with little to no preparation. They become nomads within their home nations, as did many Karen families. Families from both groups experienced internal and external displacement before resettlement in the United States. The first narratives provided here are from two Cambodian refugees. They spoke of running and hiding from Khmer Rouge soldiers and witnessing family members' deaths.

> When the Communists first came into my village . . . I knew I had to go. My wife, my children, we just ran. We ran through the rice fields and the Communists shot. First they killed two of my children. They shot again and killed my wife and both my sons. . . . I kept running for nineteen days through the jungle until I reach[ed] Thailand. From that time I cried for three years. (Cambodian refugee, male, age sixty-two)

Another Cambodian man described the first wave of executions as the Khmer Rouge entered Phnom Penh on 17 April 1975:

> All killed. The Communist killed my youngest brother first day because he in high school. Our family saw what the Communist were doing, who they killed first. We knew we must hide who we are. We tried, but my wife and all seven children were killed before we can leave the city. Another brother is tortured. He died too. The rest of my family, we must go right away. (Cambodian refugee, male, age sixty-nine)

Several Cambodian refugees reported that the emotional toil continued for decades as they and their families sought to reconnect and rebuild their lives. Many families adopted heartrending survival strategies. One high-ranking official described how he instructed his wife to disguise herself and their children:

> I tell her, we must go! You must look down! Act dumb! I dress her and my children in farmer clothes and make dirt on they feet. She cried and begged me not to leave her but I had to do it. If the Communist found us together we would all be killed. She left everything: our home, her family jewelry, her clothes. She took care of our sons and worked on the farms for three years. The Communist never knew who she was. She take care of my children. . . . She is sick with Alzheimer disease today. Now I take care of her. (Cambodian refugee, male, age seventy-four)

The Karen refugee crisis was also due to a protracted civil war that began in 1949 (Tanaka 2013); yet, their movement into Thai refugee camps did not occur until well after the Cambodian Khmer Rouge crisis ended (1975–1979). Stories are chillingly similar with regard to extensive physical and psychological hardships faced throughout initial flight and resettlement. The need to flee, hide, and flee again persists in narratives of both groups, as well as perseverance to endure unimaginable hardships in hopes of improved circumstances. The following narrative reflects the continued urgency of flight by Karen refugees, just as had been the case for Cambodian refugees:

> When I was a child, we always had to flee. We had to flee when we lived in the village, and when the enemy came to the village we had to run out to hide. When the enemy left the village we would come back. We were always running, hiding, and coming back to the village. Our lives were just to hide, float around, go here and go there to hide until we moved to the Thailand refugee camp. (Karen refugee, male, age sixty)

The chronicity of trauma, fear, and need to obscure identities, fracturing of families, and the almost constant hiding of both physical self and identity are interwoven throughout narratives.

Uncertainty also is ubiquitous in Cambodian and Karen narratives. Once families fled to refugee camps, the near-constant fleeing and hiding morphed into dull, inactive confinement in police stations (Lewis 2001, 2008) and camps (Chandler 2000; Lewis 2001; Tanaka 2013). For both groups, enclosed Thai camps became their immediate refuge from violence. Horrifying violence gave way to impoverishment, dependency, and lack of opportunity for education and independence. The desperation and perseverance that mobilized them to flee their homes became a sudden, impenetrable gridlock that halted their freedom (see Chandler 2000; Tanaka 2013).

Early Days of Escape

Although the Western world knew of the wars waging in Southeast Asia in the mid-1970s, many in the midst of the turmoil were unaware of events unfolding only a few kilometers away. Genocide in Cambodia, for example, was almost unseen by those outside the nation's borders until almost three years into the darkest period of Cambodia's history. Narratives of some of the earliest people to escape to Thailand highlight the bewilderment of both Cambodian refugees and Thai citizens concerning response to the sudden influx of Cambodian refugees.

> I go to Surin, Thailand. They not too many refugee in Thailand then [mid-1975]. They don't know what to do with me. They take me to police station like I criminal or something like that. . . . Then I move to camp for refugee. I live there for eight month. I have no place to go. (Cambodian refugee, male, age sixty-two)

Others described a nomadic life in the forest or jungle. Some revealed losses of family members and friends because of stepping on landmines (in Cambodia), becoming ill, or dying from eating whatever kinds of plants could be found. One Cambodian man (age seventy-six) explained that he lost his eye and use of his left arm when his brother stepped on a mine, "One time, my brother, my family go through the jungle. Then, we hear the pop when he step on mine. He say to me, run brother. I grab my young son and we run. So I survive, my son survive, my brother–not survive." Moving forward in time to Karen families' experiences, the almost daily struggle to find food, water, and safety meant that families had little stability.

> I got to Thailand because of the war. My mother, she flee, flee, flee, flee along with my father. They have a big wide hut at the border of Thailand and Karen State, so my mother fled to Thailand when I was three years old, so I don't remember anything. They transferred us to our first refugee camp in Thailand. (Karen refugee, female, age thirty-two)

Another Karen woman described her life as a child helper to her mother. She held responsibilities at a very young age so her family could survive:

> I took care of the baby when I was just seven years old, but I helped my mom in the forest when I turned nine years old. When I was young like my son, I took care of my youngest brother, cooking on the fire outside. I boiled water for tea for my mom. Every day, I carried hot water and my brother in the rain through the forest behind my mom. (Karen refugee, female, age twenty-seven)

In spite of Thailand's history of refugee camps, Karen refugees' experiences also reflected an uncertainty and an inhospitable environment. The first response of the local Thai government was to jail Cambodian refugees, followed by establishment of rudimentary camps in 1976 (Lewis 2008). The United Nations High Commissioner for Refugees (UNHCR 2016) became involved in 1979 with the first UNHCR-formed camp in Thailand–many of the original UNHCR camps also served Karen refugees.

Life in Refugee Camps in Thailand

Cambodian and Karen refugees described dire conditions in camps: overcrowding, too little food, no privacy, families separated from each other, illnesses, injuries, and profound uncertainty. These conditions were the norm in the mid-1970s, when Cambodians first fled to Thailand.

> Life in Thai camp is very bad. Mud, everybody sick. Nobody know what to do. We have not enough food. Lot of people just hungry and scared. Lots of people miss they family. They don't know if they family dead or if they family alive. Some see baby die when crossing river. Other see baby die in jungle. Very bad. (Cambodian refugee, male, age fifty-nine)

Although the last Cambodian refugees left the camps in Thailand in 1999 (United Nations High Commissioner for Refugees 1999), conditions across many UNHCR-affiliated camps were remarkably similar when Karen refugees arrived years later: "There were a lot of people in the camp. We walked on dirt roads. Our house was made of bamboo and the roof was made with leaves. We never had enough food and sometimes the Burmese soldier attacked people" (Karen refugee, male, eighteen). Initial settlement into a refugee camp provided little stability as the Thai government and international aid agencies struggled to accommodate the overflowing, inadequate, and exceedingly temporary refuge provided in Thailand.

As camps continued to swell and overflow, the UNHCR expanded their global crisis interventions to four major camps and numerous satellite camps (Chandler 2000; United Nations High Commissioner for Refugees 2016).

> I am in one camp with one of two my older children–one die already. The International Red Cross finally come to help because we have nothing, know nothing. My wife in a different camp with our small child. The Red Cross know we all need help to find family. They [Red Cross] look at list and then move my wife to camp with me. It is bigger camp and it have more help from outside and it have some doctor. We get ration of rice but only this much [holds cupped hand to indicate the amount]. We still have not enough but we survive. (Cambodian, male, age seventy-five)

Eventually, life for Karen refugees improved in the camps. For example, there was increased tolerance toward foraging for vegetables and other food items in and around the camp; although, this was not uniform across all camps. Many Karen refugees spoke of moving from one camp to another and shared how camps seemed different in terms of opportunity for personal choice and independence. Tanaka (2013) reported that many younger Karen refugees, born in camps, knew no other life. The younger Karen refugees (ages eighteen and twenty-one) in our study described childhood memories playing soccer, attending occasional classes, and participating in religious practices. One woman, who was a young adult in the camps, described two very different camp experiences:

> I remember a lot about the first camp I lived in. We had much more freedom than the other camps. We could go anywhere to collect vegetables in the forest, and we also had a school there. But the second camp was not free and [was] close to the highways so we had a fence around us and we cannot leave. If the guards found out, the Thai soldiers would arrest us if they know we went out of the camp to find vegetables or food in the forest like bamboo shoots, mushrooms, and squirrels. (Karen refugee, female, age thirty-two)

Another Karen refugee (age eighteen) described his family's struggle to provide enough money and food to survive. He said:

> All we have is rice, with yellow rice. We would cook it with yellow beans and make our soup with fish paste, oil, salt, all of that. But all the other foods, like meat, we have to go and find these on our own. If my dad made money, we

would buy food from the store. They didn't give us any meat to eat. Only salt, fish paste, and oil. No vegetables. They gave us the food once per month. My mom went with my dad to buy meats. The store was really close to our home. It was not a big store; it was really small in the camp. Not many people had money to buy food. (Karen refugee, male, age eighteen)

By the time Karen refugees began to arrive in Thailand, the number of major camps had grown from four to nine along the Thai/Burmese border with multiple satellite camps struggling to provide a semblance of stability in the face of massive internal movement of refugees from one camp to another (United Nations High Commissioner for Refugees 2016). Both groups revealed similar stories of deprivations, lack of opportunities, and very limited sustenance.

A Continuation of Instability

Although many (both Cambodian and Karen) spoke of returning to their homelands, most readily accepted resettlement in a host nation. Many referenced paperwork and interviews prior to being admitted to the United States. Narratives of Cambodian refugees were filled with frustration as they were interrogated regarding allegiance with Communist forces. One man described meetings with resettlement groups:

The German, the French, the United States . . . they all come and interview me about going to their country. They keep asking me, "Are you Communist or non-Communist?" I tell them I surveyor for land development. I work for CIA. I tell them I no Communist! It the Communist that kill my family! It the Communist that destroy everything! I no Communist! I tell them over and over. (Cambodian refugee, male, age sixty-one)

In the rush to meet basic needs for shelter and food, psychological needs were overlooked (Mollica et al. 1993). Sensitivity to traumatic experiences was often absent in quests for containment and processing of the sheer number of people fleeing to Thailand (Boehnlein et al. 1985). A powerful relationship developed whereby expedient actions to transform refugees into compliant groups gained importance over humanitarian responses (Ong 1995). A disregard for familial losses inflicted further pain and suffering, as suggested in the following narrative.

I have to list all the name of my family; it don't matter they dead, I still have to write it all down. Because I now single, everybody gone, I can come to U.S. I can come alone. If my family live, I cannot go. What can I do; I have no choice, I have no home, nothing. (Cambodian refugee, male, age sixty-one)

Karen refugee families expressed less suspicion and doubt that resettlement agencies would help them. Many believed remaining in their homes in Burma put their families at risk of torture, rape, conscription into the rebel army, lifelong persecution, and even death. Decisions to flee were both conscious and necessary choices. While some explicitly discussed their experiences witnessing and fleeing the visible torture of family members and neighbors, others described leaving their homes to avoid potential attacks on loved ones. Karen refugees' experiences were diverse, with some describing decisions to leave homes prior to being forced by soldiers: "We left the camp because we wanted more freedom and we wanted our children to be educated. Over there, even when you graduate grade 12, you cannot speak English and we need to learn English" (Karen refugee, female, age thirty-two).

Older family members continued to wield power over decisions regarding movement in and out of camps. Younger refugees were less aware of the turmoil and uncertainty surrounding resettlement, and their memories focused on family actions and the desire to "go back" to their home country. Protected by their families from much of the discord, they sometimes found adventure in resettlement processes. One young person, when questioned about the airplane journey from Thailand to the United States, responded:

> It was fun! Because it was our first time being in an airplane, so it was fun in some ways but in other ways we didn't know what to do. Other people asked us, "What kind of food do you want?" or "Do you want juice?" We were hungry, but we didn't even know what to ask for or what the food was. (Karen refugee, male, age eighteen)

Once they had escaped the destruction, terror, and torture of the internecine wars of Cambodia and Burma and made their way through multiple refugee camps, refugees' identities continued to be subjected to negotiation, transformation, reconstruction, and redefinition as their lives began in the United States (Lewis 2010). The imbalance of power in refugees' lives is an incessant theme, but it is one we believe can be addressed by rethinking current systemic barriers to thriving upon resettlement and making space for refugees' voices.

Starting Over

Physically and psychologically challenged by the ordeal of life and escape under extremely harsh conditions, Cambodian and Karen refugees' identities revolve around who they were prior to fleeing home. Left with no place to go, they sought refuge from outsiders. Narratives describe processes of starting over and ways events can overwhelm one's ability to face the outside world. One Cambodian man spoke about resettlement in the United States:

> I come here because of Communist. I first go to Thailand and finally go here [the United States] August 23, 1976. I arrive in California but come to Alabama right away because this where my sponsor live. I have hard time at first. I cry a lot. Finally I move to Pennsylvania for two years. . . . I go to Pennsylvania with my girlfriend. But after six years that relationship fail. So I come back to Alabama. (Cambodian refugee, male, age fifty-nine)

His story unfolded over two months of interactions (shortly after Lewis began her engagement with Cambodian families). His narrative reflects a thoughtful, purposeful journey toward resettlement and rebuilding from fractured lives and demonstrates a reclaiming of his agency:

> In 1985 I still don't speak much English, can't drive, have no skill but save some money and try to find quiet place to live. . . . Most people came here because of seafood. You don't need no skill for seafood. So I buy over 100 acre. I split the land up for family, Cambodian family. . . . This a good place, close to seafood, unskill work here. I have good spiritual life here, peaceful, quiet. (Cambodian refugee, male, age fifty-nine)

A Karen refugee similarly described early days of resettlement in the United States as filled with sadness, hope, and strength as she struggled to adjust:

> Every day I trust God. Sometimes I am very sad, when I pray and read the Bible, it is very good. I feel like I have strength, I am stronger. When you are sad, you are weak. You don't want to go anywhere and you just stay inside thinking too much. (Karen, female, age thirty-two)

Members of both groups expressed sadness, lamented loss of home and country, struggled to find meaningful employment, and strove to maintain close family relations; yet, they also engaged in collective rebuilding.

Teaching Their Children: Identities Intersect

Older family members impart wisdom to younger generations, perhaps one of the most revered intergenerational exchanges an older family member can provide. Through actions and stories, they teach how to interact with others and share foodways that impart health, language, history, and culture (Spivey and Lewis 2016). Refugees balance learning about host cultures and the need for younger family members to adapt in order to thrive. One elderly Cambodian woman described her frustration and pride. She said her grandson "only know computers and don't know Khmer [language] anymore." Her grandson answered, "Why should I learn to read and write Khmer? It has no use here." He continued his reasoning: "I'm better off spending my time learning computers. They [computers] will help me get better grades and a job. I know it is important to stay close to my family and be happy being Khmer. But, I need to move up."

Shortly after this exchange, the grandmother highlighted his accomplishments and his acceptance at a prestigious university. Her frustration at his reluctance to learn the Cambodian language and her pride in his abilities to navigate sociocultural processes reflect a dichotomy of adhering to traditions and embracing and mastering life as an active member of U.S. society. This duality can be seen in the following accounts of younger individuals who recognize the need to straddle both cultural ideologies: "Everybody in my family works. And, us kids all go to high school or college. Before, maybe kids would just do things around the house for the parents. Now, we get good educations so we can buy them a better house" (Cambodian refugee, female, age twenty-four). Another added:

> Our parents do a lot for us so we can concentrate on school. We won't be able to give our parents the same kind of care they give our grandparents because we will have professional jobs. But, that's okay, because with our jobs we can afford to buy them a big house so we can all live together. (Cambodian refugee, female, age nineteen)

The above narratives reflect refugees' continued agency in maintaining beliefs relating to filial piety (respect and care for elders) and strategies for adapting to one's environment. Straddling cultures by adjusting one's behavior to suit the context of the interactions was a common thread, especially among younger Cambodian refugees (Lewis 2010). Karen refugees also report shifting from adherence to newly adopted American cultural traditions when away from family yet retaining cultural traditions when with family and fellow Karen neighbors.

> I can be American, I can be Karen. If I go to an American friend's home, I can be American. If I go to Karen people's house, I can be Karen. If I go to Karen people's house I will sit on the floor. If I come to American house, I sit on the sofa. (Karen refugee, male, age eighteen)

Another young Karen parent added: "We teach our children, always, always even if you live in a different culture, never lose your culture . . . always show your tradition to other people. All Karen people teach this" (Karen refugee, female, age thirty-two).

In many ways, Cambodian and Karen refugee families report the need to "live two lives" and balance retention of customs from their home countries and assimilation into an American cultural milieu. Members of both groups stressed the importance of their agency in maintaining family traditions, even when those traditions were adapted to fit day-to-day life in the United States.

Family Traditions

Family provides space for collective identity and for sharing, forming, and transforming selves, identities, and memories. The sharing of traditions provides ways to continue the restructuring of identity as a unique group (as Cambodian or as Karen people). Family context provides a forum for cultural strength, knowing one's history, and rebuilding lives. One Cambodian refugee described her family's importance and its growth: "My family is my life. We came to this country broken and not sure who we would become. But my family has survived very well. We are most of us together now. We have grown because of children born and new family members coming together" (Cambodian refugee, female, age sixty-eight).

A common statement made by many Cambodian refugees was that all Cambodians are one family. This blurring of family boundaries was apparent when one Cambodian refugee man spoke of the role of family and community: "The Khmer [Cambodian] way is for families to help each other. When a family has a problem, all the families help. They bring food or wash the clothes" (Cambodian refugee, male, age sixty-four). A similar sentiment was found with Karen families who stressed the importance of sharing food, language, and religious practices. One young Karen refugee described the importance of religious traditions:

> We pray; my family prays every night before we go to sleep. When we lived in the refugee camp in Thailand, we prayed one time in the morning, and one time before sleep at night. We always do that and we are friendly to others. My family is a Christian family; we go to church together every week. We eat rice [he laughs]; that's the most important food because we eat it every day. It's part of our life. (Karen refugee, male, age eighteen)

Another Karen refugee relayed her views on her children's ability to speak the Karen language:

> It is important for my kids to know they are Karen people because we don't want to lose our Karen identity. If they don't speak Karen, we have a saying, "If you lost your language, you also lost your people." I think the language is the most important thing. (Karen refugee, female, age thirty-two)

The struggles faced by these families reflect two remarkably different groups who fled internecine wars several decades apart. Yet, their needs remain quite similar: food and shelter, a place to feel safe and secure, and power to hold on to traditional cultural patterns while adjusting to and adapting aspects of cultural patterns found in the host nation. These needs are known, and many are addressed with varying levels of success. Needs that tend to be unmet, though, are associated with feelings of acceptance by members of the host nation rather than pressures to conform.

Refugees' sense of control and agency is not often expressed directly, but regaining control of their lives not only depends on time and patience but also depends on support from their host community. Space is needed to maintain one's difference—in language, in dress, in foodways, and in religion. Space, though, is oftentimes overlooked by aid agencies assisting refugees to quickly assimilate into the United States. One Karen refugee (age forty-three) offered sage advice for meeting the needs of others. He said, "Whenever they see a visitor they must offer them something to eat. They should also be nice to other people even if they do not know them." The ultimate unmet need of the refugees described in this chapter is the need to be kind to others and to get to know them as neighbors and as brothers and sisters living together. Respect for agency and autonomy in rebuilding culturally relevant and responsive communities could provide opportunities for refugee families to cease straddling two cultures and embrace and integrate both.

U.S. Policies and Response to Refugees

Resettlement in the United States is not the end of refugees' journeys. Families endure relentless transitions and pressures as they negotiate their responsibilities as immigrants (proud of their culture and heritage) and loyal, respectful guests who may become U.S. citizens. Refugees did not choose to come to the United States but were assigned to the United States by strangers. They were not asked their preference of resettlement country. Friends and even immediate family members may be resettled in other countries (e.g., Australia, New Zealand, Canada, or Finland). Resettlement agencies, governmental decision makers, and community members involved in aspects of resettled refugees' daily lives should consider the powerlessness refugees often face and meet them with opportunities for empowerment, self-governance (Walters 2015), and mutual respect for their own decisions. Importantly, the logistical, emotional, and seemingly quotidian demands refugees face following arrival to the United States must be contextualized within personal histories of persecution, oppression, and forced displacement. Refugees' narratives must be considered in such a way that their agency is not filtered out by a governmental lens that assumes a myopic view of power (Walters 2015) residing above but not within the refugees themselves.

With the passage of the Displaced Persons Act of 1948, more than 5,000,000 persons fleeing Communist regimes were resettled in the United States. Since then, the Refugee Act of 1980 has allowed the United States to resettle more than 3 million refugees from Southeast Asia (United States Department of Health and Human Services 2012b). The United States continues to respond to and control the experiences of refugees and facilitate resettlement processes. Although more than thirty years separates the experiences of Cambodian and Karen refugees, their stories reveal inherent flaws in U.S. resettlement processes. The unmet needs of refugee families remain remarkably similar. Many governmental and nongovernmental agencies engage with the resettlement process; yet, issues faced by Cambodian refugee families (i.e., trust of the U.S. health system, limited job opportunities, adaptations in intergenerational relationships, and substandard housing) continue as issues for Karen families. The governance of refugees as material goods or assets to be "budgeted" not only disrespects their human rights to agency but also creates a false sense of ownership and overall management of goods instead of consideration of families with values, skills, and hopes for their futures.

Although refugees' narratives have revealed that they retain some levels of power over their lives, there is highly structured control exerted throughout the resettlement process. Federal agencies (e.g., the State Department and the Office of Refugee Resettlement) manage initial steps of refugee programs, including decisions regarding who to prioritize for resettlement and funding processes. Local groups engage as individual states and communities who then turn to nongovernmental, nonprofit agencies to welcome and resettle families. The remaining level of power still resides with the refugees themselves as they navigate and negotiate the rebuilding of their lives but can be subjugated by the power hierarchy.

In addition to meeting the cognitive demands, refugees in the United States must physically adapt to their new homes and the cities, towns, or communities where they are placed. Their resettlement location may or may not be accommodating to familiar environments. Some regions of the United States provide opportunities for traditional modes of production. For example, many of the refugees in our research farmed or sold commodities in their home country. Yet, many refugees are resettled in urban areas near jobs, housing, and government-sponsored resettlement offices with no access to land.

Local resettlement agencies are the hands and feet of U.S. resettlement programs. Agencies' offices are located in major urban resettlement areas (such as Atlanta, Georgia) and employ a small staff with multiple volunteers and interns. Resettlement agencies help refugee families find housing, apply for jobs, matriculate into school, and muddle through the paperwork of taxes, their initial living stipend, and travel loan repayment. Agencies solicit funds through major campaigns, teach and facilitate citizenship classes, organize healthcare appointments, secure affordable housing for refugees, and even greet resettled families at the airport.

Refugee families are minimally supported by a temporary living stipend but are expected to become responsible and self-sufficient within eight months, at which time they must begin repaying their resettlement loan. Although critical to refugees' experiences, agencies have minimal financial support, and employees spend an exorbitant amount of human capital on fundraising efforts. Local communities' financial support, volunteerism, and overall political activism are vital. Agencies' hard work and dedication can only manifest itself within supportive communities of understanding friends and neighbors. One example of community support can be seen in the establishment by Lewis, Young, and local community partners of a series of instructional workshops to assist newly arrived refugees. That series of workshops was transformed into the Refugee Responsiveness Program in collaboration with other faculty and graduate students and a local organization that serves refugees. We see this small step in partnership building as sustainable support that is culturally responsive to the lives of refugees, adding to ethical participatory action research conducted with refugee populations (see Pittaway et al. 2010).

Conclusion

The lives of resettled refugee families are often unimaginable to those of us who have not experienced such trauma. The use of qualitative methods allows their voices to be heard and strengthens our understanding of the journey from home countries to resettlement in the United States. Every voice is unique; every exertion of power and agency tells the story of resilience and determination. Social workers, case workers, healthcare providers, friends, and other nonrefugee community members may all become part of refugees' lives in their host country. While these relationships can be nourishing, they can also be stressful, be taxing, and usurp the power of refugees who struggle with myriad transitions in relationships. Refugees' lives were often fraught with losses of friends and family members, as well as dependence upon others for help and guidance as they search for peace and safety. Regularly relying on others for help as they seek safety, a sense of community, and collective responsibility may become a learned means of survival along their journey to a third host country. However, the power within a mutually supportive way of life can collide with resettlement policies (United States Department of Health and Human Services 2012a, 2012b; van Selm; Reklev and Jumbert, this volume).

A label of "refugee" in today's world is a loaded identity. Technological advances have loosened connections that hold society together as a human family. Oftentimes, refugees fled from those who imposed the most violent, unthinkable, inhumane actions upon their neighbors. People labeled "refugees" today are some of the most resilient, unyielding, and adaptable people in our world. Rather than feeling supported and secure in their host country, they may feel further traumatized by their unfamiliar setting, lack of community, and difficulty integrating to the host culture. What is most invaluable to these families often can be found within a relationship with a listening ear, assistance with translating a confusing letter, and providing encouragement for a more hopeful future.

We strive to illuminate the lives of Karen and Cambodian refugees living in the United States through their narratives. Both groups experienced extreme violence, oppression, and persecution and were forced to flee their beloved homes. The United States can offer a new start, but resettlement will never erase their unique histories. Instead, we must consider the gravity of our responsibility to welcome families who have endured unthinkable pain into a place where they may find hope for a future. These powerful voices reflect a monumental resilience of spirit in light of the long, arduous journey they travel.

Denise C. Lewis holds a Ph.D. in gerontology from the University of Kentucky and is an associate professor in the Department of Human Development and Family Science, University of Georgia, as well as an adjunct faculty member at the Royal University of Phnom Penh, Cambodia. Lewis is a qualitative methodologist and conducts cross-cultural and transnational research with refugees and other marginalized families in the United States and elder-headed households in Cambodia. Her scholarship contributes to an understanding of intersections of families, aging, culture, and society by offering a view of diversity centered on lived experiences of immigrant/ refugee and other marginalized families.

Savannah S. Young holds a Ph.D. in human development and family science from the University of Georgia and is an ethnographic research consultant located in Redwood City, California. Since completing her studies at the University of Georgia, she has continued writing and publishing research on refugee health and family issues. She is dedicated to understanding the lives of refugee families along all stages of their journeys. Her research focuses on issues surrounding the phenomenon of forced migration and the psychology of their communities in which those forced to flee find themselves. In addition to empirical research, she is passionate about community engagement and has implemented applied outreach programs in local resettlement communities in the United States.

References

Berger, Peter L. and Thomas Luckmann. 1966. *The Social Construction of Reality: A Treatise in the Sociology of Knowledge*. New York: Doubleday.

Bernard, H. Russell. 2011. *Research Methods in Anthropology: Qualitative and Quantitative Approaches*. 5th ed. Lanham: AltaMira Press.

Boehnlein, James K., J. David Kinzie, Rath Ben, and Jenelle Fleck. 1985. "One-Year Follow-Up Study of Posttraumatic Stress Disorder among Survivors of Cambodian Concentration Camps." *American Journal of Psychiatry* 142(8): 956–59.

Bowen, Murray. 1966. "The Use of Family Theory in Clinical Practice." *Comprehensive Psychiatry* 7(5): 345–74.

Bureau of Population, Refugees, and Migration, U.S. Department of State. 2015. *Cumulative Summary of Refugee Admissions.* Accessed 1 April 2016. http://www.state.gov/j/prm/releases/statistics/251288.htm.

Chandler, David. 2000. *A History of Cambodia.* 3rd ed. Boulder: Westview Press.

Creswell, John W. 2014. *Research Design: Qualitative, Quantitative, and Mixed Methods Approaches.* 4th ed. Thousand Oaks: Sage Publications.

Dowd, James. 1980. "Social Exchange, Class, and Old People." In *Stratification among the Aged,* edited by J. Dowd, 29–42. Monterey: Wadsworth.

Eastmond, Marita. 2007. "Stories as Lived Experiences: Narratives in Forced Migration." *Journal of Refugee Studies* 20(2): 248–64.

Elder, George H. Jr. 1985. *Life Course Dynamics: Trajectories and Transitions, 1968–1980.* Ithaca: Cornell University Press.

Geiger, Martin, and Antoine Pécoud. 2013. *Disciplining the Transnational Migration of People.* London: Palgrave MacMillan.

Ghorashi, Halleh. 2007. "Giving Silence a Chance: The Importance of Life Stories for Research on Refugees." *Journal of Refugee Studies* 21(1): 117–32.

Lewis, Denise C. 2001. "From Cambodia to the United States: The Disassembly, Reconstruction and Redefinition of Khmer Identity." *Southern Anthropologist* 28(1): 28–49.

——. 2008. "Types, Meanings, and Ambivalence in Intergenerational Exchanges among Cambodian Refugee Families in the United States." *Ageing and Society* 28(5): 693–715.

——. 2010. "Cambodian Refugee Families in the United States: 'Bending the Tree' to Fit the Environment." *Journal of Intergenerational Relationships* 8(1): 5–20.

McCubbin, Hamilton I. 1979. "Integrating Coping Behavior in Family Stress Theory." *Journal of Marriage and Family* 41(2): 237–44.

Mills, C. Wright. 2000 [1959]. *The Sociological Imagination.* 40th anniversary ed. New York: Oxford University Press.

Mollica, Richard F., Karen Donelan, Svang Tor, James Lavelle, Christopher Elias, Martin Frankel, and Robert J. Blendon. 1993. "The Effect of Trauma and Confinement on Functional Health and Mental Health Status of Cambodians Living in Thailand-Cambodia Border Camp." *Journal of the American Medical Association* 270(5): 581–86.

Office of Refugee Resettlement, U.S. Department of Health and Human Services. 2016. *FY 2015 Served Populations by State and Country of Origin (Refugees Only).* Accessed 1 April 2016. http://www.acf.hhs.gov/orr/resource/fy-2015-served-populations-by-state-and-country-of-origin-refugees-only.

Ong, Aihwa. 1995. "Making the Biopolitical Subject: Cambodian Immigrants, Refugee Medicine and Cultural Citizenship in California." *Social Science and Medicine* 40(9): 1243–57.

Patton, Michael Q. 2015. *Qualitative Research and Evaluation Methods: Integrating Theory and Practice.* 4th ed. Thousand Oaks: Sage Publications.

Pittaway, Eileen, Linda Bartolomei, and Richard Hugman. 2010. "'Stop Stealing Our Stories': The Ethics of Research with Vulnerable Groups." *Journal of Human Rights Practice* 2(2): 229–51.

Pittaway, Eileen, Chrisanta Muli, and Sarah Shteir. 2009. "'I Have A Voice–Hear Me!' Findings of an Australian Study Examining the Resettlement and Integration Experience of Refugees and Migrants from the Horn of Africa in Australia." *Refuge* 26(1): 133–46.

Robinson, Denise L. 1997. "Family Stress Theory: Implications for Family Health." *Journal of the American Academy of Nurse Practitioners* 9(1): 17–24.

Seponski, Desiree M., J. Maria Bermudez, and Denise C. Lewis. 2013. "Creating Culturally Responsive Family Therapy Models and Research: Introducing the Use of Responsive Evaluation as a Method." *Journal of Marital and Family Therapy* 39(1): 28–42.

Sleijpen, Mariake, Hennie R. Boeij, Rolf J. Kleber, and Trudy Mooren. 2016. "Between Power and Powerlessness: A Meta-Ethnography of Sources of Resilience in Young Refugees." *Ethnicity and Health* 21(2): 158–80.

Spivey, Savannah E. and Denise C. Lewis. 2016. "Harvesting from a Repotted Plant: A Qualitative Study of Karen Refugees and Foodways." *Journal of Refugee Studies* 29(1): 60–81.

Tanaka, Akiko. 2013. "Assessment of the Psychosocial Development of Children Attending Nursery Schools in Karen Refugee Camps in Thailand." *International Journal of Early Childhood* 45(3): 279–305.

United Nations High Commissioner for Refugees (UNHCR). 1999. *Cambodian Refugee Camps in Thailand Now Empty*. Accessed 1 April 2016. http://www.unhcr.org/en-us/news/briefing/1999/3/3ae6b81cc/cambodian-refugee-camps-thailand-empty.html.

——. 2016. *Thailand*. Accessed 1 April 2016. http://www.unhcr.org/en-us/thailand.html.

United States Department of Health and Human Services. 2012a. *Divisions-Refugee Assistance. Office of Refugee Resettlement.* Accessed 1 April 2016. http://www.acf.hhs.gov/programs/orr/resource/divisions-refugee-assistance.

——. 2012b. *Office of Refugee Resettlement. The Refugee Act.* Accessed 1 April 2016. http://www.acf.hhs.gov/programs/orr/resource/the-refugee-act.

Walters, William. 2015. "Reflections on Migration and Governmentality." *Journal für kritische Migrations und Grenzregimeforschung* 1(1): 1–25.

Wolcott, Harry F. 2008. *Ethnography: A Way of Seeing.* 2nd ed. Lanham: AltaMira Press.

9

"Giving Cases Weight"

Congolese Refugees' Tactics for Resettlement Selection

Marnie Jane Thomson

"Sister, sister!" a woman called to me in Swahili as I was walking toward the main road in Nyarugusu refugee camp in Tanzania. "Sister Marnie! It worked. Do you remember? It worked."

Nabisa was chasing after me, so I turned around to go meet her. We hurried back to her plot because she had left her children at home when she had seen me pass, and she did not want to leave them alone for long. Nabisa and her children were among the more than 70,000 Congolese refugees who were living in Nyarugusu camp in 2013. The camp opened in 1996, and the majority of its Congolese residents originate from South Kivu; they fled violence during the First and Second Congolese Wars and the violence that has continued in the east of the Democratic Republic of Congo. UN camps in Tanzania have been their home for two decades. In recent years, United Nations High Commission for Refugees (UNHCR) resettlement has increased–beginning in 2012 with the enhanced resettlement for Congolese refugees and group resettlement to the United States for approximately 30,000 Congolese living in Tanzania began in July 2015.[1] This chapter is an ethnographic account of how the Congolese view, navigate, and seek to influence the power dynamics of UNHCR resettlement selection in Nyarugusu camp.

"Forgive me, what worked? Please remind me," I asked Nabisa.

Nabisa explained that her resettlement case was proceeding smoothly now. That is what she meant by "it worked." The actions she had taken had been met with her desired result. As she reminded me of her case, I recalled our encounter.

"It really worked?" I asked, "Your case is going forward?"

"Yes, I have already signed."

Having signed meant that Nabisa had an actual resettlement case. It meant that UNHCR representatives in Nyarugusu camp had selected her for resettlement. When we first met at the end of November 2012, she had only ever presented her case to protection officers. By the time we met again in June 2013, she had completed several interviews with resettlement officers and her case had been passed along to regional headquarters for further review. Nabisa expected that the next step would be to learn which country had preliminarily accepted her application, followed by interviews with that country's immigration officers.

For Nabisa and the other residents of Nyarugusu camp, resettlement is part of the humanitarian system that governs their lives. Humanitarianism is a system premised on global inequalities (Blommaert 2001; Fassin 2010; Fassin and d'Halluin 2007; Redfield 2012; Sandvik 2008; Ticktin 2006), whereby international NGOs, and sometimes state organs, seek to ameliorate human suffering in areas deemed to be in crisis (Agier 2010; Barnett 2005, 2010; Barnett and Weiss 2008a, 2008b; Fassin and Pandolfi 2010; Feldman and Ticktin 2010; Redfield 2013; Ticktin 2011a). In refugee camps, the humanitarian apparatus brings relief and aid and also becomes a system of power, bureaucracy, governance, and regulation (Agier 2008, 2011; Dunn 2012; Malkki 1995; Turner 2010). For many Nyarugusu residents, resettlement not only is about relocating to a more wealthy nation but also represents a legal way to escape the humanitarian system that restricts their movement, employment opportunities, commerce, livelihoods, and more (Horst 2006a; Sandvik 2011).

As the humanitarian regime has become increasingly institutionalized since the 1990s through attempts to create global standardization, regulation, and evaluation (Barnett 2005; Dunn 2012; Hilhorst 2002, 2003; Leader 1998; Stein 2008; and van Selm; Sandvik, this volume), so too has resettlement through the UNHCR's commitment to procedural consistency and transparency across the globe (Sandvik 2010: 41–44). The *Resettlement Handbook,* most recently updated in 2011, "sets out standardized methodologies for identifying resettlement needs and expediting resettlement processing" in 428 pages. Bureaucratic rationalization and compartmentalization can create opacity as much as transparency (Thomson 2012), and regulation can privilege procedure and consistency to the detriment of humanitarian goals (Barnett 2005; Stein 2008). Despite this, refugees do not view the resettlement process as a cold, distant bureaucratic machine (cf. Kibreab 2004).

Instead they recognize that people–UNHCR representatives and immigration officials–are making decisions every step of the way.

Even though Congolese refugees are removed from the decisions made about their cases, they do what they can to fortify their own cases against possible rejection. Inequalities between aid providers and aid recipients are readily apparent in the camp, but refugees do not view power to be entirely confined to people in certain positions. Power is exercised by all involved through their actions (Foucault 1980). Scholarship on refugee agency has focused on refugee deception, cheating, and trickery (Jansen 2008; Kibreab 2004); coping by means of mobility (Horst 2006b); gendered usage of silence and muted voice (Thomson 2013); enacting new forms of citizenship (Turner 2005; 2010); and utilizing the camp as a livelihood option (Jansen 2015). In contrast with these analyses of refugee agency, and in line with this volume's argument that resettlement is a form of humanitarian governance, this chapter focuses on interstices of refugee agency and resettlement selection.

Agency–as exerted by refugees in this context–entails intentional pursuit of their goals through specific undertakings (Ortner 2006). This does not mean, however, that refugees believe that they can actively achieve resettlement on their own (cf. Jansen 2008). The actions refugees can take are limited, akin to James Scott's "weapons of the weak," small-scale acts of resistance that often go unnoticed or unrecognized as such (see also Vera Espinoza; Lewis and Young, this volume). Rather than nibbling away at the humanitarian structure in the camp, however, refugees approach the resettlement process with weapons of defense, not attack. Their form of resistance is to defy powerlessness. Refugees act in refusal to wait idly as someone else determines their futures. Within the constraints of the resettlement process, Nyarugusu residents speak of *kuipa kesi uzito,* giving the case weight, or sometimes they say they are *kuzidisha viwango vya kesi,* increasing the level or status of the case, to describe their efforts to be selected.

In this chapter, I describe my encounters with Nabisa to show how Congolese refugees seek to fortify their cases for resettlement. Nabisa's story is unique; every person in Nyarugusu camp has a unique story. They have different experiences in Congo, in the camp, and in the resettlement process. In other words, Nabisa's story is neither representative of the people I have met in Nyarugusu camp nor representative of the Congolese refugee experience as a whole. But individual stories like Nabisa's shed light on the larger social processes at work in the camp, in this case, the power dynamics of resettlement selection. Through her story, I outline five ways in which Congolese exercise their limited power to actively seek to influence resettlement selection in Nyarugusu camp. They are (1) telling convincing stories of fleeing due to persecution, (2) reporting persecution in the camp, (3) lying or cheating, (4) paying bribes and committing fraud, and (5) soliciting higher powers. While this list is not exhaustive, these were the undertakings Nyarugusu residents most commonly discussed with me. They are not seen as ways to cheat or game the resettlement process; rather, camp residents view them as efforts to increase the likelihood of being selected. The chapter sections follow in the order of the actions listed, preceded by a brief section on methodology.

Methodology

Nabisa sought me out through a mutual friend, another Congolese refugee, to tell me about her case for resettlement. We set up a day and time that worked for both of us and met in the room of the main hospital that I occasionally used to speak with people who were not comfortable speaking in their homes or in public locations of the camp.[2] Most of the time this occurred when people did not want their neighbors to overhear the stories they were telling me or to even know that they were meeting with me. This is how my research often proceeded. I would meet someone, often through a friend, and we would set up a time and place to meet and converse. Congolese refugees often sought me out again to update me on their life happenings or would stop me if they saw me in the camp, as Nabisa did.

I am a cultural anthropologist, and I have spent more than two years conducting research refugee camps, aid compounds, and government offices in Tanzania. My research focuses on refugee experiences of violence and dislocation and the politics of humanitarian intervention in both Tanzania and the Democratic Republic of Congo. In addition to my fieldwork in Tanzania, I have conducted fieldwork elsewhere in the Great Lakes Region of Africa and at UNHCR regional and global headquarters. But my primary research site is Nyarugusu camp in Tanzania, where I have been conducting ethnographic research since 2008.

My research is qualitative, and I have spoken with several hundred individuals. My interviews are informal. I let refugees, aid workers, and government officials take the lead and usually only ask questions for clarification or if there is something I would like to know more about. Here and elsewhere I translate my conversations as literally as I can to convey word choice and meaning as accurately as possible. My fieldwork also consists of anthropology's classic method of participant observation, by which we seek to understand the "imponderabilia of actual life," the minute details that can only be grasped through participating and observing in daily activities (Malinowski 1922:18–19). In Nyarugusu camp, participant observation included fetching water, cooking, going to the market, going to work with friends earning incentive salaries from aid agencies, collecting food rations, and visiting friends, along with other ways to pass the time.

Telling Convincing Stories of Fleeing Due to Persecution

The one thing that all refugees in Nyarugusu camp must do to qualify for resettlement is tell their own story of persecution. That day in November 2013 when I met with Nabisa in one of the hospital offices, she began by telling me how she first fled. "First I was married in 1991. I gave birth to three children. In the war in 1996, I lost my husband and children." She fled from South Kivu province to Tanzania and returned to Congo in 1999 by herself. She stayed with a friend in Bukavu, the capital of South Kivu, but she did not find her husband or her children. Not knowing what became of her family preoccupied her every thought. She could not continue to suffer that way, she explained, so she found another husband.

Nabisa had five children with her second husband. From Bukavu, they moved to Goma, the capital of North Kivu province, for her husband's job. He was a driver for Rwandan businessmen. Their business was based in Gisenyi, the Rwandan town across the border from Goma. Nabisa's husband drove a large vehicle for them, often to transport kitenge fabrics, East African patterned swaths of cloth, between Kampala and Gisenyi/Goma. "We lived a good life," Nabisa told me.

> I had a store in our house. I sold kitenge fabrics, oil, sugar, and powered soap. But the Congolese government and citizens did not like that my husband was working for the Rwandans because they had invaded our country. One night we were all startled awake by voices outside. It was around one a.m. They forced themselves inside our door. I ran to our children's room and got under the bed with all of our children. We heard them beating my husband in the living room. They were government soldiers and *Mai Mai* [militia]. They were there for three hours before we heard them leave. They killed him.

Nabisa fled with her children that night. They went to the Katindo airport, where she explained the situation to the night guard, who let them stay the night in the waiting area. In the morning, she and her children crossed the border into Gisenyi. She had no trouble at the border, and the Rwandans helped them find food and transport to Bujumbura. Nabisa does not recall how long she stayed in Bujumbura. "I had become a different person then," she told me. "I was very confused. I felt as though my head had exploded. I became very mean, and all I could remember was the brutal death of my husband."

One night a man named Kapa found her wandering in a street in Bujumbura. He bought them bread to eat. "Kapa saw that I needed to go to a refugee camp," Nabisa told me. He took them to Manyovu, the Tanzanian town on the border of Burundi, where he handed Nabisa and her family over to the immigration authorities. UNHCR came to collect them from the immigration office and brought them to Nyarugusu camp.

Camp residents often began their stories in a similar manner. They told me why they fled, who they lost along the way, and how they arrived in the camp. Many knew that I was interested in these stories. But others, like Nabisa, who sought me out on their own accord also began their stories this way. "Why did you flee?" was often the first question that UNHCR representatives and Tanzanian government officials asked when they met with refugees in order to determine refugee status. Article One (A) of the 1951 Refugee Convention defines a refugee as follows:

> A person who is outside his or her country of nationality or habitual residence; has a well-founded fear of persecution because of his or her race, religion, nationality, membership of a particular social group or political opinion; and is unable or unwilling to avail himself or herself of the protection of that country, or to return there, for fear of persecution.

Narrations of flight allow interviewers to determine whether or not the asylum seeker fled due to persecution. Any other reason for fleeing, including widespread war or violence, would not legally qualify the asylum seeker for official refugee status. For example, Nabisa's narration of the first time she fled demonstrated the trauma of fleeing in the midst of war but would not provide the explanation of persecution required by the definition of a refugee.

Nabisa explained to me that she and her children were awarded refugee status sometime after they arrived in the camp. I asked her when this was. It was 2008. That year Tanzania began conducting refugee status determination (RSD) interviews with new arrivals even though they had not technically revoked their prima facie policy for Congolese nationals by which all new arrivals from Congo are granted refugee status (Betts 2013: 117–34). Nabisa understood why I was asking about the timeline. She explained that there were fifty-seven cases that were being considered, and she was the last person to receive official refugee status.

Official refugee status was important to Nabisa and other camp residents because it provides them with the means to receive food rations in the camp and entitles them to UNHCR provisions and services. Nabisa emphasized that UNHCR Protection together with the Tanzanian Ministry of Home Affairs extended refugee status to her and her family. She even recalled the name of the zonal commissioner at the time. She remembered his name for the same reason that she remembered Kapa's: their actions directed the course of her life. Without Kapa, she would not have made it to Tanzania. Without the approval of the zonal commissioner, she would not have the official title of refugee.

Official refugee status was important to Nyarugusu residents for another reason: it is the first prerequisite needed to qualify for resettlement. According to the *UNHCR Resettlement Handbook,* "The applicant must be determined to be a refugee by **UNHCR"** (emphasis in original, UNHCR 2011: 9). As a result, refugees who are seeking resettlement know that they will have to retell the story of their escape and, in doing so, convince UNHCR representatives that their reasons for fleeing constitute persecution. To do this, they often adopt narrative styles specific to the resettlement interview process using chronological accounts with exact dates and times that differ from the metaphorical speech they often use to communicate violence and trauma in everyday life (Lynch 2013). Even before their cases are passed on to the resettlement unit, refugees will begin narrating their stories in the more detailed, technical, and literal style required by the UNHCR.

Refugees craft letters about their persecution that they try to deliver to the UNHCR. In these letters, they explain why they fled and why they cannot go back. Their hope is that these letters will spur the protection unit to call them for an interview. They often write and submit many letters in the hope that one will be seen. They also go to the UNHCR offices in the camp seeking out protection and resettlement officers to hear their stories. This has become more difficult in recent years since a system has been implemented whereby camp residents need to have a token indicating that they were summoned by the UNHCR to be seen by a representative. Otherwise, security guards will not allow them inside the fence that now surrounds the office. These efforts illustrate how camp residents are active not just in crafting their story but also in seeking ways for it to be heard, or read in the case of their letters.

Nabisa did not stop narrating her story after having been awarded refugee status. She continued to seek out protection officers and could name every person to whom she had told her story. According to her, there was one protection officer who was trying to help her pass her case along to the resettlement unit, but the others had not been helpful. Camp residents discuss the dispositions of all the UNHCR officers in the camp. They view such knowledge as power, and they want their cases to be heard by the most sympathetic and action-driven representatives. This shows how they conceive of telling their stories as a form of power, an act of swaying UNHCR representatives into action on their cases.

Reporting Persecution in the Camp

After telling the story of how and why she fled, Nabisa began describing her life in the camp. In speech that was typical of Nyarugusu residents, she described life in the camp as difficult. Often Congolese people will tell me that they have many problems. Nabisa told me that she has no peace, no security in the camp. This phrasing is also common. Nabisa said:

> I am a single mother with five children. To raise them, to clothe them, to feed them, to provide them with their various needs, it is very difficult. I have no life. I have no job. I am a woman, on my own, raising all these children. Men have come to my house at night looking to force me into having sex with them.

This has occurred three times, by three separate men. Her children yelled and made a lot of noise, attracting neighbors and Congolese security guards, who notified the Tanzanian police force in the camp. Each time the police caught the perpetrator, and he was held in the jail for only one or two days. The police have told me that they do not accept bribes, but among camp residents it is widely acknowledged that they will release prisoners if they receive payment. Since Nabisa was not invited to a hearing for any of these three men, she assumed that they had bribed the police. She has seen them since they were arrested at her home: "They are still here, walking around the camp." Because the crimes were sexual offenses, she also reported them to the International Rescue Committee (IRC) office for sexual and gender-based violence (known in the camp as SGBV or GBV). While reporting rape and sexual assault often does little to alleviate the violence women like Nabisa have experienced in the camp and elsewhere, the legal, medical, and therapeutic practices used at the SGBV name, authorize, and legitimize victims' experiences of sexual violence (Hyndman 2000: 79; Ticktin 2011b). The reports produced can be used in resettlement cases. Nabisa made a point to tell me that she knew that SGBV still had those reports.

There was another incident when people came to break into her house at night. She woke up, which scared them away. She went straight to the police after that. The police came with her to her place and decided it would be best for her to go stay in the Departure Center with the asylum seekers for seven days.[3] The police conducted an investigation of her house during that time but did not find anything. She and her children returned home after the police concluded the investigation. Nabisa does not know who tried to break into her house, she never saw them. But she sees the men who sexually assaulted her from time to time. They make threats that they "will show her" or get revenge for putting them in jail.

Stories of persecution within the camp help refugees demonstrate that resettlement is their only option for a better future. Although many camps span generations and Nyarugusu has been open for more than twenty years, the UNHCR considers camps to be temporary stopgaps on the road to providing a permanent resolution. Persecution in the camp creates a sense of urgency to find a solution. According to the UNHCR, there are three "durable solutions" available to refugees: repatriation to their country of origin, local integration in the country of asylum, and resettlement to a third country.

In 2015 Tanzania naturalized almost 162,000 Hutu refugees who have been living in self-sustaining settlements since they fled Burundi in 1972,[4] but the government has not extended local integration as a possibility to any refugees living in the camps. With local integration eliminated, voluntary repatriation and resettlement remain as the only options for Nyarugusu residents. When Nabisa and I met, UNHCR had suspended all repatriation convoys to Congo because of a resurgence of violence in the Kivu provinces.[5] Even with this moratorium, however, repatriation loomed in the camp as an ever-present threat particularly because although the enhanced resettlement of Congolese refugee had begun in 2012, it took a couple of years before it gained traction in Tanzania. In this context, stories of persecution within the camp illustrated that refugees cannot endure any longer and need an immediate change. Knowing that refugee protection is UNHCR's central mandate, camp residents' stories illustrated that their safety and security could not be ensured through repatriation or staying in the camp. They sought to show that resettlement was the only solution that could ensure their safety and protection.

The week before we met, a protection officer called Nabisa and interviewed her about her problems. She told him everything that she told me. He asked Nabisa where she has reported her problems. She said that she has reported to the IRC social workers for vulnerable people, SGBV, and the police. Nabisa credited SGBV seminars for helping her to reduce the effects of the trauma she has endured. She was also taking medicine to help her cope with the anxiety and depression she suffered as a result of these traumatic events. Every week she goes to the outpatient clinic where we first met to renew her prescription.

Refugees expect the question about reporting because they have friends who have been through the process. Reporting their problems more than once to various offices increases their chances of finding a camp authority who will vouch for them. Many residents told me that they befriended Tanzanian aid workers or government officials who work in the camp. Yet this tactic can also backfire. Aid workers often complained to me that refugees inundate them with their problems and are using them not for friendship but as a means to qualify for resettlement. Conversely, refugees have complained that Tanzanians accuse them of being disingenuous and only interested in resettlement. When frequent reporting causes such resentment, refugees worry that the aid workers might try to jeopardize their cases. Most refugees reason that this gives them more cause to report to as many places as possible, so that when a UNHCR representative asks them where they have reported, they can mention a number of offices.

Refugees report their problems in the camp to various camp officials not only because they anticipate that UNHCR representatives will ask them about it but also because they realize that doing so strengthens their credibility. UNHCR officials are required to question and assess refugees' character (Kagan 2003, 2006). Within the humanitarian structure of the camp, refugees occupy the bottom rung of the hierarchy of credibility (Stoler 1992). The approval and assistance of camp officials can help refugees climb this social ladder. Refugees are not the only ones seeking to build credibility in the resettlement process; humanitarian agents are as well (Sandvik 2008). Finding camp officials who will vouch for them, therefore, builds credibility not only for refugees but also for the UNHCR officers who forward their cases to their colleagues and superiors.

Nabisa had the police reports and showed the protection officer, but she did not have any of the SGBV documents in her possession. The protection officer told her to come back once she had obtained the documents. Refugees recognize the power of official paper trails, knowing they record the past and can reframe and redirect the future (Yngvesson and Bibler Coutin 2006). Yet they do not fetishize documents produced by camp authorities in the way that Gastón Gordillo has described for the ID papers in the Argentinian Chaco (2006). In other words, refugees understand that documents do not have the ability in and of themselves to determine the outcome of the resettlement process. They know that the resettlement officials make the decisions. Documents from UNHCR implementing partners allow resettlement officials to diffuse their individual agency in making decisions about refugee cases (Hull 2003). Refugees collect and submit these documents for the same ends. The documents show that camp officials confirm that certain events did indeed occur in the camp. Documentation extends the authority and credibility of its authors–aid workers and government representatives– to the refugees.

Lying and Cheating

Nabisa and I never discussed lying and cheating, even though there is much discussion about these issues in and around the camp. The default view among aid workers and government officials tends to be that refugees are deceptive (Daniel and Knudsen 1995; Jubany 2011; Kibreab 2004; Sandvik 2008; Zetter 1991). UNHCR officers have told me stories about refugees lying about their family composition, giving false names, falsifying documents, and fabricating stories in order to qualify for resettlement (see also Jansen 2008; Sandvik 2011, 2012, 2013). For example, one UNHCR resettlement officer told me that she had no sympathy for refugees who try to add their neighbor to their case because they received 30,000 Tanzanian shillings (roughly the equivalent of seventeen U.S. dollars) to do so. Another resettlement officer told me about a woman who continually told him that she was not a prostitute even though he kept telling her that admitting it would not hurt her case. She never admitted it, and her case was denied. Tanzanian Red Cross staff members have told me that many people in the camp did not flee because of war; they only came to Tanzania in search of qualifying for resettlement elsewhere.

A few refugees admitted to me that they had lied in their resettlement interviews. The lies people admitted to were usually about family composition. When speaking about lying in regard to resettlement, however, camp residents usually spoke of people they knew rather than themselves.

"Most of the people I know who were resettled made up stories and a few refugees with genuine concerns were rejected. Some of those who were resettled have since visited the DRC once or twice," a man who repatriated to Congo but whose family remains in Nyarugusu camp, told me. According to his experience, the UNHCR awards resettlement to those who lie, not those with what he thought were genuine fears of repatriation. This mirrors Bram Jansen's concern that refugees who do not cheat or lie may suffer because of UNHCR officials' exposure to such fabrications (Jansen 2008: 576). But who gets to decide who is lying or cheating and who is not? Who gets to decide what is fraud and what is not? Who gets to decide who is genuinely vulnerable? Who gets to decide what genuine vulnerability entails?

Lying and cheating highlight and reinforce the power inequalities of the resettlement process. Unlike Scott's weapons of the weak,[6] refugees' lies and deception do not chip away at the power structure in the camp. By lying or cheating, refugees do not deprive resettlement officers of anything. Instead, they themselves assume the risk of rejection. To fabricate evidence of being raped or attacked in the camp, refugees must cause bodily harm to themselves or to other camp residents. Most were too afraid of retribution to accuse Tanzanian aid workers of causing them harm or creating insecurity, whether or not such an incident actually occurred.

Moreover, camp residents insist that cheating in resettlement does not work without the collaboration of aid workers in the camp. As one resettled refugee in the United States told me:

> Most refugees would not know where to start in fabricating insecurity in the camp. Somebody with power must cover for the camp residents in order to make them appear truthful. Tanzanian staff members are suspicious of Congolese refugees in all kinds of ways. They would never easily accept lies or falsified information without being in on it.

In fact, it is part of aid workers' responsibilities to investigate these matters and to question the refugees (Jubany 2011; Kagan 2003; Kagan 2006). According to this viewpoint, refugees do not lie, cheat, or deceive because aid workers are faceless entities to which they have no obligations (cf. Kibreab 2004). It is quite the opposite. Refugees feel obligated to the aid workers who offer to help them with the fabrication of narratives that will afford them resettlement. This can contribute to their efforts to forge friendships with the Tanzanian aid workers in the camp, and it also contributes to refugees' willingness to pay bribes and partake in fraud.

Paying Bribes and Committing Fraud

After her interview with the protection officer, Nabisa went to the SGBV office to collect the documents. Inno, the SGBV representative who she encountered, refused to give her the documents without a bit of money for *kula chapati,* which literally translates to "eating chapati" but can also be used to indirectly ask for a small bribe. He said this in front of his supervisor, Nabisa told me. The supervisor was Tanzanian, but Nabisa did not know if Inno was Congolese or Tanzanian. She told me that she begged them for the documents, but they still refused. "Everything in my life is begging," Nabisa told me. She described the hardships that camp residents suffer, including chiggers that burrow their way into people's toes and that live in the dust and the mud brick houses that refugees must build (Thomson 2015), sleeping on a straw mat on the ground rather than a mattress, and little to no salary for the same work that Tanzanians do. In Nabisa's case, she traveled to Kasulu and Kigoma with her church as a choir member and a prayer woman, and while the Tanzanians serving the same positions were paid, she and the other Congolese refugees were not.

Nabisa then asked me for money. She only needed a small amount to give to Inno in exchange for her SGBV documents. We agreed upon 5,000 Tanzanian shillings, roughly the equivalent of three US dollars at the time. The bribes that I usually heard about were hundreds of thousands of shillings, that is, hundreds of dollars paid to government officials in exchange for refugee status or preferential treatment or to Tanzanian UNHCR representatives in exchange for forwarding cases on to resettlement or resettlement case numbers.[7] Nabisa explained that she had no money whatsoever and that she and her children lived entirely on the rations provided in the camp. Because I could afford it, I gave her the money.[8] There was no guarantee that it would get her the documents or that if she did get them that she would then qualify for resettlement.

The UNHCR would call both Nabisa's and Inno's actions fraudulent. The *UNHCR Resettlement Handbook* defines resettlement fraud as

> fraud committed in the context of resettlement processing, and may include ongoing fraud that was initially committed at an earlier stage of refugee processing. This can be defined for operational purposes as *"the intentional misrepresentation or concealment of facts or evidence material to the resettlement process with the intent of obtaining a resettlement or other benefit for the refugee concerned or for another individual who otherwise would not be entitled to be resettled or to obtain such a benefit."* (UNHCR 2011: 128, emphasis in original)

The handbook also distinguishes between two types of fraud, internal and external. Internal refers to fraud committed by employees or anyone in a contractual relationship with the UNHCR. External refers to fraud committed by anyone who is not in a contractual relationship with the UNHCR. According to the handbook, it "may be perpetrated by refugees, asylum seekers, criminals, host government officials, resettlement government officials, implementing partners, NGOs, IOM staff or others, and may take a variety of forms" (UNHCR 2011: 129). Various kinds of external fraud are described and include identity fraud, family composition fraud, document fraud, material misrepresentation fraud, and bribery (UNHCR 2011: 129–30).

Refugees tended to talk about the bribes that camp authorities demand in exchange for selection for resettlement. I heard stories of national UNHCR staff selling resettlement case numbers to fellow Tanzanians. Both refugees and expatriate aid workers told me stories of large sums being paid to UNHCR and government representatives for the purposes of resettlement. I knew a few families who had paid large bribes without seeing any results. Refugees who could not afford such bribes disclosed that they would pay them if they had the means.

This stance is echoed by refugees throughout Nyarugusu camp. They have accepted that fraud is a part of the resettlement process. The *UNHCR Resettlement Handbook* states, "Corruption and fraud in the resettlement process hurts all those involved, and it is in the common interest of everyone involved to cooperate at all levels to detect, respond to, and prevent fraud" (UNHCR 2011: 127–28). Nyarugusu residents do not see it that way. They are aware that Tanzanian aid workers are jealous that resettlement is not available to them. A few Tanzanian aid workers have admitted this to me as well. Congolese refugees believe this is part of the reason that resettlement fraud exists–it is a way for Tanzanian aid workers to benefit from resettlement, a system they are involved in but excluded from the end result of.[9]

Nabisa did not see any other way to obtain the documents she needed. The safeguards against fraud and corruption as outlined in the *UNHCR Resettlement Handbook,* such as submitting a complaint to a locked box, directly reporting to the Inspector General's Office, or contacting the Legal Affairs Section to report implementing partners (UNHCR 2011: 133–34, 138–39, 141), did not even occur to her as options. Even if they had, Nabisa had no reason to believe that reporting Inno for soliciting a bribe would help her get the documents she needed. If anything, reporting fraud seemed much more risky to most refugees than partaking in it. Those who were reported and their colleagues could jeopardize refugees' cases or seek retribution by other means.

From the Congolese perspective, bribery does not point to the immorality of refugees but rather implicates corrupt camp officials. They have seen it work in the past for their friends. They are often willing to partake in it for these reasons, even if they know that it is explicitly not allowed in the resettlement process.

Soliciting Higher Powers

Another action that camp residents undertake, often in addition to other methods or when they do not seem to be working, is to elicit higher powers to sway the decisions of resettlement officials. Some pray to God and others pay witchcraft practitioners. If camp residents talk about lying indirectly, then they talk about using witchcraft in the abstract. Whereas stories about lying included specific details about the lies, stories about witchcraft did not include any details about the curses or magic. The most detail I ever heard was that sometimes people pay practitioners to come sit outside their resettlement interviews in order to manipulate the interviewers. While no one has ever admitted to me that they used witchcraft for resettlement purposes, many have told me that they prayed to God. I often heard, "It is in God's hands now" or "If God wants, it will be." People spoke about resettlement as "a gift from heaven" or "the grace of God." The belief is that God will grace them if they have served him well. Neither of these calls to higher powers are infallible, but many residents believe that these avenues are their only means of influencing the actions of those involved in resettlement selection.

Nabisa did not disclose to me whether she turned to witchcraft or religion in regard to her case. From our conversation, though, it was clear she believed in both. She explained how the chiggers were especially bad in her home compared to her neighbors', and the only possible explanation was witchcraft. She followed that by explaining how she did "the work of Christ" with the Tanzanian Evangelist church she attended. For many in the camp, organized religion and witchcraft were neither antithetical nor mutually exclusive (Pels 2003). In the context of resettlement, soliciting higher powers whether religious or magical were ways that refugees sought to hedge against the possibilities for rejection.

Conclusion

At our first meeting, Nabisa promised to let me know what happened with the SGBV documents and her case. By the time I left the camp a few weeks later in December 2012, I heard through our mutual friend that Nabisa did not have any news to share. When we crossed paths again in June 2013, her exclamations that "it worked" meant that the money allowed her to get the documents from Inno, as he promised it would. With those documents, the protection officer passed her case along to resettlement, as he promised he would.

Most Congolese refugees know that there is nothing that will guarantee them resettlement. It does not matter how many documents they collect or how much they pay in bribes. Nor does it matter how truthful their refugee claims are or how elaborate their lies are. There is no magic formula for being selected. The process is imperfect. It is laden with politics. It was created by people and is implemented by people.

The power dynamics of resettlement selection are far from straightforward. Power is exercised and negotiated at every step along the way, which is why Congolese refugees do not just sit and wait, hoping to be identified as having resettlement needs. They take action, reporting instances of persecution, building their credibility, and doing all they can to build a solid case and influence decision makers' actions. The power in telling stories of persecution lies in UNHCR officials recognizing these stories as legitimate fears of persecution. Likewise, the power in reporting problems in the camp lies in establishing a network of camp officials who extend their credibility to refugees and UNHCR resettlement officers through the documentation of these problems. Congolese refugees do not view lying or bribing as committing fraud but as part of a flawed, intrinsically human system. They elicit higher powers through witchcraft and prayer to sway resettlement officials' decisions. Refugees undertake all of these efforts—(1) telling convincing stories of fleeing due to persecution, (2) reporting persecution in the camp, (3) lying or cheating, (4) paying bribes and committing fraud, and (5) soliciting higher powers—to give weight to their resettlement case, that is, to make their cases more likely to be selected for resettlement.

Resettlement selection allows little room for refugee agency (as also illustrated by Garnier; Losoncz; Darrow; Reklev and Jumbert; and Jubilut and Zamur, this volume). The five tactics outlined in this chapter illustrate refugees' attempts to sway resettlement officers' decisions. Their willingness to lie, cheat, bribe, and commit fraud is not an attempt to take advantage of generosity, but rather a symptom of the injustices of the system. From the refugees' point of view, aid workers' concern should not be for refugees who do not falsify information but for those who do not have access to aid workers willing to collude with them. Refugees would not have to fabricate stories of persecution if their own stories were deemed worthy of resettlement. Refugees are well aware that there must be a selection process of some sort because resettlement opportunities are limited. The one thing that most Nyarugusu residents agreed upon, however, was that if there was another opportunity afforded to them that was even half as attractive as resettlement they would take it. But in the current situation for refugees in Tanzania, there are no other options. Even if camp life were not so harsh and restrictive, the desperation for resettlement would wane.

Nabisa learned that she had been accepted for resettlement in the United States in 2013, and she and her family moved there in 2014. Hers was a successful case, but not all are. The stakes are high. A successful case holds the promise of a better life and a pathway to citizenship. A rejected case carries the threat of enduring indefinitely in the camp with the inevitability of repatriation to Congo. Resettlement selection decisions may represent aid workers' power over refugee lives, but for refugees, being selected signals the ability to regain control of their own lives.

When Nabisa and I reunited that day in 2013 and hurried back to her plot together, I met her children for the first time. They were sitting outside, on the red ground, eating *ugali*, or *fufu*, a staple food in the Great Lakes region. It is a porridge made from flour, typically maize or cassava, and eaten with meat stew or vegetables with a sauce. But Nabisa's children were eating it plain, just the yellow USAID cornmeal cooked with water, without accompaniments. Her weapons of defense–her story of fleeing, her reports of persecution in the camp, her willingness to pay a bribe in exchange for documents–were used to fortify her case for resettlement in an effort to free herself and her children from life in a refugee camp, including its meager rations. It was a refusal to languish indefinitely in the humanitarian system.

Marnie Jane Thomson is Visiting Assistant Professor of Anthropology at Washington and Lee University and was the recipient of the first Society for Applied Anthropology (SfAA) Human Rights Defender Award. Her research focuses on Congolese refugee experiences of violence and dislocation to reveal the politics of humanitarian intervention in both Tanzania and the Democratic Republic of Congo. Her recent publications include "Black Boxes of Bureaucracy: Transparency and Opacity in the Resettlement Process for Congolese Refugees," *Political and Legal Anthropology Review* and "Mud, Dust, and *Marougé:* Precarious Construction in a Congolese Refugee Camp," *Architectural Theory Review.*

Notes

1. The enhanced resettlement for Congolese refugees is an international project and still ongoing. It was slow to start in Tanzania, with only approximately 500 resettlement cases submitted in 2013 to nine different countries. The group resettlement project is solely for those going to the United States, and this has been slowed by President Trump's 2017 travel bans. See Thomson 2017 for more on the effects of the travel bans in Nyarugusu camp.

2. The room was part of the outpatient clinic of the hospital, where camp residents could visit with doctors on Tuesdays and Thursdays. On the other days, the outpatient clinic was used for private counseling sessions.

3. The Departure Center is supposed to be where refugees stay the night before embarking on a repatriation convoy. Since Tanzania's change in admittance procedures, new arrivals who report to government officials are now housed in the Departure Center until the National Eligibility Committee decides whether or not to award them refugee status. The police must have assumed this would be a safe place for Nabisa and her family because they would be surrounded by hundreds of other people sleeping in the same area.
4. In Tanzania, there is a marked difference between refugee camps and settlements. In the settlements, refugees were given land to farm and there has been no continued aid presence for decades. The settlements are self-sustaining, whereas the camps are managed by aid agencies and the Tanzanian government. For an ethnographic account of the Burundian settlements, see Malkki 1995.
5. In November 2012, the Rwandan-backed militia group M23 had seized Goma, the capital of North Kivu, which captured the attention of not only the UN but the international media as well.
6. Scott's analysis of Malay peasants whose lying meant that they paid a mere fraction of their taxes and thus had tangible effects for the power structure.
7. I have not substantiated these claims. As an anthropologist, the importance of these claims are not whether they can be proven but that they exist and that many refugees believe them to be true. For more about pay-for-resettlement claims in Kenya and Uganda, see Browne 2006; Human Rights Watch 2002; Refugee Law Project 2002, 2005. For excellent academic analyses of these claims, see Sandvik 2011, 2013.
8. This was the only time that a refugee asked me for bribe money and the only time I gave such money. One could view it as transactional, in the way that some researchers pay their informants for their participation. I do not do that, nor do I view it that way. It is possible, however, that Nabisa planned to give me her story in exchange for the money. My interpretation, however, is that she saw someone who might be able to give her this money. I viewed it as the decent thing to do because I could, and it might help. Many refugees admitted to me that they had paid bribes to aid workers, usually in much larger amounts. Sometimes it worked; sometimes it did not.
9. While a number of Tanzanian aid workers told me that this sort of bribery occurs, none of them admitted to partaking in it or accepting bribes. See Sandvik 2011 for a discussion on how forbidden practices such as fraud can also be seen as normative practices within the humanitarian apparatus.

References

Agier, Michel. 2008. *On the Margins of the World: The Refugee Experience Today.* Cambridge: Polity.

——. 2010. "Humanity as an Identity and Its Political Effects: A Note on Camps and Humanitarian Government." *Humanity* 1(1): 29–46.

——. 2011. *Managing the Undesirables: Refugee Camps and Humanitarian Government.* Cambridge: Polity.

Barnett, Michael. 2005. "Humanitarianism Transformed." *Perspectives on Politics* 3(4): 723–40.

——. 2010. *The International Humanitarian Order*. New York: Routledge.

Barnett, Michael, and Thomas G. Weiss, eds. 2008a. *Humanitarianism in Question: Politics, Power and Ethics*. Ithaca: Cornell University Press.

——. 2008b. "Humanitarianism: A Brief History of the Present." In *Humanitarianism in Question: Politics, Power, Ethics*, edited by M. Barnett and T. G. Weiss. Ithaca: Cornell University Press.

Betts, Alexander. 2013. *Survival Migration: Failed Governance and the Crisis of Displacement*. Ithaca: Cornell University Press.

Blommaert, Jan. 2001. "Investigating Narrative Inequality: African Asylum Seekers' Stories in Belgium." *Discourse & Society* 12(4): 413–49.

Browne, Peter. 2006. *The Longest Journey, Resettling Refugees from Africa*. Sydney: University of New South Wales Press.

Daniel, Valentine E., and John C. Knudsen, eds. 1995. *Mistrusting Refugees*. Berkeley: University of California Press.

Dunn, Elizabeth. 2012. "The Chaos of Humanitarian Aid: Adhocracy in the Republic of Georgia." *Humanity* 3(1): 1–23.

Fassin, Didier. 2010. "Inequality of Lives, Hierarchies of Humanity: Moral Commitments and Ethical Dilemmas of Humanitarianism." In *In the Name of Humanity: The Government of Threat and Care*, edited by I. Feldman and M. Ticktin, 238–55. Durham: Duke University Press.

Fassin, Didier, and Estelle d'Halluin. 2007. "Critical Evidence: The Politics of Trauma in French Asylum Policies." *Ethos* 35(5): 300–29.

Fassin, Didier, and Mariella Pandolfi, eds. 2010. *Contemporary States of Emergency: The Politics of Military and Humanitarian Interventions*. New York: Zone Books.

Feldman, Ilana, and Miriam Ticktin, eds. 2010. *In the Name of Humanity: The Government of Threat and Care*. Durham: Duke University Press.

Foucault, Michel. 1980. "Two Lectures." In *Power/Knowledge: Selected Interviews and Other Writings, 1972–1978*, edited by C. Gordon, 78–108. New York: Pantheon Books.

Gordillo, Gaston. 2006. "The Crucible of Citizenship: ID-Paper Fetishism in the Argentinian Chaco." *American Ethnologist* 33(2): 162–76.

Hilhorst, Dorothea. 2002. "Being Good at Doing Good? Quality and Accountability of Humanitarian NGOs." *Disasters* 26(3): 193–212.

——. 2003. *The Real World of NGOs: Discourses, Diversity and Development*. London: Zed Books.

Horst, Cindy. 2006a. "Buufis amongst Somalis in Dadaab: The Transnational and Historical Logics behind Resettlement Dreams." *Journal of Refugee Studies* 19(3): 143–157.

——. 2006b. *Transnational Nomads: How Somalis Cope with Refugee Life in the Dadaab Camps of Kenya*. New York: Berghahn Books.

Hull, Matthew S. 2003. "The File: Agency, Authority and Autography in an Islamabad Bureaucracy." *Language and Communication* 23: 287–314.

Human Rights Watch (HRW). 2002. *Hidden in Plain View: Refugees Living without Protection in Nairobi and Kampala*. New York: Human Rights Watch Publications.

Hyndman, Jennifer. 2000. *Managing Displacement: Refugees and the Politics of Humanitarianism.* Minneapolis: University of Minnesota Press.

Jansen, Bram J. 2008. "Between Vulnerability and Assertiveness: Negotiating Resettlement in Kakuma Refugee Camp, Kenya." *African Affairs* 107(429): 569–87.

———. 2015. "'Digging Aid': The Camp as an Option in East and the Horn of Africa." *Journal of Refugee Studies* 29(2): 149–165.

Jubany, Olga. 2011. "Constructing Truths in a Culture of Disbelief: Understanding Asylum Screening from Within." *International Sociology* 26(1): 74–94.

Kagan, Michael. 2003. "Is Truth in the Eye of the Beholder? Objective Credibility Assessment in Refugee Status Determination." *Georgetown Immigration Law Journal* 17(3): 367–416.

———. 2006. "Frontier Justice: Legal Aid and UNHCR Refugee Status Determination in Egypt." *Journal of Refugee Studies* 19(1): 45–68.

Kibreab, Gaim. 2004. "Pulling the Wool over the Eyes of the Strangers: Refugee Deceit and Trickery in Institutionalized Settings." *Journal of Refugee Studies* 17(1): 1–26.

Leader, Nicholas. 1998. "Proliferating Principles, or How to Sup with the Devil without Getting Eaten." *International Journal of Human Rights* 2(4): 1–27.

Lynch, Emily. 2013. "Mudende: Trauma and Massacre in a Refugee Camp." *Oral History Forum* 33: 1–26.

Malinowski, Bronislaw. 1922. *Argonauts of the Western Pacific: An Account of Native Enterprise and Adventure in the Archipelagoes of Melanesian New Guinea.* Prospect Heights: Waveland Press.

Malkki, Liisa. 1995. *Purity and Exile: Violence, Memory and National Cosmology among Hutu Refugees in Tanzania.* Chicago: University of Chicago Press.

Ortner, Sherry. 2006. *Anthropology and Social Theory: Culture, Power, and the Acting Subject.* Durham: Duke University Press.

Pels, Peter. 2003. "Introduction: Magic and Modernity." In *Magic and Modernity: Interfaces of Revelation and Concealment,* edited by B. Meyer and P. Pels. Stanford: Stanford University Press.

Redfield, Peter. 2012. "The Unbearable Lightness of Expats: Double Binds of Humanitarian Mobility." *Cultural Anthropology* 27(2): 358–82.

———. 2013. *Life in Crisis: The Ethical Journey of Doctors without Borders.* Berkeley: University of California Press.

Refugee Law Project (RLP). 2002. *Refugees in the City: Status Determination, Resettlement, and the Changing Nature of Forced Migration in Uganda.* Kampala: Refugee Law Project.

———. 2005. "'A Drop in the Ocean': Assistance and Protection for Forced Migrants in Kampala.* Working paper no. 16, Kampala: Refugee Law Project.

Sandvik, Kristin Bergtora. 2008. "The Physicality of Legal Consciousness: Suffering and the Production of Credibility in Refugee Resettlement." In *Humanitarianism and Suffering: The Mobilization of Empathy,* edited by Richard Ashby Wilson and Richard D. Brown, 223–44. Cambridge: Cambridge University Press.

———. 2010. "A Legal History: the Emergence of the African Resettlement Candidate in International Refugee Management." *International Journal of Refugee Law* 22(1): 20–47.

———. 2011. "Blurring Boundaries: Refugee Resettlement in Kampala–Between the Formal, the Informal and the Illegal." *PoLAR: Political and Legal Anthropology Review* 34(1): 11–32.

———. 2012. "Negotiating the Humanitarian Past: History, Memory, and Unstable Cityscapes in Kampala, Uganda." *Refugee Survey Quarterly* 31(1): 108–22.

———. 2013. "Rights-Based Humanitarianism as Emancipation or Stratification? Rumors and Procedures of Verification in Urban Refugee Management in Kampala, Uganda." In *Worlds of Human Rights: The Ambiguities of Rights Claiming in Africa,* edited by B. Derman, A. Hellum, and K. B. Sandvik, 257–276. Leiden: Koninklijke Brill.

Scott, James C. 1985. *Weapons of the Weak: Everyday Forms of Peasant Resistance.* New Haven: Yale University Press.

Stein, Janice Gross. 2008. "Humanitarian Organizations; Accountable–Why, to Whom, for What, and How?" In *Humanitarianism in Questions: Politics, Power, Ethics,* edited by Michael Barnett and Thomas G. Weiss, 124–43. Ithaca: Cornell University Press.

Stoler, Ann Laura. 1992. "'In Cold Blood': Hierarchies of Credibility and the Politics of Colonial Narratives." *Representations* 37: 151–89.

Thomson, Marnie Jane. 2012. "Black Boxes of Bureaucracy: Transparency and Opacity in the Resettlement Process of Congolese Refugees." *PoLAR: Political and Legal Anthropology Review* 35(2): 186–205.

———. 2015. "Mud, Dust, and Marougé: Precarious Construction in a Congolese Refugee Camp." *Architectural Theory Review* 19(3): 376–92.

———. 2017. "Revoked: Refugee Bans in Effect." In *Maintaining Refuge: Anthropological Reflections in Uncertain Times,* edited by David Haines, Jayne Howell, and Fethi Keles, 95–102. American Anthropological Association, Committee on Refugees and Immigrants.

Thomson, Susan. 2013. "Agency as Silence and Muted Voice: The Problem-Solving Networks of Unaccompanied Young Somali Refugee Women in Eastleigh, Nairobi." *Conflict, Security & Development* 13(5): 589–609.

Ticktin, Miriam. 2006. "Where Ethics and Politics Meet: The Violence of Humanitarianism in France." *American Ethnologist* 33(1): 33–49.

———. 2011a. *Casualties of Care: Immigration and the Politics of Humanitarianism in France.* Berkeley: University of California Press.

———. 2011b. "The Gendered Human of Humanitarianism: Medicalising and Politicising Sexual Violence." *Gender and History* 23(2): 250–65.

Turner, Simon. 2005. "Suspended Spaces–Contesting Sovereignties in a Refugee Camp." In *Sovereign Bodies: Citizens, Migrants and States in the Postcolonial World,* edited by T. B. Hansen and F. Stepputat, 312–362. Princeton: Princeton University Press.

———. 2010. *Politics of Innocence: Hutu Identity, Conflict and Camp Life.* New York: Berghahn Books.

United Nations High Commission for Refugees (UNHCR). 2011. *UNHCR Resettlement Handbook.* Geneva: UNHCR.

Yngvesson, Barbara, and Susan Bibler Coutin. 2006. "Backed by Papers: Undoing Persons, Histories and Return." *American Ethnologist* 33(2): 177–90.

Zetter, Roger. 1991. "Labelling Refugees: Forming and Transforming a Bureaucratic Identity." *Journal of Refugee Studies* 4: 39–63.

10

The Politics of Resettlement

Expectations and Unfulfilled Promises
in Chile and Brazil

Marcia A. Vera Espinoza

Introduction

Refugee resettlement is a process of multiple negotiations, happening at different levels and times. In this chapter, I explore the relationship between resettled refugees and the different actors involved in the program in two Latin American countries, Chile and Brazil. I do so by identifying and discussing the tensions among actors (refugees; the United Nations High Commissioner for Refugees, UNHCR; nongovernmental organizations, NGOs; and governments) and by asking how these power relationships affect the resettlement experience, both before and after refugees arrive to the host country. The chapter builds on long-time ethnographic fieldwork to trace the perceptions and everyday encounters between Colombian and Palestinian refugees and the institutions running the resettlement programs in Chile and Brazil, exploring how resettlement as humanitarian governance is negotiated, performed, and resisted at the local level. Both countries are stimulating case studies: they are considered emergent resettlement countries and share a history of exile, as thousands of people fled each country because of the oppression suffered under dictatorship regimes, while both countries have also engaged in enforcement of their refugee national laws after their return to democracy.

The negotiations and power relationships involved in refugee resettlement have been explored in an interdisciplinary body of literature, covering different stages of the resettlement process and different locations, and it is a core concern of this volume (Shrestha 2011; Sandvik 2011, 2012; Thomson 2012; Thomson, this volume). This chapter aims to contribute to this debate, exploring the experiences of resettled refugees in emergent host counties in South America. Both Colombian and Palestinian refugees and the organizations involved in resettlement in Chile and Brazil created a set of expectations regarding resettlement even before refugees arrived. The chapter discusses how these expectations varied (or not) between groups and host countries, how they developed translocally between the first country of asylum and the third host country, and how they shaped the resettlement experience when those expectations were unmet.

On the one hand, refugees' expectations of resettlement turned into claims of "unfulfilled promises" generating frustration and mistrust between refugees and the resettlement program's actors. On the other hand, the resettlement organizations' unmet expectations lead to problematic representations of refugees' intentions and behavior. I argue that, due to the tensions that emerged between actors and refugees' disappointment in the host country, refugees' radical uncertainties (Horst and Grabska 2015) created by displacement and conflict extended into resettlement, shaping their experience as one of unsettlement (see also Lewis and Young, this volume). The discussion of these expectations and the negotiations that took place between refugees and the organizations involved exposes the contradictions of resettlement as an instrument of governance at the local level.

The following sections introduce the chapter's concept and methods and provides a brief background on Brazil's and Chile's resettlement programs. The expectations of resettled refugees and of resettlement organizations, developed and experienced translocally, are then contrasted and discussed, showing how unfulfilled promises on both sides sustain resettled refugees' unsettlement.

Concepts and Methods

This research mainly draws upon interconnected strands of scholarship in human geography, anthropology, and political science, among other related disciplines. In this chapter, I draw from this volume's understanding of power as the "relational effect of social interactions" (Allen 2003) to explore the temporal and spatial consequences of the negotiations between refugees and the organizations involved in refugee resettlement. Drawing on the work of Shrestha (2011) and Hyndman (2000) on the asymmetrical hierarchies and paradoxes of humanitarian work, this chapter focuses on the power imbalances between refugees and the resettlement program, shedding light on the local (and translocal) dynamics of humanitarian governance (see Garnier, Sandvik, and Jubilut, this volume). A starting point in the recognition of the politics of resettlement is that this durable solution is a discretionary response taken by states, which involves the UNHCR at various levels (see also van Selm, this volume).

This means that power imbalances are embedded in refugee resettlement at the supranational and state level shaping the dynamics of resettlement (Sandvik 2011; Shrestha 2011; Garnier, Sandvik, and Jubilut, this volume). At the same time, these power imbalances are deepened in negotiations at the local and individual levels, through mechanisms such as the control of information and the perpetuation of waiting and uncertainty (Biehl 2015). While power imbalances in resettlement have been increasingly explored in refugee studies (Thomson 2012; Sandvik 2011; Harrell-Bond 2002), they have been underexplored in emerging resettlement countries such as Chile and Brazil.

In the discussion of the empirical data, I emphasize the significance of scale for the exploration of the negotiations among actors involved within different levels and spaces of the resettlement process. In this context, I use the lens of "translocality" to review both the spatial and temporal interconnectedness of the refugee experience within and beyond the national boundaries of the resettlement country. According to Greiner and Sakdapolrak (2013: 373), translocality is used to "describe socio-spatial dynamics and processes of simultaneity and identity formation that transcend boundaries–including, but also extending beyond, those of the nation state." This notion is relevant to enhancing the understanding of resettlement as an experience that starts in the first country of asylum, at the moment the refugee receives the information about resettlement, and develops in multiple localities.

Finally, throughout the chapter I discuss refugees' experiences as those of "unsettlement," drawing on the literature about uncertainty in forced migration (El-Shaarawi 2015; Brun 2015; Biehl 2015; Griffiths 2014). Uncertainty is understood here as the "imperfect knowledge of current conditions" and the "unpredictability of the future" (Williams and Baláž 2012: 168). Unsettlement, on the other hand, is discussed as the condition by which refugees' feelings of uncertainty and instability, resulting from experiences of displacement, extend and normalize into resettlement (Vera Espinoza, forthcoming). I argue that the power imbalances of refugee resettlement contribute to the experience of unsettlement.

This chapter draws on data collected in two extended periods of fieldwork in Chile and Brazil between 2012 and 2014 as part of a larger doctoral research project.[1] I implemented a qualitative driven mixed methods methodology (Mason 2006), which included eighty semistructured interviews with resettled refugees and other actors involved in the resettlement program (including governments, UNHCR, NGO staff, and others related to refugee assistance). I also conducted a survey with eighty-six resettled refugees across both countries, some of whom also participated in the interviews, and I carried out participant observation in two of the implementing agencies in each country. I analyzed the data obtained from the three methods separately and then brought them together through triangulation, comparing and contrasting the data and revealing the nuances (and contradictions) of the resettlement process.

Background

Chile and Brazil are pioneers in implementing resettlement programs in South America. Chile received the first group of refugees from the former Yugoslavia in 1999, while Brazil hosted a small group of refugees coming from Afghanistan in 2002. In 2004, resettlement emerged with a regional approach as part of the Mexico Plan of Action (MPA) adopted by twenty countries of Latin America and the Caribbean in the context of the twentieth celebration of the 1984 Cartagena Declaration. With the longstanding Colombian conflict in the background, the aim of resettlement was to enable the countries of the Southern Cone to contribute to relieving the burden of refugees received by Colombia's neighboring countries (Nogueira and Marques 2008). From 2004 to today, five countries of the region–Chile, Brazil, Argentina, Uruguay, and Paraguay–resettled more than 1,500 refugees from within the region and from outside the boundaries of Latin America (Ruiz 2015). The number is small compared with global resettlement needs. UNHCR estimated that by 2017 the needs for refugee resettlement were over 1,190,000 persons, a considerable 72 percent increase in comparison with 2014 (UNHCR 2016). However, the innovative efforts of Latin America to foster resettlement based on the principle of solidarity has been praised as a model of South-South cooperation and dialogue among states that can improve refugee protection (Harley 2014; see also Vera Espinoza 2018).

The emergence of resettlement in the framework of the MPA also responds to specific political momentum and is motivated by specific political goals. In the case of Brazil, since the country's redemocratization, there has been an aim to reach subregional leadership in refugee protection (see also Jubilut and Zamur, this volume). In Chile, resettlement was considered a "gesture" to the international community acknowledging the protection given to Chileans in exile during Augusto Pinochet's dictatorship (Daneri 2008). Both countries estimated that taking the lead on regional resettlement would position them as good players in relation to international cooperation and humanitarian burden sharing (Jubilut and Carneiro 2011). As a former member of the UNHCR in Brazil told me, "Everything related to refugees is political. The assistance may be humanitarian, but the drive is political. . . . And there was an ambition by both Brazil and Chile to be the first ones offering resettlement in the region."

The solidarity resettlement program was mainly aimed to protect Colombian refugees. Since 2005, more than 5,500 Colombian refugees with specific protection needs have been resettled to a third country, 20 percent of which have been resettled in countries of the Southern Cone (UNHCR 2010: 20). Most of them have come from the first countries of asylum such as Ecuador or Costa Rica, and a smaller number of Colombians have been resettled from Panama and Venezuela.

In 2007, Chile and Brazil opened the resettlement program to those from outside the boundaries of Latin America and decided to resettle a group of Palestinian refugees living on the borders between Iraq, Jordan, and Syria. This program became known as the Humanitarian Resettlement Programme (see Vera Espinoza 2017). Between September and October 2007, Brazil received 108 Palestinians refugees from the Ruwaished refugee camp in Jordan. Chile, on the other hand, received 117 Palestinian refugees coming from the Al Tanf refugee camp on the border between Iraq and Syria (Ruiz 2015).

In terms of design and implementation of resettlement, in Chile and Brazil the program relies on a tripartite structure that includes the participation of the government of each country, the UNHCR, and NGOs that act as implementing agencies (see Ruiz 2015; Bijit 2012; Jubilut and Carneiro 2011). The program in both countries received contributions and technical support from Norway, Canada, and the United States (Guglielmelli-White 2012).

In this chapter, I discuss how unmet expectations of both resettled refugees and members of the program in each country created tension and mistrust between them, affecting the resettlement experience.

Displacement and the Construction of Expectations

Leaving the first country of asylum or the refugee camp and arriving in the resettlement country is an experience full of anxieties and expectations. The construction of expectations emerged as a constant theme in the narratives of resettled refugees I interviewed in both Chile and Brazil. These expectations emerged as important in shaping refugees' decisions to take up resettlement as well as through their actual experiences of resettlement. In this section, I briefly discuss how these expectations were constructed in a context of uncertainty and then explore how they turned into "unfulfilled promises."

Expectation is usually understood as a strong belief that something will happen (Oxford English Dictionary 2007). The refugee studies literature has largely referred to the different range of expectations that refugees develop about their resettlement experience, both in Latin America (Bessa 2006; Bijit 2012) and in other contexts (Kenny and Lockwood-Kenny 2011; Westoby 2009; Marete 2012). In addition, the UNHCR and service providers have recognized that one of the biggest challenges of resettlement is what they refer to as "unrealistic expectations" (van Selm 2013). The refugees I interviewed based their expectations about third-country resettlement on what other people said (organizations and other refugees) but also on the meanings that they created from their own experiences–including hopes and aspirations. From the interviews with both Colombian and Palestinian refugees, I identified four key factors in the construction of refugees' expectations predeparture: the emergency that framed their resettlement decision (see also Kenny and Lockwood-Kenny 2011), the lack of clear information provided in the first country of asylum or in the refugee camp, the information given by family and friends resettled in other countries (see Horst 2006), and time spent in the places where they were first displaced.

These factors also shaped their uncertainties predeparture. Uncertainty appeared in refugees' narratives as a constitutive element of their experiences of displacement (Biehl 2015) but also as predominant during the events prior to departure for the resettlement country (El-Shaarawi 2015). That is to say, expectations of refugees were generated in a context of long-term uncertainty (Horst and Grabska 2015).

Rabah's experiences predeparture help to exemplify how some of the factors above shaped expectations in the context of Palestinian refugees. Rabah is 1 of the 108 Palestinian refugees resettled to Brazil from the Rwaished camp. They were the last group in the camp, and they witnessed with resignation the resettlement of others. During the five years' wait in the camp, Rabah experienced all the factors mentioned above, creating double-edged emotions from great happiness to anger:

> I was sitting there, waiting every day. Seeing how my friends were taken to other countries and I was still there. . . . One day, they called us for a meeting and that day I couldn't take it anymore and I took the chair and broke it on the floor. I was so angry because of waiting! . . . So when that lady [UNHCR officer] came to a meeting to talk about vegetables and cleaning, I told her, "We need neither vegetables nor cleaning, we just need to get out of here! I don't want to die here! I am going mad." I didn't want to argue with her. I was nervous, angry. . . . I broke the chair and I felt sad because of that. After that, she came back and told me about the opportunity of Denmark and sent me to go to the Italian hospital in Jordan to take the medical exams. When they sent you there it meant that you may go soon. She left me dreaming, living again! I knew about Denmark because I had a friend resettled there. That night I couldn't sleep thinking about going there, dreaming. I was so happy! . . . When the group from Denmark came to the camp they didn't know about us [Palestinians]; they had come for the Kurds. Why did she lie to me? They told me that just to calm me down?! (Rabah, Palestinian Refugee in Brazil)

In his narrative, Rabah explored the different sources of uncertainty experienced in the refugee camp in relation to resettlement, such as inconsistency and lack of information, sudden changes in resettlement options, and unclear selection criteria. As a result, Rabah described constant feelings of anxiety about the possibilities of leaving the camp, desperation at not knowing how or when, and resentment because of what he perceived as the "UN's constant lies." Rabah's desperation was a response to the bureaucratic system that decided his resettlement. As El-Shaarawi (2015) explores through her research with Iraqi refugees in Egypt, the resettlement process predeparture becomes another source of uncertainty that is both spatial and temporal, since refugees are uncertain of where they will go and when. The uncertainty experienced by the Palestinian refugees while waiting at the Rwaished camp revealed that refugees constructed their expectations abstractly, around the need to leave the camp and the sparse information they received, rather than around their aspirations of resettlement in Brazil. This is also because when the possibility of resettlement in Brazil was presented, there was no other real option and otherwise they would have to stay in the desert.

Waiting (Brun 2015; Khosravi 2014) and uncertainty (Horst and Grabska 2015) also characterized the predeparture resettlement process of refugees who came to Chile from the Al Tanf camp between Iraq and Syria. Although their decision was also framed by the need to leave the appalling conditions in the camp, they did not have the extra pressure of being the last group there. Instead, their main doubts were related to accepting resettlement in Chile, or waiting, again and for an indeterminate time, for the option of resettlement in another country. In the case of both Palestinian groups, the information that the refugees received about the host countries was crucial in their decision to take the resettlement option, considering that most refugees told me they knew nothing about Chile and very little about Brazil.

In this context, another difference between the Palestinian groups in each country was their source of information about resettlement. For Palestinians resettled in Brazil, there was no selection mission, and the information was provided by members of the UNHCR in Jordan. In the case of the Palestinian refugees resettled in Chile, they received information about the resettlement country directly from the institutions involved in the program who participated in the mission to the Al Tanf camp. In both cases, the information received in relation to the entitlements of the resettlement programs framed their expectations about the host countries. The account of Aziza facilitates discussion of the context of these expectations:

> We had a meeting before the interview. We went, sat in front of a big screen, and saw Chile. What did we see? . . . We saw the beach, kids playing, everything pretty. We asked about the program, and they said that they would give us around US$500, and that would be enough because you can eat and rent. And that we all would get a passport as well. (Aziza, Palestinian refugee in Chile)

Most Palestinian refugees built their expectations about resettlement around what they referred to as the "UNHCR's promises." Refugees recognized that those promises were ambiguous but did ensure that all their basic needs would be covered, that they would have access to housing, language classes, and, eventually, naturalization. Interviewees also referred to the promise of family reunification. Refugees in both countries also told of being promised that the monthly stipend they received would be enough to cover their basic needs and that access to rights would be guaranteed. In addition, resettlement also sparkled aspirations, independently of the host country, since it was perceived as the only solution for finally leaving the camp and hoping for a better future.

Despite the differences in the patterns of displacement between Palestinian and Colombian refugees, similar factors influenced Colombian refugees' expectations about resettlement. In most of the cases, the resettlement option came as the last resort when persecution found them again in the first country of asylum. Expectations were therefore constructed in a context of emergency and fear, in which Chile and Brazil did not represent the most attractive options but were indeed the only options. The narratives of Paula (resettled in Chile) and Daniela (resettled in Brazil) illustrate how these elements framed their expectations:

> After we received death threats we told everything to the authorities and they moved us almost immediately here. The only delegations that came to Ecuador at that time were Chile and Brazil . . . and I was a bit disappointed because my dream was to go to another place, I don't know, like Canada or Sweden. But when I realized that those weren't an option, we thought we should just take whatever comes because we needed to protect our children. (Paula, Colombian refugee in Chile)

> We didn't know how we were going to get here; we only knew that we will have some guarantees. . . . They told us many things, everything very pretty. Based on that we decided to accept [to go to Brazil]. (Daniela, Colombian refugee in Brazil)

Similar to the Palestinian refugees, Paula and Daniela described how they built their expectations about resettlement in Chile and Brazil in the context of an emergency and based on vague information about the program. Unlike Palestinian refugees, Colombians did have some knowledge about Chile and Brazil. These countries would not have been their first choices, which is why the information provided by the resettlement organizations, even if vague, was key in their decision to accept the offer of resettlement. Being resettled within Latin America–a region characterized by inequality–generated another source of uncertainty, and the information provided by the resettlement organizations was the only resource for people to cope and manage these uncertainties (see Griffiths 2013).

In the case of the Colombian refugees, their expectations were also influenced by the time spent in the first country of asylum. Most of the Colombian refugees that I interviewed in Chile and Brazil had spent between two and eight years in the first country of asylum (Ecuador, Costa Rica, or Venezuela), and before they were persecuted in those countries, some of them enjoyed their life there. As Milena, a Colombian refugee resettled in Chile, told me, "I didn't want to leave Ecuador. I would have stayed, because I liked it there. . . . But we had to leave because we were in danger." In some cases, the process of local integration in the first country of asylum was disrupted by persecution and violence.

In the case of both Colombian and Palestinian refugees, the expectations created were related to the aspirations of socioeconomic stability and security, firmly relying on what the organizations offered as part of the resettlement program. But whereas, to Colombian refugees, security was related mainly to physical protection, in the case of Palestinians, security was understood as the guarantee of their rights. Both groups aspired to have a stable living standard. It is relevant to note that expectations were more or less similar across genders.

The discussion of refugees' experiences predeparture enhances our understanding of how refugees framed their expectations, what these expectations were, and the pivotal role that the information provided in the first country of asylum or displacement had in refugees' acceptance of resettlement. Information as a key factor in the creation of expectations reveals how it became a mechanism of coercion that put in question how voluntary the acceptance of the resettlement option was. The next section briefly explores how these expectations turned into "unfulfilled promises" affecting the relationship between actors and the resettlement experience.

Refugees' Unmet Expectations

The expectations that refugees generated predeparture clashed with their experiences in the host countries, and, soon after arrival, they turned into complaints of unfulfilled promises. As the Palestinian groups in each country arrived roughly at the same time in 2007–2008, their perceptions postarrival in Chile and Brazil seemed to be more similar than those of Colombian refugees, whose perceptions varied depending on their year of arrival.

The complaints of the Palestinian refugees in Chile focused on the lack of accuracy of information given to them in the Al Tanf camp by the Chilean commission (composed of members of the UNHCR, the government, and the implementing agency) and how this contrasted with their socioeconomic situation in the resettlement country. Rahal highlighted some of the main issues:

> Here it is different to what I thought it would be. Very different. . . . I thought that in this country I would have a good situation and that I could live fine. But when we arrived, finding a job was difficult and we worked so much for very little money. (Rahal, Palestinian refugee in Chile)

While Palestinian refugees criticized the lack of accurate information, staff from the resettlement program in Chile stated that all the information was given but that refugees may have misunderstood what was said in the camp. Regardless of the reason, unmet expectations had a direct impact on refugees' experiences of resettlement and their relationship with service providers. Refugees perceived that the organizations lied to them about the country, particularly in relation to the high cost of living and the stipend that they would receive. This perception created mistrust of institutions involved in resettlement and added a layer of tension to their daily relationship (Hynes 2003; Daniel and Knudsen 1995).

Palestinian refugees faced their unmet aspirations with fears of further downward social and occupational mobility after two years in the refugee camp. Most of them had had jobs and a stable socioeconomic situation in Iraq. However, after years of displacement, Palestinian refugees faced a new beginning in Chile with the difficulty of learning a new language and the challenge of finding stable employment (Bijit 2012).

As with their counterparts in Chile, Palestinian refugees in Brazil showed great frustration in relation to unmet expectations but also great disappointment with their current life in Brazil. Mahfoud was one of the oldest Palestinians in Brazil, at sixty-seven years old. As with other Palestinian refugees in vulnerable situations, Mahfoud was uncertain about his future or where he was going to live after the announcement that the UNHCR would stop supporting elderly and vulnerable Palestinians at the beginning of 2014. Mahfoud's account illustrates some of the promises made by the UNHCR staff in Jordan and his frustrations over the unmet promises:

> They told me, "Look there in Brazil you are going to study Portuguese, you will find a house, you will have a job, everything." And nothing [was accomplished]! Nothing! . . . The problem is the UNHCR, nobody else. The UNHCR doesn't want to help us, they don't want us to work, they don't want anything to do with us, and they just want to leave us here. If we die, we die. If we live, we live. Two hundred reales per month? What am I? A cat? I am not a cat, I am a man! (Mahfoud, Palestinian refugee in Brazil)

Mahfoud's criticism underscores how the mistrust toward the UN, developed predeparture in the refugee camp, extended into the resettlement country once refugees faced the unfulfilled expectations. Palestinian refugees in Brazil, as in Chile, blamed the UN agency for providing unclear and misleading information about the resettlement country, but they also criticized the UNHCR approach in relation to their current situation. The quotation above emphasizes that the mistrust inculcated toward the UN system goes beyond the boundaries of the specific places of displacement and develops translocally, shaping the complex relationships and dynamics between refugees and service providers (see Greiner and Sakdapolrak 2013; Hynes 2003). As in Chile, the focus of their anger and apathy was the UNHCR and the implementing NGOs, and, to a lesser extent, they also blamed the government, demonstrating the relational aspect of power. Even though it was the governments who accepted their resettlement in the first place, refugees' daily contact predeparture was with the UNHCR and with the implementing agencies in the host country, who they identified as direct recipients of UNHCR funds.

For Mahfoud, as for other Palestinian refugees in both study sites, the uncertainty and instability experienced during displacement did not end with a durable solution in Brazil but instead became a constant, extending the temporal and spatial limits of uncertainty (El-Shaarawi 2015) and shaping the experience as one of unsettlement. Mahfoud's case was particularly acute because, being sixty-seven years old, he felt powerless. His major frustrations were related to his lack of self-sufficiency, precisely one of the main goals of the resettlement program in the country. He did not have permanent housing, and he was dependent on other people.

While the expectations of Palestinians in Chile and Brazil were similar, their conditions in the resettlement country five or six years after arrival were very different. While most of the Palestinian families interviewed in Chile were relatively socially and economically settled, those interviewed in Brazil, particularly the elderly, were unemployed and living in conditions of societal marginalization (no secure income, lack of access to some social programs, risk of being homeless, and poor language skills). Palestinian refugees in Chile had most of their immediate material needs covered and had at least one source of income per household. In addition, all the families had their own house after the government managed to include them in national housing subsidies. In Brazil, only one of the Palestinian families I interviewed managed to access a housing subsidy. Some young families and single refugees seemed to be doing better in Brazil, having secured jobs and built important social networks.

In the case of Colombian refugees in both countries, perceptions about the accomplishment of expectations were more diverse than in the case of Palestinian resettled refugees. However, there was a consensus that the information given by the resettlement organizations was rather superficial and misleading, portraying both countries' socioeconomic situation and access as better than they really were, particularly in relation to housing and jobs. Colombian refugees in Chile also highlighted issues related to cultural differences and discrimination, while Colombians in Brazil focused on the poor quality of the Portuguese classes and the barriers to accessing higher education. Some refugees in both countries also spoke about their security concerns due to the arrival of large numbers of Colombians in both host countries.

Exploring how expectations were constructed and how they turned into unfulfilled promises shows that refugees are not static within their own experiences. Refugees' expectations were also revealed as coping mechanisms and expressions of hope, particularly in the period of predeparture, as suggested by Horst and Grabska (2015), but also as a negotiation tool of power and resistance against the bureaucracies of resettlement once in the host country. They were central to refugee claims and active forms of organization (see Moulin 2012). In all these forms, expectations were at the center of the sometimes tense relationship between the resettlement program and the Palestinian and Colombian refugees in both countries.

Expectations, as shown in this chapter, are a translocal expression of the refugee experience, as they were spatially developed in one or multiple places and they shaped the communication with the organizations involved pre- and postresettlement (Westoby 2009; Fanjoy et al. 2005). Finally, exploring refugees' expectations reveals the pivotal role of information as an instrument of power that can produce "protracted uncertainty" (Biehl 2015), by which limited knowledge, waiting, and instability marked the experience of refugees both in the first country of asylum and in the resettlement country.

Resettlement Organizations' Expectations and Power Imbalances

Whereas the previous section focused on refugees' expectations, this section explores the way in which refugees were discursively constructed by members of organizations involved in resettlement through their own expectations. While some expectations were based on the program's objectives, the assumptions about refugees' behavior were shaped by hegemonic discourses about what "refugeeness" should be. I explore some concrete examples of how these representations play out in relation to the program's aim of self-sufficiency before discussing the different understandings of refugee protection. Each actor based her or his aspirations and assumptions on her or his experiences and rationale, together with structural (and budgetary) constraints.

Refugee Mentality and the Hegemonic Discourses about Self-Sufficiency

During my fieldwork at both research sites, I interviewed twenty people directly involved in the resettlement program as staff (or former members) of the organizations in each country.[2] While all of them expressed commitment to refugee protection and highlighted the well-intentioned aims of the resettlement program, some of the staff members held contradictory views about refugees. These representations of refugees affected and shaped their work, resulting in either a victim-savior approach (Harrell-Bond 2002) or the need to overcome what they called "refugee mentality." These two ideas emerged in the interviews in both countries and were evident while exploring the expectations held by the resettlement program in relation to the refugees' integration process. For example, one of the goals of the resettlement program in both countries was refugee self-sufficiency, which was understood by the implementing agencies as economic autonomy and refugees finding employment as key to their integration. This notion of self-sufficiency was even considered during the selection process, as both countries recognized that one of the criteria was "integration potential" (Guglielmelli-White 2012). NGO staff in Chile and Brazil explained that this potential was assessed in terms of previous experience, personal relationships, family composition, and willingness (and capacity) to work. As the resettlement coordinator of one of the NGOs in Brazil told me:

> We have to select people with a perspective of fast integration. . . . Against our will we are discriminating against families with high vulnerability because we don't have the capacity to work with them. At the moment of the selection, we privilege people that after a year can be economically self-sufficient. (resettlement coordinator of an implementing agency, Brazil)

It is worth noting that the expectations held by the resettlement organizations in relation to self-sufficiency and access to the labor market were not different from what the refugees themselves wanted. However, there was a gap between the assumptions of refugees and the program about what type of job they should access and how and when they should get it. In the case of Palestinian refugees in both countries and the Colombians in Brazil, language was an explicit barrier along with the type of employment (sometimes completely different from refugees' previous experience or aspirations). Additionally, refugees faced obstacles validating previous academic degrees and other issues related to age, gender barriers, or family dynamics that may have delayed their access to the job market.

Furthermore, there was a difference in what the institutions and refugees understood by self-sufficiency. For the program in both countries, self-sufficiency was related to economic stability. For refugees, self-sufficiency involved economic autonomy as well as agency and ownership of their resettlement process. For example, refugees raised demands in relation to what they considered unmet promises (discussed earlier) as well as a desire for citizenship and equal access to rights. This attitude was sometimes considered ungrateful by the resettlement organizations and explained away as due to their "refugee mentality." The notion of "refugee mentality" that emerged from the interviews was associated with the belief that refugees were used to being assisted and unable or unwilling to develop their own livelihood projects. This rhetoric was more common when referring to Palestinian refugees but was also used to explain the behavior of some Colombian refugees. The quotations below show how this idea was framed in the narratives about the program in each country:

> There was a change in the attitude of the [Palestinian] beneficiaries that I placed around the second half of 2009. Because Palestinians always had a refugee mentality, you know, that the "international community own us." . . . So, at the beginning there was a constant asking and asking. (resettlement analyst, Ministry of Interior, Chile)

> You have that Colombian refugee that was so long in Venezuela; I don't know . . . we usually said that those are the most likely to return or the ones that want to extend the financial assistance. Because when they are in the first country of asylum, they are being assisted as well, so they don't want to stop being assisted. They are used to it. (resettlement coordinator of an implementing agency, Brazil)

In the case of Palestinian refugees, the resettlement organizations associated their refugeeness with living in a refugee camp, because "they were getting all their basic needs covered there." This view focuses only on the basic assistance refugees received, decontextualizing that help from the appalling conditions in which refugees were living in the middle of the desert, unwillingly and unable to leave. As Malkki (1996) argues, these types of views depoliticize refugees and remove them from their historical context, reducing them to humanitarian subjects. I argue that in the case of Chile and Brazil, depending on refugee compliance in what was expected from them, their refugeeness made them either "universal victims" worthy of help and protection (Rajaram 2002) or "ungrateful" subjects who were used to claiming and unwilling to integrate (Moulin 2012).

The narratives that construct refugees as recipients of assistance (Rajaram 2002; see also Sigona 2014) do not account for how refugees themselves construct their own identities and agency. Most of the Palestinian refugees that I interviewed constructed their refugeeness in relation to their own narratives, relational settings, and historical processes, with being part of the Palestinian diaspora, displaced from their homeland (Doraï 2002). Indeed, their collective refugeeness was not only a humanitarian issue but also a political issue that demanded recognition, and a solution, from the international community. In this context, their refugee status, as they did with their expectations, was used as an instrument of power negotiation and resistance to claim part of the life they had lost. However, refugees did not see their refugeeness as being linked to continuous assistance but indeed as a reminder that their lives were disrupted and put on hold because of a displacement that they did not want.

Protection versus Integration: Framing the Good Refugee

Expectations surrounding what constituted the "good refugee" that emerged from the organizations' narratives were also related to the resettlement program's main objective: refugee protection. This notion of protection is mainly understood as legal protection (Helton 2003) in line with the requirements of the 1951 Refugee Convention. The resettlement program in both countries understood protection as the reestablishment of basic rights by taking people out of dangerous or appalling situations in the context of a humanitarian emergency. This emphasis is evident in staff members' narratives of implementing agencies in both countries:

> Ok, I agree that you had to leave behind relatives, parents, brothers, I don't know, friends, your life and a particular environment . . . but the program is not designed to provide you the life you used to have. The program is there to save your lives, you know? (former interpreter in an implementing agency, Chile)

> When you asked me for the main objective of the program, I told you about the goal of autonomy, mainly through insertion to the labor market. However, thinking in the bigger picture, the main aim before anything else is the one of protection. And that is pretty much something that they can get in Brazil. (staff member in an implementing agency, Brazil)

According to these accounts, protection is understood in relation to refugees' safety in the host state, the recognition of refugee status, and the state's decision to grant them a residency permit. This understanding of protection that prevails as the main goal of the resettlement program in both countries conveniently dismisses refugees' demands in relation to their substantial integration. The accounts of implementing agencies focused on the idea that refugees were safe in the host countries and therefore should be thankful. Indeed, refugees were thankful for Chile's and Brazil's protection, but they understood protection as needing to include the rights that they could not access and the accomplishment of unfulfilled promises. Between both understandings of what should be the scope of protection emerged the well-known paradox between refugee protection and refugee integration: legal status does not necessarily guarantee substantial citizenship and/or belonging (Da Lomba 2010; Hyndman 2011). Hence, it can be argued that resettlement as a durable solution does not necessarily mean the end of the refugee cycle, and many refugees found themselves living in a condition of prolonged uncertainty.

Furthermore, in both countries narratives emerged about the "ungrateful subject" (Moulin 2012), those refugees who appraised the *gift* of humanitarian protection as not sufficient without equal access to rights and services in the host country. Moulin argues that refugee resistance goes against the gratitude expected by hosts in relation to the *gift of protection* granted by the sovereign authority. In her analysis, she argues that expectations of gratitude by hosting societies are based on the premise that by providing freedom and protection, the refugees must be self-sufficient and obedient.

The trade-off between protection and refugee compliance to the "laws of gratitude" suggested by Moulin shaped to an extent the relationship between resettlement organizations and refugees. This tension was not exclusively between Palestinian refugees and the resettlement program. Colombian refugees were, to a lesser extent, also regarded under the lens of the "good and thankful refugee."

In this context, Colombian and Palestinian refugees who complained about unmet promises or who requested more attention from the organizations were deemed as "problematic," as "ungrateful," or as having the previously discussed refugee mentality. An example of this rhetoric was the case of Eugenia and her family, who developed a tense relationship with one of the NGOs in Brazil when the family actively demanded written communication, either on paper or by email, from the NGO. I discussed this case several times with members of the NGO, and they thought Eugenia and her family were "making noise" to get more assistance. They told me that they had never before received a request for written communication from refugees and that they did not have time to answer her directly.

Eugenia's request for written communication was not outside the possibilities of the NGO. However, there was no interest in responding. This case, and the service providers' narratives, showed that, on the one hand, there is mistrust in relation to the true intentions of the refugees' demands (Daniel and Knudsen 1995). On the other, none of the NGOs involved in resettlement expressed the need to be accountable to refugees (see Harrell-Bond 2002). They were accountable to the UNHCR, the donors, and the governments through different types of reports and daily communication, but not to the beneficiaries.

The NGO's refusal to provide the information in writing as requested by Eugenia resituated her in the position of *waiting*. This waiting leaves refugees expecting information from others, unaware of how long they may have to wait and uncertain of what they should or should not wait for. The wait for clear information puts the refugee on hold, reducing their negotiating power. As Bourdieu (2000: 228) argues, waiting implies submission and is "one of the ways of experiencing the effects of power . . . making people wait, . . . delaying without destroying hope . . . is an integral part of the exercise of power." That is to say, to be a refugee is to be subordinated to the will of others (Auyero 2012): the countries, the international organizations, the host society, and even the NGOs.

Some staff members unintentionally reinforced this exercise of power during their daily encounters with refugees by providing (or not providing) specific information or by making decisions that changed some of the terms and conditions of the program. Refugees were constantly reminded that the resettlement organizations set the dynamics of their relationship, since they were the ones facilitating mobility into the country; they provided their subsistence allowance and enabled, for example, their applications to certain entrepreneurship credits or benefits. In this context, control over information was crucial for defining the power structures within resettlement (See Harrell-Bond 1999, 2002). As one former staff member of the program told me, "Access to information is a right, but in the context of resettlement [it] is treated as a privilege."

In Brazil, some organization members recognized the need to improve and standardize the information provided to resettled individuals in the host country and to make transparent the criteria used for specific decisions, because the ad hoc approach in place was guided by the personal affinity between staff and certain refugees. In Chile, the delivery of information was also weak and needed to be harmonized. One refugee, Paula, told me that in order to know what was happening she used to go to the NGO's premises every week to check if there was a new service, information, or activities available. Basically, information was indeed provided, but on request only.

The performance of the resettlement organizations in Chile and Brazil vis-à-vis refugees exemplifies what I call the paradoxes between the politics of humanitarianism and the politics of belonging. The resettlement program has been designed and implemented based on the emergency and the need, expressed by the organizations, to provide immediate relief to victims of displacement, in line with common understandings of humanitarianism (Barnett and Weiss 2008). At the same time, however, the program demanded that refugees adopt the passive role of a humanitarian subject who complied with the logic of gratitude and the responsibility of self-sufficiency as the main means of integration.

Conclusion

This chapter explored the power imbalances in the resettlement process of Colombian and Palestinian refugees in Chile and Brazil, showing how these were developed at different scales of the refugee experience: from the discretionary decision of both states to resettle to the exercise of power through the control of information. The findings discussed in this chapter support the suggestion that the humanitarian structure of refugee protection has institutionalized, depoliticized, and silenced the figure of the refugee (Rajaram 2002; Malkki 1996; also Sandvik, this volume) and has exacerbated the power imbalances between the resettlement organizations and refugees (Hyndman 2000; Harrell-Bond 1999). Consequently, the processes and interventions of NGOs have been shaped in a way that encourages the mistrust and resentment expressed by refugees.

This chapter traced these power imbalances by looking at the expectations of both refugees and the organizations involved, showing how these interactions contributed to refugees' experiences of unsettlement by extending and normalizing refugees' uncertainties in the host country, while regulating how these uncertainties are "framed and made sense of" (Biehl 2015: 70).

This discussion adds new dimensions to the understanding of refugees' experiences by exploring the pivotal role of interactions in resettlement and the role of organizations as part of the resettlement experience. The analysis of the experiences of resettlement in these two Latin American countries is more relevant than ever. The prospects of the Global Compact on Refugees and the shift on humanitarian governance to reinforce protection in the regions of origin place new emphasis in South-South responses and in emerging resettlement countries such as Chile and Brazil. As such, refugee resettlement has global and regional implications as well as local and individual ones that go beyond the emergency of taking refugees out of the camp or dangerous zones. Through the study of resettlement in Chile and Brazil, this chapter contributes to the understanding of this durable solution in emergent resettlement countries, showing that the power imbalances of resettlement as a humanitarian tool are transversal across host countries and affect resettled refugees of different origins equally.

Dr. Marcia A. Vera Espinoza is a postdoctoral research associate in the ERC-funded project Prospects for International Migration Governance (MIGPROSP). She is based in the Department of Politics at the University of Sheffield, where she also teaches modules on migration and forced displacement. Her work has been published in *Global Policy*, *Forced Migration Review*, and *Development Policy Review*.

Notes

1. I would like to thank the editors for their valuable comments. This chapter builds on sections of my doctoral research, which is titled "Experiences of 'Unsettlement' Exploring the 'Integration' of Palestinian and Colombian Refugees Resettled in Chile and Brazil." The research was supported by the Chilean National Commission of Scientific and Technology and fieldwork grants from the Royal Geographical Society (with IBG) Slawson Award, the Society for Latin American Studies (SLAS), and the Sheffield Institute for International Development (SIID). The research was given ethical approval by the University of

Sheffield ethics committee in 2012 before the beginning of the fieldwork. All the interviews, participant observation, and surveys were conducted after informed and written consent was given. All the data provided by the participants has been treated confidentially. In order to protect refugees' identity and confidentiality, their names have been replaced with pseudonyms.

2. I also interviewed another sixteen informants who were involved in refugee assistance or related to the program—either through formal or informal partnerships.

References

Allen, John. 2003. *Lost Geographies of Power*. Oxford: Wiley-Blackwell.

Americas. 1984. "Cartagena Declaration on Refugees, Colloquium on the International Protection of Refugees in Central America, Mexico and Panama." 22 November. In *Annual Report of the Inter-American Commission on Human Rights*, OAS (1984–1985).

Auyero, Javier. 2012. *Patients of the State: The Politics of Waiting in Argentina*. Durham: Duke University Press.

Barnett, Michael, and Thomas G. Weiss. 2008. *Humanitarianism in Question: Politics, Power, Ethics*. Ithaca: Cornell University Press.

Bessa, Thais. 2006. *Resettlement in Brazil*. REFVIEW. Geneva: UNHCR.

Biehl, Kristen Sarah. 2015. "Governing through Uncertainty: Experiences of Being a Refugee in Turkey as a Country for Temporary Asylum." *Social Analysis* 59(1): 57–75.

Bijit, Karina. 2012. "El Proceso de Integración Social de los Refugiados Palestinos Reasentados en la Región de Valparaíso, Chile." *Si Somos Americanos. Revista de Estudios Transfronterizos* 12(1): 155–80.

Bourdieu, Pierre. 2000. *Pascalian Meditations*. Stanford: Stanford University Press.

Brun, Cathrine. 2015. "Active Waiting and Changing Hopes: Toward a Time Perspective on Protracted Displacement." *Social Analysis* 59(1): 19–37.

Da Lomba, Sylvie. 2010. "Legal Status and Refugee Integration: A UK Perspective." *Journal of Refugee Studies* 23(4): 415–36.

Daneri, Carmen Gloria. 2008. Sesion Especial Sobre Temas de Actualidad del Derecho Internacional de los Refugiados. El Refugio en Chile. Santiago.

Daniel, Errol Valentine, and John Chr. Knudsen. 1995. *Mistrusting Refugees*. Berkeley: University of California Press.

Doraï, Mohamed Kamel. 2002. "The Meaning of Homeland for the Palestinian Diaspora: Revival and Transformation." In *New Approaches to Migration? Transnational Communities and the Transformation of Home*, edited by N. S. Al-Ali and K. Koser, 87–95. London: Routledge.

El-Shaarawi, Nadia. 2015. "Living an Uncertain Future: An Ethnography of Displacement, Health, Psychosocial Well-Being and the Search for Durable Solutions among Iraqi Refugees in Egypt." *Social Analysis* 59(1): 38–56.

Fanjoy, Martha, Hilary Ingraham, Cyrena Khoury, and Amir Osman. 2005. *Expectations and Experiences of Resettlement: Sudanese Refugees' Perspectives on Their Journeys from Egypt to Australia, Canada and the United States*. Cairo, Egypt: American University in Cairo Forced Migration and Refugee Studies Program.

Greiner, Clemens, and Patrick Sakdapolrak. 2013. "Translocality: Concepts, Applications and Emerging Research Perspectives." *Geography Compass* 7(5): 373–84.

Griffiths, Melanie. 2013. "Living with Uncertainty: Indefinite Immigration Detention." *Journal of Legal Anthropology* 1(3): 263–86.

——. 2014. "Out of Time: The Temporal Uncertainties of Refused Asylum Seekers and Immigration Detainees." *Journal of Ethnic and Migration Studies* 40(12): 1991–2009.

Guglielmelli-White, Ana. 2012. *A Pillar of Protection: Solidarity Resettlement for Refugees in Latin America.* New Issues in Refugee Research 239. Geneva: UNHCR.

Harley, Tristan. 2014. "Regional Cooperation and Refugee Protection in Latin America: A 'South-South' Approach." *International Journal of Refugee Law* 26(1): 22–47.

Harrell-Bond, Barbara. 1999. "The Experience of Refugees as Recipients of Aid." In *Refugees: Perspectives on the Experience of Forced Migration,* edited by A. Ager, 136–38. London: Pinter.

——. 2002. "Can Humanitarian Work with Refugees Be Humane?" *Human Rights Quarterly* 24(1): 51–85.

Helton, Arthur. 2003. "What Is Refugee Protection? A Question Revisited." In *Problems of Protection. The UNHCR, Refugees and Human Rights,* edited by N. Steiner, M. Gibney, and G. Loescher, 19–36. New York: Routledge.

Horst, Cindy. 2006. "Buufis amongst Somalis in Dadaab: The Transnational and Historical Logics behind Resettlement Dreams." *Journal of Refugee Studies* 19(2): 143–57.

Horst, Cindy, and Katarzyna Grabska. 2015. "Introduction: Flight and Exile—Uncertainty in the Context of Conflict-Induced Displacement." *Social Analysis* 59(1): 1–18.

Hyndman, Jennifer. 2000. *Managing Displacement: Refugees and the Politics of Humanitarianism.* Minneapolis: University of Minnesota Press.

——. 2011. *Research Summary on Resettled Refugee Integration in Canada.* Ottawa: UNHCR.

Hynes, Tricia. 2003. *The Issue of "Trust" or "Mistrust" in Research with Refugees: Choices, Caveats and Considerations for Researchers.* New Issues in Refugee Research 98, Geneva: UNHCR.

Jubilut, Liliana, and Wellington Carneiro. 2011. "Resettlement in Solidarity: A New Regional Approach towards a More Humane Durable Solution." *Refugee Survey Quarterly* 30(3): 63–86.

Kenny, Paul D., and Kate Lockwood-Kenny. 2011. "A Mixed Blessing: Karen Resettlement to the United States." *Journal of Refugee Studies* 24(2): 217–38.

Khosravi, Shahram. 2014. "Waiting." In *Migration: The COMPAS Anthology,* edited by B. Anderson and M. Keith. Oxford: COMPAS. Accessed 22 June 2018. http://compasanthology.co.uk/wp-content/uploads/2014/04/COMPASMigrationAnthology.pdf.

Malkki, Liisa. 1996. "Speechless Emissaries: Refugees, Humanitarianism, and Dehistoricization." *Cultural Anthropology* 11(3): 377–404.

Marete, Julius. 2012. "The Resettlement Journey of Somali and Sudanese Refugees from Camps in Kenya to New Zealand." *Oxford Monitor of Forced Migration* 2(1): 48–52.

Mason, Jennifer. 2006. "Mixing Methods in a Qualitatively Driven Way." *Qualitative Research* 6(1): 9–25.

Moulin, Carolina. 2012. "Ungrateful Subjects? Refugee Protest and the Logic of Gratitude." In *Citizenship, Migrant Activism and the Politics of Movement*, edited by P. Nyers and K. Rygiel, 54–72. New York: Routledge.

Nogueira, Maria Beatriz, and Carla Cristina Marques. 2008. "Brazil: Ten Years of Refugee Protection." *Forced Migration Review* (30): 57–58.

Oxford English Dictionary. 2007. 6th ed. Oxford: Oxford University Press.

Rajaram, Prem Kumar. 2002. "Humanitarianism and Representations of the Refugee." *Journal of Refugee Studies* 15(3): 248–64.

Ruiz, Hiram. 2015. *Evaluation of Resettlement Programmes in Argentina, Brazil, Chile, Paraguay and Uruguay.* Geneva: UNHCR.

Sandvik, Kristin Bergtora. 2011. "Blurring Boundaries : Refugee Resettlement in Kampala—between the Formal, the Informal, and the Illegal." *PoLAR: Political and Legal Anthropology Review* 34(1): 11–32.

———. 2012. "Negotiating the Humanitarian Past: History, Memory, and Unstable Cityscapes in Kampala, Uganda." *Refugee Survey Quarterly* 31(1): 108–22.

Shrestha, Christie. 2011. *Power and Politics in Resettlement: A Case Study of Bhutanese Refugees in the USA.* New Issues in Refugee Research 208. Geneva: UNHCR.

Sigona, Nando. 2014. "The Politics of Refugee Voices: Representations, Narratives, and Memories." In *The Oxford Handbook on Refugee and Forced Migration Studies*, edited by E. Fiddian-Qasmiyeh, G. Loescher, K. Long, and N. Sigona, 369–382. Oxford: Oxford University Press.

Thomson, Marnie Jane. 2012. "Black Boxes of Bureaucracy: Transparency and Opacity in the Resettlement Process of Congolese Refugees." *PoLAR: Political and Legal Anthropology Review* 35(2): 186–205.

UNHCR. 2010. *The Mexico Plan of Action to Strengthen International Protection of Refugees in Latin America Main Achievements and Challenges during the Period 2005–2010.* Geneva: UNHCR.

———. 2011. *UNHCR Resettlement Handbook.* Geneva: UNHCR.

———. 2016. *UNHCR Projected Global Resettlement Needs 2017.* Geneva: UNHCR.

van Selm, Joanne. 2013. *Great Expectations: A Review of the Strategic Use of Resettlement.* Policy Development and Evaluation Service. Geneva: UNHCR.

Vera Espinoza, Marcia. 2017. "Extra-regional Refugee Resettlement in South America: The Palestinian Experience." *Forced Migration Review* 56: 47–49.

———. 2018. "The Limits and Opportunities of Regional Solidarity: Exploring Refugee Resettlement in Brazil and Chile." *Global Policy* 9(1): 85–94.

———. Forthcoming. *Unsettled Refugees: Understanding Uncertainty as Part of the Integration Experience.*

Westoby, Peter. 2009. The *Sociality of Refugee Healing: In Dialogue with Southern Sudanese Refugees Resettling in Australia–Towards a Social Model of Healing.* Seaholme: Common Ground Publishers.

Williams, Allan, and Vladimir Baláž. 2012. "Migration, Risk, and Uncertainty: Theoretical Perspectives." *Population, Space and Place* 18(2): 167–80.

Conclusion

The Moral Economy of the Resettlement Regime

Astri Suhrke and Adèle Garnier

The international regime for resettlement of refugees examined in this volume has three important characteristics.

First, the regime is *state-centric*. That is, the number of refugees resettled depends on the decision of national governments to offer resettlement places. The United Nations High Commissioner for Refugees (UNHCR) can plead and prod, but the final decision lies with the states. This makes for a *structurally fragmented* regime.

Second, the resettlement regime is *normatively diverse*. National governments develop and apply their own criteria for selection. While national criteria are informed by UNHCR assessments of vulnerability and need for protection, they also reflect the national interests of the participating states

Third, UNHCR is heavily *dependent* on a handful of countries for resettlement; this group partly overlaps with another very small group of states that provides most of the funding for UNHCR activities worldwide.

Why are these features important, and what do they tell us about the moral economy of the resettlement regime? Closer up, each feature is complex.

Structural Fragmentation

UNHCR has a central role in this regime. The agency assesses resettlement needs, articulates core standards for selection of candidates for settlement, and does the initial screening in preparation of lists of cases that are presented to countries offering places. Assessment of needs is made annually, based on the number of refugees in first asylum areas that are considered at risk and requiring resettlement. This number is then whittled down very considerably with a view to how many cases "the traffic will bear" and the capacity of UNHCR to process. In 2015, for instance, the initial need assessment figure was close to one million places, but the agency planned to submit cases totaling only around 125,000 persons and noted that it had capacity to process around 70,000 (UNHCR 2014c: 9). That figure seems relatively stable even across the early phase of the Syrian War, hovering between 60,000 and 90,000 annually.

Countries participating in UNHCR resettlement programs decide on the number to accept annually, typically in the form of national quotas (hence the term "quota refugees"). As several chapters in this book show, quotas and criteria for eligibility are determined through national political processes as expressed in national law and regulations. The identities of the main resettlement countries have not changed markedly over time, and their annual programs have an element of stability, although dramatic change can occur as a result of domestic politics (e.g., the United States suspended its resettlement program with UNHCR at the beginning of the Trump administration; see Cellini; Darrow, this volume) or as a crisis response to a massive outflow of refugees.

UNHCR can advocate more resettlement offers, pleading the case of vulnerable refugees in protracted displacement situations, the strain imposed on countries of first asylum, and the dangers refugees are exposed to when trying to circumvent the slow and limited regular resettlement process. This it does. What the agency cannot do is authoritatively regulate the number of places available. When new places open up, this is typically in response to sudden, large outflows that have a political and humanitarian impact in the traditional resettlement countries in North America, Europe, and Australasia. As discussed by Jubilut and Zamur; and Vera Espinoza, in this volume, some Latin American states recently joined the traditional group of resettlement countries. Yet the places offered were few, and, tellingly, the change was in large measure due to ambitions of the Brazilian government to play a larger role on the regional as well as the global humanitarian scene.

The number of placement offers is foundational to the entire resettlement regime. The limited influence of the agency in this respect constitutes a structural fragmentation of the regime. The point was implicitly recognized in UNHCR's recent policy initiative called Strategic Use of Resettlement (SUR) as discussed by van Selm in this volume: unable to generate more places, UNHCR explored ways of generating a multiplier effect from the offers on hand at any particular time.

Norm Diversity

The structural fragmentation arising from the state-centric determination of resettlement offers is compounded by the diversity of national eligibility criteria, as Cellini summarizes in this volume. Admittedly, UNHCR has made significant efforts to standardize criteria for resettlement. The agency has articulated principles of particular protection needs and vulnerability to inform participating states and has developed corresponding guidelines for its officials interviewing candidates in the field. The guidelines are centered on categories of risk (see Sandvik, this volume), that is, refugees deemed to be at risk while in first asylum due to physical or legal insecurities, medical needs, or gender, age, or family characteristics, and thus in need of resettlement. The application of a generally uniform set of criteria as a first filter in the selection of candidates injects a measure of consistency and fairness in the resettlement process as a whole.

Getting on the UNHCR list of candidates, however, does not automatically mean resettlement, and certainly not immediately. To be accepted, a candidate also has to fit the national criteria for eligibility in a given resettlement country. In the normal course of things, national selection missions, usually composed of immigration officials, visit the relevant sites to peruse lists of candidates prepared by UNHCR, screen candidates who fit with national criteria determined by the political authorities at home, and then make their pick.

As this book shows, national criteria for eligibility can be both more general and more specific than the UNHCR criteria for refugees at risk that land candidates a place on the agency's resettlement list in the first place. US legislation, for instance, has a category that privileges persons "of special humanitarian interest to the United States." Danish selection missions in refugee camps in Jordan at one point were specifically looking for Kurds for resettlement, rejecting Palestinians on UNHCR's list. The Netherlands and Canada both have criteria related to the ability of refugees to integrate well in their new homelands (though exceptions are routinely made in Canada, per operational guidelines to immigration staff; see Garnier, this volume). Japan has possibly the most restrictive integration criteria of all, at one point accepting only (Buddhist) Karen refugees who were young and had few children. The program was later expanded slightly but still permitted only Burmese speakers (and hence Buddhists). Australia has four different categories of visas for quota refugees. Norway and Sweden have slots for witnesses who have testified for the International Criminal Court, and Norway also for persons who have become refugees due to their association with the international pen club (PEN).

The diversity in national eligibility criteria helps to accommodate the diversity in the global refugee population and as such strengthens the overall protection function of the regime. On the other hand, it interjects considerable uncertainty and unpredictability in the selection process. This is particularly the case when sudden, massive refugee outflows change national assessments of intake capacity and priorities. Quota resettlement of refugees at risk may be put on the backburner, or particular groups may be privileged when national selection missions work outside the lists prepared by UNHCR (as happened during the Indochinese refugee crisis in the 1970s). Overall, the diversity in national eligibility criteria limits the ability of UNHCR to manage the resettlement process according to commonly constructed criteria of fairness and need. This weakens the regime's protection function.

Dependence

While UNHCR possesses considerable power relative to refugees by virtue of its screening role in the initial selection process, in relation to participating states the agency is in a position of extreme dependence. UNHCR is heavily dependent on a very small number of countries for both resettlement places and general funding. Arguably, this is the most important constraint on the agency's ability to develop the international resettlement regime, whether through expansion of the program or the application of greater consistency in the criteria for eligibility. The agency has almost no core funding but must raise funds through voluntary contributions for its global operations. Funding comes primarily from governments through annual contributions as well as in response to particular appeals issued by the agency during the year to support refugee emergencies. Most of the funding is earmarked for particular purposes, and it is never enough.

To illustrate, let us look at data for 2013—a somewhat normal year before the Syrian refugee crisis erupted (UNHCR 2014a: 13). In this year, the agency reported 3.16 billion dollars in revenue, of which almost all (3.11 billion) was from voluntary contributions. There was a large shortfall—the revenue covered about 61 percent of the agency's budget for that year.

Slightly over half (52 percent) of the voluntary contributions came from three donors: The United States, Japan, and the European Union. The U.S. contribution was singularly important, totaling 1 billion dollars, or one-third of the total, far ahead of the next two—Japan (252 million) and the European Union (213 million). The remaining donors in the top ten category were, with the exception of Kuwait, all European countries. The contribution of each hovered around the 100 million dollar mark. Altogether, only ten governments accounted for 82 percent of virtually all the agency's revenue.

Dependence on a few key governments is even more marked in the resettlement field. Again, looking at 2013, three countries accounted for a staggering 85 percent of the approximately 93,000 refugees resettled that year. These were the United States, Australia, and Canada. The United States alone took well over half (almost 60,000). Australia and Canada took around 10,000 each. The remaining countries in the top ten resettlement countries were European (with the exception of New Zealand). Their intake was in the range of 1–5000 refugees each.

The dependence on a small number of states for both general financing and for the resettlement program holds the refugee agency in a vicelike grip. Forceful advocacy for resettlement is discouraged by the recognition that its major supporters are already either providing critical financing or keeping the resettlement program afloat by offering spaces–and sometimes both. Some major supporters appear to pursue a trade-off policy by taking in a relatively large number for resettlement, but not contributing much funding to UNHCR's general operations (Canada and Australia),[1] or is a generous donor but has a very restrictive resettlement policy (Japan). Whichever direction the agency looks, there is heavy dependence on a few states and shortfalls of resources related to needs.

The Moral Economy of Dependence

What are the political implications of this dependence? Let us take a leaf from the literature on moral economy, which explores behavior in societies that exist on a small margin of survival. As James Scott (1976) has demonstrated, such societies may explode in rebellion, but the norm is risk-averse behavior, as manifested in cautious and conservative practices. Citing R. H. Tawney's classic description of the Chinese peasant who stands "permanently up to the neck in water, so that even a ripple is sufficient to drown him," Scott shows that such a person, in a word, does not make waves.

The same would seem to hold true for organizations. Dependence on annual contributions from a few, often fickle, governments to maintain a vast global operation would generate strong disincentives to innovate and take risk. Indeed, UNHCR is famously cautious and risk averse, sensitive to its executive committee, and particularly careful to maintain the relationship with its key supporters.[2] Caution is particularly relevant for resettlement, which constitutes a very small part of the agency's overall operations. To illustrate: the 93,000 refugees who were resettled in 2013 stood in contrast to the almost 42.9 million "persons of concern" to UNHCR that year (UNHCR 2014b). Pressure from the agency for more resettlement places might jeopardize its access to funds to support the tens of millions "of concern" who require immediate protection and assistance.

UNHCR's embrace of the status quo is also evident in its role in the New York Declaration on Refugees and Migrants adopted by the UN General Assembly in September 2016, where emphasis on resettlement is limited. An annual resettlement target of 10 percent of the world's refugees was included in the draft UN secretary-general's report prepared for the Summit leading to the Declaration. This target was removed from the final report following political negotiations (Ferris 2016; Garnier 2016). Prior to the 2016 Summit, a UNHCR-sponsored conference in Geneva aiming to identify "alternative pathways" to asylum for Syrian forced migrants generated a muted response from states (Crisp 2017). Crisp notes that advocacy for voluntary repatriation enjoys a far greater level of support in the international community than resettlement. Also of note in the lead-up to the New York Declaration was UNHCR's "fear of mandate competition" (Betts 2016), in particular the growing role of the International Organization for Migration (IOM), which would compete for resources and support in the state-centric regime. The UN Summit gave recognition to the traditionally more strongly state-driven IOM as a UN agency. Some states have since signaled a preference for IOM rather than UNHCR in what would be a typical refugee operation, such as the decision of Bangladesh to ask IOM, and not UNHCR, to coordinate assistance to Rohingya refugees (IOM 2017).

Another troubling development from an organizational perspective was the announcement by the Trump administration in early December 2017 that the United States was withdrawing altogether from the cooperative structure established to implement the migration-focused elements of the New York Declaration at the UN Summit (Wintour 2017). Washington justified the decision with reference to the primacy of national sovereignty in matters of migration, thus underscoring the state-centric nature of that regime and the related vulnerability of an agency like UNHCR.

The structure of dependence makes it eminently rational for UNHCR to embrace an organizational strategy where resettlement is maintained as a small "niche" program, designed for refugees in situations of grave risk. In practice, resettlement on a large scale has taken place only when mass outflows have been of particular political or humanitarian interest to rich and powerful coalitions of states. This happened in response to some of the twentieth-century mass outflows in Europe (after the Russian Revolution, during the Cold War) and in Asia (after communist victories in Indochina). The current difficulties of finding permanent places for refugees from Syria and the Horn of Africa, now crowding into camps and informal settlements in the Middle East, reflect quite different political realities. UNHCR has adjusted accordingly.

But a moral economy perspective also alerts us to broader considerations of justice. In this perspective, we should ask how resettlement practices affect the overall protection functions of the international refugee regime. The question has no easy answers and suggests difficult trade-offs. Examining the nature of these trade-offs and developing justifiable balances in practice has been, and will remain, a continuous task for the international refugee regime as a whole. Below, we can only point to some of its currents dimensions.

Resettlement may carry costs that weaken other protection functions of the international refugee regime. For a start, and as increasingly noted, there are economic costs. Resettling say, 100,000 refugees from (typically) the global South to the rich, industrialized North could provide assistance to many times that number of refugees if they remained in the South. A different kind of cost arises from the practice, used by some countries, to invoke resettlement as a justification to limit or even refuse first asylum (as Losoncz observes in this volume in the case of Australia). Resettlement on a large scale or in some forms may generate political backlash and feed xenophobic populism in host countries, especially in a context in which populism already is ripe. In Hungary, for instance, populist Prime Minister Viktor Orban organized in 2016 an antiresettlement referendum widely perceived as a sign of discontent with the European Union's pressure on member states to accept resettled candidates the European Commission had committed itself to accept (Gotev 2016). Similar sentiments pervade the current US administration (Blitzer 2017).

Yet resettlement obviously serves critically important protection functions. Resettlement protects at-risk refugees and reduces incentives for individuals to "jump the gate" and expose themselves to danger (as by crossing the Mediterranean). Resettlement also alleviates pressure on first asylum countries and thus strengthens the institution of asylum itself (the famed "protection dividend"). The case for resettlement also has a fundamental ethical rationale that tends to get lost in the din of daily controversies over refugee policy. Resettlement serves to remind rich and stable societies in a direct and visible manner of a basic humanitarian obligation to alleviate the consequences of wars elsewhere. That obligation, in turn, rests in part on the premise that indifference to the misery of others reduces the humanity of the self.

Astri Suhrke is senior researcher at the Chr. Michelsen Institute in Bergen, Norway, and visiting fellow at the Asia-Pacific College of Diplomacy at the Australian National University in Canberra. A political scientist, she has focused on the social, political, and humanitarian consequences of violent conflict and strategies of response. She has also written about strategies of postwar reconstruction and state building, with particular reference to Afghanistan. Her most recent books are *When More Is Less. The International Project in Afghanistan* (2011) and *The Peace In Between: Post-War Violence and Peacebuilding* (coedited anthology, 2012).

Adèle Garnier is a lecturer at the Department of Modern History, Politics and International Relations, Macquarie University, Australia. She has a Ph.D. in politics from the University of Leipzig, Germany and Macquarie University and has held research positions at the Interuniversity Research

Centre for Globalization and Work (CRIMT), Université de Montréal, Canada, and the Group for Research on Migration, Ethnic Relations and Equality (GERME), Université Libre de Bruxelles, Belgium. She has published in *Refuge,* the *Journal of Ethnic and Migration Studies,* and *WeltTrends.*

Notes

1. Canada's financial contribution to UNHCR has significantly expanded since the mid-2000s. As of 2017, it is in the top ten of UNHCR donors. At the same time, the proportion of Canadian funding tied to specific projects has increased, while funding for general operations has slightly declined (Grayson and Audet 2017).
2. Only in one period did UNHCR gain a reputation for showing innovation and strong advocacy. That was during Sadako Ogata's tenure as High Commissioner (1991–2001), which among refugee activists is considered "a golden period" in the agency's history. In retrospect, the main innovations appear to be modest: introduction of temporary protection for refugees from the Balkan Wars and a call for greater attention to the root causes of refugee outflows.

References

Betts, Alexander. 2016. *U.N. Refugee Summit: Abstract Discussions in the Face of a Deadly Crisis.* Refugees Deeply, 12 September 2016. Accessed 7 December 2017. https://www.newsdeeply.com/refugees/community/2016/09/12/u-n-refugee-summit-abstract-discussions-in-the-face-of-a-deadly-crisis.

Blitzer, Jonathan. 2017. "How Stephen Miller Single-Handedly Got the US to Accept Fewer Refugees." *New Yorker,* 13 October. Accessed 6 December 2017. https://www.newyorker.com/news/news-desk/how-stephen-miller-single-hand edly-got-the-us-to-accept-fewer-refugees.

Crisp, Jeff. 2017. *New York Declaration on Refugees: A One-Year Report Card.* Refugees Deeply, 18 September 2017. Accessed 6 December 2017. https://www.newsdeeply.com/refugees/community/2017/09/18/new-york-declaration-on-refugees-a-one-year-report-card.

Ferris, Elizabeth. 2016. *The Global Summit on Refugees and Migrants: The Pesky Level of Ambition.* Kaldor Centre for International Refugee Law, 14 September. Accessed 6 December 2017. http://www.kaldorcentre.unsw.edu.au/publication/global-summit-refugees-and-migrants-pesky-issue-level-ambition.

Garnier, Adèle. 2016. *The Future of Refugee Resettlement: Will the September Summits Make Any Difference?* Norwegian Centre for Humanitarian Studies. Accessed 6 February 2017. http://www.humanitarianstudies.no/2016/09/28/the-future-of-refugee-resettlement-will-the-september-summits-make-any-difference/.

Gotev, Georgi. 2016. *Hungary Readies Attack on Juncker over Migration Referendum.* Euractiv, 20 September. Accessed 6 December 2017. http://www.euractiv.com/section/justice-home-affairs/news/hungary-readies-attacks-on-juncker-over-migration-referendum/.

Grayson, Catherine-Lune, and François Audet. 2017. "Les Hauts et les Bas du Financement Canadien au HCR: Quelle Aide et pour Quels Réfugiés?" *Refuge* 33(1): 62–76.

International Organization for Migration (IOM). 2017. *IOM Appeal: Rohingya Refugee Crisis September 2017–February 2018*. Accessed 6 December 2017. https://www.iom.int/sites/default/files/country_appeal/file/IOM-Rohingya-Appeal-October-2017_0.pdf.

Scott, James C. 1976. *The Moral Economy of the Peasant: Rebellion and Subsistence in Southeast Asia*. New Haven: Yale University Press.

United Nations High Commissioner for Refugees (UNHCR). 2014a. *Report of the United Nations High Commissioner for Refugees Covering the Period 1 July 2013–30 June 2014*. Accessed 6 December 2017. http://www.unhcr.org/en-au/excom/unhcrannual/54352ea59/report-united-nations-high-commissioner-refugees-covering-period-1-july.html.

———. 2014b. *UNHCR Global Trends 2013*. Accessed 6 December 2017. http://www.unhcr.org/5399a14f9.pdf.

———. 2014c. *UNHCR Projected Global Resettlement Needs 2015*. Accessed 6 December 2017. http://www.unhcr.org/en-au/protection/resettlement/543408c4fda/unhcr-projected-global-resettlement-needs-2015.html?query=globalpercent20needs percent20assessment.

Wintour, Patrick. 2017. "Donald Trump Pulls US out of UN Global Compact on Migration." *The Guardian*, 3 December. Accessed 5 December 2017. https://www.theguardian.com/world/2017/dec/03/donald-trump-pulls-us-out-of-un-global-compact-on-migration.

Annex

Current Refugee Resettlement Program Profiles

Amanda Cellini

Introduction

This annex was designed to provide profiles of countries that have resettlement programs as of fall 2016. Twenty-seven countries are profiled, covering five continents. Programs profiled range from pilot programs to countries with established annual quotas, demonstrating that there is no single or universal way for a country to implement a refugee resettlement program.

The profiles are structured around eight categories that aim for ease of understanding and comparison between national programs:

1. the dates of the country's resettlement program
2. statistics from the total number of refugees resettled in recent years
3. the countries of origin of the largest number of resettled refugees in recent years
4. the refugee's status after resettlement
5. the regulatory basis for the resettlement program
6. the main selection criteria specifically for resettled refugees
7. the main national actors regarding resettlement
8. the role of United Nations High Commissioner for Refugees (UNHCR)

It should be noted that information regarding the refugee's status after resettlement has been kept to a minimum for clarity in comparison. Additionally, with regard to the category on selection criteria, the criteria listed are what are required *in addition* to the broader categories in which resettled refugees are admitted.

The information provided is intended to be a guide for further research and thus is not exhaustive. National resettlement programs are diverse in many regards: the programs profiled vary in their stage of establishment, legal grounding, and willingness to resettle different profiles of refugees as referred by UNHCR and other institutions. The public availability of information on a given program is reflected in the volume of information provided in each profile.

Information for this annex on issues of national policy largely draw upon the most recent *UNHCR Resettlement Handbook* country profiles. Supplemental information came from national offices responsible for immigration and refugee policy and UNHCR studies commissioned to evaluate pilot resettlement programs. All sources consulted can be found in the reference list at the end of the annex. Those looking for additional information, especially for European countries, would be wise to consult the Know Reset project (http://www.know-reset.eu), the European Migration Network (https://ec.europa.eu/home-affairs/what-we-do/networks/european_migra tion_network_en), and the European Resettlement Network (http://resettle ment.eu/). Additional resources on private sponsorship and the new joint IOM and UNHCR venture Emerging Resettlement Countries Joint Support Mechanism (ERCM) can also be found in the reference list.

The statistics used in the profiles reflect departures of individuals selected for resettlement as measured by the UNHCR Resettlement Statistical Database Portal, updated as of 30 September 2017. This is done for a few reasons: first, because the database collected data for all countries, from 2003 to 2017, offering a reliable source for comparisons between countries. Second, the annex aimed to measure how many refugees were actually resettled—a number that is often quite lower than the state's stated annual quotas for resettlement. It proved difficult, if not outright impossible, to find statistics on how many refugees were resettled to a specific country directly from governments: some countries were incredibly transparent with the information; some countries had publicly available statistics on refugees in the country but not disaggregated for resettlement; some countries shared statistics but did not keep information broken down by year; and many did not respond to repeated requests for statistical information. In the end, although an imperfect measure, statistical data from UNHCR for departures was used for every country except two where the national statistics were available and noticeably diverged from the UNHCR statistics. The sources for those two countries, Australia and Canada, are listed in the references.

Argentina

Date of resettlement program
Solidarity resettlement program, 2005–current

Number of refugees resettled since 2005

2017	0	2010	23
2016	0	2009	8
2015	0	2008	78
2014	21	2007	32
2013	7	2006	19
2012	5	2005	31
2011	24		

Source: Departures, UNHCR Resettlement Statistical Database Portal

Origin of largest resettled groups in last ten years
Colombia, El Salvador

Status after resettlement

Residency status	Temporary residency for two years.
Status of legal rights	Legal residents with authorization to perform paid work.

Regulatory basis

Domestic basis	Immigration Law 25.871, General Law for the Recognition and Protection of Refugees 26.165. The law complies with the 1951 Convention and Additional Protocol and provides that the term "refugee" shall also apply to persons who have fled their country of nationality or habitual residence, should they be stateless, because their lives, safety, or freedom have been threatened by generalized violence, foreign aggression, internal conflicts, massive violations of human rights, or other circumstances that have seriously disturbed the public order.
International basis	Memorandum of Understanding with UNHCR signed June 2005.

Main selection criteria

Selection procedure	UNHCR referral via selection missions and dossier selection (rarely used).
Eligibility criteria	Criteria include need for legal and physical protection, survivors of violence and torture, women in situations of risk, children and adolescents, and refugees without the prospect of local integration in the country of first asylum.
Admissibility criteria	No additional criteria.

Main national actors for resettlement

Sets resettlement quota	National Refugee Committee (CONARE) includes one representative from each of the Ministry of the Interior, Ministry of Foreign Affairs, International Trade and Worship, Ministry of Justice, Security and Human Rights, the National Institute Against Discrimination, Xenophobia and Racism, Ministry of Social Development, and a nonvoting representative from UNHCR and civil society.
	No formal legal procedure to determine annual quota and composition; no deadline.
Implements resettlement	CONARE and associated UNHCR-appointed organizations.

The role of UNHCR

Referrals	Refers cases to CONARE.
Selection missions	Funds cost of selection mission and transport.
Implementation	Sets up partner agency to implement refugee resettlement program and provides necessary funding.

Australia

Date of resettlement program
Ad hoc since 1950s; formal program: 1977–present[1]

Number of refugees resettled since 2001
The program year runs 1 July–30 June. Format: the first figure is the total of resettled refugees in a particular year. The figure in brackets is the total of

refugees admitted by Australia that year, including the special humanitarian visa program and "onshore protection" (refugee status obtained in Australia following an asylum claim).

2016–17	6,642 (12,049)	2008–09	6,499 (13,414)
2015–16	6,730 (17,555)	2007–08	6,004 (12,825)
2014–15	6,002 (13,756)	2006–07	6,003 (12,902)
2013–14	6,501 (13,768)	2005–06	6,022 (13,836)
2012–13	12,012 (20,019)	2004–05	5,511 (12,988)
2011–12	6,718 (13,759)	2003–04	4,134 (13,603)
2010–11	5,998 (13,799)	2002–03	4,376 (12,119)
2009–10	6,003 (13,756)	2001–02	4,160 (12,349)

Source: Karlsen (2016); DIBP 2017: 72.

Origin of largest resettled groups in past ten years
Afghanistan, Bhutan, Democratic Republic of Congo, Ethiopia, Eritrea, Iran, Iraq, Myanmar, Somalia, Syria

Status after resettlement

Residency status	Permanent residency.

Regulatory basis

Domestic basis	Refugees are termed "humanitarian migrants" in the Australian context.
	Australia shares responsibility for protecting refugees and resolving refugee situations through its Humanitarian Program, which includes two parts:
	The offshore (resettlement) component offers resettlement for people outside of Australia who cannot be repatriated or locally integrated and are in need of humanitarian assistance.
	The onshore (asylum or protection) component offers protection to people in Australia who meet the refugee definition as set out in the 1951 Convention relating to the Status of Refugees.
	The national legislative framework for defining refugee status for asylum seekers (the onshore component) and the criteria for accepting refugees and other humanitarian entrants (under Australia's offshore resettlement program) is based on

the Migration Act of 1958 and the 1994 Migration Regulations.

There are five refugee and humanitarian visas

Refugee visa (subclass 200): for people who are subject to persecution in their home country and are in need of resettlement.

In-country Special Humanitarian Program visa (subclass 201): for people who have suffered persecution in their country of nationality or usual residence and who have not been able to leave that country to seek refuge elsewhere who are in need of resettlement.

Global Special Humanitarian Program visa (subclass 202): for people who, while not being refugees, are subject to discrimination and human rights abuses in their home country.

Emergency rescue visa (subclass 203): offers accelerated processing for people who satisfy the refugee criteria and whose lives or freedom depend on urgent resettlement.

Women at risk (subclass 204): for female applicants and their dependents who are subject to persecution or are of concern to UNHCR.

Main selection criteria	
Selection procedure	UNHCR referral via selection missions.
Eligibility criteria	Applicants must meet the threshold criteria of persecution or substantial discrimination. In addition, the applicant must demonstrate compelling reasons regarding the degree of persecution or discrimination, the extent of their connection to Australia, whether there is any other suitable country other than Australia able to provide settlement and protection from persecution, and Australia's resettlement capacity. Criteria include women at risk and priority to specific populations via multiyear resettlement commitments (e.g., Iraq and Syria).
Admissibility criteria	Medical examinations are required.

Private sponsorship

Background	The Special Humanitarian Program (SHP) is for people outside their home country who are subject to substantial discrimination amounting to gross violations of their human rights in their home country and their application can be proposed by an Australian citizen, permanent resident, eligible New Zealand citizen, or an organization based in Australia. These applicants are not referred by UNHCR but may be registered by them.
	Special Humanitarian Program applicants can be privately sponsored under the Community Support Program if they have a functional level of English, have been offered employment, or are considered job-ready. Their application must be proposed by an approved proposing organization that is a well-established community organization in Australia that has entered a deed of agreement with the Department of Immigration and Border Protection. This includes financial commitments.

Main national actors for resettlement

Sets resettlement quota	Each year, the Australian government decides the size and the regional composition of the Humanitarian Program, taking into consideration advice from UNHCR.
Implements resettlement	The Humanitarian Program is administered by the Department of Immigration and Border Protection. The Department of Social Services is the federal government agency with the responsibility for settlement services. The Department of Education and Training has responsibility for foundational skill programs.

The role of UNHCR

Referrals	Refers cases.
Selection missions	Assists in the facilitation of selection missions.

Belgium

Date of resettlement program
Ad hoc since 1950s; ad hoc agreements since 2009; annual quota since 2013

Number of refugees resettled since 2009

2017	1,014	2012	1
2016	456	2011	19
2015	276	2010	2
2014	32	2009	54
2013	100		

Source: Departures, UNHCR Resettlement Statistical Database Portal

Origin of largest resettled groups in past ten years
Democratic Republic of Congo, Eritrea, Iraq, Palestine, Syria

Status after resettlement

Residency status	Permanent residence based on refugee status.
Status of legal rights	As refugee status can only be granted in Belgium, the individual must submit an asylum application upon arrival as a formality, and within days refugee status will be granted.

Regulatory basis

Domestic basis	The asylum procedure and the competencies of asylum institutions are governed by the Aliens Act of 15 December 1980. There are no specific provisions on resettlement in the Belgian legislation, as resettlement can be handled within existing legislation.

Main selection criteria

Selection procedure	UNHCR referral via selection missions and dossier selection.
Eligibility criteria	Criteria include meeting the refugee criteria as defined in Belgian Aliens Act and ability to articulate an individual need for protection in relation to country of origin.
Admissibility criteria	All cases are screened and cleared by the Security of the State; public order threats are also considered.

Main national actors for resettlement

Sets resettlement quota	The final decision for the annual quota belongs to the State Secretary for Asylum and Migration.
Implements resettlement	The two main operational authorities, the Office of the Commissioner General for Refugees and Stateless Persons (CGRS) and the Federal Agency for the Reception of Asylum-Seekers (Fedasil), fall under the State Secretariat for Asylum and Migration.

The role of UNHCR

Referrals	Refers cases to CGRS.
Selection missions	Assists in the preparation of selection missions.

Brazil

Date of resettlement program
Solidarity Resettlement Program, 2002–present

Number of refugees resettled since 2002

2017	2	2009	0
2016	31	2008	23
2015	0	2007	8
2014	21	2006	78
2013	7	2005	32
2012	5	2004	19
2011	24	2003	31
2010	0	2002	0

Source: Departures, UNHCR Resettlement Statistical Database Portal

Origin of largest resettled groups in past ten years
Angola, Colombia, Democratic Republic of Congo, Palestine, Syria

Status after resettlement

Residency status	Temporary residency permits.
Status of legal rights	Refugee status.

Regulatory basis

Domestic basis	The Brazilian Refugee Act (Law 9.474/97) defines refugees according to the 1951 Convention and the Cartagena Declaration criteria. It creates a sole legal status for refugees in the country, treating equally refugees who were recognized through refugee status determination (RSD) procedures and those resettled to Brazil.
International basis	Memorandum of Understanding with UNHCR, 1999.

Main selection criteria

Selection procedure	UNHCR referral via selection missions and dossier selection (rarely used).
Eligibility criteria	To qualify for resettlement, the refugee must be recognized pursuant to the 1951 Convention and its 67 Protocol as well as to the Brazilian Refugees Act, be submitted for resettlement by UNHCR, and belong to one of the following categories as established by the Memorandum of Understanding for the Resettlement of Refugees in Brazil noted above. Criteria include those with legal and physical protection needs, survivors of violence and torture, women at risk, refugees without local integration prospects, and those with strong links with other refugees already in Brazil.
Admissibility criteria	No additional criteria.

Main national actors for resettlement

Sets resettlement quota	The Brazilian Resettlement Program relies on a tripartite structure that involves government, civil society, and UNHCR in specific roles in accordance with the Memorandum of Understanding for the Resettlement of Refugees in Brazil (1999). The National Committee for the Refugees (Comitê Nacional para os Refugiados–CONARE), presided over by the Ministry of Justice, is composed of five other governmental bodies, civil society, and UNHCR coordinate actions.
Implements resettlement	There is no formal procedure or timeframe to determine the annual quota; in practice it is decided in coordination among CONARE, UNHCR, and nongovernmental organizations (NGOs).

The role of UNHCR

Referrals	Refers cases to CONARE.
Selection missions	Funds cost of selection mission and transport.
Implementation	Sets up partner agency to implement refugee resettlement program and provides necessary funding.

Canada

Date of resettlement program
Ad hoc since 1950s; annual quota since 1978

Number of refugees resettled since 2006

2017	N/A	2011	12,945
2016	46,700	2010	12,098
2015	20,045	2009	12,457
2014	12,875	2008	10,804
2013	12,210	2007	11,155
2012	9,655	2006	10,651

Source: IRCC (2017); UNHCR (2017b).

Origin of largest resettled groups in past ten years
Afghanistan, Bhutan, Burma, Burundi, Colombia, Congo, Ethiopia, Eritrea, Iran, Iraq, Somalia, Syria

Status after resettlement

Residency status	Permanent residence.

Regulatory basis

Domestic basis	Immigration and Refugee Protection Act, LC 2001 ch. 27, s.12(3), s.38(2) s.95–99 and Immigration and Refugee Protection Regulation SOR 2002/227, s.144–147, and operational guidelines exempt resettled refugees from the application of the "ability to establish" criteria that otherwise applies to permanent residents (see also Garnier, this volume)
	Canada has three resettlement streams:
	Government-assisted refugees, typically UNHCR-referred refugees who receive income support from the government for their first year in Canada.

Privately sponsored refugees, refugees and persons in refugee-like situations identified and supported for their first year in Canada by organizations and individuals.

Blended Visa Office–referred refugees, UNHCR-referred refugees who are matched with a private sponsor; income support comes partially from the government and partly from the private sponsor for their first year in Canada.

Main selection criteria	
Selection procedure	Canada will only consider an applicant for resettlement as a refugee if they are referred by UNHCR, another designated "referral organization," or a designated private sponsor.
Eligibility criteria	The applicant must meet the criteria of the 1951 Convention or the Humanitarian-protected Persons Abroad Class and have no reasonable prospect of a durable solution in a country other than Canada.
Admissibility criteria	They must pass a medical examination and criminal and security screenings. Resettled refugees are exempted from inadmissibility on the basis of "excessive demand" on the Canadian health system otherwise applying to prospective permanent residents.

Private sponsorship	
Background	Private sponsorship is currently an option, via two distinct channels:
	Privately sponsored refugees, refugees and persons in refugee-like situations identified and supported for their first year in Canada by organizations and individuals.
	Blended Visa Office–referred refugees, UNHCR-referred refugees who are matched with a private sponsor; income support comes partially from the government and partly from the private sponsor for their first year in Canada. This program was established in 2013.

Main national actors for resettlement

Sets resettlement quota	An annual resettlement range is established by the Minister of Immigration, Refugees, and Citizenship, following consultations with provincial governments, and then the proposed resettlement level is submitted as part of a report on overall immigration levels to Parliament annually in November.
Implements resettlement	Canada's resettlement program is administered by Immigration, Refugees and Citizenship Canada and Québec's Ministère de l'Immigration, de la Diversité et de l'Inclusion.

The role of UNHCR

Referrals	Refers cases.
Selection missions	Assists in the facilitation of selection missions.

Chile

Date of resettlement program
Solidarity resettlement program; 1999–current

Number of refugees resettled since 2003

2013	3	2007	119
2012	0	2006	34
2011	0	2005	75
2010	114	2004	163
2009	65	2003	87
2008	145		

Source: Departures, UNHCR Resettlement Statistical Database Portal

Origin of largest resettled groups in past ten years
Colombia, Palestine

Status after resettlement

Residency status	Permanent residence.

Status of legal rights	Granted refugee status with authorization to perform paid work.

Regulatory basis

Domestic basis	Law Decree No. 1094 of 1975; Supreme Decree No. 597 of 1084; Supreme Decree No. 2518 of 1998; Law Decree No. 20430 of 2010.
International basis	Framework Agreement for the Resettlement of Refugees in Chile with UNHCR signed in 1999.

Main selection criteria

Selection procedure	UNHCR referral via dossier selection (ten or fewer cases) and selection missions (more than ten cases).
Eligibility criteria	The refugee must meet the criteria contained in the 1951 Convention and 67 Protocol and must not be able to return to their country of origin or to remain safely in their country of asylum. Criteria include need for legal or physical protection, victims of violence and/or torture, women at risk, those with special needs, and refugees without local integration prospects in the country of first asylum.
Admissibility criteria	No additional criteria.

Private sponsorship

Background	NGOs, churches, communities, and individuals are authorized to sponsor refugees for resettlement in Chile, in agreement with the Ministry of the Interior. The sponsor shall take up the responsibility of travel arrangements, installation, and integration of resettled refugees and of the dependents.

Main national actors for resettlement

Sets resettlement quota	Ministry of the Interior and Ministry of Foreign Relations establishes an annual resettlement target in consultation with UNHCR.
Implements resettlement	The Ministry of Health, the Ministry of Education, the Ministry of Housing, the Ministry of Labor, the Ministry of Foreign Affairs, the Ministry of the Interior, UNHCR, and local NGOs, including Vicaria de Pastoral Social.

The role of UNHCR

Referrals	Refers cases to the government of Chile.
Selection missions	Funds cost of selection mission and transport.
Implementation	Sets up partner agency to implement refugee resettlement program and provides necessary funding.

Czech Republic

Date of resettlement program
Ad hoc since 1950s; emergency programs since 2005; annual program since 2008

Number of refugees resettled since 2005

2017	0	2010	48
2016	22	2009	17
2015	20	2008	46
2014	4	2007	8
2013	1	2006	0
2012	25	2005	15
2011	0		

Source: Departures, UNHCR Resettlement Statistical Database Portal

Origin of largest resettled groups in past ten years
Afghanistan, Chechnya, Cuba, Iran, Myanmar, Syrian, Uzbekistan

Status after resettlement

Residency status	Permanent residency.
Status of legal rights	Czech authorities cannot grant asylum to persons outside of Czech territory, so resettled refugees must formally apply for international protection upon arrival.

Regulatory basis

Domestic basis	Act No. 325/1999 Collection of Laws on Asylum (latest amendment entered into force 3 December 2015). Resolution No. 745 of 27 June 2008 adopted the National Resettlement Program Concept, the framework for implementation of resettlement programs.

International basis	Bilateral international agreement with UNHCR, which entered into force 10 April 2010.

Main selection criteria

Selection procedure	UNHCR referral via selection missions and dossier selection.
Eligibility criteria	Criteria corresponds with the criteria upon which refugee status is granted in the Czech Republic: Asylum Act of the Czech Republic, the 1951 Convention, and 1967 Protocol and includes priorities of humanitarian aid policy, migration policy priorities, foreign policy priorities, and integration aspects.
Admissibility criteria	No additional criteria.

Main national actors for resettlement

Sets resettlement quota	Minister of the Interior, based on input from the intra-agency working group for resettlement, UNHCR, IOM, and other civil society actors.
Implements resettlement	Department for Asylum and Migration Policy within the Ministry of Interior.

The role of UNHCR

Referrals	Refers cases to Department for Asylum and Migration Policy.
Selection missions	Assists in the facilitation of selection missions.
Implementation	Participates in the implementation of the resettlement program.

Denmark

Date of resettlement program
Ad hoc since 1950s; annual quota 1979–2005; three-year flexible quota program 2005–2016 [suspension of program in 2016]

Number of refugees resettled since 2003

2017	5	2009	488
2016	317	2008	403
2015	486	2007	480
2014	332	2006	750
2013	471	2005	454
2012	324	2004	379
2011	606	2003	520
2010	386		

Source: Departures, UNHCR Resettlement Statistical Database Portal

Origin of largest resettled groups in past ten years
Afghanistan, Bhutan, Colombia, Democratic Republic of Congo, Myanmar, Somalia

Status after resettlement

Residency status	Temporary residence permit valid for five years.

Regulatory basis

Domestic basis	Section 7 of the Danish Aliens Act provides the legal basis for refugee status eligibility in Denmark; section 8 provides the legal basis for the Danish resettlement program.

Main selection criteria

Selection procedure	UNHCR referral via selection missions and dossier selection.
Eligibility criteria	The resettlement quota is divided into four categories:

A geographical category (primarily refugees offered resettlement following in-country selection missions);

An emergency and urgent category (refugees who are in an immediate risk of *refoulement* to their country of origin and/or who risk assaults in their country of stay);

A medical category under the Twenty-or-More program (refugees with special medical needs); and

	Families who are accepted on a dossier basis together with a person accepted as a medical case under the Twenty-or-More program.
	Criteria include sexual minorities, families with children, adults with educational needs, women at risk with children, and human rights defenders.
Admissibility criteria	Section 8(5) of the Danish Aliens Act requires a health examination and consent for health information to be transmitted to the Danish Immigration Service and the local council of the municipality to which the individual will be resettled and the requirement of signing a declaration concerning the conditions for resettlement.

Main national actors for resettlement

| Sets resettlement quota | The quota is established through the Danish annual budget; the Minister of Justice decides the allocation of the quota and location of in-country selection missions following recommendations of the Danish Immigration Service. |
| Implements resettlement | The Ministry of Children, Gender Equality, Integration and Social Affairs have the principal responsibility for the reception and integration of foreign citizens. Municipalities offer a three-year mandatory integration program on behalf of the government. The Danish Refugee Council, Danish Red Cross, United Churches Integration Service, and various other NGOs participate. |

The role of UNHCR

| Referrals | Refers cases to Danish Immigration Service. |
| Selection missions | Assists in the facilitation of selection missions. |

Finland

Date of resettlement program
Ad hoc since 1950s; annual program since 1985

Number of refugees resettled since 2003

2017	1033	2009	710
2016	928	2008	675
2015	964	2007	714
2014	1,011	2006	548
2013	665	2005	584
2012	763	2004	727
2011	574	2003	443
2010	543		

Source: Departures, UNHCR Resettlement Statistical Database Portal

Origin of largest resettled groups in past ten years
Afghanistan, Democratic Republic of Congo, Iraq, Iran, Myanmar, Syria

Status after resettlement

Residency status	Temporary residency permit for four years.
Status of legal rights	Refugee status is granted and individuals are eligible for the integration measures outlined in the Act on the Advancement of Integration 1999 (2011). Unlike others who receive international protection, those resettled are specifically granted a municipality of residence directly upon arrival.

Regulatory basis

Domestic basis	The Finnish Aliens Act (2004), sections 90–92 and the Act on the Promotion of Immigrant Integration (2011). Under section 106 of the Aliens Act, refugee status is granted to an alien who has been admitted to Finland for resettlement under the refugee quota based on refugee status.

Main selection criteria

Selection procedure	UNHCR referral via selection missions and dossier selection.
Eligibility criteria	Criteria include need of international protection regarding the home country, need of resettlement from the first country of asylum, and assessment of admitting and integrating the person into Finland.

Admissibility criteria	Inadmissibility criteria include an obstacle in terms of public order, security, health, or Finland's international relations.

Main national actors for resettlement

Sets resettlement quota	The Minister of the Interior decides on the allocation of the refugee quota after consultation with the Ministry of Foreign Affairs and the Ministry of Employment and the Economy. Parliament makes the final decision on the annual quota and the resources for admitting resettled refugees to Finland when the state budget is approved.
Implements resettlement	The Finnish Immigration Service is the operational authority implementing the decision on the annual resettlement program quota. The Ministry of Employment and the Economy settles refugees in the municipalities that have made a reception decision, and various government branches and voluntary organizations collaborate at the municipal level in organizing reception.

The role of UNHCR

Referrals	Refers cases to the Finnish Immigration Service.
Selection missions	Assists in the facilitation of selection missions.

France

Date of resettlement program
Ad hoc since 1950s; annual case quota since 2008

Number of refugees resettled since 2000

2017	1,763	2012	84
2016	1,328	2011	42
2015	700	2010	217
2014	378	2009	179
2013	100	2008	276

Source: Departures, UNHCR Resettlement Statistical Database Portal

Origin of largest resettled groups in past ten years
Afghanistan, Ethiopia, Iraq, Iran, Palestine, Russia, Syria

Status after resettlement

Residency status	A ten-year residency permit is awarded after refugee status is recognized in France.
Status of legal rights	Legal residents with authorization to work and access social benefits.

Regulatory basis

Domestic basis	Code on the Entry and Stay of Foreigners and Asylum Law (CESEDA), 2004 (last modified 2011).
International basis	Framework Agreement between Government of the French Republic and UNHCR, 4 February 2008.

Main selection criteria

Selection procedure	UNHCR referral via dossier selection and, as of 2014, in-country selection missions.
Eligibility criteria	Meeting the refugee definition of Article 1 of the 1951 Geneva Convention. Forecasts are established each year for specific categories, including vulnerable women, unaccompanied children, medical cases, victims of violence, and urgent need for legal or physical protection.
Admissibility criteria	The absence of threats to security and public order is carefully reviewed by authorities; specialized security services are systematically consulted during the review of a case.

Private sponsorship

Background	Since 2017, NGOs, churches, communities, and individuals are authorized to sponsor persons who have fled Syria or Iraq and who currently reside in Lebanon for resettlement in France, in agreement with the Ministry of the Interior and the Ministry of Foreign Affairs and International Development. The sponsor shall take up the responsibility of travel arrangements, installation, and integration of resettled refugees and of the dependents.

Main national actors for resettlement

Sets resettlement quota	The Director-General for Foreign Nationals (Directorate of Asylum) oversees the resettlement program, both at the policy and operational levels, and is accountable to the Ministry of the Interior.
Implements resettlement	The Office for the Protection of Refugees and Stateless Persons (OFPRA) is the only authority authorized to grant international protection, offered only on French territory. The French Office for Immigration and Integration (OFII) assists with coordinating integration.

The role of UNHCR

Referrals	Refers 100 dossier submissions a year.
Selection missions	Assists in the facilitation of selection missions.

Germany

Date of resettlement program
Ad hoc since 1950s; annual quota since 2012

Number of refugees resettled since 2003

2017	2,248	2009	2,064
2016	1,229	2008	0
2015	2,097	2007	3
2014	3,467	2006	10
2013	1,092	2005	14
2012	323	2004	29
2011	22	2003	82
2010	457		

Source: Departures, UNHCR Resettlement Statistical Database Portal

Origin of largest resettled groups in past ten years
Iraq, Iran, Syria, Somalia

Status after resettlement

Residency status	Three-year residence permit.
Status of legal rights	Refugee protection status is not offered. Entitled to gainful employment, participation in language and integration classes as well as social benefits like German nationals. As long as social welfare is used, residence is restricted to the district where those resettled were assigned to live.

Regulatory basis

Domestic basis	Section 23(4) of the Residence Act addresses resettlement.

Main selection criteria

Selection procedure	UNHCR referral via selection missions.
Eligibility criteria	Criteria for selecting persons to be resettled is based on the admission directive issued by the Federal Ministry of the Interior in consultation with the federal states. In 2016, this included the preservation of family unity, family, or other ties in Germany conductive to integration, ability to become integrated, and the need for protection.
Admissibility criteria	Criteria for inadmissibility include conviction of crimes regarded in Germany as intentional offenses and evidence indicating association with or support for criminal or terrorist organizations.

Private sponsorship

Background	Section 68 of the Residence Act established the Regional Admissions Program, run in fifteen of sixteen regions, in Germany. Established in 2013, the program allows the sponsorship of persons by German citizens or residents with family links for admission to Germany on humanitarian grounds with a two-year renewable residence permit. Sponsors are responsible for travel costs and have full financial liability for five years, except for healthcare.

Main national actors for resettlement

Sets resettlement quota	The Federal Ministry of the Interior, the Federal Office for Migration and Refugees (BAMF), and the Federal Foreign Office.
Implements resettlement	The Federal Ministry of the Interior, BAMF, and the Federal Foreign Office are responsible for implementing the resettlement program. The interior ministries of the federal states and the local authorities (foreigners' authorities and social welfare authorities) are allocated responsible for looking after the resettled persons once they arrive in Germany, depending on the states' population and budget situation (Königstein Key).

The role of UNHCR

Referrals	Refers cases to BAMF.
Selection missions	Assists in the facilitation of selection missions.
Implementation	Assists in the implementation of the resettlement program.

Hungary

Date of resettlement program
Pilot program established in late 2012

Number of refugees resettled since 2012

2017	0	2014	4
2016	4	2013	0
2015	2	2012	1

Source: Departures, UNHCR Resettlement Statistical Database Portal

Origin of largest resettled groups in past ten years
Egypt

Status after resettlement

Residency status	Identity papers are issued upon arrival and issuance can take up to a few months.

Status of legal rights	Refugee status is granted after arrival.

Regulatory basis

Domestic basis	The framework for resettlement is found in Act LXXX of 2007 on Asylum, section 7(5). Governmental Decree 1139/2011 is meant to guarantee the practical implementation of the resettlement program of 2012.
International basis	The Hungarian government announced its decision to become a resettlement country in October 2010 and confirmed its commitment through a pledge submitted to the Ministerial Conference organized by UNHCR in Geneva in December 2011.

Main selection criteria

Selection procedure	UNHCR referral via selection missions.
Eligibility criteria	Refugee groups meeting criteria for European Refugee Fund subsidies.
Admissibility criteria	No additional criteria.

Main national actors for resettlement

Sets resettlement quota	The Hungarian government.
Implements resettlement	The resettlement program is the responsibility of the Ministry of the Interior and the Office of Immigration and Nationality (OIN).

The role of UNHCR

Referrals	UNHCR refers cases to OIN.
Selection missions	Assists in the facilitation of selection missions.

Iceland

Date of resettlement program
Ad hoc since 1950s; annually since 1996; annual quota since 2007

Number of refugees resettled since 2003

2017	47	2009	0
2016	56	2008	29
2015	13	2007	30
2014	4	2006	0
2013	0	2005	31
2012	9	2004	0
2011	0	2003	24
2010	6		

Source: Departures, UNHCR Resettlement Statistical Database Portal

Origin of largest resettled groups in past ten years
Afghanistan, Cameroon, Colombia, Former Yugoslavia, Iraq (Palestinians), Syria, Uganda, Zimbabwe

Status after resettlement

Residency status	Temporary residence permit valid for four years.
Status of legal rights	Refugee status.

Regulatory basis

Domestic basis	Article 44 of the Icelandic Act on Foreigners.

Main selection criteria

Selection procedure	UNHCR referral via selection missions and dossier selection.
Eligibility criteria	Criteria: recognized under UNHCR mandate and are described by the Act on Foreigners in Iceland as a refugee. Focus has been on protection cases, including women at risk and medical needs; focus from 2016 will be on refugees from Syria. Dossier selection has occurred since 2010.
Admissibility criteria	No additional criteria.

Main national actors for resettlement

Sets resettlement quota	The government of Iceland decides the quota in close consultation with the Ministry of Welfare.
Implements resettlement	The Icelandic Refugee Committee is the consultative body on quota refugees. The Ministry of Welfare (former Ministry of Social Affairs), through the Icelandic Refugee Committee, is responsible for the selection, admission, and integration of refugees in Iceland, while working in close cooperation with other relevant ministries. The Icelandic Refugee Committee is composed of members from the Ministry of the Interior, the Ministry of Welfare, the Ministry of Foreign Affairs, and the Red Cross of Iceland. Municipalities and support families play a large role in integration.

The role of UNHCR

Referrals	Refers cases to Iceland Refugee Committee and Directorate of Immigration.
Selection missions	Assists in the facilitation of selection missions.

Ireland

Date of resettlement program
Ad hoc since 1950s; program based since 1998; annual quota since 2005

Number of refugees resettled since 2003

2017	266	2009	194
2016	359	2008	89
2015	178	2007	107
2014	98	2006	119
2013	62	2005	116
2012	40	2004	64
2011	36	2003	43
2010	20		

Source: Departures, UNHCR Resettlement Statistical Database Portal

Origin of largest resettled groups in past ten years
Democratic Republic of Congo, Myanmar (Rohingya), Somalia, Sudan, Syria

Status after resettlement

Status of legal rights	Persons admitted to Ireland under the resettlement program are not granted refugee status within the meaning of the 1951 Convention; they are granted "programme refugee" status under section 24 of the 1996 Refugee Act, as amended. While a "programme refugee" does not get Geneva Convention Status, they get the same rights and entitlements that are attributable to a convention refugee under section 3 of the Refugee Act 1996, as amended.

Regulatory basis

Domestic basis	Provision for participation in UNHCR led resettlement programs was made in section 24 of the 1996 Refugee Act, as amended. The Government Decision of November 1998 marked the beginning of Ireland's resettlement program. The Government Decision of June 2005 expanded the resettlement program to an annual quota.

Main selection criteria

Selection procedure	UNHCR referral via selection missions and dossier selection.
Eligibility criteria	Group resettlement is preferred (individual cases are rare), unaccompanied child cases are not accepted, mix of women at risk, persons with disabilities, and other special needs cases, and community leaders and spiritual leaders are favored.
Admissibility criteria	Must possess a valid travel document; if not a holder of an Irish Travel Document, must apply for a valid entry visa.

Private sponsorship

Background	Based on a decision of the Ministry of Justice, a program for the private sponsorship of refugees for resettlement to Ireland ran from March to December 2014. Irish citizens of Syrian origin or Syrian residents in Ireland were eligible to sponsor relatives

with specific vulnerabilities under the Syrian Humanitarian Admission Program (SHAP). Refugee status determination was not required. Persons were admitted on humanitarian grounds and were offered two-year renewable residence permits. Sponsors were responsible for travel and the full financial liability for the duration of stay.

Main national actors for resettlement

Sets resettlement quota	The annual quota is determined by the government. Decisions regarding the country of origin/country of first asylum are made by the Minister for Justice and Equality in consultation with the Department of Foreign Affairs and Trade and UNHCR.
Implements resettlement	The Department of Justice and Equality has responsibility for the resettlement policy.

The role of UNHCR

Referrals	Refers cases to the Resettlement Unit, Office for the Promotion of Migrant Integration, and Department of Justice and Equality.
Selection missions	Assists in the facilitation of selection missions.

Japan

Date of resettlement program
Pilot program, 2010–2014; formal resettlement program announced from 2015

Number of refugees resettled since 2010

2017	29	2013	18
2016	18	2012	0
2015	19	2011	18
2014	23	2010	27

Source: Departures, UNHCR Resettlement Statistical Database Portal

Origin of largest resettled groups in past ten years
Myanmar

Status after resettlement

Residency status	Residence permit valid for four years.
Status of legal rights	The status of a long-term settler (*teijusha*) is given upon arrival in Japan.

Regulatory basis

Domestic basis	1981 Immigration Control and Refugee Recognition Act.
	The government of Japan's Cabinet Agreement of 16 December 2008 forms the basis for the admission of the resettled refugees and the structure of the pilot project. The 19 December 2008 Detailed Implementation Arrangements for the Admission of Refugees through a Pilot Resettlement Project, revised in both 2012 and 2013, outlined the specific details on the admission and the settlement support to be provided under the pilot. Japan grants humanitarian residence status based on a political decision through a cabinet agreement. Acceptance of refugees based on a cabinet agreement can, in principle, be terminated by a government decision, as admission is not based on an obligation under an international convention or entrenched in Japanese law. Resettled refugees under the Pilot Resettlement Project were admitted to Japan under conditions like a cabinet agreement.

Main selection criteria

Selection procedure	UNHCR referral via selection missions and dossier selection.
Eligibility criteria	The 2008 Cabinet Agreement stated that the pilot project beginning in 2010 was to offer resettlement to Myanmarese refugees who are granted temporary asylum in Thailand, fulfilling the following criteria: Individuals recognized by UNHCR to need international protection and recommended to Japan to provide protection;
	Individuals with the ability to adjust to Japanese society and with likelihood to obtain a job to maintain his/her livelihood and his/her spouse and children;
	The government of Japan also outlined additional preferred characteristics of the candidates: to be relatively young, to be Karen speakers, and ideally

only have a few children. This was expanded in 2013 to include Burmese speakers, and the definition of family was broadened; in 2014, Myanmarese refugees from Malaysia were included.

Admissibility criteria	At the discretion of the government.

Main national actors for resettlement

Sets resettlement quota	In 2012, the government of Japan established the Resettlement Expert Council to assess the pilot project and make recommendations for the future.
Implements resettlement	The Implementation Decision does not specify which ministry or agency is specifically responsible; in practical application, the Ministry of Foreign Affairs, the Agency for Cultural Affairs, and the Ministry of Health, Labor, and Welfare have taken on the responsibility for the implementation of resettlement.

The role of UNHCR

Referrals	Refers cases.
Selection missions	Assists in the facilitation of selection missions.
Implementation	Assists in the implementation of the resettlement program.

The Netherlands

Date of resettlement program
Ad hoc since 1950s; annual quota since 1983

Number of refugees resettled since 2003

2017	1948	2009	347
2016	689	2008	580
2015	428	2007	425
2014	743	2006	327
2013	362	2005	479
2012	262	2004	252
2011	479	2003	129
2010	430		

Source: Departures, UNHCR Resettlement Statistical Database Portal

Origin of largest resettled groups in past ten years
Bhutan, Burundi, Democratic Republic of Congo, Eritrea, Ethiopia, Iraq, Myanmar

Status after resettlement

Residency status	Five-year temporary residence permit.
Status of legal rights	Holders of a temporary residence permit for asylum have the same access to healthcare, social security, and the labor market as citizens.

Regulatory basis

Domestic basis	There are no specific arrangements in law for people who are resettled in the Netherlands. Asylum in the Netherlands is granted on the basis of the 2000 Aliens Act; Article 29 identifies grounds for admittance.
	The Decree of the Minister of Justice of 24 June 2010 sets out Dutch resettlement policy, including quota, selection procedure, arrival, and status given to resettled refugees. Decree of 19 May 2000 transfers responsibility for resettled refugees to the Minister of Justice. Decision 7 February 2012, Policy Framework of Resettlement 2012–2015, established the resettlement quota.

Main selection criteria

Selection procedure	UNHCR referral via selection missions and dossier selection.
Eligibility criteria	Criteria include the willingness and ability to integrate into Dutch society.
Admissibility criteria	Inadmissibility criteria include the individual constitutes a threat to public policy or national security.

Private sponsorship

Background	A working group of NGOs has proposed space for 100 private resettlement spaces to be sponsored by civil society during 2018–2019 in addition to the Dutch annual resettlement quota. The organizations would offer settlement and integration support in collaboration with local municipalities.

Main national actors for resettlement

Sets resettlement quota	The government established a quota to be administered over a four-year basis.
Implements resettlement	The Ministry of Security and Justice is responsible for resettlement policy and coordinates the contact between the government of the Netherlands and UNHCR. Operational issues are handled by the Dutch Immigration and Nationalization Service, which operates under the authority of the Ministry of Security and Justice. The Netherlands Agency for the Reception of Asylum Seekers is responsible for the orientation and reception of resettled persons.

The role of UNHCR

Referrals	Refers cases to Immigration and Naturalization Service (IND).
Selection missions	Assists in the facilitation of selection missions.
Implementation	Assists in the implementation of the resettlement program.

New Zealand

Date of resettlement program
Ad hoc since 1940s; annual quota since 1987

Number of refugees resettled since 2003

2017	801	2009	675
2016	895	2008	894
2015	756	2007	629
2014	639	2006	622
2013	682	2005	307
2012	719	2004	107
2011	477	2003	351
2010	535		

Source: Departures, UNHCR Resettlement Statistical Database Portal

Origin of largest resettled groups in past ten years
Afghanistan, Bhutan, Colombia, Myanmar, Palestine, Sri Lanka, Syria

Status after resettlement

Residency status	Permanent residence.
Status of legal rights	Afforded same rights as other permanent residents and citizens.

Regulatory basis

Domestic basis	The Immigration Act 2009 provides the statutory basis by which New Zealand determines who it has obligations to under the 1951 Convention and 67 Protocol, the 1984 Convention against Torture, and the 1966 Covenant on Civil and Political Rights. The New Zealand Refugee Resettlement Strategy was approved by the New Zealand government in 2012.

Main selection criteria

Selection procedure	UNHCR referral via selection missions and dossier selection.
Eligibility criteria	Refugees considered for resettlement must be recognized as mandated refugees and referred by UNHCR. Criteria include women at risk, medical/disabled (including a specific number of spaces for those with HIV/AIDS), and UNHCR priority protection.
Admissibility criteria	Factors considered include immigration policy, credibility, settlement, risk, and medical assessments.

Private sponsorship

Background	The government has agreed to a pilot Community Organization Refugee Sponsorship Category for twenty-five refugees in 2017–2018, in addition to the annual quota. As of this writing, potential sponsoring community organizations were requested to register with the government.

Main national actors for resettlement

Sets resettlement quota	The composition of the refugee quota is agreed to annually by the Minister of Immigration and the Minister of Foreign Affairs, following submissions by UNHCR.

Implements resettlement	The Refugee Quota Branch is the branch of Immigration New Zealand (INZ) that is tasked with operating the Refugee Quota Programme. INZ, in turn, sits within the Ministry of Business, Innovation and Employment.

The role of UNHCR

Referrals	Refers cases to INZ.
Selection missions	Assists in the facilitation of selection missions.

Norway

Date of resettlement program
Ad hoc since 1945; annual quota since 1980s

Number of refugees resettled since 2003

2017	1,698	2009	1,367
2016	3,149	2008	22
2015	2,220	2007	978
2014	1,188	2006	871
2013	938	2005	636
2012	1,137	2004	859
2011	1,258	2003	1,856
2010	1,088		

Source: Departures, UNHCR Resettlement Statistical Database Portal

Origin of largest resettled groups in past ten years
Bhutan, Eritrean, Iraq, Myanmar, Syria

Status after resettlement

Residency status	Temporary residence permit valid for three years.
Status of legal rights	Legal resident with refugee status.

Regulatory basis

Domestic basis	Immigration Act of 2008, nr. 35, paragraph 28.

Main selection criteria

Selection procedure	UNHCR referral via selection missions and dossier selection takes priority.
Eligibility criteria	Cases submitted by the Norwegian Ministry of Foreign Affairs, international criminal courts with which Norway has witness resettlement agreements, Norwegian PEN, or Norwegian NGOs with a presence in areas where UNHCR is not represented may also be considered. Criteria include need for resettlement, women at risk, vulnerability due to gender identity or sexual orientation, families with children under the age of eighteen, and the ability to integrate.
Admissibility criteria	Inadmissibility criteria include falling within the scope of Article 1D or E of the Refugee Convention, having committed a crime against peace, a war crime, or a crime against humanity, having committed a serious nonpolitical crime outside of Norway's borders prior to admission, having been guilty of acts contrary to the purposes and principles of the UN, issues of fundamental national interests, or posing a danger to Norwegian society.

Main national actors for resettlement

Sets resettlement quota	After consultation with other ministries and NGOs, the Norwegian Directorate of Immigration (UDI) proposes a quota. By 15 December the Parliament decides the state budget, including the total size of the next year's quota and the Ministry of Justice and Public Security decides the allocation of the quota.
Implements resettlement	Settlement of refugees in municipalities is managed by the Directorate of Integration and Diversity. The municipalities facilitate the two-year introduction program.

The role of UNHCR

Referrals	Refers cases to UDI.
Selection missions	Helps facilitate selection missions.

Paraguay

Date of resettlement program
Solidarity resettlement program, 2010–current

Number of refugees resettled since 2010

2017	0	2013	0
2016	0	2012	0
2015	0	2011	13
2014	0	2010	13

Source: Departures, UNHCR Resettlement Statistical Database Portal

Origin of largest resettled groups in past ten years
Colombia

Status after resettlement

Residency status	Temporary residence permits valid for three years.

Regulatory basis

Domestic basis	General Law 1938 on Refugees of 2 July 2002 defines and regulates refugee status in accordance with the 1951 Convention, its 1967 Protocol, and the 1984 Cartagena Declaration on Refugees.
International basis	In 2007, Paraguay signed a Memorandum of Understanding on Resettlement of Refugees with UNHCR, which established the criteria under which refugees may qualify for resettlement to Paraguay.

Main selection criteria

Selection procedure	UNHCR referral via selection missions
Eligibility criteria	Criteria include refugees under the terms of the 1951 Convention, 1967 Protocol, and other regional instruments, in particular the Cartagena Declaration of 1984. Special consideration will be given to the resettlement needs of refugees from Latin America.
Admissibility criteria	No additional criteria.

Main national actors for resettlement

Sets resettlement quota	The National Commission for Refugees (CONARE), in consultation with the UNHCR Regional Office for Southern Latin America, sets the annual quota.
Implements resettlement	The resettlement program is coordinated by CONARE. The various public actors involved in CONARE include the Ministry of Foreign Affairs, the Interior Ministry via the Department of Immigration and Department of Informatics of the National Police, the National Secretariat for Housing and Habitat, the Ministry of Public Health and Social Welfare, the Ministry of Education and Culture, and the Ministry of Justice and Labor via the National Professional Career Development Service and the National Employment Education and Training Service.

The role of UNHCR

Referrals	Refers cases to CONARE.
Selection missions	Funds cost of selection mission and transport.
Implementation	Sets up partner agency to implement refugee resettlement program and provides necessary funding.

Portugal

Date of resettlement program
Ad hoc since 1950s; annual quota since 2007

Number of refugees resettled since 2007

2017	70	2011	28
2016	12	2010	24
2015	39	2009	26
2014	14	2008	5
2013	6	2007	12
2012	21		

Source: Departures, UNHCR Resettlement Statistical Database Portal

Origin of largest resettled groups in past ten years
Afghanistan, Democratic Republic of Congo, Eritrea, Iraq, Ivory Coast

Status after resettlement

Residency status	Residence permit valid for five years.
Status of legal rights	Refugee status is granted.

Regulatory basis

Domestic basis	Asylum Law No. 27/2008 of 30 June 2008 is the most relevant legal instrument in terms of national legislation defining refugee status eligibility and includes a specific provision on resettlement in chapter III, section V. Resolution of the Council of Ministers No. 110/2007 of 12 July 2007 established a resettlement quota of a minimum of thirty persons per year in Portugal.

Main selection criteria

Selection procedure	UNHCR referral via dossier selection.
Eligibility criteria	Criteria include women at risk, unaccompanied minors, survivors of violence or torture, and those experiencing legal and physical protection needs.
Admissibility criteria	Those with a criminal background and those found to pose a threat to Portugal's public order or international relations will not be accepted.

Main national actors for resettlement

Sets resettlement quota	Government of Portugal.
Implements resettlement	The Immigration and Border Service within the Ministry of the Interior is responsible for the provision and implementation of the Portuguese resettlement program.

The role of UNHCR

Referrals	Refers cases to the Immigration and Border Service.
Selection missions	Helps facilitate selection missions.
Implementation	Assists in the implementation of the resettlement program.

Romania

Date of resettlement program
Annual quota since 2008

Number of refugees resettled since 2008

2017	11	2012	0
2016	0	2011	0
2015	2	2010	38
2014	44	2009	0
2013	0	2008	0

Source: Departures, UNHCR Resettlement Statistical Database Portal

Origin of largest resettled groups in past ten years
Iraq, Myanmar (Kachin)

Status after resettlement

Residency status	Temporary residency permit valid for four years.
Status of legal rights	Refugee status.

Regulatory basis

Domestic basis	Law no. 122/2006 on Asylum in Romania defines who is eligible for refugee status and provides the general framework on resettlement.
	Government Decision no. 1596/2008 regulated the relevant administrative procedure for resettlement and the initial resettlement quotas. The quotas are modified through new articles introduced by subsequent government decisions (e.g., G.D. no. 239/2016 for 2016–2017).

Main selection criteria

Selection procedure	UNHCR referral via selection missions and dossier selection.
Eligibility criteria	Criteria include recognition as refugee in accordance with Article 1A of 1951 Convention and 1967 Protocol, does not benefit from effective protection or integration perspectives on the territory of the country of asylum, does not have prospects for voluntary

repatriation, and has expressly accepted to be resettled to Romania.

| Admissibility criteria | Inadmissibility criteria: presenting a threat to public order, national security, health, or public morals. |

Main national actors for resettlement

| Sets resettlement quota | A consultative body of a nonlegal nature, the "Resettlement Committee," was established in 2008 to determine the number of refugees in need of resettlement by Romania and the state where the refugees should originate from. The committee includes representatives from the Ministry of Internal Affairs and the Ministry of Foreign Affairs. The president of the committee is the general inspector of the General Inspectorate for Immigration (GII). |
| Implements resettlement | The GII is the main institution with responsibilities in the field of refugee resettlement. |

The role of UNHCR

Referrals	Refers cases.
Selection missions	Assists in the facilitation of selection missions.
Implementation	Assists in the implementation of the resettlement program.

Spain

Date of resettlement program
Ad hoc since 1978; program basis in 2012; pilot quota program 2013–2014

Number of refugees resettled since 2012

2017	422	2014	30
2016	288	2013	0
2015	92	2012	80

Source: Departures, UNHCR Resettlement Statistical Database Portal

Origin of largest resettled groups in past ten years
Colombia, Eritrea, Palestine, Sudan, Somalia

Status after resettlement

Status of legal rights	Refugee status.

Regulatory basis

Domestic basis	Law 12/2009 of 30 October 2009 regulates the right to asylum and subsidiary protection as well as making a specific reference to the possibly of establishing a resettlement program. Law 4/2000 of 11 January 2000 regulates the rights of foreign nationals in Spain. Communication of the Council of Ministers 28 July 2012 approves a resettlement program to resettle up to thirty refugees during 2013 and 2014.
International basis	There is an agreement between the Kingdom of Spain and UNHCR from 9 December 2002 by which the Spanish government shows its support for UNHCR programs and activities; no specific reference was made to UNHCR's resettlement programs.

Main selection criteria

Selection procedure	UNHCR referral via selection missions and dossier selection.
Eligibility criteria	Priorities match UNHCR Global Resettlement Solidarity Initiative.
Admissibility criteria	In-country medical screening.

Main national actors for resettlement

Sets resettlement quota	Council of Ministers
Implements resettlement	Ministry of Interior, Ministry of Employment and Social Security, Spanish Red Cross, other NGOs.

The role of UNHCR

Referrals	Refers cases.
Selection missions	Assists in the facilitation of selection missions.

Sweden

Date of resettlement program
Annual quota 1950–present

Number of refugees resettled since 2003

2017	2,678	2009	1,880
2016	1,868	2008	1,558
2015	1,808	2007	1,772
2014	1,812	2006	1,571
2013	1,832	2005	1,190
2012	1,483	2004	1,645
2011	1,896	2003	873
2010	1,789		

Source: Departures, UNHCR Resettlement Statistical Database Portal

Origin of largest resettled groups in past ten years
Afghanistan, Colombia, Democratic Republic of Congo, Ethiopia, Iraq, Palestine, Somalia, Sudan, Syria

Status after resettlement

Residency status	Permanent residency.
Status of legal rights	Refugee status.

Regulatory basis

Domestic basis	The Aliens Act of 2005 sets out the criteria for the recognition of refugee status eligibility and asylum in Sweden.

Main selection criteria

Selection procedure	UNHCR referral via selection missions and dossier selection takes priority.
Eligibility criteria	Exceptional cases can be submitted by Swedish diplomatic missions and witness agreements with international tribunals. Weight is given to strategic resettlement and efforts to resolve protracted refugee situations. Medical or special needs does not disqualify a case.

Admissibility criteria	Inadmissibility criteria: if the individual constitutes a threat to public order and security.

Main national actors for resettlement

Sets resettlement quota	Annually, the Swedish parliament allocates funds for the resettlement of refugees to Sweden. Thereafter, the Ministry of Justice issues the general guidelines for the Swedish resettlement program, which must be approved by the parliament.
Implements resettlement	The Swedish Migration Agency, acting on behalf of the Swedish government, is the main actor responsible for the coordination of resettlement to Sweden. Resettled individuals will be provided support from the municipality in which they are resettled.

The role of UNHCR

Referrals	Refers cases to the Swedish Migration Agency.
Selection missions	Helps facilitate selection missions.

Switzerland

Date of resettlement program
Ad hoc since 1950s; pilot project from 2013

Number of refugees resettled since 2003

Year	Number	Year	Number
2017	409	2009	0
2016	667	2008	8
2015	92	2007	3
2014	30	2006	0
2013	0	2005	8
2012	80	2004	1
2011	0	2003	3
2010	0		

Source: Departures, UNHCR Resettlement Statistical Database Portal

Origin of largest resettled groups in past ten years
Iraq, Palestine, Syria

Status after resettlement

Legal rights	Refugee status.

Regulatory basis

Domestic basis	Asylum Act of 26 June 1998.
International basis	Agreement with UNHCR (2013).

Main selection criteria

Selection procedure	UNHCR referral.
Eligibility criteria	High protection need, Integration motivation and potential, and 40–60 percent should be women and 7 percent should be persons with physical and mental frailties.
Admissibility criteria	Security grounds and whether threat to national interest.

Main national actors for resettlement

Sets resettlement quota	The Federal Council
Implements resettlement	Federal Office for Migration, State Secretariat for Migration, cantons, NGOs.

The role of UNHCR

Referrals	Refers cases.
Selection missions	Helps facilitate selection missions.

United Kingdom

Date of resettlement program
Ad hoc basis since 1940s; program basis 2004–2007; annual quota since 2007

Number of refugees resettled since 2003

2017	4,679	2009	969
2016	5,074	2008	697
2015	1,768	2007	348
2014	628	2006	349
2013	750	2005	242
2012	989	2004	272
2011	424	2003	118
2010	695		

Source: Departures, UNHCR Resettlement Statistical Database Portal

Origin of largest resettled groups in past ten years
Bhutan, Democratic Republic of Congo, Ethiopia, Iraq, Myanmar (Karen, Rohingya), Palestine, Somalia, Syria

Status after resettlement

Residency status	Indefinite leave to remain.
Status of legal rights	Refugee status.

Regulatory basis

Domestic basis	The Nationality, Immigration and Asylum Act (2002) provides the general framework for asylum and refugee status eligibility. The Gateway Protection Program's (GPP's) legal framework for international collaboration and funding for resettlement are discussed in section 59 of this Act.

Main selection criteria

Selection procedure	UNHCR referral via selection missions and dossier selection (rarely used).
Eligibility criteria	The GPP offers a legal route for a specific number of particularly vulnerable refugees to settle in the United Kingdom each year, with a specific quota.
	The Mandate Refugee Scheme (MRS) allows refugees from around the world with close family ties with the United Kingdom to be resettled.

Admissibility criteria	Grounds for inadmissibility: committing a serious crime or being a threat to security.

Private sponsorship

Background	The basis for a sponsorship scheme was established through a ministerial arrangement under the 2010 Equality Act. In late 2016, the U.K. Fully Community Sponsorship Scheme was established under the government's resettlement pledges related to the Syrian conflict. Up to 20,000 persons fleeing Syria could be admitted under the Vulnerable Person Resettlement Scheme (VPRS) and 3,000 children and families from the Middle East and North Africa could be admitted through the Vulnerable Children's Resettlement Scheme (VCRS). Registered charities, community interest companies, and religious organizations accredited by the Home Office are authorized to sponsor persons and are responsible for financial and settlement support for the individual's first year and accommodation for the first two years.

Main national actors for resettlement

Sets resettlement quota	Quota set annually by government ministers who take into consideration available resources, the need for resettlement globally, and the impact on services at a local level in the United Kingdom.
Implements resettlement	GPP and MRS are operated by the U.K. Home Office in partnership with UNHCR. The Refugee Team is the part of the Home Office responsible for considering applications for refugee resettlement and identifying caseloads in close cooperation with UNHCR.

The role of UNHCR

Referrals	Refers all cases.
Selection missions	Assists in the facilitation of selection missions.

United States

Date of resettlement program
Ad hoc since 1940s; annual quotas since 1975; efforts made to pause and review program in 2017

Number of refugees resettled since 2003

2017	20,428	2009	62,011
2016	78,761	2008	48,828
2015	52,583	2007	32,007
2014	48,911	2006	14,382
2013	47,750	2005	23,289
2012	53,053	2004	28,253
2011	43,215	2003	13,987
2010	54,077		

Source: Departures, UNHCR Resettlement Statistical Database Portal

Origin of largest resettled groups in 2016
Bhutan, Democratic Republic of Congo, Iraq, Myanmar, Somalia, Syria

Status after resettlement

Residency status	Temporary residency for one year.
Status of legal rights	Authorized employment upon arrival; after one year, a refugee must file for adjustment of status to lawful permanent resident. Five years after admission, a refugee is eligible to apply for U.S. citizenship.

Regulatory basis

Domestic basis	A person must meet the U.S. definition of a refugee found in section 101(a)(42) of the Immigration and Nationality Act (INA), which closely follows the definition in the 1951 Convention. The INA also defines as refugees, under certain circumstances specified by the president, certain persons who are within their country of nationality, or if they do not have a nationality, the country in which they were habitually residing.

Main selection criteria

Selection procedure	Selection missions.

Eligibility criteria	The administration annually consults with the Congress on the U.S. Refugee Admissions Program providing the main national actors for resettlement to discuss the international and domestic implications of U.S. refugee policy. Nationality and regional priorities are set for each quota in tiers based on the fiscal year.
	Criteria: To qualify for resettlement in the United States, refugees must:
	Be among those refugees determined by the president to be of special humanitarian concern to the United States;
	Meet the definition of a refugee pursuant to section 101(a)(42) of the INA;
	Not be firmly resettled in any third country;
	Be otherwise admissible under U.S. law.
Admissibility criteria	Criteria for inadmissibility: health (including some communicable diseases, physical or mental disorders, and current drug abuse or addiction), criminal activity, and security grounds can prevent individuals from being resettled.

Main national actors for resettlement

Sets resettlement quota	The annual quota runs the length of the fiscal year. It is established in consultation with the president, Congress, other federal departments, and NGOs.
Implements resettlement	At the federal level, the Bureau of Population, Refugees and Migration (PRM) of the Department of State administers the U.S. Refugee Admissions Program in conjunction with U.S. Citizenship and Immigration Services (USCIS) of the Department of Homeland Security and the Office of Refugee Resettlement (ORR) of the Department of Health and Human Services (HSS). Multiple designated sponsorship agencies facilitate integration with the assistance of NGOs.

The role of UNHCR

Referrals	Refers cases for consideration for resettlement.
Selection missions	Assists the facilitation of selection missions.

Uruguay

Date of resettlement program
Solidarity resettlement program, 2009–present

Number of refugees resettled since 2009

2017	0	2012	5
2016	0	2011	0
2015	0	2010	17
2014	52	2009	14
2013	14		

Source: Departures, UNHCR Resettlement Statistical Database Portal

Origin of largest resettled groups in past ten years
Colombia, Palestine, Syria

Status after resettlement

Status of legal rights	Refugee status.

Regulatory basis

Domestic basis	Law no. 18.076, adopted in 2006, establishes the principles and rights governing the status of refugees in Uruguay, created the Refugee Commission (CORE) and its permanent secretariat, the authority in charge of defining the profiles of people to be resettled, the selection of families, and the adjudication of the refugee status in the country.
	Law no. 18.382 covers the Framework Agreement for Refugee Resettlement.
International basis	Framework Agreement with UNHCR signed June 2007.

Main selection criteria

Selection procedure	UNHCR referral via selection missions.
Eligibility criteria	Criteria: must be refugees under the terms of the 1951 Convention, the 1967 Protocol, and the Cartagena Declaration of 1984, including those with a need of legal and physical protection and those without local integration prospects, including women

at risk and a special program for those willing to be resettled to rural areas. Priority is given to refugees from Latin America.

Admissibility criteria	No additional criteria.

Main national actors for resettlement

Sets resettlement quota	The Refugee Commission (CORE) consists of representatives from the Ministry of Foreign Affairs and the Interior (National Directorate of Immigration), the University of the Republic, the legislative branch, and one representative from an NGO appointed by the Regional Representative of UNHCR and another from an NGO whose aim and practice is focused on human rights. UNHCR or its representative will act as guests, with voice but no vote.
Implements resettlement	CORE and associated UNHCR-appointed organizations.

The role of UNHCR

Referrals	Refers cases to CORE.
Selection missions	Funds cost of selection mission and transport.
Implementation	Sets up partner agency to implement refugee resettlement program and provides necessary funding.

Amanda Cellini currently works at the Peace Research Institute Oslo (PRIO) and the Norwegian Centre on Humanitarian Studies (NCHS). Previously, she has worked at the Norwegian Institute of International Affairs (NUPI) and with local resettlement organizations in the United States. She holds an M.Sc. in human rights and multiculturalism from the University College of Southeast Norway and a B.A. in international relations from Rhodes College. In 2018, she became a doctoral research fellow at the Faculty of Law, University of Oslo, researching refugee resettlement.

Note

1. Australia's first formal refugee program was introduced in 1977; the Special Humanitarian Program was introduced in 1981; the Special Assistance Category was introduced in 1992; the Humanitarian Program formally separated from

the Migration Program in 1993; the offshore and onshore components of the Humanitarian Program began to be identified separately in 1996.

References

Department of Immigration and Border Protection (DIBP). 2017. *Annual Report 2016–2017.* Canberra: Commonwealth of Australia. Accessed 18 December 2017. https://www.border.gov.au/ReportsandPublications/Documents/annual-reports/annual-report-2016-17-performance-statements.pdf.

Fratzke, Susan. 2017. *Engaging Communities in Refugee Protection: The Potential of Private Sponsorship in Europe.* Brussels: Migration Policy Institute Europe.

Immigration, Refugees and Citizenship Canada (IRCC). 2017. *Resettled Refugees: The Number of Resettled Refugees Arriving in Canada as Part of the Government of Canada's Refugee Resettlement Program.* Accessed 18 December 2017. http://open.canada.ca/data/en/dataset/4a1b260a-7ac4-4985-80a0-603bfe4aec11?_ga=1.75575509.1191729561.1480792113.

International Catholic Migration Commission (ICMC) Europe. 2017. *Private Sponsorship in Europe. Expanding Complementary Pathways for Refugee Resettlement.* Scoping paper. Brussels: (ICMC) Europe.

Karlsen, Elibritt. 2016. *Refugee Resettlement to Australia: What Are the Facts?* Research Paper Series, 2016–17. Parliament of Australia. Updated 7 September. Accessed 18 December 2017. http://www.aph.gov.au/About_Parliament/Parliamentary_Departments/Parliamentary_Library/pubs/rp/rp1617/RefugeeResettlement.

Ruiz, H. 2015. *Evaluation of Resettlement Programmes in Argentina, Brazil, Chile, Paraguay, and Uruguay.* Accessed 18 December 2017. http://www.unhcr.org/57c983557.pdf.

Treviranus, Barbara and Sakaya Osanami Torngren. 2015. *A Socio-Economic Review of Japan's Pilot Resettlement Project.* New Issues in Refugee Research, Research Paper No. 276. Accessed 18 December 2017. http://www.refworld.org/docid/558ac8ea4.html.

UN Refugee Agency. UNHCR. *UNHCR Resettlement Handbook, 2011.* Accessed 18 December 2017. http://www.refworld.org/docid/4ecb973c2.html.

——. *UNHCR Resettlement Handbook, Country Chapter–Argentina,* June 2013. Accessed 18 December 2017. http://www.refworld.org/docid/52a0775e0.html.

——. *UNHCR Resettlement Handbook, Country Chapter–Australia,* April 2016. Accessed 18 December 2017. http://www.refworld.org/docid/57a192f64.html.

——. *UNHCR Resettlement Handbook, Country Chapter–Belgium,* June 2016. Accessed 18 December 2017. http://www.refworld.org/docid/57a195ef4.html.

——. *UNHCR Resettlement Handbook, Country Chapter–Brazil,* June 2013. Accessed 18 December 2017. http://www.refworld.org/docid/52a077620.html.

——. *UNHCR Resettlement Handbook, Country Chapter–Canada,* August 2014. Accessed 18 December 2017. http://www.refworld.org/docid/541190974.html.

——. *UNHCR Resettlement Handbook, Country Chapter–Chile,* January 2002. Accessed 18 December 2017. http://www.refworld.org/docid/4666bbd32.html.

——. *UNHCR Resettlement Handbook, Country Chapter–Czech Republic,* July 2016. Accessed 18 December 2017. http://www.refworld.org/docid/57a198134.html.

——. *UNHCR Resettlement Handbook, Country Chapter–Denmark,* March 2016. Accessed 18 December 2017. http://www.refworld.org/docid/57a19a1d4.html.

——. *UNHCR Resettlement Handbook, Country Chapter–Finland,* September 2014. Accessed 18 December 2017. http://www.refworld.org/docid/541941d94.html.

——. *UNHCR Resettlement Handbook, Country Chapter–France,* July 2016. Accessed 18 December 2017. http://www.refworld.org/docid/57a19be64.html.

——. *UNHCR Resettlement Handbook, Country Chapter–Germany,* June 2013. Accessed 18 December 2017. http://www.refworld.org/docid/52a0776815.html.

——. *UNHCR Resettlement Handbook, Country Chapter–Iceland,* April 2016. Accessed 18 December 2017. http://www.refworld.org/docid/577a55014.html.

——. *UNHCR Resettlement Handbook, Country Chapter–Ireland,* May 2016. Accessed 18 December 2017. http://www.refworld.org/docid/57a19d4f4.html.

——. *UNHCR Resettlement Handbook, Country Chapter–Netherlands,* July 2016. Accessed 18 December 2017. http://www.refworld.org/docid/577a54294.html.

——. *UNHCR Resettlement Handbook, Country Chapter–New Zealand,* October 2014. Accessed 18 December 2017. http://www.refworld.org/docid/5458b4794.html.

——. *UNHCR Resettlement Handbook, Country Chapter–Norway,* July 2016. Accessed 18 December 2017. http://www.refworld.org/docid/57a1a7e14.html.

——. *UNHCR Resettlement Handbook, Country Chapter–Portugal,* July 2013. Accessed 18 December 2017. http://www.refworld.org/docid/4ecb9c000.html.

——. *UNHCR Resettlement Handbook, Country Chapter–Romania,* July 2013. Accessed 18 December 2017. http://www.refworld.org/docid/4ecb9c00d.html.

——. *UNHCR Resettlement Handbook, Country Chapter–Sweden,* September 2014. Accessed 18 December 2017. http://www.refworld.org/docid/542125334.html.

——. *UNHCR Resettlement Handbook, Country Chapter–United Kingdom of Great Britain and Northern Ireland,* September 2014. Accessed 18 December 2017. http://www.refworld.org/docid/54339eb45.html.

——. *UNHCR Resettlement Handbook, Country Chapter–The United States of America,* October 2014. Accessed 18 December 2017. http://www.refworld.org/docid/546de8414.html

——. *UNHCR Resettlement Handbook, Country Chapter–Uruguay,* July 2016. Accessed 18 December 2017. http://www.refworld.org/docid/57a1a9e34.html.

UNHCR. 2017a. *Canada's 2016 Record High Level of Resettlement Praised by UNHCR.* Accessed 18 December 2017. https://www.unhcr.ca/news/canadas-2016-record-high-level-resettlement-praised-unhcr/.

——. UNHCR. 2017b. *Emerging Resettlement Countries Joint Support Mechanism* (ERCM). Accessed 18 December 2017. http://reporting.unhcr.org/sites/default/files/Information percent20Sheet percent20on percent20ERCM percent20September percent202016.pdf.

Index

STUDIES IN FORCED MIGRATION

General Editors: Tom Scott-Smith and Kirsten McConnachie

This series, published in association with the Refugees Studies Centre, University of Oxford, reflects the multidisciplinary nature of the field and includes within its scope international law, anthropology, sociology, politics, international relations, geopolitics, social psychology, and economics.

www.ingramcontent.com/pod-product-compliance
Lightning Source LLC
Chambersburg PA
CBHW070908030426
42336CB00014BA/2330